RC 451.5 .N4 B43 1982

Behavior modification in
 Black populations

D0909531

DATE DUE

NOV 1 7 1994	
APR 3 0 1997	
MAY 6 1997	
NOV - 9 2001	
NOV 2 6 2001	

GAYLORD   PRINTED IN U.S.A.

RICHARD STOCKTON COLLEGE
OF NEW JERSEY LIBRARY
POMONA, NEW JERSEY 08240

Behavior Modification in Black Populations

PSYCHOSOCIAL ISSUES AND EMPIRICAL FINDINGS

Behavior Modification in Black Populations

PSYCHOSOCIAL ISSUES AND EMPIRICAL FINDINGS

Edited by

SAMUEL M. TURNER

Western Psychiatric Institute and Clinic
University of Pittsburgh
Pittsburgh, Pennsylvania

and

RUSSELL T. JONES

Clinical Psychology Center
University of Pittsburgh
Pittsburgh, Pennsylvania

PLENUM PRESS   •   NEW YORK AND LONDON

RICHARD STOCKTON COLLEGE
OF NEW JERSEY LIBRARY
POMONA, NEW JERSEY 08240

Library of Congress Cataloging in Publication Data

Main entry under title:

Behavior modification in Black populations.

Includes bibliographical references and index.
1. Afro-Americans—Mental health. 2. Psychotherapy. 3. Behavior modification. I. Turner, Samuel M., 1944–   II. Jones, Russell, T.,
date-   . [DNLM: 1. Behavior therapy. 2. Blacks—Psychology. WM 425
B41915]
RC451.5.N4B43   362.2'08996073   82-3746
ISBN 0-306-40867-8   AACR2

© 1982 Plenum Press, New York
A Division of Plenum Publishing Corporation
233 Spring Street, New York, N.Y. 10013

All rights reserved

No part of this book may be reproduced, stored in a retrieval system, or transmitted,
in any form or by any means, electronic, mechanical, photocopying, microfilming,
recording, or otherwise, without written permission from the publisher

Printed in the United States of America

To Brenda and Marquette Turner

and the Joneses
Walter and Alma, my parents, and
Virginia, my wife

Contributors

Victor R. Adebimpe, Northern Communities Mental Health and Mental Retardation Center, Pittsburgh, and University of Pittsburgh School of Medicine, Pittsburgh, Pennsylvania

Lloyd Bond, Learning Research and Development Center, University of Pittsburgh, Pittsburgh, Pennsylvania

A. Toy Caldwell-Colbert, Center for Personal Growth, Department of Psychology, Emporia State College, Emporia, Kansas

Leon Green, Graduate School of Applied and Professional Psychology, Rutgers University, New Brunswick, New Jersey

Gerald Groves, Department of Psychiatry, Boston University Medical School, Boston, Massachusetts, and Edith Nourse Rogers Memorial Veterans Hospital, Bedford, Massachusetts

Jack O. Jenkins, Department of Psychology, University of Georgia, Athens, Georgia

Russell T. Jones, Clinical Psychology Center, University of Pittsburgh, Pittsburgh, Pennsylvania

Lily M. Kelly, Department of Psychology, University of Georgia, Athens, Georgia

Maxie C. Maultsby, Jr., Director, Rational Behavior Therapy Center, Department of Psychiatry, University of Kentucky College of Medicine, Lexington, Kentucky

Anna Mitchell-Jackson, University of Colorado Health Sciences Center, 4200 East 9th Avenue, Denver, Colorado

Douglas Payne, Department of Psychology, University of Georgia, Athens, Georgia

Sarah Rahaim, Veterans Administration Hospital, Kansas City, Missouri

Rashad Khalil Saafir, National Institute of Mental Health, Rockville, Maryland

Carolyn M. Tucker, Department of Psychology, University of Florida, Gainesville, Florida

Samuel M. Turner, Department of Psychiatry, Western Psychiatric Institute and Clinic, University of Pittsburgh School of Medicine, Pittsburgh, Pennsylvania

Preface

During the past decade, research and practice in the field of behavior modification have experienced phenomenal growth. Behavioral intervention strategies that were considered strictly experimental a few years ago are now accepted therapeutic modalities, and behavioral methodology has been instrumental in creating an atmosphere conducive to the development of scientific rigor in the area of mental health. But behavioral influence has not been limited to mental health. There has been considerable impact in education, industry, government, and general health care.

Although behavior modification has made a significant impact on psychology in general, there has been a noticeable lack of theorizing and empirical research on issues primarily related to black populations. In fact, the black community in general, and black psychologists in particular, often have viewed behavioral approaches with suspicion. We hope that the material presented in this volume will serve to clarify what the behavioral approach is and what it is not and that it will help to foster an understanding of the behavioral approach. Moreover, empirical data demonstrating the effectiveness of behavioral procedures with black populations are presented. It is our hope that the material will provide some insight into how behavioral theory, methodology, and therapeutic strategies can be used to the benefit of black mental health in particular and the overall psychological health of the black community in general. Finally, we believe the chapters contained in this volume will serve as a catalyst for further use of behavioral principles in constructing theories of black behavior and in furthering empirical research.

The material included was purposefully selected to be of a varied nature. In addition to a chapter on behavioral theory, we have included a chapter of historical information on the treatment of black patients by the mental health professions, as well as chapters on diagnostic issues, psychosocial issues, specific clinical syndromes, education, and community-wide applicability; there is also a chapter presenting a theoretical perspective on self-defeating behavior.

We believe that behavioral theory and methodology can be used to explain and examine the significant problems confronting the black community and further the process of creating an empirical black psychology. We also believe the tools of this approach have been neglected, largely because of a lack of well-trained black psychologists and a mis-understanding of practical aspects of behavioral intervention. Over the past few years, we have witnessed an increase in the number of black psychologists, including many of a behavioral persuasion. This will un-doubtedly improve the status of behavioral approaches in the black psy-chological community. It is our hope that with the increasing number of black behaviorists and the availability of material such as that pre-sented here, some of the benefits of behavioral technology will be re-alized.

The authors wish to express thanks to the contributors for endeav-oring to meet our specific criteria. Also, the encouragement, support and insightful help of Leonard R. Pace, Senior Editor for Plenum Pub-lications, is gratefully acknowledged. Finally, we would like to express our gratitude to Deborah C. Beidel and Barbara Duffy Stewart for their technical assistance.

SAMUEL M. TURNER

RUSSELL T. JONES

Contents

Chapter 3: A Historical View of Blacks' Distrust of
Psychiatry   39

Maxie C. Maultsby, Jr.

Chapter 4: Psychiatric Symptoms in Black Patients   57

Victor R. Adebimpe

Chapter 7: Academic Improvement through Behavioral
Intervention ....

Russell T. Jones

Chapter 8: Rational Behavior Therapy ....

Maxie C. Maultsby, Jr.

Chapter 9: Modification of Interpersonal Behavior 171

A. Toy Caldwell-Colbert and Jack O. Jenkins

Chapter 10: Substance Abuse 209

Jack O. Jenkins, Sara Rahaim, Lily M. Kelly, and Douglas Payne

Chapter 13: Implementing Community Programs: The
Black Perspective in Behavioral Community Psychology .

Rashad Khalil Saafir

1

Behavior Modification and Black Populations

SAMUEL M. TURNER

INTRODUCTION

Over the past decade, behavior modification has gained widespread acceptability and respectability, both as a theoretical approach to understanding various aspects of pathological behavior and as a system of therapy. But the influence of behavioral theory has not been limited strictly to pathological behavior in the clinical arena. Behaviorists have applied their technology in a wide variety of areas including the improvement of health habits (Matarazzo, 1980), education (Semb, 1972), the environment (Witmer & Geller, 1976), economics (Agras, Jacob, & Lebedeck, 1980), communities (Liberman & Bryan, 1977), and even problems of race relations (Jones & Haney, 1981; Williams, Cromier, Sapp, & Andrews, 1971). With such widespread applicability in helping to resolve human problems, behavioral theory and practice has established itself as a useful way of conceptualizing and changing behavior on an individual, group or system-wide basis. Thus, behavior modification has proved more than a passing fad as predicted by some and is not dead as lamented by others (Krasner, 1976).

Although behavioral theory and methodology have greatly influenced psychology in general, they have not been accepted as a viable theory of behavior by either black psychologists or the black community at large. In fact, the term *behavior modification* is often viewed suspiciously and linked with such concepts as mind control and with medical interventions such as psychosurgery and pharmacotherapy. To be sure, some of the problems plaguing the behavioral approach in the black community are the same problems seen by the public at large. Nevertheless, acceptance in the black community has not kept pace with the overall progress of this approach. One obvious problem stems from the lack of

SAMUEL M. TURNER • Department of Psychiatry, Western Psychiatric Institute and Clinic, University of Pittsburgh School of Medicine, Pittsburgh, Pennsylvania 15261.

black psychologists, particularly black psychologists of a behavioral persuasion.

In this chapter, the historical background, methodology, and models of behavior modification will be reviewed. Thereafter, some of the reasons for behavior modification's tainted image in the black community, and some of the objections that have been raised by black mental health professionals will be discussed. Finally, I will attempt to dispel these objections and discuss the advantages of an objective and empirical approach to understanding behavior in general and black behavior in particular.

TERMINOLOGICAL ISSUES

Up to this point, I have used the term *behavior modification* to describe a theoretical approach to conceptualizing human behavior and behavior change strategies. However, there are several terms sometimes used interchangeably to refer to the same or similiar concepts and strategies. More specifically, *behavior modification, behavior therapy,* and *applied behavior analysis* have been used synonomously by some behaviorists and independently by others. Presently, there exist three journals bearing these names *(Behavior Modification, Behavior Therapy, Journal of Applied Behavior Analysis)* and several others making use of some variation of the three terms. This might imply that they deal with different subject matter. Yet, a quick review will reveal that, although slight variations exist, the journals deal basically with the same type of material. The terminological issues have been the source of some controversy in recent years among behaviorists. The source of the controversy is partly rooted in the fact that there is no unified behavioral theory. Rather, behavioral theory is comprised of various principles derived from the laboratories of experimental psychology, in particular principles of learning.

In attempting to make a distinction among the terms, Stolz, Wienckowski, and Brown (1975) asserted that the term *behavior therapy* refers primarily to clinical interventions where clients are seen on a one-to-one basis. Hence, the application of behavior principles to remedy behavioral pathology by a therapist in an individual session would be an instance of behavior therapy. Stolz *et al.* (1975) add that behavior modification procedures are directed at "changing the environment and the way people interact rather than by intervening directly through medical procedures (such as drugs) or surgical procedures (such as psychosurgery)" (p. 1,028). They further assert that in behavior modification there is a heavy use of operant principles and eschewal of mediational constructs such as anxiety. An examination of the behavioral literature, however, will reveal that operant principles are part of most behavioral programs, and behavior change procedures that are not identified as operant will be referred to as behavior modification procedures. A distinction based on these issues does not appear to be satisfactory.

Franzini and Tilker (1972) defined behavior therapy in a fashion similar to that of Stoltz *et al.* (1975). The term *behavior therapy* is deemed to be appropriate when it is used to help resolve problems on an individual basis via one–to–one contact with a therapist. On the other hand, behavior change procedures involving efforts to alter social institutions or groups are properly labeled *behavior modification*. However, this seems to be a rather limited definition of therapy. Consider the instances of group and family therapy. When a behaviorist engages in these therapies, surely he is employing behavior therapy, albeit directed at more than one individual. The problem appears to be centered around the idea that the term *therapy* should be employed when we are referring to the treatment of emotional difficulties. As we shall see, behavioral strategies are used to resolve many other types of problems. Furthermore, the above distinctions are not consonant with the manner in which behaviorists have traditionally viewed the terms. In much of the early literature, the terms *therapy* and *modification* were used interchangeably (e.g., Franks, 1969; Kanfer & Phillips, 1970; Krasner, 1976). In 1969, Gordon Paul described behavior modification as a subarea of a larger domain of behavioral influence. This subarea of influence relies on behavioral principles to alter human behavior. Considering Paul's division and the above discussion, the term *behavior modification* would be an overall term for any behavioral change strategy employing behavioral principles, and behavior therapy would be a subset of behavior modification in the clinical arena.

The third term, *applied behavior analysis*, has been described (Franzini & Tilker, 1972) as the application of operant principles in behavior change procedures. As previously stated, principles of operant conditioning are inherent in most if not all behavioral strategies. Such a distinction would appear to serve no useful purpose. The differentiation of behavior modification and behavior therapy as described above appears to be somewhat more meaningful. In view of Paul's (1969) distinction, we have chosen to use the term *behavior modification* in the title of this book in order to reflect the wide diversity of topics covered. Yet, the reader will find the terms used interchangeably throughout the various chapters. This is the case in most of the behavior literature, and perhaps, as Calhoun and Turner (1981) concluded, distinguishing between the terms has little advantage.

A DEFINITION OF BEHAVIOR MODIFICATION

Ever since the popularization of behaviorist doctrines in the late 1950s and early 1960s, there has been much acrimonious debate over the definition of behavior modification. Early definitions such as the one proposed by Eysenck (1959) argued that behavior modification can be distinguished from other approaches because its bases are in modern learning theory. Similarly, a later definition by Wolpe (1976) claimed that behavior therapy is based on principles and paradigms of learning. These strong claims of a learning theory basis for behavior modification have been the center of the debate over definition (e.g., Breger & McGaugh, 1966; Eysenck, 1972). A major contribution to the ambiguity surrounding the definition of behavior modification derives from the fact that a monolithic behavior modification is nonexistent. What appears to exist is a variety of distinctly divergent approaches. Indeed, Davison and Neale (1974) pointed out that behavior modification is "an attempt to study abnormal behavior by drawing on the methods used by experimental psychologists in their study of abnormal behavior" (p. 485). This is the essential element of most definitions of behavior modification in the past few years. That is, behavior modification represents a commitment to the use of experimental methods in the study of human behavior. This is embodied in a recent definition proposed by Kazdin and Hersen (1980), which states that behavior modification is characterized by these four points:

1. A strong commitment to empirical evaluation of treatment and intervention techniques
2. A general belief that therapeutic experiences must provide opportunities to learn adaptive or prosocial behavior
3. A specification of treatment in operational and, hence, replicable terms
4. An evaluation of treatment effects through multiple-response modalities, with particular emphasis on overt behavior

In summary, behavior modification may be characterized by the use of methods and theories (including learning theories) of experimental psychology in the study of human behavior, normal and abnormal. The behavioral approach is further characterized by an unyielding commitment to the scientific method and has had an immeasurable influence in bringing some measure of scientific rigor to the field of mental health.

THE PHILOSOPHICAL DOCTRINE OF BEHAVIORISM

What is the relationship of behavior modification to the philosophical doctrine of behaviorism? Behavior modifiers typically refer to themselves as behaviorists; do they mean to imply that they adhere to the principles of philosophical behaviorism? While we will not endeavor to present a detailed thesis on philosophical behaviorism here, some brief explanatory comments may prove useful.

Prior to the emergence of behaviorism, psychology has been dominated by introspectionism and concerned itself with such mentalistic contructs as consciousness, mind, and soul. The nineteenth century witnessed the blossoming of a mechanistic and materialistic approach in the biological sciences. Coupled with objective methods of inquiry, significant advances were made in this area (Kazdin, 1978). These movements within the biological sciences touched upon psychology through the mutual and overlapping areas of physiology and zoology. The emergence of objectivism in psychology is embodied in the concept of behaviorism. According to Kazdin (1978), this was "primarily a methological revolt to establish the scientific basis of psychology" (p. 49).

The name most closely identified with behaviorism is that of John B. Watson, who put forth the tenets of behaviorism in his classic 1913 paper, "Psychology as the Behaviorist Views It." Other significant behaviorists who have influenced all of psychology include Skinner, Hull, Thorndike, and Guthrie. Behaviorism as a philosophical doctrine disavowed the existence of mind, consciousness, and soul (Kantor, 1969). Basically, human beings are considered to be a collection of responses shaped by biological and environmental factors. It should be noted, however, that there are different versions of behaviorism. Metaphysical behaviorism (sometimes referred to as *radical behaviorism*) represents the rejection of mental events and such concepts as mind. Methodological behaviorism chooses to ignore the question of such events for want of the methodology to study them scientifically. Analytical behaviorism assumes that the discussions of such terms are really statements about behavior (Mace, 1910, cited in Eysenck, 1972). Modern-day behaviorists, for the most part, operate at the level of methodological and analytical behaviorism (Erwin, 1978). While behavior modification as we know it today is not equivalent to the behaviorism espoused by Watson, it does appear that Watsonian behaviorism spurred the growth of behavior modification, and it is the emphasis on objective inquiry that cements behavior modification's relationship to philosophical behaviorism.

MODELS OF BEHAVIOR MODIFICATION

Having reviewed briefly some background issues in the development of behavior modification, I now turn to a discussion of the various models of behavior subsumed under the behavioral rubric. I noted earlier that there is no single set of principles on which behavior modification is based. Rather, the behavioral model is comprised of several theories. In fact, one source of the terminological confusion discussed earlier can be directly attributed to the existence of multiple models. Yet, it is the existence of many different models, continual refinement of older models, and the emergence of new ones to accommodate newly acquired information that make the behavior movement truly a scientific approach to understanding human behavior. Let us turn now to a discussion of individual models.

OPERANT (INSTRUMENTAL) CONDITIONING

Principles of operant conditioning can be found throughout psychology as well as in the usage of the lay public. For almost half a century, operant conditioning has been the dominant force within psychology, shaping the behavior of adherents and foes alike. Operant conditioning is most often associated with the name of B.F. Skinner and is sometimes referred to as Skinnerian psychology. The single most authoritative source on operant conditioning is Skinner's *The Behavior of Organisms: An Experimental Analysis,* published in 1938. For a complete understanding of operant psychology the reader is also referred to *Schedules of Reinforcement* (Ferster & Skinner, 1957).

The essence of operant psychology is that behavior is a function of its consequences. Consequences are stimuli that follow the occurrence of responses made by the organism. Technically, the nature of a given consequence is determined by its functional relationship to behavior. That is to say, if a stimulus or event serves to increase the probability of occurrence of a given behavior, it is said to be a positive reinforcer. When the probability of behavior is decreased by a given consequence, the consequence functions as a punisher. Behavior can be reinforced positively or negatively. Positive reinforcement occurs when the probability of a behavior is increased by the presentation of a stimulus or event. An example would be a child who works harder on his math problems as a result of his teacher's patting his head and telling him that he is doing well. Another everyday example of positive reinforcement is the receipt of a paycheck for a week's work. In most circumstances, failure to receive a paycheck will probably result in decreased work behavior (extinction).

When a behavior increases, contingent on the removal of a particular stimulus, it is said to have been negatively reinforced. An example would be cessation of nagging behavior following engagement in dishwashing behavior on the part of a reluctant teenager.

Punishment is commonly defined as the presentation of an aversive event (corporal punishment) or the removal of a positive reinforcer (television watching, use of the car). It must be remembered that punishment is defined by its effect on behavior, and the instances cited above are defined as punishment if (and only if) they result in a decrease in the behavior on which they are contingent.

The concepts of reward and punishment have been discussed briefly because they form the heart of the operant approach. Although the description provided is quite simple, the technology of operant conditioning is based upon complex usage of reinforcement and punishment and the two concepts combined with other strategies such as shaping, chaining, stimulus control, and extinction. The interested reader is referred to the original sources cited above as well as to Bandura (1969), Craighead, Kazdin, and Mahoney (1976), and Whaley and Malott (1971).

The operant approach to behavior is a comprehensive approach and in its extreme form is most closely related to metaphysical behaviorism. From this perspective, the organism for all intents and purposes is at the mercy of its environment. The embodiment of operant principles in social engineering can be found in Skinner's *Walden Two*. One does not have to accept the extreme interpretation of operant principles to acknowledge their obvious contribution to our understanding of human behavior. Such principles are not only a part of formal behavior modification programs, but can be found throughout our educational system, industry, government, and everyday interactions. Operant principles are active in all of the subsequent models of behavior I shall discuss, even though they are not always formally acknowledged.

CLASSICAL (RESPONDENT) CONDITIONING

The principles of classical conditioning emanate from the work of Pavlov and other Russian reflexologists. By now, every student who has had psychology 101 or some equivalent is familiar with Pavlov's studies with salivating dogs (Pavlov, 1927). This early work significantly contributed to the move toward objectivism in psychology and ultimately to behavior modification. Clinical behavioral procedures are heavily based on this model, and it is particularly prominent in the explanation of neurotic behavior patterns including phobias and other avoidance behavior.

Classical conditioning is an associationist approach to understanding behavior. Basically, the arrangement of various stimuli (association) in the environment determines how the organism will respond. This is particularly so when emotional arousal is involved. In essence, the acquisition of a response is determined by the arrangement of the stimulation, the biological state of the organism, and the individual's response repertoire (Kanfer & Phillips, 1970).

The now famous case of Little Albert will serve as an illustration of how fear can be classically conditioned. Little Albert was an 11-month-old boy with no prior fear of white rats. He was placed in a room into which a white rat was introduced. Subsequently, the presence of the rat was paired with a loud, aversive noise. Within a short period of time, Little Albert avoided (was afraid of) the rat. Moreover, his fear generalized (stimulus generalization) to other white furry objects (e.g., a rabbit, a Santa Claus mask, Watson & Rayner, 1920). Although this study is totally unacceptable by today's standards of experimental conduct, it provided a powerful demonstration of the direct application of principles derived in the laboratory to human behavior. An analogous illustration in modern-day terms would be the individual involved in an accident who develops a fear of driving that subsequently generalizes to include fear of riding in cars or any other motorized vehicle. Such an individual would be said to have a conditioned emotional reaction and a conditioned avoidance response.

Therapeutically, aversive conditioning principles comprised of escape, avoidance, and punishment paradigms are based on principles of classical conditioning. Counterconditioning procedures (e.g., systematic desensitization, implosion) are also strongly identified with the principles of classical conditioning.

In distinguishing classical conditioning from operant conditioning, it might be helpful to remember that in classical conditioning the emphasis is on stimuli or, more correctly, the association of various stimuli. On the other hand, operant conditioning is primarily concerned with responses and particularly with the consequences elicited by a given response. Together, they provide the early foundation of behavior modification, and, since they are theories of learning, the roots of behavior modification's claim to be the application of principles of learning can be understood.

SOCIAL LEARNING THEORY

Principles of operant and classical conditioning can be invoked to explain many aspects of human behavior. However, no one learning theory can account for all patterns of behavior. For instance, neither operant or classical principles can explain the phenomenon of no-trial learning or the acquisition of language. Moreover, the previously discussed theories give little attention to symbolic or self-regulatory processes. Essentially, the individual is viewed as a passive actor in his environment.

Social learning theory (Bandura, 1969; 1977a) acknowledges the role of central mechanisms in behavior control but also retains much of operant and classical conditioning. Whereas these principles are viewed as operative, the individual assumes more control in creating his own environment. In social learning theory, we can see a marked departure from philosophical behaviorism. Although the social learning theorist retains a commitment to empiricism and objectivity, he has introduced the notion that behavior can be influenced symbolically and that cognitive variables serve to mediate behavior.

A central element of social learning theory is the concept of vicarious learning. Bandura (1969) argues that virtually all behavior learned through direct experience can be learned through observation, or vicariously. It is through the mechanisms of observational learning that no-trial learning and acquisition of language can be explained. The term most widely used in the behavior literature to describe this process is *modeling*. The concept of imitation (and even the psychoanalytic concept of identification) roughly approximates the behavioral concept of modeling. Simply put, modeling is the vicarious acquisition or extinction of behavior.

A concrete example should suffice to illustrate the process in its most elementary form. Ralph brings his teacher an apple and receives a nice smile, a thank you, and a pat on the head. Charles observes this taking place, and the next day he shows up with an apple. Alternatively, Mary observes Johnny receiving punishment (a spanking) because he runs ahead of his parents in the street. Although Mary has run ahead of her parents before, after observing Johnny's fate she ceases such behavior.

As the examples illustrate, vicarious experience may serve to facilitate the occurrence of certain behavior (disinhibitory effects) or to decrease the likelihood of certain behavior occurring (inhibitory effects). In addition, the learning of completely new responses (i.e., responses not already in the repertoire) is possible on a vicarious basis.

Even emotional responses can be acquired vicariously. Witness the instance of a young mother walking her small child. When confronted by a small dog, the mother responds with fear behavior (withdrawal, frightened look, tightening of muscles). When the child is confronted with a small dog the next day, he responds as his mother did, even though he had not feared dogs in the past.

The modeling process is governed by the rather complex operation of attentional processes, retention processes, motor reproduction processes, and incentive and motivational processes. These variables are discussed at some length by Bandura (1969, 1977a). First, in order for an individual to acquire behavior exhibited by a model (i.e., vicariously), he must attend to, recognize, and differentiate the features of the model's response (attentional processes). Second, in order for the information obtained to be used, it must be retained. Such memory operations as rehearsal and symbolic coding are instrumental in determining whether new material is retained for future use (retention processes). Third, the utilization of symbolic representations (imaginal and verbal) to guide behavior is determined by whether the necessary components are available in the repertoire (motor reproduction processes). Finally, when conditions are favorable, the individual is motivated to engage in all the necessary operations to acquire, retain, and reproduce modeled behavior (incentive and motivational processes). As can be seen, some of these processes are distinctly cognitive and as such represent a major divergence from operant and classical theory. But it should be remembered that the strong commitment to objectivism is retained. Modeling procedures can be employed as behavior-change procedures with individuals or groups. The principles of vicarious learning have been incorporated into numerous clinical procedures and into the educational setting (see Rosenthal, 1976 for a review).

COGNITIVE BEHAVIOR MODIFICATION

If social learning theory represents a movement away from doctrinaire behaviorism, cognitive behavioral approaches would seem to represent a complete break. Behaviorists, at least since Skinner (see Skinner, 1953), have recognized the existence and importance of cognitive behavior and private events. It is crucial to understand that the behaviorist rejected such events as outside the realm of an objective science because they could not be directly observed, measured, and manipulated. It is not true that they believed them to be nonexistent or unimportant. Of course, our technology has advanced to the extent that we can now measure some private events (e.g., GSR, EKG, sexual arousal in males and females). In many instances, there are specific patterns of correlation among these private events and other behavior. Hence, they are no longer strictly private.

Recently, Bandura (1977b) argued that all learning occurs through the process of something referred to as "perceived self-efficacy." Self-efficacy develops as a function of the individual's mastery experiences. However, once developed, it appears to operate as a nontangible cognitive structure that serves as a mediator of all behavior. Such a conception of behavior has not received wide support among behaviorists, and the cognitive movement in general has been the subject of polemical assault (cf. Ledwidge, 1979; Wolpe, 1976a,b). It can be argued that such a conception of behavior certainly appears to represent a complete break with the rigid objectivism characterizing behavior modification.

The concept of self-control is an integral part of the cognitive movement. Embodied in the concept of self-control is the idea that individuals can control or change their own behavior by the conscious manipulation of rewards and punishment. A major part of self-control is the concept of self-reinforcement—the individual reinforcing himself to produce a behavior change. Although there are numerous studies purporting to demonstrate the effects of self-reinforcement, there is a dispute as to whether self-reinforcement, as employed in extant studies, occurs in the absence of external factors (cf. Bandura, 1978; Jones, Nelson, & Kazdin, 1977; Rachlin, 1974). The concept of self-control alone can be subsumed under the rubric of operant theory. However, as employed in some cognitive theories, it appears to be outside the realm of what is typically viewed as behaviorism. Although quite popular, cognitive theories at this time enjoy little experimental support. It shall be interesting to see what unfolds during the next decade.

PROBLEMS WITH THE IMAGE OF BEHAVIOR MODIFICATION

When behavior modification emerged in the late 1950s and early 1960s, it was accompanied by the typical unfounded claims and over-zealousness of new movements within a scientific discipline. Therefore, it is not surprising that unsupported claims were the rule rather than the exception, much like what we have seen with biofeedback in recent years and what appears to be happening in biological psychiatry today. Yet, behavior modification has withstood the test of time and persists today, neither a faded fashion nor a moribund bit of history. To the contrary, it has matured into a discipline capable of recognizing its limitations on a theoretical and practical plane (e.g., Hersen, 1979). Moreover, it has shown the willingness to reassess old positions, incorporate new findings, and continually assess its efficacy (cf. Kazdin & Hersen, 1980; Kazdin & Wilson, 1978).

Behavior modification has always been characterized by a commitment to the scientific method in psychological research. The fact that this commitment led to the gathering of indisputable data on the effectiveness of behavioral procedures helped it to weather the storm of often impassioned attacks from other theoretical schools. But this unswerving commitment to the scientific method and use of technical language has also helped to create an image of behavior modifiers as inhuman, uncaring, mechanistic, and controlling individuals whose ultimate aim is to produce conformity at all cost. Part of this perception, or more accurately misperception, is due to the fact that many behavioral principles were generated in the experimental laboratory with animals (e.g., Skinner's pigeons, Pavlov's dogs). In addition, the behavior modifier has consistently used the language of control and coercion in his literature. This is unquestionably associated with a negative public image. Often when he refers to behavior modification, the lay reader has images of the depictions in such works as *A Clockwork Orange* and *The Manchurian Candidate*. Clearly, the ability to alter and control behavior, as depicted in these works and the callous manner in which it is employed are cause for concern. However, these examples of attempts to change and control behavior do not represent behavior modification as we know it. Moreover, these examples are not realistic in terms of how behavior can be influenced or changed.

Further to illustrate the problem of image, a citation from the *New York Times* reported in an article by Turkat and Forehand (1980) relating to the Patty Hearst incident will be informative. (Hearst, a California heiress, was linked to a series of crimes involving the self-styled "Symbionese Liberation Army"; Hearst claimed she was abducted and forced to participate.) The May 28, 1974 article reported that behavior modification can produce behavior change by

> sensory deprivation or sensory overstimulation (i.e., by binding or blindfolding the subject and confining him to a soundproof dark-room) . . . or by subjecting him to unrelenting noise or light or other sensations. The infamous Chinese water torture falls into the second category. (p. 446)

If the reader recalls the theories of behavior previously discussed, it can easily be seen that there is nothing in the above quotation that necessarily links the procedures discussed to behavior modification. Although such procedures no doubt modify behavior just as psychosurgery, electroconvulsive shock, or psychotropic drugs do, they do not qualify as behavior modification strategies as they do not fit into the behavioral conception of behavior change.

It is a peculiar irony that the very essence of the behavioral approach (commitment to the scientific method) has helped to create a negative public image. In their quest for knowledge and eagerness to demonstrate the potency of their behavior change strategies, the behavior modifiers forgot an important point: language also has an influence on behavior. In this instance, it appears to have been a negative influence on the public at large. To use the terms *conditioning, shaping, aversive control, positive control, extinction,* and *stimulus–response,* to mention a few, does not sit well with those of us concerned with humanistic values. I believe that most behaviorists do have such values but simply failed to realize the impact of their language. During the past few years, we have witnessed a turnaround in this regard. There has been much concern with our public image, and apparently this has produced some positive results. A recent article by McGovern, Fernald, and Calhoun (1980) revealed that, although humanistic therapies were viewed as warmer and friendlier, behavior therapies were viewed as more effective. Time will tell whether we are witnessing a true trend of improvement in image.

BEHAVIOR MODIFICATION AND THE BLACK COMMUNITY

If behavior modification has a tainted image in the community at large, it is even more strongly deprecated in the black community. Why is this the case? I have already alluded to the problem of a lack of black psychologists in general and blacks of a behavioral persuasion in particular. Since many blacks are served by clinics primarily staffed by blacks (mostly nondoctoral), the black lay public has not had an opportunity to become familiar with behavioral approaches. Too often, white therapists are viewed with suspicion, particularly when they attempt to employ strategies that are potentially intrusive, without full explanation of intent.

I have stated that the public at large is concerned with the issue of behavior control. Similarly, Bandura (1974) commented that there

> is growing public concern over manipulation and control by psychological methods. Some of these fears arise from expectations that improved means of influence will inevitably be misused. Other apprehensions are aroused by exaggerated claims of psychological power couched in the language of manipulation and authoritarian control. (p. 859)

Issues of control are doubly important in the black community. Who has influence and how that influence is used to mold the behavior and opinion of our children are considered matters of survival. The black community is justifiably suspicious of powerful behavior change procedures. It is easy to understand why this is the case. The history of the black man and his treatment in America is less than flattering to the white majority. He has been denied the opportunity to create his own destiny and has been subjected to a cruel manipulation aimed at keeping him "in his place." Thus, behavior manipulation of any sort is viewed with suspicion.

The theories of behavior cited earlier in this chapter can be used to account for some behavior in black Americans. It can be strongly argued that black Americans have been conditioned to believe that they are inferior, that black is ugly, and white is beautiful. The experiences of blacks in America during the 1960s, when police power was abused to discredit and quash black organizations, serve to remind us that when the tools of control exist, they surely will be used. It has even been argued that there is a conspiracy to deny the black man political influence in America. Thus, whenever a black gains significant influence, there is a movement begun to discredit him. When the experience of black Americans is combined with the human tendency to be suspicious of methods of mind or behavior control, it can easily be understood why blacks are skeptical of behavior modification.

IS BEHAVIOR MODIFICATION A THREAT?

The theories of the behavioral approach, like all other theories, account for certain aspects of behavior but not all. Moreover, like most good theories, they are constantly being revised to accommodate new empirical information. The behavior change strategies based upon these theories have proved to be powerful in many instances when correctly employed.

The potential for abuse is inherent in behavioral strategies, just as it is in those derived from other schools. For example, it is common knowledge that surgery (e.g., hysterectomy) is performed in many instances when it is unnecessary and that minor tranquilizers are often prescribed in an injudicious fashion. Similarly, verbal psychotherapy has been shown to be detrimental under certain circumstances. Is the surgical procedure responsible for unnecessary hysterectomies? Is the availability of minor tranquilizers responsible for their abuse? Finally, is the existence of verbal psychotherapy responsible for its misuse? The answer is obviously no to all of the above questions. The same applies to behavior modification. It is incumbent upon a scientific discipline, society, and our legal institutions to monitor the use of tools of a given profession. In recent years we have seen a great awareness and willingness on the part of behavior modification theorists to be responsible for the use of behavioral strategies (Stolz & Associates, 1978; Stuart, 1981; Stuart & Davison, 1975.). Similarly, public and governmental concern has served to correct some obvious abuses (Wexler, 1973). Despite some instances of abuse of behavioral strategies, the overall positive impact of behavior modification is obvious from the available literature (Turner, Calhoun, & Adams, 1981).

Behavioral procedures have been used for the betterment of blacks and the black community much more than is usually realized. This will become evident upon reading the ensuing chapters. To illustrate this point, I shall cite several references. A study by O'Donnell and Worell (1973) reported the use of systematic desensitization to reduce racial prejudice in white college students. More recently, Frederiksen, Jenkins, Foy, and Eisler (1977) reported the use of a social skill training program to alter explosive and antisocial behavior among black patients in a Veterans Administration hospital. In a similar vein, Hersen, Turner, Edelstein, and Pinkston (1975) used an individualized social skills training program to help reintegrate a chronic and regressed black schizophrenic back into the community. In the educational setting, numerous studies benefiting black students have been conducted in which black students were all or part of the subject population. An example is a token reinforcement program to help black students in a remedial reading program (Staats, Minke, & Butts, 1970). Similarly, a token economy program was used to teach writing skills to a Head Start class of predominantly black students (Miller & Schneider, 1970).

On a larger scale, O'Connor (1977a) has outlined a detailed behavioral model designed to alter race and sex discriminatory behavior patterns on a group basis. Similarly, behavioral strategies were found to be useful in altering racially discriminatory behavior in a large government agency (O'Connor, 1977b).

I began this section by raising a question: "Is behavior modification a threat, and, particularly, is it a threat to the black community?" I believe the answer to that question is no. On the other hand, behavior modification can be misused and misapplied just as any therapeutic procedure may be subject to misuse. In answering the same question, Jackson (1976) commented that from a theoretical perspective, behavior modification has an advantage for blacks because, in its definition of psychopathology, the basis of the problem is not in intrapsychic conflict. He further concluded that

> the fact that it was not formulated on white middle class Europeans but evolved through work with clients who were not, as the charge has been made, youthful, attractive, verbal, and successful, is a positive reinforcer of why its assessment process has included consideration of the standard of behavior deemed appropriate by the subculture of the individual. (p. 366)

In 1972, my good friend and colleague William Hayes wrote a chapter entitled "Radical Black Behaviorism," which was included in an edited volume by Jones (1972). In my opinion, this paper has not received the attention from black psychologists that it deserves. Therefore, I will spend some time here discussing several points made by Hayes in this work. Within the black psychological movement, there is a call for a "black psychology" which Hayes attributes to the failure of American psychology adequately to consider cultural and racial factors. There can be no doubt that the indictment of American psychology is justified, and ample illustration of this failure will unfold in subsequent chapters. In addressing this issue, Hayes argues that because most black psychologists are trained at white institutions and because there is a disparity of approaches among black psychologists, a cohesive body of knowledge is not likely to emerge. He goes on to state: "If an unbiased understanding of black behavior is to emerge, it must be radically different from previous explanations offered by psychology" (Hayes, 1972, p. 52).

I certainly concur with the above statement. It seems clear to me that if a responsible psychology is to emerge that considers the unique aspects of subcultures in its conception of behavior, it must be different from traditional psychological approaches. It is my feeling that if we have a true science of human behavior, we will then have a psychology that is truly comprehensive and unbiased. Hayes proposes that this science of human behavior can be achieved through radical black behaviorism. It should be noted that the term *radical* is used here in a descriptive sense, and not from the philosophical viewpoint of radical or metaphysical behaviorism discussed earlier. Essentially, this radical black behaviorism is a restatement of the primary ingredient of behaviorism. It is characterized by a rejection of mentalistic constructs and a commitment to objectivism. Moreover, Hayes argues that "a science of human behavior should have a lot to say about the nature of the problem but it should also lead to concrete suggestions for the solution of the problem" (p. 57). I believe the behavioral approach fulfills this requirement. The chapter in this volume by Leon Green will serve as an excellent example of what Hayes meant by that statement.

SUMMARY

I have presented a brief overview of behavior modification, its roots, and the various models of behavior subsumed under the behavioral rubric. Behavior modifiction is defined as the application of principles generated in experimental psychology, and particularly learning theories. Further, it is characterized by a firm commitment to objectivism and empiricism. It is in the latter characteristics that it is most closely associated with philosophical behaviorism. Although there is some terminological confusion with the use of other terms such as *behavior therapy* and *applied behavior analysis,* there is essentially little difference. Hence, the literature shows that they are used interchangably. We chose the term *behavior modification* because we believe it is more reflective of the broadest view of behavioral principles.

Behavior modification is often associated with such procedures as psychosurgery, ECT, psychopharmacology, and "mind control." It is clear that while these procedures change or influence behavior, they do not fit into any of the behavioral models we have discussed. Moreover, psychosurgery, ECT, and psychopharmacology are medical procedures employed by members of the medical profession, principally psychiatrists. Behavior modification is unquestionably a product of psychology and is primarily employed by clinical psychologists.

Behavioral treatment strategies are subject to abuse and misuse just as those of other orientations are subject to such abuse and misuse. It is incumbent upon the discipline to police the use of behavioral procedures, and it is the responsibility of society to determine what it believes to be morally and legally acceptable conduct on the part of behavioral scientists. Behavior modification, through the Association for Advancement of Behavior Therapy (1977), has shown it is willing to act responsibly in providing guidelines for the proper use of behavioral strategies. Other professional, government, legal, and social groups have also acted to curb some of the obvious abuses in the past (e.g., American Psychological Association, 1977). In response to what are justifiable criticisms, there have appeared numerous works designed to explicate the ethics of behavior modification (e.g., Stolz & Associates, 1978).

Black psychologists have been particularly concerned about the applicability of behavioral techniques to black clients. Yet, I have argued, as others have (e.g., Hayes, 1972; Jackson, 1976), that the behavioral approach provides the mechanism through which a psychology of the black experience can be formulated. Moreover, the behavioral approach is the only one within psychology that has properly recognized subcultural differences in its assessment strategies. Finally, the literature contains numerous instances of behavioral procedures benefiting black clients, both individuals and groups. Therefore, I must conclude that much of the criticism emanates from blacks holding other theoretical positions and from a misunderstanding of what behavior modification actually is. I hope this text will serve to eliminate this problem and will act as a catalyst in generating interest in behavior modification on the part of black behavioral scientists.

REFERENCES

Agras, W. S., Jacob, R. G., & Lebedeck, M. The California drought: A quasi-experimental analysis of social policy. *Journal of Applied Behavior Analysis*, 1980, *13*, 561–570.

American Psychological Association. *Ethical standards of psychologists:* 1977 Revision. Washington, D.C.: American Psychological Association, 1977.

Association for Advancement of Behavior Therapy. Ethical issues for human service. *Behavior Therapy*, 1977, *8*, 763–764.

Bandura, A. *Principles of behavior modification.* New York: Holt, Rinehart, & Winston, 1969.

Bandura, A. Behavior theory and the models of man. *American Psychologist*, 1974, *29*, 859–869.

Bandura, A. *Social learning theory.* Englewood Cliffs, N.J.: Prentice-Hall, 1977. (a)

Bandura, A. Self-efficacy: Toward a unifying theory of behavior change. *Psychological Review*, 1977, *84*, 191–215. (b)

Bandura, A. The self system in reciprocal determinism. *American Psychologist*, 1978, *33*, 344–358.

Breger, L., & McGaugh, J. L. Learning theory and behavior therapy: A reply to Rachman and Eysenck. *Psychological Bulletin*, 1966, *65*, 170–173.

Calhoun, K. S., & Turner, S. M. Historical issues and current perspectives in behavior therapy. In S. M. Turner, K. S. Calhoun and H. E. Adams. (Eds.), *Handbook of clinical behavior therapy.* New York: Wiley, 1981.

Craighead, W. E., Kazdin, A. E., & Mahoney, M. J. *Behavior modification: Principles, issues and applications.* Atlanta: Houghton Mifflin, 1976.

Davison, G. C., & Neale, J. *Abnormal psychology: An experimental clinical approach.* New York: Wiley, 1974.

Erwin, E. *Behavior therapy: Scientific, philosophical, and moral foundations.* Cambridge: Cambridge University Press, 1978.

Eysenck, H. J. Learning theory and behavior therapy. *Journal of Mental Science*, 1959, *105*, 61–75.

Eysenck, H. J. Behavior therapy is behavioristic. *Behavior Therapy*, 1972, *3*, 609–613.

Ferster, C. B., & Skinner, B. F. *Schedules of reinforcement.* New York: Appleton-Century-Crofts, 1957.

Franks, C. M. *Behavior therapy: Appraisal and status.* New York: McGraw-Hill, 1969.

Franzini, L. R. & Tilker, H. A. On the terminological confusion between behavior therapy and behavior modification. *Behavior Therapy*, 1972, *3*, 279–282.

Frederiksen, L. W., Jenkins, J. O., Foy, D. W., & Eisler, R. M. Social skills training to modify abusive verbal outbursts in adults. *Journal of Applied Behavior Analysis*, 1976, *9*, 117–125.

Hayes, W. A. Radical black behaviorism. In R. L. Jones (Ed.), *Black psychology.* New York: Harper & Row, 1972.

Hersen, M. Limitations and problems in the clinical application of behavioral techniques in the psychiatric setting. *Behavior Therapy*, 1979, *10*, 65–80.

Hersen, M., Turner, S. M., Edelstein, B. A., & Pinkston, S. G. Effects of phenothiazines and social skills training in a withdrawn schizophrenic. *Journal of Clinical Psychology*, 1975, *31*, 588–594.

Jackson, G. C. Is behavior therapy a threat to black clients? *Journal of the National Medical Association*, 1976, *68*, 362–367.

Jones, R. L. *Black psychology.* New York: Harper & Row, 1972.

Jones, R. T. & Haney, J. I. A body-behavior conceptualization of a somatopsychological problem: Race. In R. M. Lerner and A. Rossnagel (Eds.), *Individuals as contributors to their development: A life span perspective.* New York: Academic Press, 1981.

Jones, R. T., Nelson, R. E., & Kazdin, A. E. The role of external variables in self-reinforcement: A review. *Behavior Modification*, 1977, *1*, 147–178.

Kanfer, F. H., & Phillips, J. S. *Learning foundations of behavior therapy.* New York: Wiley, 1970.

Kantor, J. R. *The scientific evolution of psychology.* Chicago: Principia, 1969.

Kazdin, A. E., *History of behavior modification. Experimental foundations of contemporary research.* Baltimore: University Park Press, 1978.

Kazdin, A. E., & Hersen, M. The current status of behavior therapy. *Behavior Modification*, 1980, *4*, 283–302.

Kazdin, A. E., & Wilson, G. T. *Evaluation of behavior therapy: Issues, evidence and research strategies.* Cambridge, Mass.: Balinger, 1978.

Krasner, L. On the death of behavior modification: Some comments from a mourner. *American Psychologist*, 1976, *31*, 387–388.

Ledwidge, B. Cognitive behavior modification: A step in the wrong direction? *Psychological Bulletin*, 1979, *85*, 353–375.

Liberman, R. L. & Bryan E. Behavior therapy in a community mental health center. *American Journal of Psychiatry*, 1977, *134*, 401–406.

McGovern, H. N., Fernald, C. D., & Calhoun, L. G. Perceptions of behavior and humanistic therapies. *Journal of Community Psychology*, 1980, *8*, 152–154.

Matarazzo, J. D. Behavioral health and behavioral medicine: Frontiers for a new health psychology. *American Psychologist*, 1980, *35*, 807–817.

Miller, L. K., & Schneider, R. The use of a token system in project head start. *Journal of Applied Behavior Analysis*, 1970, *3*, 213–220.

O'Connor, R. D. Treatment of race and sex discriminatory behavior patterns. In G. A. Harris, (Ed.), *The group treatment of human problems.* New York: Grune & Stratton, 1977. (a)

O'Connor, R. D. Status of initial training, change and prevention portion GAO's antidiscrimination program. Draft Report to the United States General Accounting Office, December, 1977. (b)

O'Donnell, C. R., & Worell, L. Motor and cognitive relaxation in the desensitization of anger. *Behaviour Research and Therapy*, 1973, *II*, 473–481.

Paul, G. Behavior Modification research: Design and tactics. In C. M. Franks (Ed.), *Behavior Modification: Appraisal and status*. New York: McGraw-Hill, 1969.

Pavlov, I. *Conditioned reflexes*. New York: Oxford University Press, 1927.

Rachlin, H. Self-control. *Behaviorism*, 1974, *2*, 94–107.

Rosenthal, T. L. Modeling therapies. In M. Hersen, R. M. Eisler, & P. M. Miller (Eds.), *Progress in behavior modification*, Vol. 2. New York: Academic Press, 1976.

Semb, G. *Behavior analysis and education*. Lawrence Kansas: The University of Kansas Support and Development Center for Follow Through, Department of Human Development, 1972.

Skinner, B. F. *The behavior of organisms: An experimental analysis*. New York: Appleton-Century-Crofts, 1938.

Skinner, B. F. *Walden two*. New York: Macmillan, 1948.

Skinner, B. F. *Science and human behavior*. New York: Macmillan, 1953.

Staats, A. W., Minke, K. A., & Butts, P. A token-reinforcement remedial reading program administered by black therapy-technicians to problem black children. *Behavior Therapy*, 1970, *1*, 331–353.

Stolz, S. B., & Associates. *Ethical issues in behavior modification*. San Francisco: Jossey-Bass, 1978.

Stolz, S. B., Wienckowski, L. A., & Brown, B. S. Behavior modification: A perspective on critical issues. *American Psychologist*, 1975, *7*, 1027–1048.

Stuart, R. B. Ethical guidelines for behavior therapy. In S. M. Turner, K. S. Calhoun, & H. E. Adams (Eds.), *Handbook of clinical behavior therapy*. New York: Wiley, 1981.

Stuart, R. B., & Davison, G. C. Behavior therapy and civil liberties. *American Psychologist*, 1975, *7*, 755–763.

Turkat, I. D., & Forehand, R. Critical issues in behavior therapy. *Behavior Modification*, 1000, *1*, 445–404.

Turner, S. M., Calhoun, K. S., & Adams, H. E. (Eds.). *Handbook of clinical behavior therapy*. New York: Wiley, 1981.

Watson, J. B. Psychology as the behaviorist views it. *Psychological Review*, 1913, *20*, 58–177.

Watson, J. B., & Rayner, R. Conditioned emotional reactions. *Journal of Experimental Psychology*, 1920, *3*, 1–14.

Wexler, B. B. Token and Taboo: Behavior Modification, token economies, and the law. *California Law Review*, 1973, *61*, 81–109.

Whaley, D. L. & Malott, R. W. *Elementary principles of behavior*. Englewood Cliffs, New Jersey: Prentice-Hall, 1971.

Williams, R. L., Cromier, W. H., Sapp, G. L., & Andrews, H. B. The utility of behavior management techniques in changing interracial behaviors. *The Journal of Psychology*, 1971, *77*, 127–138.

Witmer, J. F., & Geller, E. S. Facilitating paper recycling: Effects of prompts, raffles and contests. *Journal of Applied Behavior Analysis*, 1976, *9*, 315–322.

Wolpe, J. Behavior therapy and its malcontents-I. Denial of its bases and psychodynamic fusionism. *Journal of Behavior Therapy and Experimental Psychiatry*, 1976, *7*, 1–5. (a)

Wolpe, J. Behavior therapy and its malcontents-II. Multimodal electicism, cognitive exclusivsm and "exposure empiricism." *Journal of Behavior Therapy and Experimental Psychiatry*, 1976, *7*, 109–116. (b)

2

Psychosocial Aspects of the Therapeutic Process

ANNA MITCHELL-JACKSON

THE IMPORTANCE OF SOCIAL AND CULTURAL EXPERIENCES ON THE DEVELOPMENT OF TREATMENT APPROACHES AND MODELS

Cognitive, conative, and coping skills are influenced by a multitude of factors. Most salient among these factors are cultural and psychosocial influences. The manner in which information is organized and processed is affected by these factors as well as the way that behavior is categorized and understood. The purpose of this chapter is to describe the potential impact of cultural, social, and psychological variables on the conceptualization of behavior, on the development of psychotherapeutic models of treatment, and on psychotherapeutic process. Three major premises will be advanced in this chapter. They are as follows:

1. Behavior can best be understood from a multilevel perspective, for example, an interaction among biological, psychological, sociological, and cultural factors. However, cultural factors become more influential in shaping behavioral responses as the organism matures.
2. Psychosocial factors influence much of what transpires in the psychotherapeutic encounter.
3. The black culture is sufficiently different from Euro-American culture for misunderstanding of behavioral processes and functions to have occurred. This misunderstanding has resulted in problems in service delivery and treatment approaches.

Each premise will be explored in an effort to understand the subtleties and complexities of cultural factors in psychotherapeutic operations.

ANNA MITCHELL-JACKSON • University of Colorado Health Sciences Center, 4200 East 9th Avenue, Denver, Colorado 80262.

UNDERSTANDING BEHAVIOR

Historically in Western civilization, behavior has been conceptualized alternately as biologically based, psychologically based, or socially based. Rarely, until the last two or three decades, has behavior been conceptualized as the product of the interaction of these three factors. Each of the three factors has had its period of ascendancy, and each has incorporated the other framework to a varying degree (Boring, 1929; Hempel, 1966; Young, 1966).

Models for understanding behavior have closely followed beliefs about human functioning extant at the times the models were proposed—for example, overt observable behavior (Skinner, 1953, 1974; Watson, 1913), relevance and immediacy (Kohler, 1959; Perls, Hefferline, & Goodman, 1951; Polster & Polster, 1973), internal conflicts (Freud, 1953, 1964). Each model developed has set forth basic principles as central explanatory concepts. These central concepts have been expanded to include ideas about human learning and interaction. However, there has been a striking absence of cultural factors as explanatory concepts. The relative absence of cultural factors in this regard can be seen in three prominent therapeutic approaches: behavior therapy (Bandura, 1969; Kazdin, 1978; Levis, 1970), psychoanalytically oriented therapy (Freud, 1953, 1964; Horney, 1939; Sullivan, 1953), and gestalt therapy (Kohler, 1959; Perls *et al.*, 1951; Polster & Polster, 1973). While these approaches have not formally incorporated psychosocial variables in the body of the theories of behavior derived, each has utilized cultural variables to differing degrees in assessing therapeutic outcome (Freud, 1953, 1964; Kazdin, 1975; Perls *et al.*, 1951). In addition, definitions of normality have been included in each theory to assess treatment outcome. The definitions have proved to be especially relevant in looking at the impact of cultural variables on therapeutic process.

CONCEPT OF NORMALITY

Normality has been defined in various ways. It has been defined as health, as optimal functioning, as proximity to the ideal (e.g., average), and as process. Recently, normality has been equated with the social well-being of the individual (Offer & Sabshin, 1966). In the concept of normality as health, behavior is considered to be within normal limits when no manifested pathology is present. In other words, normality is defined as an absence of disabling symptoms. In this conceptualization, the emphasis is placed on the treatment of symptoms which interfere with the adequate functioning of the individual. Many names have been applied to this approach; Offer and Sabshin (1966) call it the *medical model.* In the concept of normality as optimal functioning, the normal person is equated with the ideal person (Maslow, 1954; Rogers, 1961). Self-actualization is the ultimate goal of treatment, and the emphasis is placed on the development of a healthier character structure. Treatment results are measured in terms of proximity to the "ideal." This approach has been labeled the *idiographic model.* Normality as average functioning has received considerable attention. From this perspective, it is conceived of as the middle range between two extremes. In the concept of normality as process, the focus has been one of temporal progression. What is normal is seen as fluctuating and changing over time. When normality is viewed as social well-being, the focus has been on social betterment, improvement of life circumstances, and modification of social and political forces in the treatment process. However, notions of cultural pluralism are not incorporated.

The degree to which the person's adjustment is perceived as adequate in the long run is a rating of the approximation of the specified behavioral patterns to those extant in the "major" society and not within the individual's own culture. Normality, then, is conceived of as congruence with societal standards. In this context, mental health can be defined as the person's optimal social capacity, taking the major culture as a referent. This view has direct implications for the development of service delivery systems. What also appears to be germane is that cultural factors have been couched within a particular frame of reference, that of the Western European mode of thought. There is considerable evidence, however, that other cultural influences affect responses within the western world. Notable among these are black, Chicano, and Native American cultural systems. These cultural systems are group- rather than individual-oriented and have different philosophical constructs governing their views of the world and of interpersonal interaction. A possible schema for comparing the cultural aspects of the three cultures in relation to five constructs—view of man, group ethos, time concept, tradition, and respect for age—is presented in Table 1. From a perusal of this table, it can be seen that a different emphasis is placed on interaction, achievement, and responsibility. The focus will be on the psychosocial influence of black behavior in subsequent discussions. This will encompass potential impacts of black socialization experiences on the therapeutic encounter and on therapy outcome.

PSYCHOSOCIAL INFLUENCES ON BEHAVIOR

To understand the cultural correlates of black culture and psychosocial influences on behavior, it is necessary to discuss African philosophy

Table 1. Aspects of Black, Chicano, and Native American Cultures with Reference to Philosophy about the Nature of Man, Group Ethos, Time Concepts, Tradition, and Respect for Age

Black	Chicano	Native American
Holistic view of man 　Union between the physical and spiritual 　Life cycle unending 　Harmony with nature	Holistic view of man 　Mind and body viewed as one 　Life and death not distinct—simply phases of the same cosmic cycle	Holistic view of man 　Harmony with nature
Group ethos 　Collective group responsibility 　Kinship system 　Extended family 　Shared responsibility	Group ethos 　Family-centered 　Extended family 　Subordination of the individual to the community or group	Group ethos 　Concern for the welfare of others 　Cooperation rather than competition 　Sharing of wealth
Time concept 　Elastic concept of time 　Unhurried approach 　Phenomenalist emphasis 　Time associated with events—noteworthy occurrences	Time concept 　No rigid adherence to time 　Community and family matters take precedence over other scheduled activities	Time concept 　"Time is always with us"
Tradition 　Behavior defining passages among various life stages set 　Practices governing interaction and responsibility set	Tradition 　Prescribed responses in association with age level, sex, and status	Tradition 　Tradition emphasized
Respect for age 　Knowledge associated with age 　Historical chronologers 　Oral transmission of customs	Respect for age 　Obedience and respect afforded to the elderly	Respect for age 　Skill and wisdom associated with age

which provides the substrate for Afro-American culture. In African culture, religion plays a prominent role (Mbiti, 1969; Nobles, 1972). Religion permeates all activities, beliefs, and practices. Man is viewed as a spiritual being who is inextricably a part of nature and the natural cycle. The life cycle is thought to be unending and to include members yet to be conceived as well as deceased members. There is a strong emphasis on the role of the spiritual, on adaptation, and on living in harmony with one's surroundings and with one's fellow humans. Man in the general sense is expected to adapt creatively to the natural confines of his environment, not to change or modify it. Furthermore, a union between the physical and spiritual is envisioned. No distinction is made between the spiritual, psychological, or biological features of man. In this view, feelings as well as cognitive factors become imbued with the same kind of positive attributes. A full integration of mind, spirit, and body is representative in this belief system. This is contrasted with a Western European belief system which still encompasses the concept of dualism or separateness of mind and body. The manifestations of these concepts—the importance of religion and the integration of all aspects of human nature—can be seen in Afro-American culture, where religion serves as a unifying force in the community, where feelings are liberally demonstrated during religious service, and where affective as well as cognitive and physical expressions are esteemed. Affective responses are placed on the same level as intellectual or physical prowess.

Growing out of feelings of unity with nature and the closeness of men to each other is another African value—feelings of collective responsibility. Strong kinship bonds are extant in African culture. Everyone is seen as related to everyone else, despite blood lines, and is expected to work for the survival and enhancement of the group. Strong feelings of brotherhood and shared responsibility develop out of this context. The individual possesses identity in relation to the group (Nobles, 1972). Personal achievement is not encouraged as a separate act. Achievement instead is linked to behaviors which lead to the enhancement of the tribe. Nobles (1972) states that correlates of this belief can be seen in Afro-American culture in the assumption of responsibility for and protection of fellow blacks who are not biologically related and in the network system derived as a resource for economic, social, and political coping.

Survival of the group, as well as survival of elderly members, takes on special significance in African culture. Elders in the tribe are revered for having survived and for the attainment of wisdom. Elders are involved actively in the instruction and socialization of the young. Elders are also influential in making decisions regarding directions and goals for the tribe, as well as serving as chronologers of tribal history (Nobles, 1972).

Once more, correlates of this value system can be seen in Afro-American culture. Persons, regardless of circumstances or social status, are afforded respect. Titles are always appended when addressing the elderly, and the elderly are viewed as active family members regardless of infirmities.

As salient as a unified view of man, the group ethos, and respect for age are two additional constructs—close adherence to tradition and an elastic concept of time. Practices governing religious ceremonies, interpersonal interactions, expectations, and responsibilities are clearly established. Each individual is aware of practices and is held to them. There is not a feeling of coercion, however, but one of compliance. Through the process of socialization, these customs and beliefs are internalized, to use one frame of reference, or become habitual via reinforcement, to use another frame of reference. There also are discrete practices which clearly delineate life stages or passages, for instance, from childhood to adulthood; such customs provide stability, predictability and cohesiveness.

Observance of time is not seen as important in and of itself, but as it marks the occurrence of events (Nobles, 1972). Time, then, is conceptualized as phenomenalistic. It is linked to births, deaths, and noteworthy occurrences of other kinds. The approach to life is dedicated and purposeful, but it also has an unhurried aspect. It is hypothesized that Afro-American family structure, beliefs, interactional patterns, and adaptive behavior can be understood best from the perspective of African cultural correlates. These factors will each be discussed in turn.

FAMILY STRUCTURE

Much has been presented about the black family (Dennis, 1976; Hill, 1971; Nobles, 1972; Scanzoni, 1971; and Staples, 1978). One quality of the black family that has been described is the strong extended family ties which exist both within and across generational lines. In recent times a modified extended family structure has been noted which takes the direction of separate, independently functioning, nuclear, domestic units which are linked by a system of shared assistance in times of crisis. These arrangements go beyond blood ties. The resemblance to the concept of collective responsibility in African culture is a strong one, even though a modification of the custom has taken place in an adaptive manner in response to constraints placed on it by American cultural practices. Creative adaptation has been a key factor in black family structure, for example, loss of members, economic privations, political and educational constraints.

Flexible roles within the black family serve as one such example.

Duties are less likely to be defined as man's work or woman's work, but instead as tasks that must be accomplished. The tasks are carried out by whoever is available to perform them. Again, this represents an adaptation within the family brought about by environmental circumstances and practices. Older members, as they are able, take responsibility for younger members and for the performance of duties within their capability. Interaction within the family and in the black community at large is marked by respect, cooperation, and support. To be sure, deviations occur in these behaviors as they do in any cultural group. However, it is the exceptions which have been the major focus in psychological and social literature rather than the affiliative and supportive aspects.

Afro-American parents have traditionally assumed a more egalitarian posture in the family than is the case in African culture. This can be seen as representing still another adaptation to American society. Needs of the family are decided upon and are met in a collective manner, for example, a sharing of economic and protective functions. This does not mean that areas of decision-making are mutual or not clearly defined. The opposite is the case. Each parent takes primary responsibility for an agreed-upon task. Value systems, interactional problems, and adaptive strategies mirrored in the black family are apparent in the wider black community. How the value systems are reflected in the larger black community are discussed below.

CULTURAL VALUE SYSTEMS

The five aspects of African culture—unity of all human functioning, feelings of shared responsibility, respect for age, elasticity of time, and customs governing interpersonal interactions—are observable within Afro-American culture. Illustrations of these factors are numerous. The ability to think clearly and rapidly, to speak extensively, and to "feel" are mutually respected in Afro-American culture (Nobles, 1972). No hierarchy is established among components, nor is one component more revered than another. Cognition includes not only abstract modes of thought and problem-solving, but perhaps more fully developed creative ability as well (Jackson, 1979). Easy shifts are seen as occurring among components characterizing cognition and affect without disruptions in the context of quality of responses.

Feelings of shared responsibility are illustrated amply by a sense of kinship and by protective and supportive attitudes assumed by black people toward each other. Affiliative responses are exhibited in the absence of personal acquaintance. The response to persons who may be considered strangers is one of inclusion and help. A strong need exists to assist another black person perceived to be in a distressful situation.

This need transcends clearly empathic responses, which also are present. It involves direct assistance to help the person extricate himself from the situation. It involves verbal and physical actions. Another example of this concept can be seen in the assumption of care of black children, which can be viewed from some aspects as a communal endeavor, and by the informal network systems through which help is offered. Being known by blood relationships rather than by name, (for instance, someone's son or daughter) is another illustration of a sense of brotherhood seen also in the inclusion of blood-related and non-blood-related persons in activities as though they were family members. Still other illustrations of group behavior can be seen in dancing and music where collective statements or activity are discernible.

Respect for age is adhered to closely in Afro-American culture. Use of titles, deference given to older persons, as well as recognition regardless of any perceived station in life, are illustrations of this. Black people are expected to listen to elderly members without interrupting their discourse and to consider advice carefully even though alternate decisions may be made. The black elderly have clear roles within the family, assisting in decision-making on the direction and mission of the family.

Nobles (1972) describes communal potential time (CPT) in his writing. This concept captures well the notion of temporal elasticity. Social events occur when people assemble. There is a "potential" time given for the gathering, but people feel under no constraint to get to the function right at that time. This does not imply a casual attitude regarding family or professional responsibility but a relaxed attitude toward social events. The time frame is one that is flexible but predictable.

Interpersonal interactions are complex but comprehensible. Interactions are governed by requirements for proof of loyalty, by status-free interchanges in certain instances, and by close adherence to prescribed status in other instances. An elaboration of these factors is discussed briefly below.

INTERACTIONAL PATTERNS

Interpersonal interactions are frequently characterized by candor, trust, and cooperation, although the antithesis of these behaviors also occurs. Proof of trustworthiness may be required before the evolution of the stages in the relationship can begin. Strategies by which proof is obtained are not unlike rituals in African culture whereby ability, loyalty, and stamina are tested, for instance, verbal attack, humiliation, assignment of arduous tasks. Discernible rules govern social interactions where status and achievement, except for age, may be largely disregarded.

However, age and status play prominent roles in other interactional patterns. The roles in relation to age and status have already been described. Proof of loyalty in social, political, or psychotherapeutic relationships generally occurs. In this context, opinions, values, and past activities are usually explored. Questioning about these areas may be undertaken in a casual manner (e.g., questions about where the person is from, primary involvements, feelings about other black people).

Social equality is assumed as a rule in black relationships, although there is cognizance of specific talents and areas in which mutual assistance may be given. The assumption of equality is made, in my opinion, because of the leveling influence of race (e.g., discriminatory practices can at any time modify achievement and status). Statements like "what goes up must come down" and "what goes around comes around" capture the essence of this idea. The concepts of group process and rules take into account areas of specialization of responses but not rigid stratification of members of the group. The skills possessed by individual members are expected to be used for the betterment of the group. Animosity is generated if this proves not to be the case (e.g., anger at the black middle class for perceived nonsupport and non-involvement in black causes). Interactional patterns are defined also by the context in which they occur, such as the family or the larger community, and religious, political, or informal social circumstances. Expectations for each of these situations are learned.

ADAPTIVE AND COPING STRATEGIES

In African cultures, survival of the group is paramount and necessarily precedes group enhancement. Coping strategies are related to this factor also in Afro-American culture, where adaptive skills take the direction of quick thinking under pressure and expert planning which ensures the survival of the group as well as survival of group practices and belief systems. Adaptive abilities also take the form of innovation and creativity. Innovation is expressed through inventiveness (e.g., many possible solutions to problems) and through the arts (e.g., music, literature, poetry, art, and dance) (Jackson, 1979). Expressions through artistic endeavors provide profound statements regarding the status, accomplishments, and state of the race as well as problems inherent in survival.

Adaptive skills devoted to group survival also consist of strategies by which perceived antagonists are consciously duped or are made to think that plans not in their interest really are for their benefit. Thus, adaptive skills are related to needs to master a capricious and unpredictable environment and to foster group solidarity and survival. Coping strategies come out of assessment of societal practices which are potentially malignant to black survival and evaluations of motivations considered adverse to the causes promoted by black people. One essential survival strategy that has evolved is knowing when and when not to trust and whom to trust. Since trusting and cooperation are essential components in most psychotherapeutic approaches, these prove to be highly significant in dictating the goals, directions, and success of therapeutic interventions.

The questioning and sometimes distrustful attitude on the part of black individuals has been characterized as maladaptive and pathological, even paranoid in some circumstances. Although this behavior may in fact reach pathological proportions in some individuals, there has been a tendency to label this behavior as a psychotic manifestation in black people in general (Gross & Herbert, 1969; Thomas & Sillen, 1972). The proclivity to misdiagnose and to make dispositions on the basis of inaccurate findings has indeed intensified the very issue of mistrust. A hallmark of the therapeutic encounter, regardless of theoretical perspective, is one of mutual regard and trust. When this crucial factor is in doubt from the beginning, and when this doubt has some basis in reality, for example, impressions formed on the basis of experiences with racism, a viable therapeutic alliance becomes unlikely or at best tenuous. The issue of trust in the therapeutic alliance will be discussed at this point together with those of therapist and patient expectations of treatment and the therapeutic relationship.

THE THERAPEUTIC ENCOUNTER

Examples of psychosocial aspects of psychotherapy have been described in prior discussions of the three major theories of human behavior: psychoanalytic, gestalt, and behavioral approaches. In each approach, goals for treatment have focused on factors which result in accommodation to approved social norms. Thus, psychotherapy possesses a socializing function as well as a methodology by which stress, conflict, perceptual incongruency, and faulty learning are alleviated. Some theorists have held that by reinforcement of cultural norms psychotherapeutic approaches are indeed a political process. Psychosocial aspects of psychotherapy are expressed not only in terms of the emphasis placed on goals themselves but in terms of the entire interactive process.

The establishment of a therapeutic alliance and the development and accomplishment of treatment goals are important components of therapy. Each of these components takes on added significance when black individuals are involved in treatment. Specifically, the issues of trust, expectations of receiving help, and treatment involvement may be magnified considerably. The issue of race (i.e., blackness) and how this issue is perceived by the patient and by the therapist also may be monumental issues and/or hurdles in the establishment of a therapeutic relationship. Suspicion of the motives of the therapist and doubt about the therapist's true interest and ability can be factors which impede the formation of a helping alliance and which may lead to unplanned terminations. In addition, the therapist may be viewed as not only suspect and possibly incompetent, but as administratively or politically impotent with regard to achieving goals which the patient thinks are desirable. It should be noted that these factors are important regardless of theoretical orientation. I will now examine the components of psychotherapy as well as some of the issues mentioned above in light of some cultural variables. This examination will begin with the discussion of the therapist and patient expectations of therapy.

THERAPIST AND PATIENT EXPECTATIONS OF TREATMENT

Acknowledgement has been given to the importance of expectations by participants in therapy on the rating of effectiveness of treatment (Goldstein, 1962; Lipkin, 1954). Positive expectations are associated usually with perceived positive outcome. Negative expectations are associated usually with perceived negative outcome. Positive expectancies have been translated to mean hope or confidence held by the patient. Lack of congruence between patient and therapist expectations is disruptive to the treatment process (Heine & Trosman, 1960). Therapist attitudes influence treatment process as well as patient attitudes. Therapists base expectations of effectiveness of treatment on assessment of abilities, maturational level, motivation, and diagnosis. Race, social class, age, and sex have been found to be crucial variables in determination of treatment involved and on assessment of "treatability" (Banks, 1972; Calnek, 1970; Carkhuff & Pierce, 1967; Cimbolic, 1972; Warren, Jackson, Nugaris, & Farley, 1973). An unquestioned consequence of racism has been a global devaluation of black individuals and black culture within American society at large (Thomas & Sillen, 1972). The procedure by which the devaluation/dehumanization process occurs is presented in Table 2. The possibility of the existence of a black culture outside that of the American cultural influence has been discounted. Instead, black behavior and value systems have been hypothesized to be the same as those of white individuals or, at times, as deviations from these behaviors. This view has been associated with different diagnoses and treatment involvement (Gross & Herbert, 1969; Jackson, Berkowitz, & Farley, 1974; Moss, 1967). It would follow that therapist expectations of success

Table 2.   Mechanism of Racism

Mechanisms
Identification of outgroups
Isolation of differences, for example, race, social practices, beliefs
Identification of differences as deficits
Definition of deficits as genetically based and immutable
Assignment of caste status
Rationalization and justification of discriminatory practices

with black patients may be adversely influenced by the above findings. Black patients' expectations of receiving psychological help are also likely to be low.

When engagement in therapy occurs, levels of trust and cooperation are probably tenuous, and resistance high, due to the status ascribed to black patients. Unplanned termination by either the therapist or the patient may result (Jackson, 1973). Issues of trust and stereotypic views of black ability often emerge from the discriminatory experiences of the black individual and out of overt or indirect endorsement of racist doctrines on the part of the white individual. Value judgments based on social teaching or example influence professional decision-making processes. Further discussion of how the mental health profession has viewed black people is presented in Chapter 4.

THE THERAPIST RELATIONSHIP

If therapy is to be beneficial, a therapeutic relationship or an agreement to enter into treatment must be established. A helping relationship is built on mutual regard and cooperation. The therapist must be seen by the client as skillful, trustworthy, and interested in the welfare of the client. In fact, it has been argued that the therapeutic approach is less important than the characteristics of the treatment relationship and the experience of the therapist. Although this is certainly open to debate, the relationship with the patient is a factor in all modes of therapy. The patient must view the therapist as competent, interested, and trustworthy. The patient must have enough confidence and faith in the efficacy of treatment to become involved and to carry out assignments; if he does not, disruptions occur in treatment. All of the therapist characteristics noted above may be questioned by the black patient, who may test the therapist for sincerity and competence. Status issues may become ascendant also in the relationship if therapy becomes an ongoing process. Status issues could involve such concerns as whose role in the relationship has the higher value and who is in charge of directing the relationship. In many instances, black patients may have a tendency to view the relationship as one of peer–peer rather than doctor–patient. This would be a function of the value system of cooperative interaction and collective endeavor. Needless to say, therapists must be aware of this value system if they are to deal effectively with such patients.

The goals established in psychotherapy are as a rule socially acceptable ones. Therapists probably would find it difficult or impossible to develop a contract for treatment which would be at odds with accepted social norms. Codes of ethics are in fact built upon socially and scientifically approved constructs. However, the norms selected are likely to be ones held by the therapist and not necessarily congruent with those of the patient. When this occurs, persons from different cultures are likely to be misguided and the problems which brought them to therapy intensified. The mismatch in value systems between the therapist—black or white—and the black patient is potentially sizable, since different frames of reference and beliefs are likely to be present because of professional training or experiential or cultural differences.

EVALUATION OF THERAPY EFFECTIVENESS

Persistent problems in definition, design, and measurement have obscured assessment made of therapy outcome (Meltzoff & Kornreich, 1970). The most perplexing problem has been how to define psychotherapy and behavioral change and how to control for extraneous variables. Experimental control in the form of treatment versus no treatment, matching of therapists on discipline, theoretical control of other independent variables, such as socioeconomic level, have been some methods utilized better to define therapy populations and therapy variables. Meltzoff and Kornreich (1970) have discussed these factors in some detail. Numerous instruments have been utilized to assess therapy effectiveness, noteworthy among them, evaluation of attitudinal change, level of functioning, and ratings of perceived attainment of goals by the therapist and the patient. Conflicting results obtained from all of these procedures have led to many more questions about what the therapeutic process is, how it works, and whether it is effective; if so, in what circumstances and with which patients?

Black patients are likely to evaluate therapy outcome as negative if they feel that the therapist cannot understand them or their culture or is not interested in their welfare (Warren, Jackson, Nugaris, & Farley, 1973). Greater satisfaction with treatment felt by black patients, as well as the number of treatment sessions attended, may be a function of the regard the patient has for the therapist and a perception of the therapist's regard for him. Duration of treatment and perceived effectiveness of treatment may be related in part to the race of the therapist. According to Carkhuff and Pierce (1967) and Griffith (1975), black therapeutic dyads may form longer treatment relationships and the relationships may be viewed as more gratifying.

CONGRUENCE OF CHANGE WITH PSYCHOSOCIAL EXPERIENCE

One method of assessing therapy outcome is congruence with the individual's cultural experiences. In some respects, this issue is addressed in the evaluation of level of functioning in that level of functioning is in part a measurement of social adaptation. However, social adaptation as usually defined may be at odds with the cultural experiences and belief systems of the patient. In my opinion, this situation exists with black patients when there is a tendency to ascribe white value systems to the patient, an approach that is potentially destructive and could lead to decreased levels of functioning. More effective and constructive would be a determination of the individual's personal constructs in relation to those of the black community. One possible schema for conceptualizing black cultural values has been presented. Operational definitions of component behaviors for each area would have to be developed. Global terms such as *self*, *identity*, and *self-esteem* are too unwieldy to consider. The adoption of concepts such as these would lead to problems in definition and measurement similar to those described previously. Innovations in measurement also would have to be developed, for example, a reliance on face-to-face communication that is traditional in black culture. Models of treatment may encompass procedures whereby group affiliations and group identity are facilitated, as is the case in network approaches. In addition, cross-generational considerations may have to be taken into account in setting up networks, as well as blood- and nonblood relationships. The behavioral model discussed in the previous chapter appears to be optimal in meeting the above criteria.

FUTURE CONSIDERATIONS

Evidence has been presented in this chapter in support of a psychosocial frame of reference which takes into account possible interfaces of psychosocial factors among or across levels of behavior. Tentative adaptations of this behavioral framework vis-à-vis psychotherapy also have been discussed. An Afro-American value system based upon African correlates has been discussed with the view of possible modification in therapeutic approaches. These considerations were presented for the purpose of accenting the importance of psychosocial experiences and restrictions in thinking as well as biases which influence the development of behavioral and therapy models. To the extent that psychosocial influences are sizable in conceptualization of behavior, treatment approaches, and treatment outcome, considerable rethinking and restructuring would have to occur in all of these areas.

TRAINING ISSUES AND DELIVERY SYSTEMS

Noteworthy among the areas which must be reconsidered are those of training and delivery systems. Training in psychology struggles constantly with the issue of translation of theoretical constructs into avenues of practical application. This would be no less of a problem in this instance. I will not present any revolutionary schema here beyond that already advanced. A determination would have to be made of how best to structure training so that an appreciation of psychosocial influences could be obtained. This might take the form of changes in training curricula so that course work reflects the pluralistic nature of American society and so that concentration on specific cultures represented in American society is possible. It could require as well the inclusion of practicum experiences with members of racial/cultural groups, carried out in a sufficiently flexible and intensive manner to impart both affective and intellectual knowledge of lifestyle. A complete revamping of graduate programs might have to be considered. Experience in a particular culture could constitute the first year of graduate training for clinical and counseling students in psychology. The graduate student might be required to live within the new cultural context and be paired with a member of the cultural group who would teach him about day-to-day activities and values. Evaluation of the student's progress would be made jointly by the community teacher and university faculty. This experience could be followed by formal course work which would capture the essence of these experiences and build upon them. This method combines learning with doing as well as with social contact in a manner which may prove to be more beneficial in the long run from a clinical perspective. This procedure would not compromise scientific knowledge or scientific thinking. It would, in fact, permit more critical evaluations of material presented in formal course work and would possibly stimulate the construction of alternative models of human behavior. It could promote reliance on primary data sources rather than secondary or tertiary sources.

Mental health delivery systems may have reinforced both the isolation of patients and, to some degree, a perpetuation of maladaptive behavior by a concentration on methods which may heighten problems of integration of responses and functioning. Mental health approaches have tended to focus on the individual, for example, rather than on the group or wider social context in which the individual lives, thereby intensifying difficulties of transition following treatment and perhaps producing imbalances in the behavioral repertoire of the patients. Just as behavior and maladaptive responses have multicausal components, corrections and adjustments which psychotherapy addresses may also need to be multifaceted and inclusive. Networking has been one suggestion for service delivery creating less disruption and fewer regulatory difficulties.

Behavioral problems do not develop in isolation. Problems develop in conjunction with difficulties that cut across areas of functioning—physiological, psychological, cultural. Responses to problems are not compartmentalized but are expressed across levels. Understanding of the multiple determinants of behavior as well as the development of mental health approaches and delivery systems that take multiple factors into account may prove to be theoretically sound and clinically feasible. Perhaps most salient is an appreciation of the fact that psychosocial factors permeate thinking, process, outcome, and evaluation in psychotherapy.

Summary

The purpose of this chapter has been multiple in scope. Efforts were made to review potential psychosocial impacts on behavior and to explore how models and theories of behavior and treatment approaches are influenced by sociocultural factors. Psychosocial variables were presented as recurring themes in models and as extremely influential in the development of models and treatment approaches. A possible schema for viewing Afro-American culture was presented with the intent of delineating the major value and belief systems of the culture and outlining potential problem areas and issues in treatment. The therapeutic process was discussed both from a broad perspective, vis-à-vis sociocultural factors, and specifically, from the standpoint of the black patient. Finally, issues related to the training of psychologists were discussed.

References

Bandura, A. *Principles of behavior modification.* New York: Holt, Rinehart & Winston, 1969.
Banks, W. The differential effects of race and social class in helping. *Journal of Clinical Psychology,* 1972, *28*, 90–92.
Boring, E. G. *A history of experimental psychology.* New York: Century, 1929.

Calnek, M. Racial factors in the countertransference: The black therapist and the black client. *American Journal of Orthopsychiatry*, 1970, *40*, 39–46.

Carkhuff, R. R., & Pierce, R. Differential effects of therapist race and social class upon patient: Depth of self-exploration in the initial clinical interview. *Journal of Consulting Psychology*, 1967, *31*, 632–634.

Cimbolic, P. Counselor race and experience effects on black clients. *Journal of Consulting and Clinical Psychology*, 1972, *39*, 328–332.

Dennis, R. Theories of the black family: The weak family and strong family schools as competing ideologies. *Journal of Afro-American Issues*, 1976, *4*, 315–328.

Freud, S. *The standard edition of the complete psychological works of Sigmund Freud*. London: Hogarth Press, 1953; 1964.

Goldstein, A. P. *Therapist–patient expectancies in psychotherapy*. New York: Pergamon Press, 1962.

Griffith, M. S. *Effects of race and sex of client and therapist on duration of outpatient psychotherapy*. Unpublished doctoral dissertation, University of Colorado, 1975.

Gross, H., & Herbert, M. The effect of race and sex on variation of diagnosis and disposition in a psychiatric emergency room. *Journal of Nervous and Mental Disease*, 1969, *148*, 638–642.

Heine, R. W., & Trosman, H. Initial expectations of the doctor–patient interaction as a factor in continuance in psychotherapy. *Psychiatry: Journal For The Study of Interpersonal Processes*, 1960, *23*, 275–278.

Hempel, C. G. *Philosophy of natural science*. Englewood Cliffs, N.J.: Prentice-Hall, 1966.

Hill, R. *Strengths of black families*. Washington, D.C.: National Urban League, 1971.

Horney, K. *New ways in psychoanalysis*. New York: W. W. Norton, 1939.

Jackson, A. M. Psychotherapy: Factors associated with the race of the therapist. *Psychotherapy: Theory, Research and Practice*, 1973, *10*, 273–277.

Jackson, A. M. Performance on convergent-divergent tasks by black adolescents. In W. D. Smith, A. K. Burlew, M. H. Moseley, & W. M. Whitney (Eds.), *Reflection on black psychology*. New York: University Press of America, 1979.

Jackson, A. M., Berkowitz, H., & Farley, G. K. Race as a variable affecting treatment involvement of children. *Journal of the American Academy of Child Psychiatry*, 1974, *13*, 20–31.

Kazdin, A. E. *Behavior modification in applied settings*. Homewood, Illinois: Dorsey Press, 1975.

Kazdin, A. E. *History of behavior modification*. Baltimore: University Park Press, 1978.

Kohler, W. *Gestalt psychology*. New York: New American Library, 1959.

Levis, D. J. *Learning approaches to therapeutic behavior change*. Chicago: Aldine, 1970.

Lipkin, S. Clients' feelings and attitudes in relation to the outcome of client-centered therapy. *Psychological Monographs*, 1954, *68*, No. 372.

Maslow, A. H. *Motivation and personality*. New York: Harper, 1954.

Meltzoff, J., & Kornreich, M. *Research in psychotherapy*. New York: Atherton Press, 1970.

Mbiti, J. S. *African Religion and Philosophy*. New York: Anchor, 1970.

Moss, J. Incidence and treatment variations between Negroes and Caucasians in mental illness. *Community Health*, 1967, *3* (1), 61–65.

Nobles, W. W. African philosophy: Foundations of black psychology. In R. L. Jones (Ed.), *Black Psychology*. New York: Harper & Row, 1972.

Offer, D., & Sabshin, M. *Normality: Theoretical and clinical concepts of mental health*. New York: Basic Books, 1966.

Perls, F. S., Hefferline, R., & Goodman, P. *Gestalt therapy*. New York: Julian Press, 1951.

Polster, E., & Polster, M. *Gestalt therapy integrated: Contours of theory and practice*. New York: Brunner/Mazel, 1973.

Rogers, C. R. *On becoming a person: A therapist's view of psychotherapy*. Boston: Houghton Mifflin, 1961.

Scanzoni, J. *The black family in modern society*. Chicago: University of Chicago Press, 1971.

Skinner, B. F. *Science and human behavior*. New York: Macmillan, 1953.

Skinner, B. F. *About behaviorism*. New York: Knopf, 1974.

Staples, R. *The black family: Essays and studies*. Belmont, Calif.: Wadsworth, 1978.

Sullivan, H. S. *Conceptions of modern psychiatry*. New York: W. W. Norton, 1953.

Thomas, A, & Sillen, S. *Racism and psychiatry*. New York: Brunner/Mazel, 1972.

Warren, R. C., Jackson, A. M., Nugaris, J., & Farley, G. K. Differential attitudes of black and white patients toward treatment in a child guidance clinic. *American Journal of Orthopsychiatry*, 1973, *43*, 384–393.

Watson, J. B. Psychology as the behaviorist views it. *Psychological Review*, 1913, *20*, 158–177.

Young, R. M. Scholarship and the history of the behavioral sciences. *History of Science*, 1966, *5*, 1–51.

3

A Historical View of Blacks' Distrust of Psychiatry

MAXIE C. MAULTSBY, JR.

INTRODUCTION

In 1978, I was an invited speaker at a conference on the mental health needs of American blacks, sponsored by the Department of Health, Education, and Welfare. Specifically, the conference participants were concerned about the relatively low utilization by needy blacks of readily available, federally supported mental health services. The conference was designed to address the following questions:

1. Why are emotionally needy blacks much less likely than whites to seek readily available (pay or nonpay) mental health services?
2. Why are blacks who come for psychotherapy and counseling much more likely than whites to drop out early and/or fail to benefit?
3. What are some logical and economically practical solutions to that mental health problem?

As a native black American, I viewed the answer to the first two questions as intuitively obvious. As a group, American blacks have a deeply rooted, long-standing distrust of American psychiatry. This distrust is clearly reflected by the following polar views most blacks hold about mental health. At one pole are the emotionally normal people, capable of solving and expected to solve their own emotional problems. At the other pole are the emotionally unstable people, incapable of and in need of help in solving their emotional problems. Individuals falling into the latter category are viewed as "crazy" and hence must see psychiatrists and/or other mental health professionals.[1] Regardless of their

[1] Lay people often use *psychiatrist* to refer to M.D. as well as non-M.D. psychotherapists and counselors.

MAXIE C. MAULTSBY, JR. ● Director, Rational Behavior Therapy Center, Department of Psychiatry, University of Kentucky College of Medicine, Lexington, Kentucky 40503.

race, however, people normally dislike and deny evidence that they are crazy. Many blacks, therefore, tend to avoid mental health professionals in favor of trying to solve their emotional problems by themselves.

In spite of their preference for emotional self-help, as a group blacks do not exhibit any more emotional self-help skills than white people. This fact leads to two intriguing, yet (to my knowledge) unanswered questions. Does the culturally reinforced distrust blacks have for American psychiatry reflect intuitively healthy, self-protective insight? Or is that distrust merely an interesting cultural idiosyncrasy? The following recorded facts of black American history are most likely to reveal valid answers to these questions.

THE ORIGIN OF BLACK DISTRUST OF PSYCHIATRISTS

Throughout black American history, two of the most enduring and strongly held white American beliefs have been:

1. Black people are inferior and therefore have less mental capacity than white people.[2]
2. Whether by nurture or nature, the personality structure of black Americans is hopelessly abnormal by white American standards (Thomas & Sillen, 1972).

Originally, the proponents of the idea that blacks are inferior people based their beliefs on the Biblical story of Ham. According to the book of Genesis, Ham's father Noah placed a curse on Ham's descendants that doomed them to be the servants of servants. The American Christian slave owners believed the black African "heathens" were the descendants of Ham. Since servants of servants would not have to be as intelligent as whites, seventeenth-century Christian whites assumed that God had not wasted superior brains on the Africans. Therefore, it seemed logical to the first American settlers to enslave Africans, not only to insure the economic success of the colonies, but also to insure that Ham's descendants carried out God's will. In addition, enslaving the Africans seemed the best way to make them Christians and thereby "save their condemned souls from hell." Several of the American colonies, therefore, passed

---

[2] A recent Harris Poll, part of the 50th anniversary report of the National Conference of Christians and Jews, revealed that 25% of American whites still believe that blacks are less intelligent than whites. The report is available upon written request to Harry A. Robinson, Vice President of Public Relations, National Conference of Christians and Jews, 43 West 57 Street, New York, NY 10019.

laws requiring slave owners to make their slaves Christians prior to importing them into the colony. Understandably, then, America's founding fathers gave their belief in the inferiority of blacks the support of the American Constitution. For apportioning members of the House of Representatives according to state populations, the original Constitution directed that a slave be counted as 3/5 of a white person.

By the mid-nineteenth century, increasing industrialization began to make slavery less and less profitable. This fact freed the more enlightened American Christians to begin expressing their budding doubts that God really had the American type of slavery in mind for the descendants of Ham. Consequently, in defense of both their Christian consciences and their financial investment in slavery, American slave owners began to search for scientific support for the belief that blacks were inferior people and that slavery was the most appropriate living condition for them.

There were only two groups of recognized experts on human behavior in nineteenth-century America: Christian scholars (many of whom were rethinking the Biblical story of Ham) and physicians. Then, as now in America, physicians were among the most respected, highly educated, consistently conservative, and strongly supporting of the dominant beliefs and values of their society. That fact explains why many early American physicians willingly fabricated pseudoscientific evidence in support of the popular belief in black inferiority. Then, as now, health science training did not eliminate racist beliefs (Freedman, Kaplan, & Sadock, 1978).

Typical of the nineteenth-century medical science fiction writers was Samuel G. Morton, professor of anatomy at Pennsylvania Medical College in the early 1840s. Dr. Morton claimed that the brains of people become progressively smaller as one "decends" from the Caucasian to the Ethiopian. Morton based his claim on his unreplicated measurements of the volumes of human skulls (Stanton, 1960). This belief is in accord with the nineteenth-century phenomenon known as the phylogenetic concept of race. Briefly, this form of social Darwinism held that within the races, an evolutionary process analogous to that in the animal kingdom had resulted in whites' having reached the highest stage of biological evolution. Blacks and Indians were seen as comparable to adolescents in relation to white adults. In fact, G. Stanley Hall, a proponent of social Darwinism, founder of the *American Journal of Psychology*, and first president of the American Psychological Association, described blacks and Indians as members of the adolescent races in an arrested stage of development (Hall, 1904).

Fortunately, anatomy is an empirical science and does not lend itself to enduring support for medical science fiction. Consequently, there

have always been relatively bias-free medical scientists attacking the pseudoscientific propaganda of racist anatomists such as Morton (Morais,
1967). That is perhaps one of the reasons the proslavery people turned
to physicians who specialized in mental health to find support for their
belief in the inferiority of blacks. Then, as is still the case today, the
mental health field was the least empirically based of the medical sciences;
and again there were many physicians ready to supply medical science
fiction in support of the national belief in the inferiority of blacks. Typical
of those physicians was Samuel Cartwright, a white slave owner and
native of Louisiana.

Cartwright was widely acclaimed for his discovery and description
of the following two mental disorders of blacks: *drapetomania* and *dysaesthesia aethioptica* (Stampp, 1956). Drapetomania, or "flight-from-home
madness," was the insanity that caused slaves to run away from their
"good lives" in slavery. Dysaesthesia aethioptica, "an insensibility of the
nerves, or hebetude of mind," was the mental disease that caused slaves
to try to avoid work, to destroy their masters' property, and generally
to irritate their overseers. These symptoms were in direct contrast to the
behavior of psychologically "healthy" slaves, who, Cartwright explained,
were faithful, hardworking and happy-go-lucky.

The racist medical science fiction writers of mid-nineteenth-century
America got what they considered to be solid support from the 1840
American census figures. That year marked the first time the American
government attempted to count America's mentally diseased and defec-
tive people. Much to the surprise of most northern whites, the 1840
census computed the insanity and idiocy rate of free American blacks
in northern free states to be 10 times higher than that for slaves in the
southern states. One in every 162.4 free northern blacks was reported
insane, compared to only one in every 1,558 slaves. The antislavery
climate in Maine seemed particularly bad for blacks; the 1840 census
"revealed" that one of every 14 blacks in Maine was a madman! But in
the "healthy slavery climate" in Louisiana, the 1840 census showed only
one insane slave in every 4,310. (Corrected 1840 Census Report of the
United States State Department—Jarvis, 1844, 1852).

Probably because the 1840 census was one of America's first official
attempts to falsify government statistics, the census-takers (all of whom
were white) were remarkably unskilled. Consequently, Edward Jarvis,
a physician and later president of the American Statistical Association,
easily discovered and documented their naively bungled fraud (Jarvis,
1844, 1852). For example, the 1840 census-takers reported 27 insane,
1 blind, and 2 deaf and dumb blacks in eight towns in Maine that did
not have a single black resident. Also, in New Hampshire the 1840
census-takers reported 12 insane and 3 deaf and dumb blacks in eleven

towns that had no black residents. This pattern of finding and counting nonexistent blacks was repeated throughout the northern states. But the high point of the flagrant fraud came when the census-takers officially changed the race designation of 133 white insane patients of the Worcester, Massachusetts, Insane Asylum from "white" to "black."

The Memorial of 1844 to the United States Senate (Morais, 1967) was a detailed exposé of the fraudulent 1840 census. In it, James McCure Smith, a free black American physician and graduate of the University of Glasgow, gave a complete breakdown, by state, of the 186 insane, 38 blind, and 36 deaf and dumb blacks "found" by the 1840 census-takers in northern towns that did not have any black residents. Jarvis (1852) later published a similar exposé.

The evidence of clear-cut fraud was so obvious that John Quincy Adams, former President of the United States and then a United States Representative from Massachusetts, requested a Congressional investigation. At that point, former South Carolina Senator and then-Secretary of State John C. Calhoun, whose department was in charge of the census, admitted that there were errors. However, Mr. Calhoun maintained that the errors were so numerous that they balanced each other out and therefore led to the same conclusions that would have been reached even if the figures had been honestly reported (Thomas & Sillen, 1972; Willie, Kramer, & Brown, 1973). Still, in the interest of public trust, Mr. Calhoun appointed Willian A. Weaver, the southern white who had been the superintendent of the 1840 census, to investigate further. After "careful, objective re-examination" of the 1840 census figures, Mr. Weaver concluded that no errors had been made (Thomas & Sillen, 1972). Consequently, those blatantly false census figures remained in the official government records to be cited in the psychiatric and other mental health literature throughout the world. Jarvis (1844) most accurately described the situation as "so far from being an aid to the progress of Medical Science . . . it [i.e., the 1840 census] has thrown a stumbling-block in its way which will require years to remove." Evidence of the accuracy of Jarvis's prediction was brought to light in 1851.

Using the 1840 census as the source of "objective data," an unnamed author wrote in the 1851 issue of the *American Journal of Insanity*, "Who would believe, without the facts in black and white before him, that every fourteenth colored person in the State of Maine is an idiot, or a lunatic?" In response to that inquiry, Jarvis (1852) published his most detailed account of the 1840 federal fraud, thereby reinforcing his prior (Jarvis, 1844) description of the scientific worthlessness of those census data. For the United States Government, however, the 1840 census figures were quite useful. Mr. Calhoun used them to try to persuade the British to return escaped American slaves from the "emotionally unhealthy" climate of freedom to the "emotionally healthy" climate of slavery. Fortunately, the British were unconvinced and refused to return the slaves (Morais, 1967). However, Mr. Calhoun was extremely successful in using the 1840 census figures to justify to the American Congress the annexation of and extension of slavery into the Texas Territory (Thomas & Sillen, 1972).

ATTITUDES FOLLOWING THE CIVIL WAR

Scientists in general—especially those in the mental health field—tend to discover what the current ruling class of their society already believes (Freedman et al., 1978). Therefore, it is understandable that after the American Civil War otherwise serious scientists at prestigious universities continued to write racist medical science fiction that was widely publicized and naively accepted. For example, R.B. Bean, professor of anatomy at the prestigious Johns Hopkins University, reported in the *American Journal of Anatomy* (1906), "The Negro's brain is smaller than the brains of Whites and that explains the Negro's lack of will-power, self-control, self-government, ethical and esthetic faculties" (p. 379). Then, in the much more widely read *Century Magazine*, Dr. Bean added to those claims that he was "forced to conclude it is useless to try to elevate the Negro by education" (Thomas & Sillen, 1972).

Three years later, the chairman of the anatomy department at Johns Hopkins, Franklin P. Mall, refuted Bean's medical statements. But *Century Magazine* did not think the refutation was sufficiently newsworthy to publish. Unfortunately, Mall's article had little significant impact on America's concepts of blacks' mental health. That fact was probably related in part to the year that Mall published his article. It was the same year (1909) that G. Stanley Hall, leading American advocate of social Darwinism, invited Freud to introduce America's mental health professionals to the psychoanalytic theory of personality development and the technique of psychoanalytic psychotherapy. The relative lack of empirical limits in psychoanalytic theory made it ideal for the authoritative espousal of popular racism as well as the then-popular Victorian era sexism (Broverman, Broverman, Clarkson, Rosenkrantz, & Vogel, 1970; Tennov, 1976; Thompson, 1964). However, there is no way to determine whether that fact was a significant factor in the instant national acceptance by American mental health professionals of psychoanalytic theory and techniques.

In fairness to Freud, it should be noted that there is no evidence that he shared the racist beliefs of G. Stanley Hall and the early American psychiatrists. But it is a fact that the first volume of America's *Psychoan-*

alytic Review, the first psychoanalytical periodical in English, carried three articles dealing with mental illnesses in blacks. All three supported the racist, psychiatric science fiction of Cartwright, Hall, and Calhoun (Thomas & Sillen, 1972). It is also a fact that ten years earlier, William A. White, cofounder of the *Psychoanalytic Review* and leading American psychiatrist, published the following: "In active competition with mentally superior Whites, free Blacks succumb in the unequal struggle with a rapidly increasing insanity rate" (White, 1903).

The *Psychoanalytic Review* was not the only twentieth-century, scientific American journal publishing racist science fiction. The following sampling merely scratches the surface; yet it shows that twentieth-century American psychosocial scientists, of varied professional interests, have been uniformly preoccupied with justifying the still popular American beliefs that blacks are inferior people and have hopelessly pathological personality structures, (see Bean, 1906; Bevis, 1921; Jennsen, 1969; O'Malley, 1914; Weatherly, 1910). Each sang the same old time-honored white supremacist songs.

Personal Beliefs and Research Fraud

The above cited facts of American history support the hypothesis that the distrust of American psychiatry by nineteenth-century black Americans was based primarily on intuitively healthy, self-protective insight. But did twentieth-century American blacks have valid reasons for maintaining that distrust? Again, the recorded facts of history will probably produce the most valid answer. A.R. Jensen's work (1969) deserves special discussion. When it first appeared, it received headlines in the national media, was accepted and endorsed by leading American educators; and was completely reprinted in the Congressional Record of the United States. It was used by Southern school boards as a defense in desegregation court cases, and was the basis of White House racial policy discussions (Thomas & Sillen, 1972). At last, it seemed, white America had found the long-sought scientific support needed to justify its widely held and most enduring beliefs that black people were inferior and therefore had less mental capacity than white people and that, whether by nurture or nature, the personality structure of black Americans was hopelessly abnormal by white American standards.

The main basis for Jensen's popular article was the internationally acclaimed work of Sir Cyril Burt, past president of the British Psychological Society and first psychologist to be knighted for internationally recognized brilliance and research excellence. Burt's classic paper, "Intelligence and Social Mobility," and related works seemed to confirm his own (and, later, Jensen's) strongly held personal belief that (a) IQ is genetically determined and (b) people who have low scores on IQ tests—usually poor people of all races—are mentally inferior to people who have higher scores—usually affluent white people. Sir Burt's work later became the main justification for the famous three-tier British educational system (Reik, 1979).

Four years after Jensen's 1969 article, Jensen himself accidentally discovered and published evidence indicating that, like America's 1840 census-takers, Burt had simply made up his IQ data (Dorfman, 1978; Wade, 1976). However, before Jensen's accidental discovery, Leon Kamin, a Princeton University psychologist, had been lecturing (for over two years) about his suspicions regarding Burt's work. In 1974 Kamin published good evidence that Burt had most probably falsified his data.

Hans Eysenck, claimed by Burt to have been his brightest pupil, and Jensen, Eysenck's student, have both tried to minimize and dismiss Burt's scientific fraud. They claim he "was merely guilty of certain carelessness in his reporting" (Wade, 1976). However, Dorfman's (1978) recent in-depth statistical analysis of Burt's work indicates that "beyond any reasonable doubt Burt fabricated his data." But in the time-honored tradition of former Secretary of State John Calhoun, Jensen maintained that his own conclusions would have been the same "even if Burt had never existed" (Wade, 1976). Less biased but equally competent scientists disagree with his claim (Wade, 1976). With a unanimity seldom seen among scientists, even in the same field, scientists in the varied fields cited in Jensen's (1969) article have since pointed out that Jensen inaccurately summarized many of his cited research studies. These scientists concluded that his methodology and statistical analyses were faulty and that his conclusions were unjustified (Thomas & Sillen, 1972).

In spite of Jensen and other pseudoscientific supporters of white supremacy, the percentage of Americans who believe that whites are biologically superior to blacks seems to have decreased significantly from 100 percent in 1700 (Harris & Associates, 1978). But that fact *does not* mean that blacks now have valid reasons to trust mental health professionals. To the contrary, their long-standing distrust still seems as appropriate as before.

The commitment of America's most influential mental health professionals (over 95% of whom are white) to the beliefs that blacks are inferior and have abnormal personality structures seems as strong now as it has ever been (Freedman *et al.*, 1978; Thomas & Sillen, 1972; Willie *et al.*, 1973). As a group, America's white mental health professionals have changed only the basis for justifying their commitment. Instead of fabricating anatomical or other medical science fiction to support their racist beliefs, white mental health professionals have turned largely to studies of personality structure based on psychoanalytic interviews. One of the most influential of such studies resulted in the now widely accepted work *The Mark of Oppression* (Kardiner & Ovesey, 1962).

Kardiner and Ovesey, psychoanalysts and leading proponents of "the mark of oppression" theory, maintain that American blacks do not have a single personality trait that is not derived from their difficult living condition, (i.e., life in racist America). These authors claim there is no exception to that rule. Blacks, according to Kardiner and Ovesey, "don't have any possible basis for healthy self-esteem, but they have every incentive for self-hatred" (p. 297). In addition, these psychoanalysts believe that psychotherapy or counseling for blacks is useless. They claim the only way to help blacks increase their self-esteem and stop hating themselves is to eliminate all vestiges of racial prejudice and discrimination in America.

Kardiner and Ovesey (1962) based their pessimistic conclusions about blacks on data obtained from psychoanalytic interviews of 25 blacks. Twelve of those subjects were patients receiving psychotherapy from Kardiner and Ovesey, 11 were paid subjects, and 2 were volunteers. The investigators purposely excluded successful blacks from their study and defended that exclusion with their belief that including successful blacks could not have affected their conclusions. Kardiner and Ovesey believe that successful blacks are the exception and not the rule and are, therefore, "statistically unimportant" (p. 301).

Even if Kardiner and Ovesey's claims are correct, rarely are America's mental health professionals (white or black) so naive as to believe that they alone can eliminate racism in America. Understandably, therefore, mental health professionals (white or black) who believe that blacks are hopelessly abnormal are much more likely to recommend drugs, incarceration, and electric shock therapy for emotionally distressed blacks than for emotionally distressed whites (Garfield & Bergin, 1978; Hollingshead & Redlich, 1958).

PSYCHOANALYTIC CATCH–22

Believing in "the mark of oppression" theory encourages white mental health professionals to look for and find only evidence of psychopathology in blacks. For example, Thomas and Sillen (1972) cite a study carried out at Johns Hopkins University which maintained that evidence of high self-esteem in blacks is merely a defense against low self-esteem. That study and the more poignant, yet equally ludicrous example below of racist psychoanalysis demonstrate how easily psychoanalytic theory allows any behavior by blacks to be authoritatively interpreted as evidence of pathologic personality structure, even when pathology does not exist (Freedman *et al.,* 1978). In early 1952, Prudhomme (1973), one of the first fully trained black American psychoanalysts, was briefed by a Howard University team of lawyers about their plans to initiate the now-historic 1954 *Brown vs. Board of Education* desegregation case. As a result of that meeting, Prudhomme requested that the American Psychiatric Association (APA) leadership officially support the contention that separate educational facilities are not equal. In response to this request, not only did the APA leadership refuse Prudhomme's request, but one of the "more insightful" APA officials diagnostically labelled Prudhomme's request "an example of his continuing acting-out behavior" (p. 47).

TRAINING CONSIDERATIONS

There is a popular but naive notion that referring all black patients to black mental health professionals is the best solution to racism in mental health. But that idea would not be uniformly helpful, even if it were possible to implement. The percentage of black Americans is more than four times the percentage of black mental health professionals (Billingsley, 1968; Freedman *et al.,* 1978; Willie *et al.,* 1973). America's black mental health professionals receive the same anti-black mental health training that white mental health professionals receive (Billingsley, 1968; Freedman *et al.,* 1978; Thomas & Sillen, 1972; Willie *et al.,* 1973). Freedman, Kaplan and Sadock (1978) correctly pointed out that white mental health professionals are products of racist America, and that, unfortunately, their professional training does not cure that malady. Instead, the training of white mental health professionals often exacerbates the already undesirable mental health situation blacks are forced to accept. America's white mental health professionals do over 98% of America's mental health research. Understandably, therefore, their research usually reinforces the popular racial stereotypes about blacks as individuals and as family members.

The Mark of Oppression (Kardiner & Ovesey, 1962) may well be the most obvious example of widely accepted anti-black mental health studies, but it is hardly unique. To realize how all-pervasive anti-black mental health concepts are in America's professional literature, one need only look under *black* or *Negro* in the index of almost any psychosocial textbook written by a white author.[3] Most often one sees: *See* slavery, *see* crime,

---

[3] Books authored by whites make up over 98% of the required and recommended reading for white and black students in the mental health professions.

see juvenile delinquency, *see* illegitimacy, *see* syphilis, *see* civil disorder, *see* rape, *see* murder, *see* probation and parole, *see* social welfare, *see* unwed mothers, *see* matriarchal families. One rarely, if ever, is directed to a section that even implies that normal, healthy black people exist. This fact adds convincing weight to Kardiner and Ovesey's claim that emotionally healthy or successful blacks are the exceptions to the rule of incurably pathological personality structure. Understandably, therefore, America's white mental health students usually have a biased view of black Americans, with little or no understanding of the conditions in which they must live.

Many of these views were based on conceptions of blacks prior to the Civil War. Until the end of this war, just over 114 years ago, white America legally and inhumanely prevented well over 96% of its black people from experiencing white America's concept of a healthy, stable family life (Billingsley, 1968). Even during the short period of relative black freedom in America (about one third the time spent in slavery), the federal and state public welfare laws have usually forced unemployed black males to choose between watching their families starve, stealing, and divorcing or deserting their wives (Billingsley, 1968) so the mother and children could qualify for welfare support. Still, at least 75% of black families qualify as both healthy and stable by white American standards. If one looks only at black families with incomes above the poverty level, the proportion of normal, stable black families rises above 93% (Billingsley, 1968).

Obviously, America's mental and emotional health literature about blacks focuses almost exclusively on the small percentage of psychosocially disturbed people found in every race. Then, by passing off those unrepresentative but highly scientific data as if they applied to blacks in general, white American mental health professionals confuse and mislead naive white students in the mental health professions about their future black patients. Most of those unsuspecting white students have never had significant prior personal experience with black people. Without the counterbalancing personal experiences almost all black mental health professionals get growing up in the black community, white mental health students carry grossly distorted views of blacks into treatment settings. Therefore, even the most unprejudiced and well-intentioned white mental health professionals may pose a serious threat to the mental health of their black patients (Freedman *et al.* 1978). Depending upon how thoroughly trained black mental health professionals are, they too may be unhelpful, if not equally dangerous (Cheek, 1976).

In summary, the training of most American mental health professionals (black, white, or other) is largely irrelevant to understanding and helping emotionally distressed blacks. But that training is ideal for perpetuating white America's two most enduring beliefs about blacks: That they are mentally inferior to whites, and that, whether by nurture or nature, they have an incurably abnormal personality structure.

Against that background, it is easy to see why twentieth-century, reality-oriented blacks distrust and avoid most mental health professionals, regardless of race. In addition, that self-protective action seems to be based primarily on an intuitively healthy insight into the anti-black mental health posture inherent in America's mental and emotional health care system.

OTHER REASONS FOR BLACKS' DISTRUST OF PSYCHIATRY

There are irreconcilable clashes between black cultural conditioning and basic psychoanalytic theory, the backbone of American mental health evaluation and psychotherapy. One of the most outstanding of those cultural clashes has to do with the assumed phallic stage of personality development. Most educated blacks humorously dismiss the possibilities of Oedipus and Electra complexes with: "That may be why white people are so crazy, but such nonsense doesn't have anything to do with my problem." And for uneducated blacks, the suggestion of the possibilities of those assumed complexes is one of the most reliable ways to provoke a fight. Yet in either case, psychoanalytically oriented psychiatrists can and do authoritatively interpret black behavior as being evidence of the pathologic presence of those complexes. But the recent research of Schwab (1979), indicating that psychoanalytic theory may not be the best way to understand the behavior of blacks, makes this common practice highly suspect.

The most popular American psychotherapeutic techniques create painful treatment dilemmas for blacks. Being psychoanalytically based, these techniques most often require emotion–charged, passive, dependent patient–therapist relationships. Since more than 95% of America's mental health professionals are white, the average black patient's therapist is likely to be white as well. In light of the facts cited above about current racism in American psychiatry, such passive–dependent therapeutic relationships are rarely attractive to blacks. And the following fact makes them even less appealing: The therapist–patient interactions essential for the "working through" process characteristic of psychoanalytic therapeutic relationships often resemble the old, hated, white master–black slave relationships (Freedman et al., 1978; Willie et al., 1973). Understandably, therefore, black patients have a strong tendency toward negative transference and hostile, antitherapeutic acting behavior with both white and black[4] insight-oriented therapists. That fact may partially explain why blacks are more likely than whites to be given less desirable forms of treatment, such as incarceration, electroshock therapy and mind-altering drugs (Hollingshead & Redlich, 1958; Garfield & Bergin, 1978). The negative reaction blacks have to this practice is a second important reason they distrust America psychiatry.

A reasonable remedy for this situation is to make the training of America's mental health professionals more appropriate to improving the mental and emotional health of America's blacks. That could be done easily and quickly by broadening the staff development and in-service training of practicing white and black mental health professionals to include sensitivity to cultural differences (Cheek, 1976; Katz, 1978) and techniques of culture-free psychotherapy and counseling.

WHAT AND WHICH ARE THE CULTURE-FREE PSYCHOTHERAPIES?

Culture-free psychotherapies are those which are equally effective for whites, blacks, and others, regardless of age, sex, or socioeconomic class. In America, the techniques of psychotherapy and counseling that best qualify as culture-free are the behavior and the more recent cognitive-behavior therapies. Typical examples of behavior therapy are described in Wolpe and Lazarus (1966), Goldfried and Davison (1976), and Bandura (1969). Examples of the newer cognitive-behavioral techniques are described in Meichenbaum (1977), Mahoney (1977), Foreyt and Rathzan (1978), Ellis (1962), Ellis and Grieger (1977), and Maultsby (1977, 1978, 1979, 1982).

Unfortunately, many psychotherapists unwittingly want their patients to accommodate to them, or to their life-style (Pinderhughes, 1973). Consequently, merely using a culture-free psychotherapy may not always be sufficient for ideal therapeutic results when psychotherapists and patients are of different races. As Jones (1972), Freedman *et al.* (1978), Cheek (1976), and Katz (1978) point out, therapists (white, black, or other) often do not understand their own racial prejudices. Consequently, even culture-free techniques of psychotherapy can be misused to the patients' disadvantage if therapists desire their patients to adapt to their life-styles. Therefore, when therapists and patients are of different races, the most nearly ideal techniques of psychotherapy and counseling will be those which are both culture-free and self-help-

---

[4] Prior to the Civil War, free American blacks also owned slaves.

oriented. One such technique is rational behavior therapy (RBT; see Chapter 8).

The self-help focus of RBT meets the culturally determined need blacks have to help themselves emotionally. In addition, the self-help focus eliminates the "one-down" role patients traditionally have in psychotherapy. And of most importance, the self-help focus puts patients in appropriate charge of the direction, rate, and extent of therapeutic change. Thereby, patients and therapists are as well protected as possible from the potential barriers to therapeutic progress each other's racial biases might otherwise create. Unfortunately, research-tested techniques of emotional self-help in professionally delivered mental health services are both recent and relatively rare (Maultsby, 1971, 1978, 1979; Maultsby, Costello, & Carpenter, 1976; Maultsby, Winkler, & Norton, 1975). The behavior and cognitive-behavior therapies mentioned above usually include self-help maneuvers. But (to my knowledge) none of them has been tested in comparative outcome studies involving exclusively black populations. Obviously this is an important area for future mental health research.

All of my psychiatric training, practice, and research has been in mental health facilities where the patient populations are over 90% white but from all social classes. Nevertheless, my experiences (Maultsby, 1971, 1975, 1978; Maultsby & Graham, 1974; Maultsby et al., 1975; Maultsby et al., 1976), as well as those of my white and black colleagues (Brandsma, Maultsby, & Welsh, 1979; Ross, 1978; Ruhnow, 1977; Schwager, 1975), indicate that whites (especially poor whites) often prefer culture-free, self-help-oriented techniques of psychotherapy and counseling to traditional psychoanalytically based techniques. In addition, poor whites and blacks usually benefit from those techniques of psychotherapy and counseling as much as they do from the traditional insight-oriented techniques.

CONCLUSION

In examining the history of how the black man has been viewed by the mental health professions in America, it must be concluded that he has been viewed and treated in a most derogatory fashion. In fact, it would appear that, rather than attempting to understand the unique position of the blacks in our society, American mental health professionals have made a continuous, concerted effort to depict blacks as something less than human beings. Certainly, there have been strong efforts toward proving the inferiority of the black man's intellectual potential and the inferiority of his personality structure. Although these efforts were always couched in scientific respectability, closer examination has shown that the results of such studies usually reflected the racial bias of the investigator rather than the data. The most recent example of outright fraud can be seen in the revelation that Sir Cyril Burt fabricated much of his data on the relationship of social mobility and intellectual ability (Dorfman, 1978; Wade, 1976). Also, extensive examination of Jensen's (1969) work reveals numerous methodological inadequacies as well as interpretive errors (Thomas & Sillen, 1972).

Given the background that has just been described, the relevant question at this time is whether black Americans can obtain appropriate mental health services. Although the answer to that question cannot be conclusively given, it is a safe bet that the services provided at this time are inadequate. There can be no doubt that both black and white therapists (trained in our traditional programs) are ill-equipped to deal with problems presented by black patients. There is little emphasis in the training programs on the cultural differences between white and black populations. Therefore, it must be concluded that the distrust of mental health professionals by blacks is totally warranted. Furthermore, in view of its history, this distrust is considered to be healthy.

However, the situation is not hopeless, as there is a growing number of black researchers and clinicians, an increasing fund of empirical data, and the existence of relatively culture-free therapeutic modalities. Many chapters in this book reflect the growing availability of information on black behavior patterns, as well as the effective use of treatment techniques to help black patients with emotional problems.

REFERENCES

Bandura, A. *Principles of behavior modification.* New York: Holt, Rinehart & Winston, 1969.

Bean, R. B. Some racial peculiarities of the negro brain. *American Journal of Anatomy,* 1906, *5,* 353–415.

Bevis, W. M. Psychological traits of the southern negro with observations as to some of his psychoses. *American Journal of Psychiatry,* 1921, *1,* 69–78.

Billingsley, A. *Black families in white America.* Englewood Cliffs, N.J.: Prentice-Hall, 1968.

Boyd, N. Black families in therapy. *Psychiatric Spectator,* Sandoz: 1979, *11,* 21–25.

Brandsma, J. M., Maultsby, M.C., & Welsh, R. *The outpatient treatment of alcoholism; A review and comparative study.* Baltimore: University Park Press, 1979.

Broverman, I. K., Broverman, D. M., Clarkson, F. E., Rosenkrantz, P. S., and Vogel, S. R. Sex role stereotypes and clinical judgments of mental health. *Journal of Consulting and Clinical Psychology,* 1970, *34,* 1–7.

Burt, C. Intelligence and social mobility. *British Journal of Statistical Psychology,* 1961, *14,* 3–24.

Cheek, D. *Assertive black, puzzled white.* San Luis Obispo, Calif.: Impact Publishers, 1976.

Dorfman, D. T. The Cyril Burt question: New finds. *Science,* 1978, *201,* 1177–1186.

Ellis, A. *Reason and emotion in psychotherapy.* New York: Lyle Stewart, 1962.

Ellis, A., & Grieger, R. (Eds.), *R.E.T.: Handbook of rational emotive therapy*. New York: Springer, 1977.

Foreyt, J., and Rathzan, D. *Cognitive behavior therapy*. New York: Plenum Press, 1978.

Freedman, A. M., Kaplan, H. I., & Sadock, B. J. *Modern synopsis of comprehensive textbook of psychiatry II*. Baltimore: Williams & Wilkins, 1978.

Garfield, S. L., and Bergin, A. C. *Handbook of psychotherapy and behavior change*, (2nd ed). New York: Wiley, 1978.

Goldfried, M. S., and Davison, G. C. *Clinical behavior therapy*. New York: Holt, Rinehart & Winston, 1976.

Hall, G. S. *Adolescence* (Vol. 2). New York: Appleton, 1904.

Harris, L. A., & Associates. A study of attitudes toward racial and religious minorities and toward women. Prepared for the National Conference of Christians and Jews; study number S2829B, November, 1978.

Hollingshead, A. B., & Redlich, F. C. *Social class and mental illness*. New York: Wiley, 1958.

Jarvis, E. Insanity among the coloured populations of the free states. *American Journal of Medical Science*, 1844, *8*, 71–83.

Jarvis, E. Insanity among the coloured population of the free states. *The American Journal of Insanity*, 1852, *8*, 268–282.

Jensen, A. R. How much can we boost I.Q. and scholastic achievement? *Harvard Educational Review*, 1969, *39*, 1–123.

Jones, F. The Black psychologist as consultant and therapist. In R.L. Jones (Ed.), *Black psychology*. New York: Harper & Row, 1972.

Kamin, L. *Science and Politic IQ*. Potomac, Maryland: Erlbaum, 1974.

Kardiner, A., & Ovesey, L. *The mark of oppression*. New York: World Publishing, 1962.

Katz, J. H. *White awareness*. Norman, Okla.: University of Oklahoma Press, 1978.

Mahoney, M. J. Personal science: A cognitive learning therapy. In A. Ellis & R. M. Grieger (Eds.), *Handbook of theory and practice*. New York: Springer, 1977.

Mall, F. P. On several anatomical characters of the human brain said to vary according to race and sex. *American Journal of Anatomy*, 1909, *9*, 1–32.

Maultsby, M. C. Systematic written homework in psychotherapy. *Psychotherapy, Theory, Research and Practice*, 1971, *8*, 195–198.

Maultsby, M. C. Patients' opinions of the therapeutic relationship in rational behavior therapy. *Psychological Reports*, 1975, *37*, 795–798. (a)

Maultsby, M. C. *Help yourself to happiness through rational self-counseling*. New York: Institute for Rational Living, 1975. (b)

Maultsby, M. C. The evolution of rational behavior therapy. In J. L. Wolfe and E. Brand (Eds.), *Twenty years of rational therapy*. New York: Institute for Rational Living, 1977.

Maultsby, M. C. *A million dollars for your hangover*. Lexington, Ky: Rational Self-Help Books, 1978.

Maultsby, M. C. Rational behavior therapy in groups. In G. M. Gazda (Ed.), *Innovations in group psychotherapy*. Springfield, Ill.: Charles C Thomas, 1979.

Maultsby, M. C. Rational behavior therapy. In S. M. Turner and R. T. Jones (Eds.), *Behavior therapy and black populations: Psychosocial issues and empirical findings*. New York: Plenum Press, 1982.

Maultsby, M. C., & Graham, D. T. Controlled study of the effects on self-reported maladaptive traits, anxiety scores and psychosomatic disease attitudes. *Journal of Psychiatric Research*, 1974, *10*, 121–132.

Maultsby, M. C., Winkler, P. J., & Norton, J. C. Semiautomated psychotherapy with preventative features. *Journal of the International Academy of Preventative Medicine*, 1975, *Fall*, 27–37.

Maultsby, M. C., Costello, R. T., & Carpenter, L. C. Classroom emotional education and optimum health. *Journal of the International Academy of Preventative Medicine*, 1976, *Dec.,* 24–31.

Meichenbaum, D. *Cognitive-behavior modification: An integrative approach.* New York: Plenum Press, 1977.

Morais, H. M. *The history of the negro in medicine.* New York: Publishers Company, 1967.

O'Malley, M. Psychosis in the colored race. *Journal of Insanity*, 1914, *71*, 309–336.

Pinderhughes, G. A. Racism and psychotherapy. In C. V. Willie, B. M. Kramer, & B. M. Brown (Eds.), *Racism and mental health.* Pittsburgh: University of Pittsburgh Press, 1973.

Prudhomme, C., & Musto, D. F. Historical perspectives on mental health and racism in the United States. In C. V. Willie, B. M. Kramer, and B. M. Brown (Eds.), *Racism and mental health.* Pittsburgh: University of Pittsburgh Press, 1973.

Reik, M. Cyril Burt's data on I.Q.: Taxing the numbers. *Frontiers of Psychiatry*, 1979, *9*, 5.

Ross, G. Reducing irrational personal traits, trait anxiety and interpersonal needs in high school students. *Journal of measurement and evaluation in guidance*, 1978, *11*, 44–50.

Ruhnow, M. Federal Probation Officer, North District of Texas. Personal Communication, 1977.

Schwab, J. J. In Lipsitt, D. R. Major issues in mental health, *Psychiatric Opinion*, 1979, *16*, 40–43.

Stampp, K. M. *The peculiar institution: Slavery in the ante-bellum South.* New York: Knopf, 1956.

Stanton, W. *The Leopard's spots. Scientific attitudes toward race in America, 1815–1859.* Chicago: University of Chicago Press, 1960.

Tennov, D. Psychotherapy: *The hazardous cure.* Garden City, N.Y.: Anchor Press, 1976.

Thomas, A., & Sillen, S. *Racism and psychiatry.* New York: Brunner/Mazel, 1972.

Thompson, C. *Interpersonal psychoanalysis.* In M. R. Green (Ed.), *Interpersonal Psychoanalysis.* New York: Basic Books, 1964.

Wade, M. I.Q. and heredity: Suspicion of fraud beclouds classic experiment. *Science*, 1976, *194*, 916–919.

Weatherly, D. G. Race and marriage. *American Journal of Sociology*, 1910, *15*, 433–454.

White, W. A. Geographic distribution of insanity. *Journal of Nervous and Mental Disease*, 1903, *30*, 258–279.

Willie, C. V., Kramer, M. B., & Brown, B. S. *Racism and mental health.* Pittsburgh: University of Pittsburgh Press, 1973.

Wolpe, J., & Lazarus, A. A. *Behavior therapy techniques.* New York: Pergamon Press, 1966.

4

Psychiatric Symptoms in Black Patients

VICTOR R. ADEBIMPE

INTRODUCTION

Dissatisfaction with psychiatric diagnosis dates back to the finding of Masserman and Carmichael (1938) that 40% of in-patients from a university hospital required a major revision in their diagnosis one year later. That report ushered in four decades of research into the reliability of various assessment procedures (Ash, 1949; Beck, 1962; Feighner, Robins, Guze, Woodruff, Winokur, & Munoz, 1972; Woodruff, Goodwin, & Guze, 1974), culminating in the third edition of the American Psychiatric Association's *Diagnostic and Statistical Manual* (1980). The major novelty of this manual, (that is, the specification of defined criteria for each diagnostic category) is an attempt to minimize differences in the perceptual and conceptual habits of clinicians, and reflects the preoccupation of the antecedent research with this aspect of the general problem of diagnostic errors. This approach assumes that there is a relatively high degree of homogeneity among patients with regard to symptoms and the diagnostic criteria for any psychiatric illness or that such variations as might exist will be clinically insignificant and will not lead to misdiagnosis.

However, several transcultural and multiethnic studies clearly demonstrate that such an assumption is not necessarily valid: every situation in which there is cultural diversity should be investigated for this potential source of errors. This chapter will draw attention to some of these studies, describe some symptoms which are of different diagnostic significance in blacks as compared to whites, and suggest ways of increasing diagnostic accuracy with this group of patients.

VICTOR R. ADEBIMPE ● Northern Communities Mental Health and Mental Retardation Center, Pittsburgh, and University of Pittsburgh School of Medicine, Pittsburgh, Pennsylvania 15261.

Transcultural and Interethnic
Variations in Symptom Patterns

The evidence that clusters of symptoms for a disease may not be identical in various groups comes from cross-cultural and international studies. For example, national differences have been reported by Murphy (1965) in the symptomatology of depression and schizophrenia. In a survey of the symptoms of endogenous depression in European countries, ideas of influence and religious preoccupation were reported relatively infrequently among the French, Germans, and Austrians. Preoccupation with poverty was common among the Polish and the French, but less prominent among the Germans. Self-accusation and guilt feelings were common among the Germans, but suicidal tendencies, agitation, anorexia, and somatic preoccupation were the most frequently reported symptoms. In a similar survey of schizophrenic symptoms, this group of investigations found that the distribution of symptoms appeared to vary with social, cultural, observational, and perceptional factors (Murphy, Wittkower, Fried, & Ellenberger, 1963).

That patients in the same country may show similar diversity in symptom patterns has also been documented. Murphy (1974) found that Canadians of British origin differ from those of French origin not only with respect to symptomatology, but also in the frequency, course, and probable treatability of mental illness. This phenomenon has also been observed in Hawaii, which has an even more heterogenous population. According to Katz and Sandborn (1976), patients from different ethnic groups manifest psychosis differently, and there are clear variations in emotional and behavioral patterns in all groups. The differences are more prominent in emotional states (hostility, anxiety, depression, and apathy) than in the cognitive and perceptual aspects of psychosis. The Hawaii-Caucasian psychotic is more "emotional" than the Hawaii-Japanese, as well as more schizoid, withdrawn, and retarded. The Japanese and Filipino differ primarily in a factor called "disorganized hyperactivity," in which the latter obtained higher scores.

From the above studies, one may infer the following: (1) that the diagnostic implications of some symptoms may differ from one group to another, (2) that clinicians working in ethnically diverse populations must familiarize themselves with symptom characteristics of each group, and (3) that diagnostic manuals should not be written as though one set of diagnostic criteria were necessarily valid for all ethnic groups.

In the United States, research findings such as those mentioned above have contributed to a vague awareness of cultural influences on various aspects of diagnosis and treatment. Leighton (1972) has commented on the general neglect of these factors by psychiatrists and their habit of concentrating on intrafamilial and interpersonal aspects, while assuming a cultural homogeneity which does not exist. Leighton maintains that symptomatology does not differ much from one culture to another, but he concedes that there are differences in the symbolic and behavioral means of expression, as well as in culturally determined causes and culturally accepted treatments.

Writing specifically about the black patients, Gary (1976) has enumerated some of the deficiencies of contemporary research and practice: (a) its use of inappropriate and unreliable instruments, (b) a tendency to underemphasize culture and to deny its importance, and (c) a reluctance to treat racism as a variable. In spite of this awareness that diagnostic norms derived from whites may not be entirely suitable for blacks, there is, to my knowledge, no body of data to guide clinicians in minimizing errors in their daily practice. There is also an unfortunate tendency to assume that appeals for greater attention to this issue are unfounded or based on subjective impressions and anecdotal data. It is therefore pertinent to inquire, *first,* if there is any reason to expect subtle differences between blacks and whites in the clinical presentation of symptoms, *second,* if specific symptoms have different diagnostic weights in the two groups, and *third,* if these differences are reflected in the levels of diagnostic accuracy attained in both groups.

Are There Racial Differences in Symptom Patterns?

Although the types of interethnic variations in symptoms described above have not been clearly documented for black and white groups in the United States, there is some indication that they probably exist. Liss, Welner, Robins, and Richardson (1973) studied the psychiatric records of 256 patients who had been labelled "undiagnosed" during their index admissions and retrieved data on 223 psychiatric symptoms as well as 137 nonsymptom variables such as family history, onset of illness, personal history, and so forth. Twelve symptoms were found to occur at a significantly higher frequency among blacks, and one among the whites. Recorded more frequently for black patients were dull affect, delusions of body change, delusions of grandeur, delusions of passivity, auditory hallucinations, visual hallucinations, psychomotor retardation, concrete interpretation of proverbs, decreased need for sleep, increased speech, fighting, and a vague history of illness. Depressed affect was recorded more frequently for whites. When the two groups of patients were diagnosed according to research criteria, however, no significant differences were found in the percentages of patients in different diagnostic categories; this fact suggested the need to find the association of the above symptoms with diagnosis in the two groups. It was found that there was a greater association between symptoms and diagnosis in whites than in blacks. For example, a positive association was found only in white patients between auditory hallucinations and schizophrenia, visual hallucinations and schizoaffective illness, dull affect and organic brain syndrome, delusions of grandeur and mania. A negative association between depressed affect and mania was found only in white patients. The authors, after considering other possibilities, concluded that these findings suggest that a different pattern of psychiatric symptoms is characteristic of the black and white groups.

Although these findings are suggestive, and these conclusions consistent with the results obtained in cross-cultural and interethnic studies, the sample is not typical and probably should be used only cautiously as a basis for generalization. Moreover, if pairs of black and white patients had been matched for social class, age, and sex, these factors (rather than race) might have accounted for some or all of the observed symptom differences (Derogatis Covi, Lipman, Davis, & Rickels, 1971; Tonks, Paykel, & Klerman, 1970). A replication of this study on a large sample of matched patients may yield more conclusive results.

The implications of the second part of the study cited above were nonetheless significant. For example, if auditory hallucinations are positively associated with a final diagnosis of schizophrenia in whites, but not in blacks, less weight must be assigned to that symptom in making a diagnosis of schizophrenia in a black patient. The finding that "there was a greater association between symptoms and diagnosis among whites" simply means that symptom clusters currently in use have greater validity for whites than blacks. Accurate clinical assessments of black patients depend, therefore, on an awareness of those symptoms and signs which have a different diagnostic significance for them. In the following sections, I will discuss those symptoms which appear most often to mislead clinicians in the diagnosis of schizophrenia, depression, and mild mental retardation in black patients.

FALSE-POSITIVE SYMPTOMS OF SCHIZOPHRENIA IN BLACK PATIENTS

Schizophrenia is diagnosed on the basis of specific groups of clinical features, such as Bleuler's (1950) four "A's" (autism, ambivalance, loose associations, disturbances of affect), Schneider's (1959) "first rank" symptoms, or the Feighner criteria (Feighner *et al.*, 1972).

Clinicians must be fully conversant with the range of phenomena included in these concepts because attitudes, behaviors, and thought processes with which the diagnostician is unfamiliar (due to his background and training) may easily appear to be variants of diagnostic criteria for this disorder.

BLEULER'S CRITERIA

Bleuler emphasized the central importance of ambivalence, autism, loose associations, and disturbances of affect, among various other features of schizophrenia. *Ambivalence* denotes the simultaneous existence of opposite feelings, thoughts, and intentions in the same patient. *Autism* means that the patient lives in a private world which is separate and different from the external reality that others experience and share. *Loose associations* are the verbal manifestations of schizophrenic thought disorder, in which connections between ideas are so disjointed that the patient's speech is difficult, if not impossible, to understand. *Disturbances of affect* are disorders of the expression of emotion. They range from a complete failure to show an emotional response to significant stimuli to the exhibition of responses which are completely inappropriate to the situation. Also, affect may remain the same over a period of time, for instance, during an interview, in which the patient discusses topics which would normally evoke a variety of facial expressions. These criteria should be carefully evaluated in black patients. For example, it is not uncommon for excitement, agitation, hypomania, or manic hyperactivity to coexist with excessive religious fervor and to reach such proportions that psychiatric hospitalization appears indicated. It is difficult to assign a diagnosis in the acute stage of such a condition, when the patient is singing, preaching, and reading the Bible aloud in the emergency room. "Speaking in tongues" in such a state is undoubtedly a form of autistic behavior, and the flow of words may be indistinguishable from loose associations, tangentiality, or word salad. Neologisms may also be present.

These features are different from the Bleulerian symptoms which they simulate, for they are ascribed by the patient to divine influences and are not regarded as strange by members of the religious group who are still in touch with conventional reality. A detailed account of the onset, nature, and duration of previous episodes, as well as a family history, should be obtained. If this information is inconclusive, diagnosis should be deferred. In my experience, those cases which are *not* acute exacerbations of schizophrenic or bipolar affective disorders usually run a benign course and become asymptomatic within a few days. In some cases, the dramatic forms of worship encouraged in certain churches in the black community will have been the precipitating factor in repeated episodes of a diagnosable psychotic illness, but this fact is usually recognized only in retrospect.

The evaluation of disturbances of affect may also pose some difficulty. A seemingly "deadpan" appearance, which has been said to be a characteristic of black patients (Carter, 1974) may be evaluated as a flat affect and interpreted as partial evidence for Bleulerian features. In order to avoid such a premature inference, this symptom should be rated while the patient speaks on various topics which are of interest to *him*. In my experience, a persistently flat affect in a black patient is more often associated with a depressive illness and is usually accompanied by psychomotor retardation. In schizophrenic patients a labile or inappropriate affect is more common.

SCHNEIDER'S FIRST RANK SYMPTOMS

Schneider's first rank symptoms consist of characteristic hallucinations and delusions, which are regarded as highly correlated with a final diagnosis of schizophrenia. The auditory hallucinations are those of the patient (a) hearing his own thoughts spoken aloud, the sounds coming from outside his head; (b) hearing voices conversing about him and referring to him in the third person; (c) having somatic delusions, and (d) experiencing delusional perceptions, in which a delusional system is ushered in by a relatively unremarkable perceptional event.

RELIGIOUS DELUSIONS

When religious delusions occur in the above form, Schneiderian first rank symptoms are usually, though not always, diagnostic of schizophrenia. The clinician should, however, be wary of phenomena which bear only a superficial resemblance to them. We have already noted the autistic forms of behavior and speech which are exhibited in the context of religious activities. Similarly, patients may hold beliefs which, to an observer, appear to be grandiose delusions but which are not easy to distinguish from concepts which certain churches expect their members to accept as evidence of their faith. Some of these beliefs may also be logical extensions of such concepts. For all their apparent strangeness, they may be widely held in the patient's community. For example, Gynther, Fowler, and Erdberg (1971) found that 58% of a sample of normal rural blacks endorsed the item "evil spirits possess me at times" on the Minnesota Multiphasic Personality Inventory. Even if these individuals had no other symptoms, such a statement would in some situations lead to a diagnosis of schizophrenia and probably to hospitalization, inasmuch as a less clearly defined symptom earned Rosenhan's pseudopatients the same penalties (Rosenhan, 1973). Clinicians should be aware that religious delusions have been reported as occurring more frequently among black patients (Singer, 1977). The details of such beliefs, with which a diagnostician may be unfamiliar, should be carefully explored and discussed with knowledgeable informants, since they acquire greater diagnostic importance when they are so bizarre that their abnormal nature is obvious to members of the same religious group.

PARANOID DELUSIONS

Like religious delusions, paranoid delusions may be falsely identified in blacks. Suspiciousness is an adaptive mechanism in a hostile environment but may become a reflex reaction to relatively benign stimuli. Well-documented experiences have created in black patients varying degrees of guardedness, distrust, and concern that ward rules, routines, and research protocols are not necessarily in their best interests. These attitudes should not automatically be interpreted as indicating a paranoid psychosis—a diagnosis which ought to be reserved for situations in which specific, bizarre paranoid beliefs are held by the patient which cannot be explained in terms of his experiences on the ward or elsewhere. Clinicians should be aware that most blacks have these feelings to some extent and may elicit unconscious defensiveness or hostility on the part of hospital staff members, who in turn may begin to act in ways which provide ample justification for the patient's suspicions. Reports of a higher frequency of paranoid schizophrenia among black patients (Figelman, 1968; Sletten, Schuff, Altman, & Ulett, 1972; Steinberg, Pardes, Bjork, & Sporty, 1977) may be a direct result of the failure to separate normal suspiciousness and its attendant lack of cooperation from their pathological counterparts.

OTHER NONSCHIZOPHRENIC HALLUCINATIONS AND DELUSIONS

Clinicians also need to be aware of the differential diagnosis of hallucinations and delusions in general. Although these symptoms are often manifestations of other illnesses which may reach psychotic proportions (e.g., temporal-lobe epilepsy, drug intoxications, alcoholic syndromes, manic-depressive illness), schizophrenia most quickly comes to mind because it is the most common form of psychosis. Unless the content of these symptoms and the context in which they appear are carefully explored, it is likely that patients who have them will automatically be labelled schizophrenic. It also follows that if they occur more frequently in the members of an ethnic group, schizophrenia will be diagnosed more often among them.

A higher frequency of hallucinations and delusions has often been reported among blacks. This appears to be true even when all diagnostic categories are taken into consideration (Vitols, Waters, & Keeler, 1963; Sletten *et al.*, 1972; Liss *et al.*, 1973; Singer, 1977). It has been suggested that the tendency of clinicians to assume that these symptoms are diagnostic of schizophrenia, instead of seeking more clues, may partly explain the higher rates of this disorder usually reported for blacks but which have not been confirmed when strict diagnostic criteria are used in making the diagnosis (Welner, Liss, & Robins, 1974). Clinicians should remember that the etiology, age of onset, family history, and course of the various psychoses are useful adjuncts in arriving at a diagnosis, and that using the category of schizophrenia as a "wastebasket" for puzzling cases may result in an irrevocably damaging treatment career for a patient who has been falsely labelled.

FEIGHNER CRITERIA

Contemporary approaches to psychiatric diagnosis emphasize not only symptom complexes but a variety of nonsymptom data. For example, according to Feighner *et al.* (1972), research patients need to meet the following criteria in order to qualify for a diagnosis of schizophrenia:

A. Both of the following are necessary: (1) a chronic illness with at least six months of symptoms prior to the index evaluation without return to the primary level of psychosocial adjustment, (2) absence of a period of depressive or manic symptoms sufficient to qualify for affective disorder or probable affective disorder.

B. The patient must have at least one of the following: (1) delusions or hallucinations without significant perplexity or disorientation associated with them, (2) verbal production that makes communication difficult because of a lack of logical or understandable organization. (In the presence of muteness the diagnostic decision must be deferred.)

   We recognize that many patients with schizophrenia have a characteristic blunted or inappropriate affect; however, when it occurs in mild form, interrater agreement is difficult to achieve. We believe that on the basis of presently available information, blunted affect occurs rarely or not at all in the absence of B-1 or B-2.

C. At least three of the following manifestations must be present for a diagnosis of "probable" schizophrenia: (1) single, (2) poor premorbid social adjustment, (3) family history of schizophrenia,

(4) absence of alcoholism or drug abuse within one year of onset of psychosis, (5) onset of illness prior to age forty.

The problems of assessing hallucinations, delusions, and affect in black patients, which we have already discussed, are of similar relevance in using the Feighner criteria. In addition, it should be noted that being single and having poor premorbid social adjustment or work history may not carry the same diagnostic weight among blacks as among whites. Similarly, to exclude patients who have abused alcohol or drugs within one year of the index admission may not be a realistic goal among black patients.

Difficulties of verbal communication are sometimes encountered in black patients which appear to indicate excessive concreteness but are in reality merely modes of expression characteristic of the lower social classes in general and of the black community in particular. This phenomenon appears similar to the "incapacity to free oneself from the major meaning of a word," which has been reported as a disorder of conceptual thinking found in schizophrenia (Hamilton, 1974). Clinicians should also be cautious in trying to assess this feature in blacks by the use of proverb interpretation. Correct interpretation of proverbs is closely related to a patient's social and educational background and premorbid intellectual functioning. Many black patients have had only a nodding acquaintance with the types of proverbs usually used in the routine mental status interview and are more likely to give interpretations which would be regarded as "concrete," thus strengthening a diagnostic impression of schizophrenia. This misapplication can be avoided by first asking the patient if he has ever used such proverbs in ordinary conversation or if he is familiar with their use by others. If any doubt exists as to his familiarity with common sayings, other tests of abstraction should be employed.

RECOGNITION OF DEPRESSION IN BLACK PATIENTS

ATYPICAL SYMPTOMS

Contemporary criteria for the diagnosis of depression in research patients (Feighner *et al.*, 1972) are as follows (A through C required):—

A. Dysphoric mood characterized by symptoms such as the following: depressed, sad, "blue," despondent, hopeless, "down in the dumps," irritable, fearful, worried, or discouraged.

B. At least five of the following criteria are required for "definite depression:" (1) Poor appetite or weight loss (positive if 2 pounds a week or ten pounds or more a year when not dieting; (2) sleep difficulty (including insomnia or hypersomnia); (3) loss of energy, e.g., fatigability, tiredness; (4) agitation or retardation; (5) loss of interest in usual activities or decrease in sexual drive; (6) feelings of self-reproach or guilt (either may be delusional); (7) complaints of or actually diminished ability to think or concentrate, such as slow thinking or mixed-up thoughts; (8) recurrent thoughts of death or suicide, including thoughts of wishing to be dead.

C. A psychiatric illness lasting at least one month with no preexisting psychiatric conditions such as schizophrenia, anxiety, neurosis, hysteria, alcoholism, drug dependency, antisocial personality, homosexuality and other sexual deviations, mental retardation, or organic brain syndrome.

(Patients with life-threatening or incapacitating medical illness preceding and paralleling the depression do not receive the diagnosis of primary depression.)

Although the above criteria are relatively unambiguous, they can be ascertained only if the clinician is able to recognize the presence of depressed mood in the first place. Carter (1974) has asserted that depression in black patients often presents with multiple somatic complaints rather than a dysphoric mood. Thus, headaches, joint pains, impotence, palpitations, and gastrointestinal symptoms may mask a depressive illness. This presentation has been reported not only among blacks but also among other patients of the lower social classes (Schwab, 1975; Schubert, 1978). Clinicians who are unaware of the significance of such somatic complaints may fail to explore clues which will lead to the correct diagnosis and may become concerned with investigating and treating a nonexistent physical illness. A high index of suspicion is required in diagnosing patients whose circumstances appear depressing (e.g., current difficulties with marriage, family, job situation, income, housing, etc.) but who maintain a stiff upper lip because of the cultural attitude that "a grown man ain't supposed to cry" (Carter, 1974).

On the other hand, clinicians should be aware of the differential diagnosis of multiple somatic complaints. The diagnosis of hysteria (Briquet's Syndrome) relies heavily on the presence of such symptoms; depressed feelings, crying easily, hopelessness, and suicidal thoughts and gestures are often also present. The symptoms of this illness, however, usually have a dramatic quality; and the age of onset, course, and mental status examination will usually differentiate it from a primary depressive illness (Woodruff et al., 1974).

SYMPTOMATIC ALCOHOLISM, DRUG ABUSE, AND SOCIOPATHY

Many patients drink alcohol, abuse drugs, and become hostile when they are depressed. Since alcohol, taken in small quantities, elevates the mood in a subgroup of patients, the cardinal symptoms of depression may be masked. Thomas and Lindenthal (1975) have pointed out the facts that (a) homicides committed by blacks involve concomitant alcohol use more frequently than do white homicides, and (b) homicides involving blacks very often result from friction in close interpersonal relationships, such as jealousy in marital partners. These features are atypical of homicides seen in whites and are indicative of underlying depression, just as alcoholism and drug abuse are sometimes depressive equivalents.

Helzer (1975) found that alcoholism is more common among the relatives of black manic men than among the relatives of their white counterparts, thus lending some support to the thesis that alcoholism secondary to affective disorder (for example, excessive drinking in the depressed phase of manic-depressive illness) may indeed be more common among black patients. The differentiation of these conditions from one another is facilitated by the recognition that sociopathic behavior usually has its onset in childhood and that a detailed account of the past history will often reveal episodes of primary affective disorder during periods of abstinence.

DIAGNOSIS OF BORDERLINE MENTAL RETARDATION

It is now well recognized that the interpretation of intelligence quotient tests must be done with the awareness that blacks have a lower average score than whites. But this fact is often forgotten in the evaluation of intelligence in black patients who obtain a full scale IQ score which would place them in the category of borderline mental retardation. This is usually discovered during the routine "workup" for some other psychiatric condition, and the patient thereby acquires a second diagnosis. Quite often, the patient demonstrates no sign of mental retardation and in some cases may prove on closer scrutiny to have a higher than average level of functioning. It has therefore been my practice to add 10 points to the reported full scale IQ in order to see if the new score does not more accurately reflect the clinical presentation and the patient's demonstrated scholastic and vocational aptitudes. This "rule of 10" has crudely but usefully served the same purpose as Williams' Black Intelligence Test of Cultural Homogeneity (Williams, 1974), which is not yet in routine use. Clinicians must remember that mental health delivery systems often segregate the mentally retarded from other psychiatric patients and that an erroneous diagnosis of this nature may lead to a series of "treatment" experiences which are irrelevant for the individual who has been mislabeled.

EFFECTS OF SYMPTOM DIFFERENCES ON DIAGNOSTIC ACCURACY

Although the symptoms discussed above are likely to lead to over-diagnosis of schizophrenia and underdiagnosis of depression in blacks, I am not aware of any studies in which the impact of these patterns on the accuracy of diagnosis has been specifically investigated. There is, however, a striking parallel between these patterns and the reported tendency to diagnose schizophrenia more frequently and affective disorders less frequently in blacks who had almost identical symptom profiles as their white counterparts (Raskin, Crook, & Herman, 1975; Simon, Fleiss, Garland, Stiller, & Sharpe, 1973). They may also be related, at least in part, to statistics of mental illness in which schizophrenia is reported to be more prevalent, and affective disorder less prevalent among blacks (Meyer, 1974; Steinberg *et al.*, 1977; Taube, 1973). There can be little doubt that such statistics are of questionable validity as long as clinicians are unaware of the types of problems discussed in this chapter. Furthermore, these differences appear to be a logical explanation of the greater frequency of misdiagnoses in blacks when patient groups which include several diagnostic categories are sampled (Welner, Liss, & Robins, 1973).

TOWARD MORE ACCURATE DIAGNOSES IN BLACKS

Although diagnostic problems in blacks have in the past been perceived as an aspect of white racism in psychiatry, it seems reasonable, from the above, to surmise that there are considerable pitfalls for even the most well-meaning and unprejudiced clinician. We have already noted that the latest diagnostic manual, DSM-III, is based on research which has as its primary aim the reduction in clinician variability, while assuming the equal validity of diagnostic criteria for all ethnic groups. If, as I have attempted to show, that assumption is unwarranted, DSM-III may not be as important a step forward for blacks and other ethnic minorities as it is for the white middle class. Clearly, more research is needed to explore fully the extent of this problem in various diagnostic categories and to find ways of solving it.

Meanwhile, it is important to explore ancillary or alternative methods of diagnostic assessment. For example, self-report questionnaires may reduce the difficulties of the initial interactions between patients and diagnosticians, which sometimes result in the collection of much less data on the black patient (DeHoyos & DeHoyos, 1965). Actuarial diagnoses by computer, consisting of the assignment of a diagnosis by comparing the index patient with thousands of other patients, would avoid basing diagnostic statements on data which are more valid for whites (Hedlund, Evenson, Sletten & Cho, 1980).

Biological markers, such as sleep studies, should prove to be "culture-free" in the identification of affective disorders (Kupfer, Foster, Coble, McPartland, & Ulrich, 1978). Behavioral methods of assessment, in which each symptom or group of symptoms is regarded as a target for intervention, avoid the problems of clustering symptoms into syndromes and are therefore of particular relevance for therapy-oriented evaluations of the black patient. These methods are discussed elsewhere in this volume. In all probability, accurate diagnoses in blacks will depend on combinations of these approaches.

REFERENCES

American Psychiatric Association. *Diagnostic and statistical manual of mental disorders*, (3rd ed.). Washington, D.C.: American Psychiatric Association, 1980.

Ash, P. The reliability of psychiatric diagnoses. *Journal of Abnormal and Social Psychology*, 1949, *44*, 272–276.

Beck, A. T. Reliability of psychiatric diagnoses: A critique of systematic studies. *American Journal of Psychiatry*, 1962, *119*, 210–216.

Bianchi, D. N., Cante, J. E., & Kiloh, L. G. Cultural identity and the mental health of Australian aborigines. *Social Science and Medicine*, 1970, *3*, 371–387.

Bleuler, E. *Dementia praecox, or the group of schizophrenias*. Translated by J. Zinkin. New York: International University Press, 1950.

Carter, J. H. Recognizing psychiatric symptoms in black Americans. *Geriatrics*, 1974, *29*, 97–99.

Cohen, R. E. Borderline conditions: A transcultural approach. *Psychiatric Annals*, 1974, *4*, 7–23.

DeHoyos, A., & DeHoyos, G. Symptomatology differentials between negro and white schizophrenics. *International Journal of Social Psychiatry*, 1965, *11*, 245.

Derogatis, L. R., Covi, L., Lipman, R. S., Davis, D. M., & Rickels, K. Social class and race as mediator variables in neurotic symptomatology. *Archives of General Psychiatry*, 1971, *25*, 31–40.

Feighner, J. P., Robins, E., Guze, S. B., Woodruff, R. A., Winokur, G., & Munoz, R. Diagnostic criteria for use in psychiatric research. *Archives of General Psychiatry*, 1972, *26*, 57–63.

Figelman, M. A comparison of affective and paranoid disorders in Negroes and Jews. *International Journal of Social Psychiatry*, 1968, *14*, 277–281.

Gary, L. E. Mental health research in the black community. In E. Cash, L. E. Gary, L. R. Mathis, and T. Thompson (Eds.), *Key mental health issues in the black community*. Washington: Institute for Urban Affairs and Research, Howard University, 1976.

Gynther, M. D., Fowler, R. D., & Erdberg, F. False positive galore: The application of standard MMPI criteria to a rural, isolated, negro sample. *Journal of Clinical Psychology*, 1971, *27*, 234–237.

Hamilton, Max (Ed.), *Fish's clinical psychopathology*. Bristol, England: John Wright, 1974.

Hedlund, J. L., Evenson, R. C., Sletten, I. W., & Cho, D. W. The computer and clinical prediction. In J. B. Sidowski, J. Johnson, and T. A. Williams (Eds.), *Technology in mental health care delivery systems*. Norwood, N.J.: Ablex Publishing, 1980.

Helzer, J. E. Bipolar affective disorders in black and white males; comparison of symptom and familial illness. *Archives of General Psychiatry*, 1975, *32*, 1140–1143.

Katz, M. M., & Sandborn, K. L. Multiethnic studies of psychopathology and normality in Hawaii. In J. Westermeyer (Ed.), *Anthropology and mental health*. The Hague: Mouton, 1976.

Kupfer, D. J., Foster, F. G., Coble, P., McPartland, R. J., & Ulrich, R. F. The application of EEG sleep for the differential diagnosis of affective disorders. *American Journal of Psychiatry*, 1978, *135*, 69–74.

Leighton, D. C. Cultural determinants of behavior: A neglected area. *American Journal of Psychiatry*, 1972, *128*, 1003–1004.

Liss, J. L., Welner, A., Robins, E., & Richardson, M. Psychiatric symptoms in black and white inpatients. I: Record study. *Comprehensive Psychiatry*, 1973, *14*, 457–482.

Masserman, J. H., and Carmichael, H. T. Diagnosis and prognosis in psychiatry. *Journal of Mental Science*, 1938, *84*, 893–946.

Meyer, N. G. Age, sex, and color variations in the diagnostic distributions of admissions of inpatient services of state and county mental hospitals, United States, 1972. Statistical Note. Washington, D.C.: *National Institute of Mental Health Biometry Branch*, 1974.

Murphy, H. B. M. The epidemiological approach to transcultural psychiatric research. In A. V. S. de Reuck and R. Porter (Eds.), *Transcultural psychiatry*. Boston: Little, Brown, 1965.

Murphy, H. B. M. Differences between mental disorders of French Canadians and British Canadians. *Canadian Psychiatric Association Journal*, 1974, *19*, 247–257.

Murphy, H. M. B., Wittkower, E. D., Fried, J., & Ellenberger, H. A. A cross-cultural survey of schizophrenic symptomatology. *International Journal of Social Psychiatry*, 1963, *9*, 237–249.

Raskin, A., Crook, T. H., & Herman, K. D. Psychiatric history and symptom differences in black and white depressed inpatients. *Journal of Consulting and Clinical Psychology*, 1975, *43*(1), 73–80.

Rosenhan, D. L. On being sane in insane places. *Science*, 1973, *179*, 250–258.

Schneider, K. *Clinical psychopathology*. New York: Grune & Stratton, 1959.

Schubert, D. S. Recognizing depression in patients with physical symptoms. *Medical Challenge*, August, 1978, 44–95.

Schwab, J. J. Amitryptiline in the management of depression and depression associated with physical illness. In Merck Sharp and Dohme: *Amitryptiline in the management of depression*, 1975.

Simon, R. J., Fleiss, J. L., Garland, B. J., Stiller, P. R., & Sharpe, L. Depression and schizophrenia in hospitalized black and white mental patients. *Archives of General Psychiatry*, 1973, *28*, 509–512.

Singer, B. D. *Racial factors in psychiatric intervention.* San Francisco: R. E. Research Associates, 1977.

Sletten, I. W., Schuff, S., Altman, H., & Ulett, G. A. A state-wide computerized psychiatric system: Demographic, diagnostic, and mental status data. *British Journal of Social Psychiatry,* 1972, *18,* 30–40.

Steinberg, M. D., Pardes, H., Bjork, D., & Sporty, L. Demographic and clinical characteristics of black psychiatric patients in a private general hospital. *Hospital and Community Psychiatry,* 1977, *23,* 128–132.

Taube, C. A. Primary diagnosis of discharges from general hospital psychiatric inpatient units, United States 1970–71. Statistical Note 68. Washington, D.C.: *National Institute of Mental Health Biometry Branch,* 1973.

Thomas, C. S., and Lindenthal, J. J. The depression of the oppressed. *M. H.: A publication of the Mental Health Association,* Summer, 1975, 13–14.

Tonks, C. M., Paykel, E. S., & Klerman, G. L. Clinical depressions among negroes. *American Journal of Psychiatry,* 1970, *127,* 329–335.

Vitols, M. M., Waters, H. G., & Keeler, M. H. Hallucinations and delusions in white and negro schizophrenics. *American Journal of Psychiatry,* 1963, *1205,* 472–476.

Welner, A., Liss, J. L., & Robins, E. Psychiatric symptoms in white and black inpatients: Follow-up study. *Comprehensive Psychiatry,* 1973, *14,* 383–388.

Welner, A., Liss, J. L., & Robins, E. A systematic approach for making a psychiatric diagnosis. *Archives of General Psychiatry,* 1974, *31,* 193–196.

Williams, R. L. Scientific racism and I.Q.: The silent mugging of the black community. *Psychology Today,* 1974, *12,* 32–41.

Woodruff, R. A., Goodwin, D. W., & Guze, S. B. *Psychiatric diagnosis.* New York: Oxford University Press, 1974.

5

A Learned Helplessness Analysis of Problems Confronting The Black Community

LEON GREEN

INTRODUCTION

The life experience of many economically deprived black Americans is largely a direct result of racial discrimination and prejudice, abject poverty, and educational, economic, social, and political control in America (Collier, 1977; Harwood, 1969). Under these conditions, it is not surprising that many experience some form of depression, hopelessness, and helplessness (Kerr, 1972; McCord, 1969). The tendency in America has been to invoke arguments of innate intellectual inferiority (Jensen, 1969) or inferior personality structure as an explanation for these behaviors (e.g., Kardiner & Ovesey, 1962). A more parsimonious and empirically testable model of hopelessness and helplessness is provided by the learned helplessness theory (Seligman, 1975, 1978). The purpose of this chapter is to present an overview of the learned helplessness model, describe how it can be used to account for numerous problems confronting economically deprived black Americans, and discuss behavior change procedures which emanate from the model. In addition, a brief discussion of depression which sometimes develops from feelings of chronic helplessness will be included. A word of caution is needed at this juncture. The discussion of learned helplessness in this chapter is not meant to imply that all black Americans suffer from this problem. Hence, this is not a deficit model of black behavior as so many previous models have been. However, the learned helplessness model is viewed as useful in explaining certain behaviors in disadvantaged black populations. It should also be noted that the model applies to any disadvantaged group, regardless of race, although the present focus in this chapter is on black populations.

LEON GREEN • Graduate School of Applied and Professional Psychology, Rutgers University, New Brunswick, New Jersey 08903.

Briefly stated, learned helplessness occurs when an individual perceives that there is no response which he can make that will affect the outcome or control of a particular situation or event (Seligman, 1975; Seligman, Klein, & Miller, 1976). The practice of racial discrimination and economic, political, and educational restrictions provide the basis for many blacks to experience helplessness. At a basic level, black people's color is often the basis for excluding them from certain housing areas (Donnerstein, Donnerstein, & Koch, 1975). Blacks are restricted and excluded from certain jobs regardless of their qualifications (Burlew, 1977; Howard & McCord, 1969) and certain schools and educational institutions regardless of level of preparation (Low, 1962; Thompson, 1962). For many black people, a perception of helplessness even extends itself to the political spheres; blacks express futility in their attempts to participate actively in the political process in America (Clark, 1965). Black persons in ghetto–slum areas may not ascertain any possibility of escaping from their plight (Harwood, 1969). Unskilled blacks who are jobless frequently perceive no chance of acquiring a job in the future. Black children in schools may perceive no means to affect the grades they receive from white teachers, especially if the teachers express a lack of confidence in their ability to learn (Bennett, 1976).

Theoretical and Empirical Bases

Learned helplessness is presented as a model to explain some of the etiological and maintenance factors of problems confronting black people in situations produced by racial discriminatory practices and resultant life conditions. Obviously, before applying a learned helplessness analysis to such problems, at least two questions should be addressed: (a) what are the major characteristics of the model and (b) what relevant research supports the model's applicability in explaining such problems?

RESPONSE–OUTCOME INDEPENDENCE

The concept of learned helplessness was derived by Seligman and his associates (Overmier & Seligman, 1967; Seligman, 1975; Seligman et al., 1976; Seligman & Maier, 1967) to describe the failure of dogs to respond in inescapable shock conditions and their subsequent failure to initiate escape behavior to eliminate shock under conditions where escape was possible. Similar effects have been produced in humans and other species (Seligman, 1975; Seligman et al., 1976). The essential condition for the occurrence of learned helplessness consists of uncontrollability based upon a perception of response–outcome (reinforcement) independence. Learned helplessness effects can be observed in motivational disturbances, cognitive disturbances, and emotional disturbances. Collectively, these disturbances produce decrements in behavioral performance.

According to Seligman (1975), learned helplessness occurs when an individual perceives independence between performance and/or reinforcement outcome. Under this condition, whether an individual responds or not, the probability of a particular outcome is the same (Maier & Seligman, 1976). In this situation, the individual perceives that his behavior cannot control the outcome or events; one cannot terminate or reduce the probability of an adverse event nor produce or increase the probability of a positively reinforcing event.

The expectation that continued responding will be independent of outcome appears to be principally responsible for producing the motivational, cognitive, and emotional disturbances of learned helplessness. In the motivational disturbance, the expectation of uncontrollability reduces response initiation to eliminate the uncontrollable event (Maier & Seligman, 1976). Individuals do not initiate responses to escape from uncontrollable events because the incentive for attempting escape is the expectation that the attempt will eliminate or reduce the occurrence of the undesirable event (Seligman et al., 1976). This is probably the basis for the passivity in learned helplessness and presumably in helplessness depression. Cognitive deficit consists of a reduction in the perception of control (Maier & Seligman, 1976). Individuals show difficulty in perceiving that their responses do affect success and failure in new situations, this occurs even though their responses actually terminate the aversive event (Seligman et al., 1976). The negative cognitive set appears to be produced by learning that responses and outcomes are independent of each other. A negative cognitive set derived from experience with learned helplessness situations interferes with an individual's ability to learn later that a contingent relationship exists between behavior and outcome on future occasions (Maier & Seligman, 1976).

UNCONTROLLABILITY AND UNPREDICTABILITY

Uncontrollable aversive events produce greater emotional disruptions than do controllable aversive events. Three kinds of learning can occur in respect to the fear or anxiety which accompanies the occurrence of an aversive event: (a) if an individual can control the events, anxiety disappears; (b) if an individual is uncertain about control of the event, anxiety remains; (c) if an individual learns he cannot control the event, helplessness depression occurs (Seligman et al., 1976). The discriminability or predictability of an occurrence of an aversive event is important here. Unpredictable aversive events produce greater emotional disturbance than predictable aversive events when controllability of the aversive event is held constant. According to Seligman (1975), this difference occurs because an unpredictable aversive event does not provide a signal or conditioned stimulus for the occurrence of the aversive event, and thus the individual has no way of knowing when it is safe (conditions under which the aversive event will not occur) or dangerous (conditions under which the aversive event will occur). If an individual cannot anticipate when the uncontrollability of an aversive event will recur, then the unpredictability of the situation's recurrence will produce generalization of the helplessness effect across similar situations and may affect dissimilar situations (Abramson, Seligman,& Teasdale, 1978).

ROLE OF ATTRIBUTION

Learned helplessness theory differentiates between *personal* and *universal* helplessness. Personal helplessness depends upon an internal attribution for the cause of the helplessness, whereas universal helplessness depends upon an *external* attribution for the cause of the helplessness (Abramson *et al.*, 1978; Seligman, 1978). In personal helplessness, a person perceives that the outcome is not contingent on any response in his repertoire but expects the outcome to be contingent on a response in the repertoire of a *relevant other*. In contrast, universal helplessness concerns situations in which a person expects the outcome not to be contingent on any response in his repertoire or in the repertoire of any relevant other.

The distinction between personal and universal helplessness is based upon Bandura's (1977a) self-efficacy model, which distinguishes between efficacy expectations and outcome-based expectations. An efficacy expectation refers to whether an individual expects that he will be able to produce or exhibit a particular response in a particular situation. An outcome expectation refers to whether an individual expects a particular response to be effective in producing a desired outcome (Bandura, 1977a). When a low efficacy expectation is coupled with a high outcome expectation, personal helplessness exists. Universal helplessness involves a low outcome expectation: no response exists that the individual or relevant others can use to produce the desired outcome in a particular situation (Abramson *et al.*, 1978). The "relevant other" concept has special relevance to the analysis of problems confronting the black community. In this regard, a black person may perceive himself as having high self-efficacy in one area but perceive his race, and thus himself, as being universally helpless in another area. Whether a black person perceives himself as personally or universally helpless has serious implications for his self-perception of competence and worth.

The *generality* and *chronicity* of learned helplessness depends upon the attribution the individual makes for noncontingency between his current acts and outcomes as they relate to future acts and outcomes (Abramson *et al.*, 1978). If a black person makes an attribution to a global or general factor, his expectation is that helplessness will occur across a wide range of situations, whereas an attribution to a specific or unique factor indicates an expectancy that helplessness will not occur across situations. Similarly, attributing helplessness to a stable (chronic) factor leads to an expectancy that in a similar situation helplessness will recur and it will be long in duration, whereas attributing helplessness to an unstable or transient factor leads to an expectation that the duration of helplessness will be short-lived or intermittent. Note that an individual's attribution affects his prediction of the recurrence of the expectancy of helplessness, whereas the expectancy of response independency determines the occurrence of the helplessness deficits (Abramson *et al.*, 1978).

HELPLESSNESS AND OTHER MODELS OF LEARNING

MODELS OF LEARNING[1]

Learned helplessness is presented as a complement to explanations of behavior based upon operant conditioning (Levis, 1976; Skinner, 1953) and social learning theory (Bandura, 1969; 1977a; 1977b; 1978). The theoretical basis of operant conditioning explains the occurrence of behavior in terms of its relationship to its contingent environmental consequences. Behavior, as an operant, is defined in terms of the changes it produces in the environment. The role an event plays in operant conditioning depends upon its functional relationship to other events (Skinner, 1953). If behavior increases on future occasions when followed contingently by an event, then reinforcement has occurred. If it decreases, then punishment has occurred. Behavior will come under the control of a stimulus event if the event reliably indicates the outcomes for exhibiting that behavior. Behavior undergoes extinction if it is not followed with some frequency by a reinforcing event. The individual's cognitions play no role in the regulation and control of behavior in this theory.

Social learning theory begins with the basic tenet that behavior,

---

[1] Respondent conditioning is not included in this analysis because an analysis of its bases is beyond the scope and space allocation for this chapter. However, see Seligman (1975) for comparisons with learned helplessness.

personal factors (cognitions, images, emotions), and environmental factors are reciprocal determinants of each other in an interdependent relationship (Bandura, 1977b). A social learning analysis adds a cognitive mediational system to operant conditioning principles and learning. Based upon social learning theory, behavior can be learned and influenced through vicarious reinforcement, modeling, self-control, cognitive representation of contingencies, cognitive expectations, and covert problem solving. More emphasis is placed upon the mutually reciprocal interactions of these means of behavioral control than is indicated in the operant theory of learning.

RESPONSE–OUTCOME LEARNING SPACE

The learned helplessness model provides data and explanations for a portion of the response-outcome learning space (Seligman, 1975) which had not been adequately explored or explained. Social learning theory and operant conditioning both provide adequate analysis and explanations for effects of continuous reinforcement, intermittent reinforcement, extinction, punishment, and differential reinforcement of other behavior. In each case the contingency either depends upon the response's occurrence (continuous and intermittent reinforcement and punishment) or nonoccurrence (extinction and differential reinforcement of other behavior). These cases represent response dependence because the probability of an outcome when a response occurs is different from the probability of outcome when a response does not occur (Maier & Seligman, 1976; Seligman, 1975). In contrast, the learned helplessness model describes situations in which the probability of an outcome is equal when the response occurs or does not occur (Seligman, 1975). Since the outcome occurs independently of the person's response, then responding is useless and the person is deemed helpless in these situations.

INTERACTION OF LEARNING MODELS

Models of learning based upon operant conditioning, social learning theory, and learned helplessness explain different aspects of the learned helplessness phenomenon and thus probably interact in explaining the cognitive-behavioral phenomenon. Learning principles derived from operant conditioning and social learning provide viable explanations for the rate of occurrence, maintenance, differential occurrence, and modes of acquisition and transmission of learned helplessness in black people. In addition, behavior change procedures rely heavily on these models. The theory of learned helplessness provides an analysis of the cognitive, emotional, and motivational deficits produced by response–outcome independence. The theory provides minimal analysis of the individual's actual behavior, except as an indirect indicant of cognitive, emotional, and motivational deficits. Even helpless behavior is affected by other environmental events in the real world which may serve to influence it. This gap in information can be filled by operant conditioning principles. Social learning theory, from a reciprocal determinism position, can provide an analysis of the mutual interactions among: (a) response–outcome independence, (b) cognitive, motivational, and emotional deficits, and (c) other environmental events that serve to maintain and increase the helplessness behavior under other conditions and in other situations.

Some illustrations depicting the interaction of these models in their explanation of learned helplessness behavior may help to clarify their interdependence. Reinforcement for exhibiting helplessness or punishment for not exhibiting helplessness can serve to maintain helplessness even after the conditions for helplessness have been eliminated. Under conditions of response–outcome independence, learned behavior which normally would produce the desired outcome will undergo extinction and thus accelerate the helplessness effect. The ability to determine which cues indicate the onset of response–outcome independence can increase the discriminability of one's behavior in the situation.

The importance of social learning in understanding learned helplessness can be seen in vicariously produced helplessness effects. When an individual observes failure produced by response–outcome independence, he can vicariously experience helplessness even though he has not been exposed to the uncontrollable events. In their investigation of vicariously learned helplessness, Brown and Inouye (1978) found that persistence on a difficult task will be lower if an individual observes a model, with similar competence, fail prior to performing the task himself. An increase in persistence is expected if an individual perceives himself as more competent than the "helpless model." Presumably, black persons may exhibit helplessness in situations in which other blacks have modeled helplessness if they perceive themselves to have similar levels of competence.

LEARNED HELPLESSNESS AND THE BLACK EXPERIENCE

Learned helplessness appears to be quite relevant to some black people's responses to racial discriminatory practices in America and their resultant life styles. Racial discriminatory practices can produce helplessness by limiting the effectiveness of any response made by the black population in a wide range of situations. When situations are controlled based upon racial discrimination, then the outcomes for the black population are the same regardless of whether they respond appropriately, inappropriately, or not at all. To the extent that black persons perceive themselves to be helpless as a function of racial discrimination (control), they will probably exhibit *universal* helplessness. To the extent that they perceive themselves to be helpless as a product of their own lack of intelligence, skills, competencies, or ability to utilize opportunities, they will probably exhibit *personal* helplessness. Some black individuals may also perceive themselves to be helpless as a function of a combination of their inabilities and the racist system in America; thus, there is no reason to gain appropriate skills since these skills may be useless in affecting outcomes in racially controlled situations. Even when helplessness is due to racial discrimination, it is important to compare the degree of perceived uncontrollability with the actual level of uncontrollability. For example, a white college professor may operate with the policy that no black person can obtain a grade higher than a C in his course. In this situation, any black student is helpless in producing responses that will change the probability of obtaining an outcome of grade A or B regardless of such variables as skill, intelligence, and amount of studying. However, obtaining outcomes of C, D, or F may be response-dependent and not governed by uncontrollable outcomes. In this case, a black student cannot control whether his performance will be evaluated as above average but can control whether his performance will be judged average or below average.

To the extent that racial discrimination is the progenitor of educational, economical, and political inequities between blacks and whites, it directly serves to increase the pervasiveness of learned helplessness in blacks. The following analysis provides a learned helplessness interpretation of problems confronting black individuals in academic settings, politics, employment attainment and job performance, the welfare system, and "ghetto–slum" life experiences. In addition, the analysis examines the links between learned helplessness and anxiety, depression, suicide, self-esteem, and self-concept.

ACADEMIC ACHIEVEMENT

It is perhaps in educational settings that young black children most readily find themselves subjected to racial discriminatory practices (Bennett, 1976; Low, 1962; Thompson, 1962) and thus to the effects of learned helplessness. Existing evidence (Bennett, 1976), indicates that white teachers have differential expectations in respect to the performance levels of black and white children. Bennett's (1976) data suggest that white teachers believe that white students will perform significantly better than black students. In this situation, black children might learn that the outcomes of their performances are not dependent upon their quality or level of academic performance, but more upon the teacher's perception of their racial status. These perceptions can have long-range consequences on the future achievement strivings of black children. Apparently, one factor in explaining the difference between white and black youths' achievement strivings lie in blacks' lower expectancy of being able to obtain their goals (Katz, 1969).

It is especially important to explore the possibility of learned helplessness when black children are given the designations of mental retardation. Presumed retardation may be learned helplessness in disguise. Apparently, this was the case with a fourth-grade black child described in *Death at an Early Age* (Kozol, 1967). According to Seligman (1975), the child may have learned that when English words are presented, there is nothing he can do right; repetitive failure increases and, over time, produces and maintains helplessness. Children's higher-order cognitive skills can be substantially retarded when they learn that responses do not produce solutions (Seligman, 1975). In this regard, when black children experience chronic failure, they may develop expectations that they will always fail in school (Seligman, 1975). Fortunately, for most black children, this failure is not consistent across subjects or teachers. Two experiments by Dweck and associates (Dweck, 1975; Dweck & Reppucci, 1973) indicate that feelings of helplessness can be under discriminative control of different teachers and different subjects.

Besides the motivational and cognitive deficits, children in academic settings who are faced with repeated failure may also exhibit emotional expressions of helplessness. Seligman (1975) reported a case of a black boy who experienced helplessness due to chronic academic failure and who would throw tantrums when presented with a word-card or a spelling book. Many times black children may receive not only punishment in the form of failure for their academic performance but also reinforcement in the form of a passing grade for being quiet and nondisruptive (Clark, 1965).

Research is needed to examine the parameters of learned helplessness in academic settings. Chronic failure combined with teachers' expectations of inadequate performance may lead to stable, global, and internal attribution. Black students will probably perceive their helplessness as a more universal occurrence in academic settings if they attribute their problems to external factors such as the teacher's prejudice, uninteresting subjects or a racist educational system.

EMPLOYMENT AND LIVING CONDITIONS

Problematic employment and living conditions are perpetuated by racially discriminatory policies. These policies force a large percentage of blacks to live in slum-ridden ghettos and deprive them of equal access to employment and economic opportunities (Clark, 1965; Harwood, 1969). Attempts to escape from ghetto residency are met with substantial racial discrimination in respect to apartment availability (Donnerstein, Donnerstein, & Kock, 1975; Harwood, 1969). Living in the ghetto, black people are exposed to poor housing conditions, suffer inadequate nutrition and health care, and face high rates of disease and early death (Clark, 1965). The unemployment rate for blacks is at least twice the unemployment rate of whites, and this discrepancy is apparently on the increase (Patterson, 1976). Since whites control economic enterprises in northern black ghettos and restrict economic opportunities, escape from the ghetto through employment is infeasible for blacks as a group (Clark, 1965; Harwood, 1969). Joblessness and living below poverty level force many blacks into the welfare system. The manner in which the welfare system is designed perpetuates poverty by prohibiting recipients from involvement in self-help enterprises to supplement their income (Smith, Burlew, Mosely, & Whitney, 1978). Nor does the current welfare system provide incentives for attempts to remove oneself from the system.

According to Clark (1964), immobility, stagnation, apathy, indifference, and defeatism are the results of this racial discrimination and institutionalization of powerlessness or, more aptly, learned helplessness. Low income, joblessness, welfare, and ghetto-slum conditions restrict many black individuals' choices and frequently expose them to outcomes independent of effort (Seligman, 1975). Uncontrollability produced by ghetto poverty experiences can also produce helplessness, which can lead to depression, passivity, and defeatism (Seligman, 1975).

POLITICAL AND LEGAL SYSTEMS

It is possible that the black population's low level of political participation and trust in the legal system are a result of learned helplessness in those situations. They often do not receive a fair trial in court, and more often than not the police appear unresponsive to their needs. Blacks do not have equal protection under the law (Clark, 1965; Smith *et al.*, 1978). Black persons are overrepresented in jail and prison populations (Smith *et al.*, 1978). These problems are exacerbated by frequent arrests, improper searches, unjustified convictions, and racially biased decisions when the problems involve interracial conflicts. Under these conditions, any legal outcome for black persons appears to be largely independent of their behavioral performance and much more a function of their race and socioeconomic status. This kind of uncontrollability probably leads to universal helplessness since the controlling factors are external and are probably perceived as external. Research is needed to test this hypothesis and to determine the relationships among type of legal outcome, socioeconomic status, and the generality and chronicity of learned helplessness.

Political involvement on the part of black Americans has been hampered by the lack of control over outcomes of their political participation (Seasholes, 1965). Not only does political involvement undergo extinction, but many blacks perceive the political outcome of their participation to be based upon "fate control" (Seasholes, 1965). In this situation, the policy outcome is the same regardless of black participation. Perception (Seasholes, 1965) of fate control corresponds to perception of uncontrollable outcomes. A study by Shorter (1976) indicates that the amount of political involvement corresponds to the black person's perception of having control over his life. He assessed students' political activity by peer ratings of their political activity in the Black Student Union and on the Kerpelman and Weiner Activity Scale, which provides an assessment of actual and desired political activity. Shorter's study demonstrates that highly political and active black students believe they have more control over their lives than relatively less politically active students. Both highly active and less active black students believe that blacks as a group do not have much control over what happens to them. However, the more politically active black students are less likely to believe that black people's lives are controlled by chance or fate than are their less-active counterparts. Highly active black students believe that powerful other people, institutions, and systems control the black population's living condition and lives (Shorter, 1976).

Whether the perception of controllability or uncontrollability is based upon fate or powerful others, it is still based upon an external attribution and forms the basis for perceived universal helplessness. Seasholes (1965) suggests that blacks who perceive their political status and insignificance to be a result of their own shortcomings attribute lack of political effectiveness to their own worthlessness. Data are needed to ascertain conditions affecting the generality of political helplessness.

THE DEFEATED: ALCOHOLISM AND DRUG ABUSE

The high rate of alcoholism and drug addiction in the black ghettos (McCord, 1969) and among black people in general (Smith et al., 1978) may be a response to uncontrollable aversive conditions due to racial discrimination, joblessness, political and legal ineffectiveness, severe poverty, inadequate education and training, and depression resulting from the inability to affect positive outcomes. McCord (1969) indicates that blacks used alcohol to relieve anxiety, to ease fatigue, and to get away from miseries of life. McCord (1969) and Smith et al., (1978) suggest that black individuals who experience the greatest amount of injustice are probably most likely to seek escape from these conditions by engaging in alcohol and drug abuse. The use of alcohol and drugs may act to temporarily reduce the emotional effects of helplessness, such as anxiety and depression. Although a definitive statement on the causes of alcoholism (Nathan, 1976) and drug abuse is currently unavailable, an investigation of the relationship between alcoholism and uncontrollable aversive events may provide some answers. Research is needed to determine whether black alcoholics who attribute their alcoholic or drug abuse problem to internal problems (personal worthlessness, stupidity, and weakness) are substantially different from those who attribute their alcoholic or drug abuse problem to external factors (joblessness and racism). It may also be important to determine whether black alcoholics and drug abusers perceive their helplessness to be due to a wide range of problems or deficit areas and whether they perceive these problems or deficit areas as stable entities.

RESULTANT COGNITIVE DEFICITS

Cognitive deficits resulting from uncontrollability produced by racial discrimination primarily involve blacks' perception of their abilities to alter their present condition. One of the major results of learned helplessness is that people may perceive that they are more helpless than the level of uncontrollability in a situation warrants. Thus, black persons exposed to the uncontrollability of racial manipulation and discrimination may not perceive *the extent* to which they can actually affect positive outcomes in academic settings, ghetto conditions, poverty, unemployment, and in the legal and political systems. The occurrence of discriminatory practices in the previous areas does not always indicate a stable occurrence or total control over contingent responding. It is important to determine the amount of control that can be achieved and effectively utilized to gain specified objectives when uncontrollable racial discrimination is in operation.

When racial discriminatory practices change or are no longer in effect, learned helplessness can interfere with blacks' learning that their efforts can and do produce desired outcomes. According to Seligman (1975), response–outcome independence is learned actively and interferes with learning that contingencies have changed. In academic settings, black students may expect to fail in mathematics even though they may now have a different teacher, different class, or new concepts. Job-less blacks may perceive that they are not able to find and obtain employment even after jobs become accessible and they have received specific training to qualify for them. Blacks may still feel helpless in obtaining the houses they desire, though their incomes are adequate and the legal system will respond justly to any charge of racial discrimination. Finally, blacks may not leave ghetto areas even after their income has substantially increased.

RESULTANT EMOTIONAL DEFICITS: DEPRESSION

The uncontrollability of aversive events and their unpredictability are at the root of emotional deficits produced by learned helplessness. The helplessness model of depression is a subset of depression and regards the expectation of response–outcome independence as a sufficient, but not a necessary, condition of depression (Abramson et al., 1978; Seligman et al., 1976). Helplessness depression is marked by symptoms of passivity, a negative cognitive set, and depressed affect. Depressed affect occurs when an individual cannot obtain a highly desired outcome or cannot avoid the occurrence of a highly aversive outcome. The helplessness model of depression is more general and does not contradict social learning models or operant models which view depression as a result of extinction procedures or loss of reinforcers (Costello, 1972; Ferster, 1973; Lazarus, 1968; Lewinsohn, Biglan, & Zeiss, 1976). The purpose here is to discuss depression only as it relates to the concept of learned helplessness.

The chronic feeling of helplessness caused by racially discriminatory practice may ultimately result in clinically significant depression. When these practices thwart their ability to achieve certain skills (including academic success, political effectiveness, legal justice, jobs, desirable housing, or escape from poverty), many blacks may feel helpless and hopeless in affecting a positive outcome. The depression which may accompany such a state of affairs is often associated with lowered self-esteem that is probably related to the attribution of causation. When unemployment is seen as a function of one's own inadequacies, self-esteem is likely to suffer greatly because an internal-personal attribution is made. On the other hand, if chronic unemployment is seen as a result of racial discrimination, then self-esteem will not suffer to the same degree since an external-universal attribution is made. The level or extent of depression depends upon the expectation of uncontrollability (Abramson et al., 1978). When depression is produced by uncontrollability, there are more global and stable attributions for continuous, recurrent, and pervasive negative events. Abramson et al. (1978) showed that depressed individuals "often make internal, global, and stable attributions for failure, and may make external, specific and perhaps less stable attributions for success" (p. 67). Even more problematic is the tendency for individuals who are depressed to perceive themselves as helpless more readily than nondepressed persons. Thus, the black individual in our society is confronted with situations that may be perceived as insoluble when, in fact, they are soluble.

BEHAVIORAL INTERVENTIONS FOR
HELPLESSNESS

During the above discourse, an argument has been made for the applicability of behavioral models in accounting for many problems confronting black people in American society. Particularly, the learned helplessness model was discussed in detail, and the development of helplessness and hopelessness was related to lowered levels of expectation, motivation, self-esteem, and the development of depression. This model, when combined with other behavioral models (e.g., operant, social learning theory) provides hypotheses which are empirically testable. In addition, the models generate behavior change strategies for remediating such difficulties. At this point, behavior change strategies designed to eliminate the learned helplessness effects will be discussed. These strategies are derived from the learned helplessness model and other behavioral theories.

ASSESSMENT

When black clients are seen in clinical settings, it is essential that the parameters for the client's perception of uncontrollability be assessed. If learned helplessness is found to be a factor, the assessment should be designed to ascertain whether the client's helplessness is based upon *internal* or *external* attributions. If the helplessness is due to racial discrimination, then external attribution is correct, but the extent of perceived helplessness may be inappropriate. If the attribution of helplessness pertains to global factors (i.e., "I'm dumb"), then the generality and pervasiveness of helplessness in unrelated areas must be assessed. If the attribution pertains to stable factors (i.e., "I will always be poor"), then the client may perceive no possibility for a change in his status. Behavioral assessment is also needed to determine the extent to which these attributions interact and exacerbate the helplessness effect. Careful examination of factors maintaining cognitive and motivational deficits and depression must be assessed. In addition, the situational variability of helplessness behavior and effects must be determined. Finally, the individual's level of self-control, his past reactions to failure and success, and his current level of skills including interpersonal skills must be ascertained.

THEORETICAL BASES OF TREATMENT

Motivational, cognitive, and emotional deficits are produced by the perception and expectation of response–outcome independence. Effective and efficient elimination of these deficits requires strategies that enhance the perception and expectation of response–outcome dependence, as well as strategies directed at the specific elimination of each deficit. However, these deficits are exacerbated by the kinds of inappropriate attributions made by an individual in response to his perception of the *cause* of his helplessness (Abramson *et al.*, 1978). Although strategies that increase the perception and expectation of response–outcome dependence will remove the basis for these inappropriate attributions, these attributions may continue, due to control and reinforcement from other environmental sources. If this latter condition occurs, then alteration of the inappropriate attributions may necessitate other specific interventions.

The unpredictability of uncontrollable outcomes increases the probability that helplessness behavior and motivational, cognitive, and emotional deficits will occur in situations in which response–outcome dependence exists. The higher the frequency of occurrence of helplessness behavior and deficits under nonhelplessness conditions, the higher the probability that helplessness behavior and deficits will be influenced and controlled by other environmental events. The elimination of learned helplessness under these conditions may require the modification of the controlling environmental events, as well as a reversal of the expectancy of noncontingency.

At a theoretical level, the elimination of learned helplessness requires a reversal of the expectancy that responding will not lead to desirable outcomes. This expectation is principally responsible for inhibiting response initiation (Seligman, 1975). Reversal of this expectation calls for strategies that will enhance a belief in response-outcome dependence and a belief that responding will lead to desirable outcomes (Seligman *et al.*, 1976).

An early proposal for the treatment of learned helplessness suggests guiding an individual in the performance of appropriate behaviors which are contingently related to desired outcomes or reinforcement (Seligman, 1975). The effectiveness of this "cure" depends upon persistent and repeated exposure to the contingency between behavior and desirable outcomes or reinforcements (Seligman *et al.*, 1976). Abramson *et al.* (1978) presented four major strategies to alleviate learned helplessness and helplessness depression. The four strategies are: (a) reduce the probability of an aversive outcome and increase the probability of a desired outcome, (b) reduce the desirability of an unobtainable outcome, (c) change the perception of uncontrollability, and (d) modify expectations of failure.

REDUCING THE PROBABILITY OF AVERSIVE OUTCOMES

When helplessness is identified as a problem in black clients and is produced by aversive external factors such as racial discrimination, poverty, and chronic unemployment, it is necessary to reduce the probability of aversive outcomes and increase the probability of desired outcomes. If this type of problem exists, treatment might involve the utilization of legal and political agencies to prevent aversive outcomes or the provision of desired outcomes, such as housing, employment, financial assistance, and legal aid. These strategies may increase expectations that responding will lead to desirable events. Repeated exposure to contingent reinforcement may further "stamp in" desirable behavior as outcome becomes more response-dependent. Put simply, positive experiences greatly enhance the likelihood that individuals will continue to respond in a manner that leads to those outcomes. Of course, the engineering of such events can present innumerable problems and must be planned on an individual basis.

Experimental evidence with black clients supporting this notion does exist. For example, Kandel and Ayllon (1976) found that black prison inmates' rate of academic achievement increased when a contingency management program was implemented. The powerful effects of contingencies based upon response–outcome dependence can be seen in a study on the control of drug-seeking behavior (Milby, Garrett, English, Fritschi, & Clark, 1978). The study consisted primarily of black addicts from a methadone program in which clients earned take-home privileges of methadone, contingent upon clean urine and productive activity. No addict lost take-home privileges and all showed significant reduction in drug-seeking behavior.

REDUCING DESIRABILITY OF UNOBTAINABLE OUTCOMES

At times, helplessness can be alleviated by making highly preferred outcomes less preferable when the situation is unlikely to change and the outcomes are not obtainable (Abramson *et al.*, 1978). Preferred outcomes may be powerful reinforcers. Strategies which reduce the desirability of a stimulus event must change the valence of the event from positive to negative. One method that is often used to alter the value of a stimulus is covert sensitization (Cautela, 1967). This procedure involves repeatedly associating various stimuli in the imagination in order to reduce or enhance the desirability of a stimulus. For example, in order to reduce the desirability of a given stimulus, it could be repeatedly paired with imagined scenes containing various aversive sensations such as nausea or experiencing unpleasant events. Through repeated pairing of positive stimuli with such aversive stimuli, the valence of stimuli can be altered from positive to negative. Of course, the process could be reversed to improve the desirability of a given stimulus. In such an instance, positive imagery would be used (e.g., imagery incorporating such elements as receiving praise).

Another method that can be used to alter desirability is modeling (Bandura, 1977b). Repeated exposure of clients to an influential model (person) who indicates a dislike for the client's preferred, but unattainable outcome should reduce the desirability of that outcome. An alternative or conjoint approach might emphasize aiding the client in developing subgoals that will prepare him for attainment of the previously unobtainable outcomes in the future.

CHANGING THE PERCEPTION OF UNCONTROLLABILITY

When outcomes are attainable but are not perceived as being attainable, it might be necessary to employ strategies designed to change the perception of uncontrollability. Outcomes may not be attainable because the client lacks the necessary behavior in his repertoire to obtain that which is obtainable (e.g., acquiring legal aid). When skills are deficient, specific skills training programs should be implemented. For example, assertiveness training might help a student effectively converse with a teacher he feels has given him an unfair grade. Similarly, performance skill training might enhance academic or job performance. Typically, skills training programs consist of multiple behavioral strategies such as modeling, behavior rehearsal, and instructions in combination with operant principles (e.g., reinforcement, shaping). Frederiksen, Jenkins, Foy and Eisler (1976) used an assertiveness training procedure consisting of behavioral rehearsal, modeling, and instruction to modify abusive verbal outbursts in two black males. Subsequent to treatment, there was an increase in appropriate social requests and a decrease in irrelevant comments, hostile comments, and inappropriate requests. Modeling and behavior rehearsal have also been used to modify black interviewing skill and work behavior (O'Connor & Rappaport, 1970).

MODIFICATION OF EXPECTATION TO FAIL

Often the necessary skills and responses required to achieve a desired outcome are in the client's repertoire, but chronic failure and consistent punishment have substantially reduced or completely eliminated the appropriate responses. When the responses are in the client's repertoire and the aversive contingencies have changed, Abramson *et al.* (1978) recommend modifying the client's expectation of failure. This could be accomplished by prompting the individual to engage in the necessary behavior. The assignment of *in vivo* tasks in a graded fashion should allow positive outcomes to occur which may help eliminate the negative expectation. In conjunction with graded tasks, self-control training to increase and maintain appropriate responses should also prove useful. One form of self-control involves the use of self-statements. Ultimately, if he is to be helped, a black client's perception of helplessness, chronic failure, and helplessness depression must be altered. Self-statements of failure based upon internal, stable and global factors must be changed to self-statements of external, unstable, and specific factors (Abramson *et al.*, 1978). Success based upon external, unstable, and specific factors must be changed to that based upon internal, stable, and global factors, thereby shifting the locus of control from the external environment to the individual. By employing a strategy in which the client makes positive statements to himself (e.g., Ellis, 1962; Fuchs & Rehm, 1977; Meichenbaum, 1977; Rehm, 1977), the durability and frequency of such statements can be increased, while negative self-statements will decrease. Through this process the individual's positive perception of himself is increased.

PREVENTION OF LEARNED HELPLESSNESS

Prevention of learned helplessness probably deserves the greatest amount of research effort, especially as preventive factors relate to changes in blacks' life conditions and responses to racial discrimination and control. Studies by Dweck and Reppucci (1973) and Jones, Nation and Massad (1977) demonstrate that when uncontrollable outcomes occur, individuals who have had prior experience with success and failure do not show deficits in motivation, cognition, and affect. However, those individuals who have not had such exposure do show such deficits. Thus, it is clear that helplessness develops when repeated failure experiences occur in the absence of success experiences. An individual will be immune to a situation which usually produces learned helplessness if he has had previous experience with this situation and was able to control the environment or if he perceived that the reinforcement in the evironment was dependent upon his behavioral performance.

CONCLUSION

The concept of learned helplessness and its application to problems experienced by members of the black community who have been subjected to general racial discrimination, poor education and housing, and lack of job opportunities have been discussed, particularly as they relate to problems that result from racial discriminatory practices in America. Again, it should be noted that our discussion is not concerned with the black community as a whole but relates to the economically, educationally, and politically disadvantaged segment of that community. The learned helplessness model is viewed as heuristic in accounting for some of the problematic behaviors and difficulty experienced by disadvantaged populations. A decided advantage of such a model is that it does not attribute causation to the individual (i.e., claiming he is innately inferior) but places the etiology squarely on the back of society, where it belongs. Moreover, the model provides strategies designed to overcome helplessness behavior. Essentially, learned helplessness is viewed as a response generated by continual experience with uncontrollable outcomes, especially uncontrollable aversive outcomes. It is when one's responses have no effect on the occurrence of outcome that helplessness develops. The effects of such a state of affairs can produce motivational, cognitive, and emotional difficulties which lead to a chronic state of helplessness behavior. My analysis has explored briefly how the learned helplessness model combines with operant and social learning models to provide a comprehensive theoretical model to account for such behavior. The existence of the helplessness phenomenon is seen as being of utmost importance in explaining problems experienced by blacks in academic settings, encounters with the political and legal systems, and in dealing with housing patterns and employment.

One advantage of this particular model is that it provides an adequate description not only of how self-defeating behavior is produced but also of how it might be reduced or eliminated. Four major approaches for eliminating helplessness have been explored: (a) changing the probability of aversive and desirable outcomes, (b) changing the desirability of unobtainable outcomes, (c) altering the perception of uncontrollability, and (d) modifying the expectation of failure. Several behavioral intervention strategies designed to accomplish these ends have been discussed.

The learned helplessness model provides a more adequate explanation of defeatist behavior in blacks than more traditional explanations. Furthermore, empirically testable hypotheses are being generated from the model, a rarity in the mental health field, particularly as it relates to black populations.

REFERENCES

Abramson, L. Y., Seligman, M. E. P., & Teasdale, J. D. Learned helplessness in humans: Critique and reformulation. *Journal of Abnormal Psychology*, 1978, *87*, 49–74.

Bandura, A. *Principles of behavior modification.* New York: Holt, Rinehart & Winston, 1969.

Bandura, A. Self-efficacy: Toward a unifying theory of behavioral change. *Psychological Review*, 1977, 84, 191–215. (a)

Bandura, A. Social learning theory. Englewood Cliffs, N.J.: Prentice-Hall, 1977. (b)

Bandura, A. The self-system in reciprocal determinism. *American Psychologist*, 1978, *33*, 344–358.

Bennett, C. E. Student's races, social class, and academic history as determinants of teacher expectation of student performance. *The Journal of Black Psychology*, 1976, *3*, 71–86.

Brown, I. Jr., & Inouye, D. K. Learned helplessness through modeling: The role of perceived similarity in competence. *Journal of Personality and Social Psychology*, 1978, *36*, 900–908.

Burlew, A. K. Career educational choices among Black females. *The Journal of Black Psychology*, 1977, *3*, 88–106.

Cautela, J. R. Covert sensitization. *Psychological Record*, 1967, 20, 459–468.

Clark, K. B. *Youth in the ghetto: A study of the consequences of powerlessness and a blueprint for change.* New York: Harlem Youth Opportunities Unlimited, Inc., 1964.

Clark, K. B. *Dark ghetto.* New York: Harper & Row, 1965.

Collier, B. Economics, psychology, and racism: An analysis of oppression. *The Journal of Black Psychology*, 1977, *3*, 50–60.

Costello, C. G. Depression: Loss of reinforcers or loss of reinforcer effectiveness. *Behavior Therapy*, 1972, *3*, 240–247.

Donnerstein, E., Donnerstein, M., & Koch, C. Racial discrimination in apartment rentals: A replication. *Journal of Social Psychology*, 1975, *96*, 37–38.

Dweck, C. S. The role of expectations and attribution in the alleviation of learned helplessness. *Journal of Personality and Social Psychology*, 1975, *31*, 674–685.

Dweck, C. S., & Reppucci, N. D. Learned helplessness and reinforcement responsibility in children. *Journal of Personality and Social Psychology*, 1973, *25*, 109–116.

Ellis, A. *Reason and emotion in psychotherapy.* New York: Lyle Stuart, 1962.

Ferster, C. B. A functional analysis of depression. *American Psychologists*, 1973, *28*, 857–870.

Frederiksen, L. W., Jenkins, J. O., Foy, D. W., & Eisler, R. M. Social-skills training to modify abusive verbal outbursts in adults. *Journal of Applied Behavioral Analysis*, 1976, *9*, 117-125.

Fuchs, C. Z. & Rehm, L. P. A self-control behavior therapy program for depression. *Journal of Consulting and Clinical Psychology*, 1977, *45*, 206–215.

Harwood, E. Urbanism as a way of Negro life. In W. McCord, J. Howard, B. Friedberg, & E. Harwood (Eds.), *Life styles in the black ghetto.* New York: W. W. Norton, 1969.

Howard, J., & McCord, W. Watts: The revolt and after. In W. McCord, J. Howard, B. Friedberg, & E. Harwood (Eds.), *Life styles in the black ghetto.* New York: W. W. Norton, 1969.

Jensen, A. R. How much can we boost I.Q. and scholastic achievement? *Harvard Educational Review*, 1969, *39*, 1–123.

Jones, S. L., Nation, J. R., & Massad, P. Immunization against helplessness in man. *Journal of Abnormal Psychology*, 1977, *86*, 75–83.

Kandel, H. J., & Ayllon, T. Rapid educational rehabilitation for prison inmates. *Behaviour Research and Therapy*, 1976, *14*, 323–331.

Kardiner, A., & Ovesey, L. *The mark of oppression.* New York: World Publishing, 1962.

Katz, I. A critique of personality approaches to Negro performance with research suggestions. *Journal of Social Issues*, 1969, *25*, 13–27.

Kerr, N. G. The black community's challenge to psychology. In R. W. Porgh, *Psychology and the black experience*. New York: Brooks/Cole, 1972.

Kozol, J. *Death at an early age*. Boston: Houghton Mifflin, 1967.

Lazarus, A. A. Learning theory and the treatment of depression. *Behaviour Research and Therapy*, 1968, *6*, 83–89.

Levis, D. J. Learned helplessness: A reply and an alternative S–R interpretation. *Journal of Experimental Psychology: General*, 1976, *105*, 47–65.

Lewinsohn, P. M., Biglan, A., & Zeiss, A. M. Behavioral treatment of depression. In P. O. Davidson (Ed.), *The behavioral management of anxiety, depression and pain*. New York: Brunner/Mazel, 1976.

Low, W. A. The education of Negroes viewed historically. In V. A. Clift, A. W. Anderson, & H. G. Hullfish (Eds.), *Negro education in America*. New York: Harper & Row, 1962.

Maier, S. F., & Seligman, M. E. P. Learned helplessness: Theory and evidence. *Journal of Experimental Psychology: General*, 1976, *105*, 3–46.

McCord, W. The defeated. In W. McCord, J. Howard, B. Friedberg, & E. Harwood (Eds.), *Life styles in the black ghetto*. New York: W. W. Norton, 1969.

Meichenbaum, D. H. *Cognitive-behavioral modification: An integrative approach*. New York: Plenum Press, 1977.

Milby, J. B., Garrett, C., English, C., Fritschi, D., & Clark, C. Take-home methadone: Contingency effects on drug-seeking and productivity of narcotic addicts. *Addictive Behaviors*, 1978, *3*, 215-220.

Nathan, P. E. Alcoholism. In H. Leitenberg (Ed.), *Handbook of behavior modification and behavior therapy*. Englewood Cliffs, N.J.: Prentice-Hall, 1976.

O'Connor, R. D., & Rapport, J. Application of social learning principles to the training of ghetto blacks. *American Psychologist*, 1970, *25*, 659–661.

Overmier, J. B., & Seligman, M. E. P. Effects of inescapable shock upon subsequent escape and avoidance responding. *Journal of Comparative and Physiological Psychology*, 1967, *63*, 28-33.

Patterson, P. Black unemployment. *Black Enterprise*. 1976, 7, 53–75.

Rehm, L. P. A self-control model of depression. *Behavior Therapy*, 1977, *8*, 787–804.

Scasholes, B. Political socialization of Negroes: Image development of self and polity. In W. C. Kvaraceus, J. S. Gibson, F. Patterson, B. Seasholes, & J. D. Grambs (Eds.), *Negro self-concept: Implications for school and citizenship*. New York: McGraw Hill, 1965

Seligman, M. E. P. *Helplessness: On depression, development and death*. San Francisco: Freeman, 1975.

Seligman, M. E. P. Comment and integration. *Journal of Abnormal Psychology*, 1978, 87, 165–179.

Seligman, M. E. P., & Maier, S. F. Failure to escape traumatic shock. *Journal of Experimental Psychology*, 1967, *74*, 1–9.

Seligman, M. E. P., Klein, D. C., & Miller, W. R. Depression. In H. Leitenberg (Ed.), *Handbook of behavior modification and behavior therapy*. Englewood Cliffs, N.J. Prentice-Hall, 1976.

Shorter, K. D. L. Towards developing black activists: The relationship of beliefs in individuals and collective internal-external control. *The Journal of Black Psychology*, 1976, *3*, 59–70.

Skinner, B. F. *Science and human behavior*. New York: Macmillan, 1953.

Smith, W. D., Burlew, A. K., Mosely, M. H., & Whitney, W. M. *Minority issues in mental health*. Reading, Mass.: Addison–Wesley, 1978.

Thompson, C. H. Problems in the achievement of adequate educational opportunity. In V. A. Clift, A. W. Anderson, & H. G. Hullfish (Eds.), *Negro education in America*. New York: Harper & Row, 1962.

6

The IQ Controversy and Academic Performance

LLOYD BOND

INTRODUCTION

Since 1950, psychologists and educational researchers have devoted immense investigative energy to research on factors hypothesized to enhance the academic performance of black students. This research represents an offshoot of a general interest on the part of psychologists and educational researchers in theories of learning and ways to optimize learning and achievement. The impetus for specific research on black student achievement has arisen from two overriding and pervasive facts: (a) it is generally acknowledged by the scientific community and by the public that the everyday conditions of the typical minority youngster's life are not conducive to high academic performance, and (b) the usual measures of academic achievement (i.e., standardized aptitude and achievement tests) indicate that black students are significantly behind their white counterparts in academic achievement. Before we consider research on the academic performance of black students, we will briefly review both the long and controversial history of the race/intelligence controversy and the recent renewed interest in this controversy resulting from the writings of Arthur Jensen.

A BRIEF HISTORY OF THE IQ CONTROVERSY

Prior to 1900 and the emergence of Alfred Binet's epoch-making work on intelligence testing, belief in racial difference in intellectual endowment was based more on historical considerations, cultural comparisons, and, perhaps, anecdotal experience than on any "scientific"

LLOYD BOND • Learning Research and Development Center, University of Pittsburgh, Pittsburgh, Pennsylvania 15260.

evidence. In general, doctrines of racially related genetic differences in intelligence were supported by reference to differences in cultural achievement. European achievements in the sciences, architecture, literature and the arts, and law were "compared" with those of the African continent (excluding extreme northern Africa), and, on the basis of this comparison alone, many scholars felt comfortable with notions of black inferiority.

By the mid-1800s, the doctrine of black intellectual inferiority was, in America, at least, well established. In fact, this doctrine had been refined to the point where the *nature* of racial differences was being delineated. In a statement remarkably similar to the position held by Jensen some 120 years later, the school board of Boston, Massachusetts, argued that, in those parts of study and instruction in which progress depends chiefly on memory, black children often keep pace with others, but when their progress comes to depend chiefly on abstract faculties such as analogic reasoning, they quickly fall behind (*Liberator*, 1846).

According to Weinberg (1977), by 1860 two additional developments contributed to genetic theories of racial differences in intelligence: imperialist expansion into both Africa and Europe. To a lesser extent, the same sentiments were evident in America, but here black inferiority was seen as one justification for slavery.

The appearance in 1859 of Darwin's *On the Origin of Species by Means of Natural Selection* was viewed by many scientists and lay persons alike as telling evidence of black intellectual inferiority. Darwin's dual notions of natural selection and survival of the fittest were translated into human society in the form of social Darwinism. Essentially, this doctrine held that natural selection tended to favor pure races, that racial prejudice was therefore adaptive since it accelerated the emergence of pure races, and that, on the evolutionary scale, whites were "further along" toward the human ideal than were other races.

The turn of the century witnessed the emergence of a new social discipline—anthropology. Its leaders, principally American, offered a dissenting view to the predominant theories regarding racial differences. A signal figure in this new discipline was Franz Boas, who for many years worked fruitlessly to establish a foundation for the scientific study of African culture. Of persons of African descent, he wrote: "We do not know of any demand made on the human body or mind in modern life that anatomical or ethnological evidence would prove to be beyond (their) powers" (1940, p. 14). Although many social scientists retained belief in the doctrine of white superiority, a significant number, if not a majority, of adherents to the young science of anthropology were in agreement with Boas's position.

THE EMERGENCE OF INTELLIGENCE TESTING

In 1904, a government commission in France, with a view to establishing special schools for the retarded and feebleminded, resolved to identify children who could not profit from the regular school curriculum. A French psychologist, Alfred Binet, was charged with developing testing procedures which would identify such children. Unlike Galton before him, who reasoned incorrectly that intelligence could be measured by assessing the acuity of the senses because information about the environment is available to the organism only through the five senses, Binet decided to attack his mission directly by having children respond to situations which required skills such as defining words, manipulating symbols in memory, interpreting proverbs, and forming judgments. Most importantly, he conceptualized intelligence as a "practical" activity, and his approach to its measurement was firmly grounded within the academic classroom setting. According to Binet, intelligence is "judgment, otherwise called good sense, practical sense, initiative, the faculty of adapting oneself to the circumstances. To judge well, to comprehend well, to reason well, these are the essential activities of intelligence" (1916, p. 43).

It is, perhaps, a safe speculation that the testing movement begun by Binet is the single most important event in the history of the superiority–inferiority controversy. Since the adaptation of Binet's testing procedures by Terman (1916) and others, questions of black intellectual endowment have been discussed almost exclusively in terms of scores on individual or group intelligence tests. It is a curious irony in the history of science that Binet, who rejected genetic arguments for differences in intelligence among races, social classes, and nationalities, began an assessment procedure which eventually would be the major support for arguments in favor of such differences.

The Binet-Simon scale, for ages 3 to 11, consisted of 30 short tests, arranged in ascending order of difficulty. A second scale, the 1911 version, introduced minor improvements and additions. A major change was the extension of the age range covered, from three years to the adult level. The preeminent figure in American adaptation of Binet's assessment techniques was Louis Terman of Stanford University. Terman's adaptation, now known as the Stanford–Binet, was published in 1916 and contained so many changes and additions as to represent an essentially new test. Several revisions, restandardizations, and renormings have occurred since then (in 1937, 1960, and 1972), but the essential character of the test—in content, administration, and scoring—has, for the most part, been preserved.

In the Stanford–Binet, psychologists, measurement specialists, and educators believed that they had arrived at a totally objective criterion by which the intelligence of individuals and groups could be compared. Both Terman at Stanford and Thorndike at Teacher's College, Columbia University, subscribed to the general notion of "innate" racial differences in intelligence. They had a profound effect upon a generation of educators who embraced both the notion of racial differences in intelligence and the fundamental and overwhelming dependence of intelligence on hereditary factors. Either by design or inadvertently, the intelligence quotient (IQ), defined as the ratio of mental age to chronological age multiplied by a scaling constant of 100, came to be imbued with almost mystical significance. It was (and is) widely believed that the Stanford–Binet and similar tests which immediately followed it somehow measured "native" intelligence or aptitude. The distinction between intelligence or aptitude and achievement was clearly drawn, and it was the former—considered immutable—that was measured by IQ tests. Terman predicted that IQ tests would reveal that which he and others already believed to be true, that is, the tests would show substantial and significant racial differences in general intelligence, differences which could not be erased by enriching one's learning environment. On the basis of IQ test results, Terman's prediction that there would be significant group differences in test scores was accurate. Consistently, black youngsters scored approximately 14 IQ points (one standard deviation) below their white counterparts. Many otherwise sophisticated psychologists accepted the size and consistency of these IQ differences at face value. They assumed that such differences represented real and innate differences in native intelligence. In fact, by the 1920s testing had become such an established and respected practice that well-known measurement specialists were arguing, on the basis of test results, for quotas on immigration from various "undesirable" races and nationalities. The notion began to emerge that not only could the tests detect innate differences in intelligence among races but that they could also detect within-race differences. Thus, "Nordics" (i.e., northern Europeans) were viewed as coming from a more superior gene pool than were Mediterranean peoples, who in turn were regarded as being genetically superior to Africans. The culmination of this movement was Congressional passage in 1924 of a general immigration statute which established quotas for each country. Predictably, immigrants from northern European countries were given higher quotas than were immigrants from eastern and southern European countries. Much of the impetus for these developments is traceable to the emergence of group intelligence tests during World War I.

GROUP INTELLIGENCE TESTS

America's participation in World War I required that army officials select and train thousands of young men for various military duties. This need resulted in the development of the first widely used group intelligence tests—the Army General Classification Test, known as Army Alpha by a group of psychologists headed by Robert Yerkes. (A second test, Army Beta, was also developed for non-English-speaking recruits.) The Army Alpha and the numerous other tests developed during the 1920s purported to measure "general intelligence" (Spearman's g) through what has come to be called a "spiral omnibus" format—"spiral" in the sense that it intermingled items purporting to measure the primary mental abilities (verbal reasoning, numerical reasoning, spatial ability, etc.) and "omnibus" in the sense that it presumably covered all such primary abilities. The most comprehensive analysis of the thousands of test results was accomplished by Brigham (1923) at Princeton University. After an extensive analysis of Alpha results by race and nationality, Brigham concluded, as had others, that racial and ethnic mean differences on the newer group intelligence test also reflected innate (i.e., genetic) differences in intelligence. Curiously, and for reasons that are unknown, Brigham completely reversed his position on the question of native intelligence years later, claiming that native intelligence is "one of the most serious fallacies in the history of science" (Downey, 1961, see also Brigham, 1930).

The Army Alpha test spurred the vigorous development of group tests of all kinds that to this date shows no sign of abating. Although many of these tests purported to be "intelligence" or "aptitude" tests, as distinct from "achievement" tests, an examination of the actual items of the two shows clearly that they are virtually indistinguishable (Cooley & Lohnes, 1976). Performance on standardized academic achievement tests had by 1950 become the criterion against which to judge the effectiveness of interventions, the academic growth of pupils, the relative worth of schools, the qualifications of applicants for advanced or professional degrees, the diagnosis of educational deficiencies—the list goes on and on. In fact, the current author was able to find very few examples of educational research in which the dependent variable was anything other than standardized nationally normed tests of overall reading or numerical ability.

World War II and the Nazi atrocities signaled a temporary end to the popularity of theories of innate racial differences in intellectual functioning. In fact, the horror of the concentration camps so appalled American academicians and lay persons alike that a radical environmentalism tended to replace the genetic theories. The extremes of this position might be stated as follows: Every human being born without obvious genetic deficiences (e.g., Down's syndrome) is infinitely malleable and, to all intents and purposes, is intellectually indistinguishable at birth from any other human being. It therefore follows that variations in the environment cause the variation which we see in measures of intelligence.

Few persons would now agree with such a totally environmentalist stance. The view currently accepted by many is that measured intelligence is a complex function of an individual's heredity and environment and that attempts to disentangle the relative contribution of each are doomed to fail.

RECENT DEVELOPMENTS

In 1969 Jensen published a now famous and highly controversial article in the *Harvard Educational Review* entitled "How much can we boost IQ and Scholastic Achievement?" This article was followed by two books (Jensen, 1972, 1973) entitled, respectively, *Genetics and Education* and *Educability and Group Differences*. Taken together, these 800 pages of writings have rekindled the fires of the IQ controversy. They have generated literally scores of responses and counterresponses in psychological and educational journals.

Essentially, Jensen concludes in the long article that the "compensatory education" efforts aimed principally at poor black youngsters had failed, possibly because these youngsters were genetically incapable of mastering traditional school subjects to any acceptable degree. Instructional technology had not failed these children; they were simply ineducable. The evidence Jensen adduced in support of this conclusion was extensive. It included, among other things, the following: (1) the within-group heritability (i.e., the proportion of population phenotypic variance that is attributable to differences in genotypes) of IQs obtained from white samples was estimated by Jensen to be in the range of .75 to .85, (2) studies of identical twins reared apart indicated that correlations between the separated twins IQs ranged from 0.62 (n = 12) to .86 (n = 53), and (3) the IQs of adopted white children more closely resembled the IQs of their biological parents than those of their adoptive parents. In the two subsequent books mentioned above, Jensen adds to these arguments the facts that (1) other minorities such as American Indians (who, according to Jensen, are even more "educationally disadvantaged" than blacks) score higher than blacks on typical IQ tests, (2) blacks perform more poorly, relative to whites, on many items judged to be "culture-free" than they do on items judged to be "culture-loaded," and (3) blacks and whites differ most on abstract reasoning or high g-loaded tests. A final argument, upon which Jensen lays great stress, involves a prediction which he claims follows from a "genetic hypothesis," namely, that since the mean score of whites on IQ tests is 100 and the mean score of blacks is 85, the siblings of two groups of blacks and whites with the same measured IQ (130, say) should "regress" to different means. Jensen reports data which tend to support these predictions from "genetic theory."

In his most recent book, *Bias in Mental Testing,* Jensen (1980) gives implied support to the genetic argument through a comprehensive psychometric analysis of test items by race and socioeconomic status. Essentially, Jensen examines three kinds of bias: bias as differential predictive validity, bias as item content which favors one group over another, and bias that results from factors external to the test itself, such as race of examiner, test-taking experience, or racial differences in personality and motivational variables.

Regarding his first definition of bias (i.e., the existence of differential predictive validity), the literature reveals that if any bias in IQ tests exists at all, it is generally in the opposite direction to that claimed by critics of IQ tests. That is, in predicting the school and job performance of blacks, the use of the white or combined IQ scores tends to predict a higher level of criterion performance for blacks than was actually attained.

Regarding the second source of bias (i.e., bias that is internal to the test itself), Jensen examines a series of criteria. These include, among other things, factor analysis of test batteries within race and socioeconomic status (SES) categories, analyses of items by race interactions, and comparisons of within-race reliabilities of various tests. In all of the analyses, none of the invalidating conditions obtained. That is to say, the factorial structure of a wide range of ability measures is similar for both races, with the first principal factor accounting for most of the variance and with similar group factors evident in both races; the relative order of item difficulties on IQ tests does not differ for blacks and whites (suggesting no item x race interactions); the items that discriminate most clearly between blacks and whites are the same items that discriminate between older and younger children within each racial group; the reliabilities of IQ and other mental ability tests appear to be as high for blacks as for whites; and finally, the largest racial differences were found not on items that are typically judged culture–specific, but on items judged to be least dependent upon cultural content.

Turning to an examination of the literature on possible biases of the third kind (i.e., biases emanating from situational factors such as race, sex, and dialect of examiner, test anxiety, test-wiseness, and coaching) Jensen concludes, "As yet no factors in the testing procedure itself have been identified as sources of bias in the test performances of different racial groups and social classes."

What is to be concluded from this massive body of evidence? Jensen postulates a "general cognitive developmental lag" among American blacks in the form of an approximately 15-point IQ difference that is unrelated to aspects of the measuring instrument, unrelated to their specific life experiences, unrelated to the quality of their education, unrelated to differences in their home and commmunity environment, unrelated to their nutrition and health care, and unrelated to any presumed psychological damage resulting from life in what (I assume) even Jensen would admit is still an essentially racist society. Although it is never stated explicitly, the implication is clear: the answer to this "developmental lag" of black folks is to be found in their genes.

The sheer bulk and apparent completeness of Jensen's writings on this tired debate are, at first blush, impressive and persuasive. Each argument listed above has, however, been shown to have serious conceptual, factual, and analytical flaws (Block & Dworkin, 1976; Kamin, 1974). Because of the impact Jensen's writings have had both among psychologists and on the public generally, it will be instructive to examine critically each point mentioned above in some detail and to discuss the many counterarguments against them.

WITHIN-GROUP HERITABILITY ESTIMATES

As has been pointed out by geneticists in general (see, for example, Lewontin, 1976; and Thoday, 1976) a within-group heritability estimate for a given trait (be it 0, 1, or anything in between) implies nothing about genetic causes for mean differences *between* groups on the trait. A simple illustration from Thoday illustrates this important point. Consider two completely inbred strains of corn. Because they are inbred by self-fertilization, there will be little or no genetic variation *within* strains. That is, within-group heritability estimates for height, say, will be close to 0.0. If one now plants seeds from each strain into ordinary potting soil, one seed to each pot, one will discover that the plants will vary in height. That is, there will be both within-strain and between-strain variation. Since the plants within each strain are genetically identical, the within-strain variability must be entirely environmental, resulting from differences in soil conditions from pot to pot. The likely average difference in height *between* the strains, however, will be due entirely to genetic causes even though the within-group heritabilities are 0.0!

The opposite experiment is even more revealing. Consider now planting two handfuls of seeds of an "open-pollinated" variety of corn.

Such corn would have considerable genetic variation in it. Now, however, we plant half of the seeds in a specially prepared soil made up of specific nutrients and the other half in soil of different composition. Since the soil is identical *within* each lot, variations in height are due entirely to genetic differences (i.e., heritability approaches 1.00). Between-lot differences in height, however, will be due entirely to differences in soil nutrients. In this case then, we have complete genetic determination within groups, yet the mean differences between groups is entirely environmental! The implications of this example for the IQ controversy should be obvious.

IDENTICAL TWINS REARED APART

In his original 1969 article, Jensen examined several studies involving identical (monozygotic) twins separated shortly after birth and reared apart. Prominent among these were the twin data of Sir Cyril Burt, which included 53 twin pairs presumably collected over a period of 50 years. In Jensen's words, these were the most comprehensive data on separated twins ever assembled, and he relied upon these data extensively in concluding that the heritability of intelligence was quite high (i.e., around 0.80). Kamin (1974) was the first to point out some unexplained inconsistencies (along with some astonishing consistencies) in Burt's data. For example, the correlation between scores on a "group test" of intelligence of 21 identical twins reared apart reported by Burt in 1955 was 0.771. In 1958, Burt reported an identical correlation even though the number of additional twin pairs had increased to "over 30." In 1966, Burt reported that he had now identified 53 such pairs and, remarkably, the correlation between IQ scores remained exactly 0.771. Added to this is the equally surprising consistency of correlations reported by Burt between monozygotic twins reared together. These correlations were all exactly .944 despite the fact that from 1955 to 1966 the size of the sample increased from 83 to 95. (For more detail on similar consistencies, as well as some inconsistencies, see Kamin, 1974.) Further, Dorfman (1978) has presented compelling evidence that other data presented by Burt on IQ and social class are equally suspicious. For example, in one instance (among many) Burt presents sets of data separated by 34 years (from 1927 to 1961) on percentages of persons in vocational categories that agree with astounding precision. In one case, the chances of getting an exact match on six different percentages he reported was 1 in 97,000,000. In short, the evidence is now undeniable, by any reasonable standard, that Burt's data were at best "adjusted" and at worst fabricated.

Kamin (1974) also reports procedural and methodological flaws in other studies of twin data reported in the literature. It should be noted, however, that these criticisms concerned strictly methodological short-comings (e.g., a high degree of similarity between the environments of separated twins) as distinct from the very fidelity of the data. It is reasonable to conclude from the above that the estimates of heritability most often quoted by Jensen and Herrnstein (1973) are probably too high.

ADOPTIVE STUDIES

In addition to twin studies, studies comparing IQ scores of adopted children with their biological and adoptive parents' IQ scores figure prominently in the IQ controversy. The reason for this should be obvious. If the IQ scores of adopted children resemble those of their biological parents (whom most have never seen) more closely than those of their adoptive parents, then presumably, genetics plays at least some part in performance on IQ tests. I will not go into detail on the four major adoption studies cited in the literature (Burks, 1928; Freeman, Holzinger, & Mitchell, 1928; Leahy, 1935; Skodak & Skeels, 1949). The interested reader is referred to the original sources and to various summaries and critiques (Goldberger, 1976; Jensen, 1969; Kamin, 1974). It is sufficient to note that all such studies were conducted within white samples in Britain and the United States, that they did not control for the *selective* placement by adoption and foster home agencies (i.e., placement intended to "match" characteristics of the biological parents with those of adoptive parents), that numerous environmental differences exist between adoptive and biological parents, and that in general the variance in environmental variables among adoptive parents was generally far less than that of the biological parents.

Let us assume that the adoptive studies cited above were methodologically excellent, that they included adequate controls for all known vitiating circumstances, but that still the correlations between adopted children's IQs and those of their biological parents were significantly higher than the correlations between adopted children's IQs and those of their adoptive parents. Would such a result have any implications for the mean difference in IQ scores between blacks and whites?

A classic, carefully designed study by Scarr and Weinberg (1976) suggests that the answer is no. Scarr and Weinberg identified 130 black and interracial children who had been adopted by advantaged white families in Minnesota. The mean IQ scores of these children, who were four years of age or older at the time of testing, was 106, 6 points above the national average, 21 points above the typical score of 85 obtained for blacks nationally, and 16 points above the mean score for blacks in the same geographical area. The investigators in this study took special care to insure against possible bias in the selection of children for adoption on the basis of the educational background of their biological parents. It should also be noted that these children showed comparable superiority in strictly school-related achievements such as vocabulary, reading, and mathematics.

The Scarr–Weinberg study is the most comprehensive study undertaken of cross-racial adoption of black infants. The study suggests that we really know little about that complex of variables in advantaged white homes and communites that results in their children's performing well on IQ and scholastic achievement tests. The study also points up the conceptual bankruptcy and extreme naiveté on the part of otherwise sophisticated researchers in presuming that once they have controlled for the crudely measured construct SES, they have wiped out all IQ-relevant differences in variables between the lives of black and white people in this country. Jensen, for example, emphasizes the fact that controlling for SES reduces the IQ score difference between black and whites by only three points. He also emphasizes that other "socio-economically disadvantaged minorities" perform better on IQ tests than do blacks. Such pronouncements presume that we know more or less completely the family, economic, and cultural factors which affect IQ test performance. The fact is that our knowledge is far from complete, and the Scarr–Weinberg study demonstrates this quite dramatically.

DIFFERENCES IN PERFORMANCE ON ABSTRACT "CULTURE-FREE" ITEMS VERSUS CULTURE-LOADED ITEMS

A major bulwark in the argument of those who believe that mean race differences in IQ scores have genetic origins is the fact that blacks perform even more poorly relative to whites on abstract reasoning items (items which tend to be judged by "experts" to be less culture-loaded) than they do on strictly "knowledge" items (those which tend to be judged more culture-loaded). Most of this research and the resulting conclusions researchers have drawn are, I think, fundamentally misguided and based upon dubious assumptions. First, it should be obvious from the foregoing discussion that, except in the most extreme examples involving, say, different languages, it is premature if not outright naive to suppose that by simple inspection, "experts" can tell which items on IQ tests are culture-free and which are culture-loaded. Our understanding of such a complex construct as *culture* is far too marginal and incomplete to allow such judgments. The notion, for example, that the manipulation of abstract geometrical figures is somehow independent of the cultural experiences of a group of children is by no means certain. We as researchers must admit that our knowledge of how environmental variables affect the development of abstract reasoning ability is simply inadequate. Moreover, given this inadequacy, to postulate *genetic* causes for observed IQ differences among groups might well represent scientific irresponsibility.

REGRESSION ESTIMATES OF SIBLING IQ SCORES

In several of Jensen's writings on the subject of race differences in intelligence, he has argued that "genetic theory," as distinct from environmental hunches and intuitions, makes a specific prediction regarding the above-mentioned sibling regression toward race means. He claims that these "genetic" predictions add support to genetic arguments and that they "may seem puzzling from the standpoint of a strictly environmental theory" (1973, p. 117). He follows this with two pages of scientifically fallacious reasoning to demonstrate the incompatibility of the differential sibling predictions with an environmental hypothesis. Many have found this particular "genetic" argument quite compelling. As has been pointed out elsewhere, however, (cf. Thoday, 1976), the fallacy in Jensen's reasoning is that he confuses genetics with statistics. If, *for any reason whatsoever,* two independent groups differ on some measure, but have similar regression equations, that is, similar sibling correlations and similar within-group heritability, then the regression toward their own mean is a *statistical* fact. The differential regressions cited by Jensen can give comfort neither to hereditarians nor environmentalists, although statisticians may feel gratified.

PSYCHOMETRIC ANALYSES

Jensen's (1980) extensive psychometric analyses in his latest book do not speak directly to the nature–nuture controversy, although they do leave the reader with the clear implication that mean race differences in IQ scores have a substantial genetic basis. What these analyses demonstrate, in fact, is that the *structure* and *pattern* of intellectual functioning of blacks and whites, as currently measured, are essentially identical and that, given this, the predictive accuracy of future performance requiring similar cognitive demands is roughly comparable for both groups. (Many seem surprised by this. I am not.) Moreover, the finding that item difficulties for a given test have the same rank order for blacks and whites and a similar rank order within age groups for blacks and whites is seen by Jensen as literally destroying the notion that group IQ differences have a substantial environmental origin.

I am not persuaded at all that this is the case. Consider, for example, the mean differences among European nationalities on the Army Beta, the nonverbal test administered to thousands of recruits during World

War I. As noted earlier, immigrants from southern Europe (e.g., Italians and Portuguese) scored significantly below those from northern Europe (e.g., Danes). Would results similar to those reported by Jensen for whites and blacks be obtained between nationalities? That is to say, would a factor analysis of the items on Army Beta reveal a similar factor structure for Portuguese and Danish recruits? Would the reliabilities be similar? Would the relative order of item difficulties be similar for the two groups? Would the items which maximally discriminate *between* the nationalities be roughly the same items which discriminate between high- and low-scoring individuals within each nationality? My suspicion is that the answer to each question is a resounding "yes." Following Jensen, then, the test was not "biased" against Portuguese and Italians; we cannot, therefore, appeal to different experiential backgrounds or differential access to information to explain the differences. They must be genetic. Certainly Brigham (1930) and Terman (1916), to mention a few, thought that they were. As indicated earlier, these psychologists felt quite comfortable with promulgating what can only charitably be described as half-baked genetic theories which eventually found their way into congressional legislation in the form of immigration quotas favoring northern Europeans.

HERITABILITY

Jensen (1969) argues that the relative contributions of environment and heredity can be ascertained by the heritability coefficient. The derivation and justification for this statistic would take us too far astray. Suffice it to say that there is by no means universal agreement (even among population geneticists) that the heritability coefficient is a useful statistic in the context of the IQ controversy. More importantly, however, the statistic tells very little of instructional importance to the practical educator who wishes to change behavior. To say that 50% (or 80%) of the IQ variance in a population is attributable to heredity (even if true) implies little, if anything, about how to improve instruction and student performance. Practically, it is simply a dead-end statistic.

STUDIES OF ACADEMIC PERFORMANCE

The foregoing discussion of what has come to be called the "IQ controversy" sets the stage for a brief examination of attempts by educational psychologists, sociologists and, more recently, cognitive psychologists and psycholinguists to study factors which influence the academic performance of black students. The bulk of this research has been nonexperimental (i.e., observational) and has therefore reported correlational rather than experimental evidence. This research, which covers the spectrum of potential causal influences from desegregation to parental income, from teacher attitudes to classroom climate and from parental linguistic style to race of peers, is incredibly varied and extensive. Weinberg's (1977) massive work, *Minority Students: A Research Appraisal,* is the most up-to-date account of nonbehavioral studies of black achievement. A complete review of this literature would require an entire volume in itself. We will, therefore, restrict ourselves to a limited selection of representative studies in each of the following broad domains: (a) characteristics of the student, (b) characteristics of the environment, and (c) characteristics of significant others. First, however, it will be useful to examine two of the views which have guided much of this research.

THE DEFICIT AND CONFLICT MODELS

Two distinct orientations which have emerged over the years in studies of academic achievement of black students are the deficit and conflict models. As is often the case, the assumptions underlying these orientations are not stated explicitly, but they can usually be inferred from the approach adopted by the investigator. The first and by far the most common model guiding research on black student academic performance is the *deficit model.* Under this hypothesis it is assumed that black students are *deficient* in critical academic skills because of a long list of environmental circumstances, including an "impoverished" intellectual environment, a deemphasis by both parents and peers of intellectual pursuits, poor instruction, and lack of parental discipline. Thus, researchers who adopt this orientation typically seek to improve academic performance by directly addressing these presumed deficiencies. The second, more recent approach—called the *conflict model* or *conflict hypothesis*—assumes that the comparatively poor educational performance of minority students results from a learning history which is in direct conflict with effective instruction. Under this model, the notion of a deficient environmental history is replaced with the belief that substantial and comparable intellectual growth and learning occurs among all children and that black (and other minority) students acquire skills and competencies which render achievement in American classrooms difficult. Perhaps the best single example of this hypothesis is to be found in the increasing literature on "black English" (Labov, 1972). The basic idea of this literature is that the linguistic styles which have evolved among American blacks constitute an essentially different language. The net result is that black students are saddled with the additional burden of learning to speak and write a new language in school. It is doubtful that one hypothesis is completely erroneous and the other completely factual. A more likely circumstance is that both are partly true.

CHARACTERISTICS OF THE STUDENT

Although the list of student characteristics which conceivably could affect student performance is virtually limitless, two have received considerable attention: (a) ethnic "learning styles" and (b) achievement motivation.

ETHNIC LEARNING STYLES

Since 1965, when Lesser and his associates conducted a study on the relative importance of ethnic and social class factors in cognitive functioning among children in the New York City area, research on ethnic learning styles has increased rapidly. The question posed by this research can be stated succinctly: Do children in various ethnic groups have distinctive learning styles that can be attributed to their group membership?

Lesser, Fifer, and Clark (1965) compared patterns in the mean scores of Chinese, Jewish, Negro, and Puerto Rican children for the verbal, reasoning, numerical, and spatial components of mental ability. He observed the following orders from high to low: (a) in verbal ability, Jewish, Negro, Chinese, and Puerto Rican; (b) in reasoning, Chinese, Jewish, Negro, and Puerto Rican; (c) in numerical ability, Jewish, Chinese, Puerto Rican, and Negro, and (d) in spatial ability, Chinese, Jewish, Puerto Rican, and Negro. The educational implications of these findings are not at all clear. An important point to note, for example, is that Lesser's results are not within-group, or ipsative, patterns. Therefore, to speak of ethnic group patterns as such is inaccurate. Lesser compared rankings of the four cognitive abilities based on social class rather than ethnic identity and found the social class rankings to be less stable. He concluded from an analysis of each group that social class had its greatest effect on the measured abilities of negro children.

The Lesser study has been widely quoted in the literature on ethnic styles, but it is questionable whether the study really addresses the issue of "learning style." In fact, actual dynamic and process differences in the acquisition of knowledge by the four compared groups were never considered. Moreover, his major conclusions have not been uniformly replicated. For example, Sitkei (1966), in a study comparing 50 white and black, middle- and lower-class youngsters who averaged 4 years of age, found that the contribution of ethnic and social class factors to performance on six of Guilford's structure-of-intellect abilities was approximately the same. Additionally, on only one of the abilities was there a greater social class effect for black children than for white children. Burnes (1970) compared within-group and within-social-class profiles of 78 black and white children in St. Louis and concluded that "there is no evidence in favor of . . . patterns of abilities within cultural-racial groups. In fact . . . configurations of scores are more similar for socioeconomic classes" (p. 499).

Backman (1970) compared ability patterns of over 3,000 twelfth-grade students of Jewish, white, black, and Asian backgrounds. She concluded that significant differences in patterns existed for both ethnic group and social class but that, in every case, the differences were quite small and of questionable practical value. A major finding of the investigation was that *sex* differences in patterns were quite striking and only slightly modified by ethnic group or social class membership. Interestingly, Lesser *et al.* (1965), using first-graders, found no such sex differences. It is possible, Backman suggests, that traditional differences observed in the ability profiles of males and females (i.e., males do perform better on numerical and spatial tasks, whereas females perform better on verbal tasks) may be largely traceable to environmental influences and thus emerge only with age.

Studies by Rivers (1970), Stokes (1970), Miller (1972), and Flaugher and Rock (1972), using essentially identical strategies (i.e., a straightforward comparison of within-group profiles), added to an already confused picture. In each case where ethnic differences in ability profiles were found, the researcher was left, for the most part, with a dead-end conclusion which had no clear instructional implications. Moreover, rarely were actual processes, environmental or otherwise, investigated in order to explain such differences. Two studies, however, those of Feldman (1969) and Marjoribanks (1972), stand out from the rest in this regard. Feldman (1969) studied the *rate* and *sequence* of the acquisition of skills necessary to perform a spatial reasoning task. Comparing Chinese, white, and black children in the fifth, seventh, and ninth grades, he found clear rate differences but no sequence differences. These results are not conclusive, however, since the study was not longitudinal. The reader may have detected a certain simplicity in the above approaches to so complex an issue as "learning style." In fact, with the possible exception of Feldman, no study cited addressed the issue of *learning* as such. Rather, the studies simply delineated current levels of cognitive performance in terms of ability profiles. Furthermore, the investigations tended to reduce the complex of forces acting on children to one monolithic variable—ethnic group membership. To be sure, most investigators suspected the presence of factors other than ethnicity, but few included any of these in their investigations.

Majoribanks (1972) considered eight variables from the home environment in an investigation of 11-year-old Canadian males of Indian, French, Jewish, Italian, and white Anglo-Saxon parents. The eight variables were (a) press for achievement, (b) press for activeness, (c) press for intellectuality, (d) press for independence, (e) press for English, (f) press for "ethlanguage," (g) mother dominance, and (h) father dominance. The rationale for inclusion of these particular variables is not of concern. The important point to note is that, in general, ethnic group effects on the four abilities investigated (verbal, number, spatial, and reasoning) were reduced considerably once home learning environmental forces were taken into account. For spatial ability, the ethnic group effect disappeared completely. Weinberg (1977) notes that the force of Majoribanks's eight-factor home environment was observed in its existing state. "There is no reason," he concluded, "why its impact could not be heightened by deliberate action. Nor is there much basis for denying the potential additional effect of that other learning environment called 'school' " (p. 63).

ACHIEVEMENT MOTIVATION

The search for important personality antecedents of differential patterns of achievement among the sexes, ethnic groups, and social classes has resulted in a burgeoning literature over the past several years. The personality variables which have been studied in addition to learning style (mentioned earlier) are self-concept (Brown, 1966; Wendland, 1968), occupational aspirations (Cosby, 1971), self-esteem (Haggstrom, 1963; Lessing, 1969), and achievement motivation (Banks, McQuater, & Hubbard, 1978). Typically, the former three (self-concept, self-esteem, and occupational aspirations) have been studied as theoretically and practically important dependent variables in their own right, without being explicit viewed as antecedent, causal factors in student academic performance.

It is primarily the latter construct, achievement motivation, which has been hypothesized to influence academic performance. Banks *et al.* (1978) draw a useful distinction between studies involving intrinsic versus extrinsic bases of motivational orientations to achievement. The distinction relates to the degree to which sustained performance on academic tasks depends on maintenance factors which have as their referents stimulus conditions or contingencies that are external to the student. The distinction may be relatively straightforward (e.g., comparing performance under conditions of external reinforcement versus no reinforcement), or it may be more subtle (e.g., comparing external stimuli such as candy and cookies, which possess inherent power to evoke and maintain performance, with those stimuli such as verbal praise, the effectiveness of which depends on an internalized system of values).

One of the relatively consistent findings in this research is that black and lower-class children are generally more dependent upon extrinsic rewards (Banks *et al.*, 1978). That is to say, unlike white or middle-class children, minority group and socioeconomically disadvantaged individuals, if they engage in sustained academic effort at all, do so under conditions of immediate and tangible external rewards, rather than intrinsic, internalized mechanisms. Theories of the origin and development of these differential reinforcement contingencies are few. Katz (1967) suggests that the inability of lower-class children to engage in sustained academic effort in the absence of immediate extrinsic reward is a result of the failure on the part of parents or other socializing agents to reinforce the internalization of such mechanisms as deferred gratification and self-control. Observational and experimental evidence for this notion, however, is relatively scarce.

Weiner and Peter (1973) have proposed a cognitive-developmental model of achievement orientation based upon the developmental theories of Piaget (1965) and Kohlberg (1969). They operationalize intrinsic reward as the ascendancy of effort (corresponding to "intent" in moral judgments) over outcome. More specifically, they hypothesized that emphasis upon effort over outcome increases linearly with time and that black and disadvantaged students lag behind their white counterparts in this respect. Their results indicated that the pattern of development was similar for both black and white students, black students tending on the average to attain each level of effort orientation one age category (three years) later than their white counterparts.

Green and Farquhar (1965) and Gurin, Gurin, Lao, and Beattie (1969) have criticized much of the achievement motivation research for the narrow conceptualization of achievement implied in most studies (virtually all studies employed academic tasks such as analogies, arithmetic items, or other indices of strictly academic achievement such as scores on standardized tests). Moreover, as Banks *et al.* (1978) note, the potential mediating variable "task interest" has been largely ignored. In those few instances where "task-liking" or task interest is specifically included, this variable was shown to have striking effects upon task persistence (Lefcourt & Ladwig, 1965) and on the amount of information sought on a subject (Williams & Stack, 1972). In a carefully designed study, Banks, McQuater, and Hubbard (1977), using a paradigm employed by Weiner and Kukla (1970) and Weiner and Peter (1973), asked 16- to 18-year-old high school students to make achievement judgments of reports about activities of other teenagers. Their results indicated that black and white students, when previously equated on task-liking, did not differ on the judgments of effort (i.e., intrinsic) orientation across levels of task-liking, but differed significantly in their concern for outcomes. More specifically, blacks showed a relatively greater tendency toward concern for the extrinsic factors of success and failure on low interest tasks. Banks *et al.* argue that although strictly academic tasks may not be specifically developed within subcultural social-learning, such tasks are probably lower on interest hierarchies of individuals denied the tools and opportunities critical to early practice and performance. The Banks *et al.* study is important in that it offers a potentially powerful explanatory mechanism (i.e., task-liking) for the ascendancy of external reward over self-reward in black and low-income children. A fuller description of some of the theoretical and methodological issues in self-reward studies is discussed later.

CHARACTERISTICS OF THE ENVIRONMENT

Brief mention should be made of the extensive literature on sociological and econometric models of student performance. These usually take the form of "educational production functions" or "input–output" analysis, in which student performance is viewed as the school "output" which results from a list of school "inputs." This list can be quite extensive, covering such factors as number of special staff in the school (Mollenkopf & Melville, 1956), "classroom atmosphere" (Goodman, 1959), instructional expenditures (Benson, Schmelzle, Gustafson, & Lange, 1965), student/teacher ratio (Kiesling, 1969), teacher salary and turnover (Burkhead, Fox, & Holland, 1967), presence of ability grouping (Bowles, 1969), building age and size (Guthrie, Kleindorfer, Levin, & Stout, 1971), and overall school size (Sommers & Wolfe, 1975). The above list represents but a small fraction of the number of variables which have been studied in these large investigations. As is typical of observational studies which differ in numerous and complex ways, both in terms of methodology, statistical analysis, and student population, very few of these global variables *consistently* predict student performance. This is so for both black and white students. Of particular concern in many sociological investigations is the effect of the contextual variable desegregation. It is perhaps worthwhile to comment on some of the more recent reviews of this extensive literature.

DESEGREGATION AND BLACK STUDENT ACHIEVEMENT

The most recent studies (and most comprehensive of the desegregation literature) are those of Weinberg (1977) and Bradley and Bradley

(1977). At least three causal themes run through much of this research. First, it is assumed that black students, as a result of desegregation, will be exposed to the presumed instructionally advantageous practices and materials of schools attended by white students. A second theme is that blacks will adopt the achievement-related values of white students and that this in turn will result in improved academic performance. A third theme is that academic performance is in part a function of self-esteem and that the development of feelings of inferiority, which a segregated education presumably engenders, is mitigated by desegregation.

The validity of these assumptions aside, the results thus far obtained present a confused and contradictory picture, confounded by numerous methodological and analytical problems. For example, many studies (see, for example, Coleman, Campbell, Hobson, Mcpartland, Mood, Weinfeld, & York, 1966) were cross-sectional, rather than longitudinal, and therefore suffer from the numerous conceptual deficiences of cross-sectional data. Those studies which were longitudinal also suffered from numerous methodological difficulties. For example, a summary of 29 desegregation studies from 1959 to 1975 reported by Bradley and Bradley (1977) revealed that 21 (72%) used a nonequivalent control group or unspecified quasi-experimental design to investigate desegregation effects. The interpretative problems involved in such designs are well known and have been spelled out in gruesome detail (cf. Lord, 1967; Cronbach, Rogosa, Floden, & Price, 1976). Moreover, problems of extensive student attrition, differing units of analysis, inadequate socioeconomic status and entering ability controls, volunteer and self-selection effects, and failures to meet the assumptions of subject and school equivalence all combined to postpone a final verdict on the effects of desegregation on black student performance. Little wonder, then, that Weinberg's (1977) extensive review showed 29 studies to conclude that desegregation resulted in higher academic performance of black students than control groups, while 19 studies resulted in no effects. Similar percentages have been reported by Crain and Mahard (1977). The most reasoned cautious conclusion regarding the effects of desegregation on black student academic achievement is provided by Crain and Mahard (1977) who state:

> The best studies have in common a recognition of an important fact about desegregation—that desegregation is not a . . . laboratory controlled experiment which is identical in Jacksonville and in Berkeley. Every case is different, and we should not expect identical results every time. Thus one answer to the question "what is the effect of desegregation on achievement" is "sometimes it works and sometimes it doesn't"—but this is true of any intervention. (p.32)

CHARACTERISTICS OF SIGNIFICANT OTHERS

Teachers and parents are typically cited as the two most important external influences on student academic growth and achievement. Parents are major socializing agents of children. As such, they control in large measure the child's introduction to language, social customs and norms, and interpersonal behavior. Teachers usually act not only as additional adult socializers but also as the child's first encounter with formal academic instruction. A summary of the major findings of research devoted to the influence of parents and teachers follows.

TEACHER ATTITUDES

A commonly held belief among lay persons and educational researchers alike is that teachers' attitudes toward a student's ability and motivation have a powerful and direct effect upon their interactions with and behavior toward that student and that these in turn affect student academic performance. There is ample evidence (Corwin & Schmidt, 1969; Elliott, 1968; Howe, 1970; North & Buchanan, 1967; Rosenthal & Jacobson, 1968; Wilcox, 1966) that teachers, both black and white, have generally negative attitudes toward minority children. Such children are viewed by their teachers as less able academically, more troublesome, lacking in motivation, and generally uneducable. What is conspicuously lacking are well-conducted, empirical observations linking attitudes to actual behavior. Common sense and intuition, however, would suggest that a connection clearly exists. Actual classroom observations by Parsons (1965), Jackson and Cosca (1974), and others (cf. United States Commission on Civil Rights, Report V, 1973) linking attitudes to behavior do exist, however, for Mexican American students. Parsons, for example, found that (1) teachers systematically ignored Mexican American children's hands in favor of calling on Anglos, (2) Anglo "helpers" aided teachers, but in no case were Mexican American children so designated, and (3) the relative frequency of verbal praise was higher for Anglo students than for Mexican American students and, conversely, the relative frequency of criticism of Mexican American students was substantially greater than for Anglo students. The essential findings of Parsons were replicated in an elaborate and large-scale observational study of 429 classrooms in 52 California schools conducted by the U.S. Commission on Civil Rights. In addition to the significantly differential praise accorded Anglo students noted by Parsons, this study also found that teachers direct questions to Anglo students 21% more often than they direct them to Mexican American students and that

Mexican American pupils generally receive significantly less overall attention from teachers.

With a few notable exceptions (Weinberg, 1977), the evidence regarding teacher attitudes and behavior toward minority students points overwhelming to a generally defeatist and negative orientation on the part of teachers toward minority students.

While the observational nature of much of this evidence precludes compelling cause-and-effect relationships, a reasonable conclusion is that the accumulated weight of such attitudes and behaviors adversely affects academic motivation and achievement. The following chapter treats further the experimental evidence on teacher behaviors and student achievement.

TEACHER RACE

Recently, that is, within the last three or four decades, considerable research on race of teacher as a factor influencing the academic performance of black students has been undertaken (Bond, 1977; Glick, 1971; Gordon, 1967; McMillan, 1967; Ohberg, 1972). The general pattern which emerges from these studies is that teacher race, *per se*, does not directly affect student performance. The conclusion is consistent with other findings mentioned earlier which suggest that black and white teachers do not differ significantly in their orientation toward black students.

CHARACTERISTICS OF THE PARENT

The awareness that parents are potent educational influences on the intellectual development of children—as distinct from the formal and professional influences of teachers—is now well established from the literature on child development and parent–child interaction. The body of research on parental behaviors which influence cognitive growth is—like much of the literature surveyed above—far too voluminous to cover in detail here. Excellent reviews are available (Hartup, 1972; Hess, 1969; Horowitz, 1975; Scott-Jones, 1979). It is sufficient here to repeat the list of variables developed by Hess (1969) that have been found to be related to intellectual development and academic achievement:

A. Intellectual relationship
   Demand for high achievement
   Maximization of verbal achievement
   Engagement with and attentiveness to the child

Maternal teaching behavior
Diffuse intellectual stimulation
B. Affective relationship
Warm affective relationship with child
Feelings of high regard for child and self
C. Interaction patterns
Pressure for independence and self-reliance
Clarity and enforcement of disciplinary rules
Use of conceptual rather than arbitrary regulatory strategies

The above list is surely not complete. In the future, for example, we can expect continuing contrastive research (black versus white parental styles, lower-class versus middle-class, etc.) of the type undertaken by Hess and Shipman (1965) to add to this increasing list.

REFERENCES

Backman, M. E. *Relationship of ethnicity, socioeconomic status, and sex to patterns of mental ability.* Unpublished doctoral dissertation, Columbia University, New York, 1970.

Banks, W. C., McQuater, G., & Hubbard, J. L. Task-liking and intrinsic–extrinsic achievement orientations in black adolescents. *Journal of Black Psychology,* 1977, *3,* 61–71.

Banks, W. C., McQuater, G., & Hubbard, J. L. Toward a reconceptualization of the social-cognitive bases of achievement orientations in blacks. *Review of Educational Research,* 1978, *48,* 381–397.

Benson, C. S., Schmelzle, W. K., Gustafson, R. H., & Lange, R. A. *State and local fiscal relationships in public eduction in California.* Report of the Senate Fact Finding Committee on Revenue and Taxation. Sacremento, California: State Senate, State of California, 1965.

Binet, A. & Simon, T. *The development of intelligence in children.* Vineland, N.J.: The Training School at Vineland, 1916.

Boas, Franz. *Language and culture.* New York: MacMillen, 1940.

Block, N. J., & Dworkin, G. (Eds.). *The IQ Controversy.* New York: Random House, 1976.

Bond, H. M. *Black American scholars: A study of their beginnings.* Detroit: Balamp Publishing, 1977.

Bowles, S. S. *Educational production functions: Final report.* Washington, D.C.: U.S. Department of Health, Education, and Welfare, Office of Education, 1969.

Bradley, L. A., & Bradley, G. W. The academic achievement of black students in desegregated schools: A critical review. *Review of Educational Research,* 1977, 43, 399–449.

Brigham, C. C. *A study of American intelligence.* Princeton: Princeton University Press, 1923.

Brigham, C. C. Intelligence tests on immigrant groups. *Psychological Review,* 1930, *37,* 158–165.

Brown, B. R. *The assessment of self-concept among four-year-old negro and white children: A comparative study using the Brown-IDS self concept referents test.* Unpublished manuscript, New York University, 1966.

Burkhead, J., Fox, T. G., & Holland, J. W. *Input and output in large city high schools.* Syracuse, New York: Syracuse University Press, 1967.

Burks, B. S. The relative influence of nature and nurture upon mental development: A comparative study of foster parent–foster child resemblance and true parent–child resemblance. In *27th Yearbook: Nature and Nurture, Part I.* Bloomington, Ind.: National Society for the Study of Education, 1928.

Burnes, D. K. S. Patterns of WISC performance for children of two socioeconomic classes and races. *Child Development,* 1970, *41,* 493–499.

Coleman, J. S., Campbell, W. Q., Hobson, C. J., Mcpartland, J., Mood, A. M., Weinfeld, F. D., & York, R. L. *Equality of educational opportunity.* Washington, D.C.: U.S. Government Printing Office, 1966.

Cooley, W. W., & Lohnes, P. *Evaluation research in education.* New York: Irvington Publishers, 1976.

Corwin, R., & Schmidt, M. Teachers in inner city schools: A survey of a large city school system. *Theory Into Practice,* 1969, *8,* 209–222.

Cosby, A. Black-white differences in aspirations among deep south high school students. *Journal of Negro Education,* 1971, *40,* 18–29.

Crain, R. L., & Mahard, R. E. *Desegregation and black achievement.* Paper presented at the Conference on Social Science and Law in Desegregation, Amelia Island, Florida, October, 1977.

Cronbach, L. J., Rogosa, D. R., Floden, R. E., & Price, G. C. *Analysis of covariance: Angel of salvation, or temptress and deluder?* Stanford, California: Stanford University, 1976.

Darwin, C. *On the origin of species by means of natural selection.* New York: Appleton, 1896.

Downey, M. T. *Carl Campbell Brigham.* Princeton: Educational Testing Service, 1961.

Dorfman, D. D. The Cyril Burt question: New findings. *Science,* 1978, *201,* 1177–1185.

Elliott, D. H. *Social origins and values of teachers and their attitudes to students from poverty backgrounds.* Unpublished doctoral dissertation, University of Pittsburgh, 1968.

Feldman, D. H. *The fixed sequence hypothesis; Ethnic differences in the development of spatial reasoning.* Unpublished doctoral dissertation, Stanford University, 1969.

Flaugher, R. A., & Rock, D. A. *Patterns of ability factors among four ethnic groups.* Paper presented at the Annual Convention of the American Psychological Association, Honolulu, Hawaii, 1972.

Freeman, F. N., Holzinger, K. J., & Mitchell, B. C. The influence of environment on the intelligence, school achievement, and conduct of foster children. *27th Yearbook: Nature and Nurture,* Part I. Bloomington, Ind.: National Society for the Study of Education, 1928.

Glick, I. D. Does teacher's skin color matter? *Integrated Education,* 1971, *9*(5), 26–30.

Goldberger, A. S. Mysteries of the meritocracy. In N. J. Block & G. Dworkin (Eds.), *The IQ controversy.* New York: Random House, 1976.

Goodman, S. M. *The assessment of school quality.* Albany, New York: State Education Department of New York, 1959.

Gordon, E. W. Equalizing educational opportunity in the public schools. *IRCD Bulletin* (Information Retrieval Center on the Disadvantaged), November, 1967.

Green, R. C., & Farquhar, W. Negro academic motivation and scholastic achievement. *Journal of Educational Psychology,* 1965, *5,* 241–253.

Gurin, P., Gurin, G., Lao, R., & Beattie, M. Internal-external control in the motivational dynamics of negro youth. *Journal of Social Issues,* 1969, *29,* 29–53.

Guthrie, J. W., Kleindorfer, G., Levin, H. M., & Stout, R. T. *Schools and inequality.* Cambridge, Mass.: MIT Press, 1971.

Haggstrom, W. C. Segregation, desegregation, and negro personality. *Integrated Education,* 1963, *5,* 19–23.

Hartup, W. W. (Ed.). *The young child* (Vol. 2). Washington, D.C.: National Association of the Education of Young Children, 1972.

Herrnstein, R. J. *IQ in the Meritocracy*. Boston: Little, Brown, 1973.

Hess, R. D. Parental behavior and children's school achievement: Implications for Head Start. In E. H. Grotberg (Ed.), *Critical issues in research related to disadvantaged children*. Princeton: Educational Testing Service, 1969.

Hess, R. D., & Shipman, W. Early experience and the socialization of cognitive modes in children. *Child Development*, 1965, *36*, 869–886.

Horowitz, F. D. (Ed.). *Review of child development research* (Vol. 4). Chicago: University of Chicago Press, 1975.

Howe, F. C. *Teacher perceptions toward the learning ability of students from differing racial and socioeconomic backgrounds*. Unpublished doctoral dissertation, Michigan State University, 1970.

Jackson, G., & Cosca, C. The inequality of educational opportunity in the southwest: An observational study of ethnically mixed classrooms. *American Educational Research Journal*, 1974, *11*, 219–229.

Jensen, A. R. How much can we boost IQ and scholastic achievement? *Harvard Educational Review*, 1969, *39*, 1–123.

Jensen, A. R. *Genetics and education*. New York: Harper & Row, 1972.

Jensen, A. R. *Educability and group differences*. New York: Harper & Row, 1973.

Jensen, A. R. *Bias in mental testing*. New York: The Free Press, 1980.

Kamin, L. J. *The science and politics of IQ*. New York: Halstead Press, 1974.

Katz, I. The socialization of academic motivation in minority group children. In D. Levine (Ed.), *Nebraska symposium on motivation*. Lincoln: University of Nebraska Press, 1967.

Kiesling, H. J. *The relationship of school inputs to public school performance in New York state*. Washington, D.C.: U.S. Department of Health, Education, and Welfare, Office of Education, 1969.

Kohlberg, L. Stage and sequence: The cognitive-developmental approach to socialization. In D. Goslin (Ed.), *Handbook of socialization: Theory and research*. Chicago: Rand McNally, 1969.

Labov, W. *Language in the inner city: Studies in the black English vernacular*. Philadelphia: University of Pennsylvania Press, 1972.

Leahy, A. M. Nature, nurture and intelligence. *Genetic Psychology Monographs*, 1935, *17*, 4.

Lefcourt, H. & Ladwig, G. The effect of reference group upon Negroes' task persistence in a biracial competitive game. *Journal of Personality and Social Psychology*, 1965, *1*, 668.

Lesser, G. S., Fifer, G. & Clark, D. H. *Mental abilities of children from different social-class and cultural groups*. Chicago: University of Chicago Press, 1965.

Lessing, E. E. Racial differences in indices of ego functioning relevant to academic achievement. *Journal of Genetic Psychology*, 1969, *115*, 160–169.

Lewontin, R. C. Race and intelligence. In N. J. Block & G. Dworking (Eds.), *The IQ Controversy*. New York: Random House, 1976.

Liberator, August 21, 1846. Quoted in M. Weinberg, *Minority students: A research appraisal*. Washington, D.C.: U.S. Government Printing Office, 1977.

Lord, F. A paradox in the interpretation of group comparisons. *Psychological Bulletin*, 1967, *68*, 304–305.

McMillan, J. H. *The influence of caucasian teachers on negro and caucasian students in segregated and racially mixed inner-city schools*. Unpublished doctoral dissertation, Michigan State University, 1967.

Marjoribanks, K. Ethnic and environmental influences on mental abilities. *American Journal of Sociology*, 1972, *78*, 323–337.

Miller, M. D. *Patterns of relationships of fluid and crystallized mental abilities to achievement in different ethnic groups*. Unpublished doctoral dissertation, University of Houston, 1972.

Mollenkopf, W. G., & Melville, S. D. *A study of secondary school characteristics as related to test scores.* Research Bulletin RB 56-6. Princeton: Educational Testing Service, 1956.

North, G. E., & Buchanan, O. L. Teacher views of poverty area children. *Journal of Educational Research,* 1967, *61,* 53–55.

Ohberg, H. G. Does the black child need a black teacher? *Integrated Education,* 1972, *10*(2), 27–28.

Parsons, T. W., Jr. *Ethnic cleavage in a California school.* Unpublished doctoral dissertation, Stanford University, 1965.

Piaget, J. *The moral judgment of the child.* The Free Press: New York, 1965.

Rivers, W. L. *The stability of differential patterns of mental abilities in children from different ethnic groups.* Unpublished doctoral dissertation, St. Louis University, 1970.

Rosenthal, R., & Jacobson, L. *Pygmalion in the classroom: Teacher expectations and pupils' intellectual development.* New York: Holt, Rinehart, & Winston, 1968.

Scarr, S. and Weinberg, R. IQ test performance of black children adopted by white families. *American Psychologist,* 1976, *31,* 726–739.

Scott-Jones, D. *Family variables associated with school achievement in low-income black first-graders.* Unpublished doctoral dissertation, University of North Carolina, 1979.

Sitkei, E. G. *Comparative structure of intellect in middle- and lower-class four-year-old children of two ethnic groups.* Unpublished doctoral dissertation, University of Southern California, 1966.

Skodak, M., and Skeels, H. M. A final follow-up study of one hundred adopted children. *Journal of Genetic Psychology,* 1949, *75,* 85–125.

Stokes, C. A. *Some effects of schooling, age, race, and socio-economic status on the cognitive development of primary school boys.* Unpublished doctoral dissertation, University of Michigan, 1970.

Sommers, A., & Wolfe, B. *Equality of educational opportunity qualified: A proeducation function approach.* Philadelphia: Department of Research, Federal Reserve Bank of Philadelphia, 1975.

Terman, L. M. *The measurement of intelligence.* Boston: Houghton Mifflin, 1916.

Thoday, J. M. Educability and group differences. In N. J. Block & G. Dworkin (Eds.), *The IQ Controversy.* New York: Random House, 1976.

U.S. Commission on Civil Rights, Teachers and Students. *Differences in teacher interaction with Mexican American and Anglo students.* Report V: Mexican American Education Study. Washington, D.C.: Government Printing Office, March 1973.

Weinberg, S. *Minority students: A research appraisal.* Washington, D.C.: U.S. Government Printing Office, 1977.

Weiner, B., & Kukla, A. An attributional analysis of achievement motivation. *Journal of Personality and Social Psychology,* 1970, *15,* 1–20.

Weiner, B., & Peter, N. A. Cognitive-developmental analysis of achievement and moral judgments. *Developmental Psychology,* 1973, *9,* 290–309.

Wendland, M. M. *Self concept in southern negro and white adolescents as related to rural-urban residence.* Unpublished doctoral dissertation, University of North Carolina, 1968.

Wilcox, P. R. Teacher attitudes and student achievement. *Teachers College Record,* 1966, *68,* 371–379.

Williams, J., & Stack, J. Internal-external control as situational variables in determining information seeking by negro students. *Journal of Consulting and Clinical Psychology,* 1972, *39,* 127.

7

Academic Improvement through Behavioral Intervention

RUSSELL T. JONES

INTRODUCTION

As the preceding chapter demonstrates, the black child's academic performance may be negatively influenced by a host of factors, ranging from personal variables to teacher expectations. Given the fact that academic performance is of major importance in predicting future success, methods of mitigating the influence of these factors are essential. This chapter will therefore be devoted to techniques used to combat those factors that inhibit the establishment and maintenance of academic performance.

Inasmuch as the classroom is typically a place where formal teaching of academic behavior is conducted, it is a prime target for behavioral intervention. Unfortunately, for reasons discussed earlier, the classroom has been found to be a source of less than positive experiences for some children. Children from "disadvantaged" backgrounds, for example, often experience early failure and tend to find the classroom itself either aversive or neutral, but certainly not reinforcing (Smith, 1973). Culturally different children may thus suffer from the harsh effects of an inadequate educational experience and may often be forced to drop out without acquiring the necessary survival skills for competing in society. Given the inept status of many urban schools (Silberman, 1970), techniques for decreasing the growing number of ill-prepared young people are urgently needed. To obtain this goal, the behavioral approach—a radical departure from traditional approaches—is advocated.

Viewing behavior from a behavioral perspective assumes that behavior, both desired and undesired, is learned and that, through the application of various learning principles, it can be modified. However, rather than assuming, as teachers, parents, and other change-agents often do, that behavior can be effectively modified without formal and

RUSSELL T. JONES ● Clinical Psychology Center, University of Pittsburgh, Pittsburgh, Pennsylvania 15260.

systematic application, the extreme importance of systematization is stressed. As a result, behavior is functionally analyzed (a) by objectively defining the behaviors of interest, (b) by assessing the parameters of the behaviors (when and where they occur and their frequency, duration, and magnitude) and (c) by ascertaining the cause of the behaviors (in terms of antecedent and consequent events). Constant and consistent assessment, conducted in the hope of specifying the parameters of the behavior of interest before, during, and after intervention, is considered essential to evaluation of the effect of intervention.

The purpose of this chapter is to provide the reader with an overview of several widely used behavioral techniques which, in conjunction with this assessment, have been found to be effective in enhancing academic performance (i.e., teacher attention, token reinforcement, self-control, group contingencies, and punishment).[1]

Teacher Attention

One of the simplest and least expensive of these techniques is teacher attention (including verbal praise, smiles, frowns, handshakes, and pats on the back), which has been shown to influence student behavior, both desired and undesired. If applied systematically, this attention can be used to increase a host of desired academic behaviors. However, when unsystematically applied, it may increase undesired behavior. Major benefits stemming from the use of teacher attention are its relative ease of application in classroom settings as well as its demonstrated effectiveness in altering behavior. Behaviors found to improve significantly following its administration include studying behavior (Hall, Lund, & Jackson, 1968), attending behavior (Broden, Bruce, Mitchell, Carter, & Hall, 1970; Hawkins, McArthur, Rinaldi, Gray, & Schaftenaur, 1967), and test performance (Witmer, Bornstein, & Dunham, 1971).

An example of an effective application of teacher attention to the enhancement of task-relevant behavior as well as to the reduction of disruptive behavior is provided by Ward and Baker (1968). In this study, teacher attention and praise were employed to increase the task-relevant, productive behavior of 12 first-grade black students who attended an urban public school. During a 5-week baseline, the frequency of deviant behavior was recorded. Deviant behaviors included inappropriate talking, out-of-seat behavior, aggression, and inattentive behavior. Task-relevant behavior included time-on-task, listening, and question an-

---

[1] For a more comprehensive description of these and other programs, the interested reader is referred to Jones and Kazdin (1981) and Kazdin (1977).

swering. Three groups of children were used to assess the effects of treatment. An experimental group was comprised of three boys, all of whom demonstrated a high frequency of disruptive classroom behavior, and one withdrawn and inattentive girl. Each of two control groups consisted of four randomly selected subjects. Treatment, which consisted of teachers systematically ignoring deviant behavior and systematically reinforcing task-relevant, productive behavior with attention and praise, was initiated for the experimental group during week 6 and extended for a seven-week period. A series of four weekly seminar–discussions were held with the three experimental teachers to facilitate their understanding and application of behavioral techniques, with special focus on teacher attention.

The results showed that, as teachers increased the proportion of attention which was directed toward the task-relevant behavior of experimental subjects, disruptive behavior decreased. A drop in deviant behavior from 74% during baseline to 57% during the last five weeks of treatment attests to the effects of teacher attention in decreasing deviant behavior. Although a number of methodological confounds exist, including the possibility of improper application of contingent attention and the possibility of differential observations of treatment subjects, this study demonstrates the potential use of teacher attention in enhancing task-relevant behavior.

However, it should be noted that inappropriate child behavior may often be a result of the teacher's attending to undesired behavior and

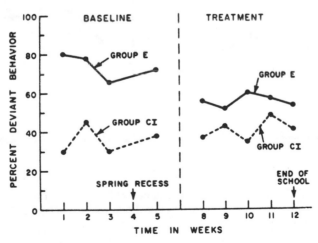

Figure 1. Deviant behavior of Group E and Group Cl. From Ward & Baker (1968); reprinted with permission.

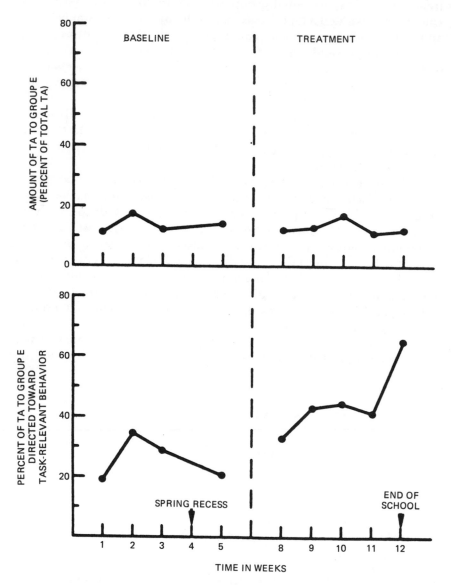

Figure 2.   Teacher attention to Group E. Amount of TA directed toward Group E and percent of attention to Group E directed toward task-relevant behavior. From Ward & Baker (1968); reprinted with permission.

the teacher's ignoring of desired behavior (Thomas, Presland, Grant, & Glynn, 1978). Indeed, many teacher–child interactions have been found to be of a negative nature, a situation which may result in the development and maintenance of negative patterns of interaction (Madsen, Madsen, Saudargas, Hammond, & Egar, 1970). Therefore, teachers should strive to become more sensitive to students' needs as well as to react more positively and more systematically to students' behavior.

In summary, teacher attention has been demonstrated to be an effective technique, when systematically applied, in enhancing academic behavior. Given its low cost/benefit ratio, coupled with its relative ease of application, systematic use of teacher attention should certainly be encouraged.

Token Reinforcement

In those situations in which contingent teacher attention may not be powerful enough to curb deviant patterns of learned behavior or to establish new behaviors, a stronger technique might be in order. One such technique is token reinforcement, which has been found to be extremely effective in enhancing performance on academic tasks (for excellent reviews, see Kazdin & Bootzin, 1972; McLaughlin, 1975; O'Leary & Drabman, 1971).

The token economy is a behavioral program designed to increase desired responses through reinforcement with stars, points, poker chips, and other types of tokens. Following students' demonstration of desired behaviors, tokens redeemable for small toys, candy, free time, or other reinforcing objects or activities are contingently administered. Several advantages of the use of tokens in the classroom include their relative ease of application during ongoing teaching sessions, their ability to bridge the delay between a response and a reinforcer (where they serve as a generalized secondary reinforcer), and their potential use in teaching children academic skills such as counting. Because of the assumption that academic performance will improve if students are taught such skills as working quietly, following directions, and paying attention to the teacher, many token programs have been directed toward increasing such behaviors. Subsequent to the initial demonstration of this technique at the Ranier State School in Washington (Birnbrauer & Lawler, 1964), it has been shown repeatedly to improve academic achievement.

An example of the employment of a token economy with a group of predominantly black children (70%) is provided in a study which was carried out by Miller and Schneider (1970) in a Head Start class. This study was designed to develop a method of teaching initial elements of handwriting, the effectiveness of which was experimentally evaluated by the comparison of a treatment and a control group. The following skills were taught to the experimental group: (a) holding a pencil correctly, (b) drawing straight lines at different angles, (c) drawing curved lines at different angles, (d) drawing freehand lines and (e) drawing various shapes. In this group, correct responses, as determined by the teacher or an aide, were followed by the delivery of tokens (on a small fixed-ratio schedule). Tokens could be used to buy tickets, which were exchanged for reinforcing activities during play periods. Reinforcers consisted of snacks and access to a "funroom" (where a variety of toys were kept), an art area, an outdoor play area, and a movie room. The effectiveness of this program in maintaining desired responses was evaluated by the employment of periods of contingent reinforcement (when the preceding procedure for reinforcement was followed) and noncontingent reinforcement (when 25 tokens were given to each child). Achievement tests were administered to both groups at the beginning and the end of the program in order to assess the overall effectiveness of the token reinforcement system.

On the posttest achievement measure, significant gains were made by subjects in the experimental group, whereas minimum gains were evidenced by control group subjects. Additionally, experimental subjects responded at a higher rate when reinforcement was contingent than

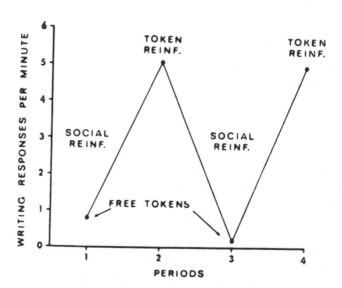

Figure 3. Mean rate of responding with and without contingent token reinforcement. Each point represents the mean rate for 10 children during a 30-minute study period. From Miller & Schneider (1980); reprinted with permission.

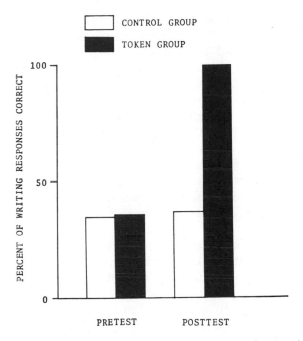

Figure 4. Comparison of pretest and posttest achievement scores for the token group and control group. Token group bars are averages for seven children present at both tests; control group bars are averages for 11 children present at both tests. From Miller & Schneider (1968); reprinted with permission.

when it was noncontingent. Although the possibility of a number of methodological shortcomings exists (e.g., differential regression among treatment and control groups), the potential of this technique is demonstrated.

In addition to handwriting skills, a number of other behaviors have been modified through the use of token reinforcement. Academic behaviors which have been altered include arithmetic, spelling, vocabulary, letter discrimination, and reading and writing (Ayllon & Roberts, 1974; Chadwick & Day, 1971; Glynn, 1970; Lahey & Drabman, 1974; Lovitt & Curtiss, 1969; Staats, Minke, Finley, Wolf, & Brooks, 1964; Surratt, Ulrich, & Hawkins, 1969; Wilson & McReynolds, 1973). Substantial gains have also been found on a number of standardized tests, including the Metropolitan Reading Test, the Wide Range Achievement Test, and the California Test of Mental Maturity (Ayllon & Kelly, 1972; Bushell, 1974; Kaufman & O'Leary, 1972; Rollins, McCandless, Thompson, & Brassell, 1974).

Indeed, both employment of token reinforcement during the

administration of a standardized test, The Metropolitan Achievement Test (Ayllon & Kelly, 1972), and the implementation of a token program (involving either "reward" or "response cost" procedures) prior to testing (Kaufman & O'Leary, 1972), resulted in significant improvements. In the first study, subjects receiving token reinforcement had each subtest checked and were given a token (which could be exchanged for back-up reinforcers following the completion of the test) for each correct response. Subjects receiving the standard procedure were given the test according to the instructions provided in the test manual. Employment of token reinforcement during administration of the test resulted in significantly better performance by both trainable mentally retarded children and children of normal intelligence than did standard conditions. In the second study, each student in the "reward" class began rating periods without tokens but could receive them for following rules. In the "response cost" class, each student began rating periods with a specified number of tokens but could lose them for not following the rules. Employment of token reinforcement resulted in mean gains of 0.6 grades on the reading portion of the Wide Range Achievement Test (Kaufman & O'Leary, 1972). The magnitude of change in this study was demonstrated by a comparison with an equivalent group of students at

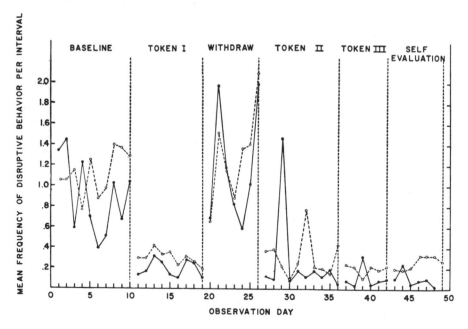

Figure 5. Comparison of daily mean disruptive behavior in reward and cost classes; reward (—●—), cost (---○---). From Kaufman & O'Leary 1972; reprinted with permission.

the hospital who lost 0.2 grades on this reading test over the same time period.

Notwithstanding the success experienced with the use of token reinforcement, it should be employed with extreme prudence. It must be remembered that some students do not respond positively to token reinforcement for a variety of reasons, including their lack of the requisite skills and the use of insufficient reinforcement by the teacher (Kazdin, 1977). Another important consideration is the determination of back-up reinforcers (i.e., what tokens may be exchanged for). Often teachers determine *a priori* what tokens will be redeemable for, independent of their demonstrated effect on behavior. The teacher who finds, to his surprise, that bubble gum does not result in increased accuracy of answering problems could have obviated this occurrence simply by asking the student what he liked. Finally, teachers should be aware of potential undesired behaviors, such as hoarding and stealing, which may result from the use of tokens. This technique should be employed only following a careful analysis of students' needs, capabilities, and limitations. Thus, the teacher or parent should carefully consider the characteristics of the student population in deciding how and when to employ token reinforcement.

SELF-CONTROL

Techniques in which the student may serve as the major change-agent fall under the rubric of self-regulation and are often designated as self-control procedures (see Karoly, 1977; O'Leary & Dubey, 1979, and Rosenbaum & Drabman, 1979, for reviews). Such procedures have offered an array of valuable techniques with which to enhance behavioral change through use of the logic that a person is able to alter the probability of a response which he wishes to control by initiating another response or contingency. For example, a child who desires to increase his rate of working arithmetic problems may tell himself that he will engage in "fun time" only after this goal is reached. Although there exist a host of definitional, theoretical, and methodological issues (Bandura, 1978; Jones, 1980), the self-control model is typically regarded as consisting of three major components: (a) self-monitoring, whereby the person observes his performance on a given task, (b) self-evaluation, in which the person compares his performance with the performance of others or with some externally imposed standard, and (c) self-reinforcement, whereby the person self-administers a reinforcer following the completion of some specified task or self-administers a punisher contingent upon a poor performance (Kanfer, 1975, 1976). Recently, self-control strategies have received an increasing amount of attention. Consequently, a literature which demonstrates the success of self-control strategies in the modification of academic behavior has rapidly developed (Mahoney & Thoresen, 1974).

A demonstration of the employment of a self-control technique is provided by Glynn, Thomas, and Shee (1973). Eight children, randomly selected from a second-grade class, served as experimental subjects. During daily 30-minute class reading lessons, each subject's on-task behavior was observed. On-task behavior was defined as looking at the teacher or blackboard, reading to the teacher, and/or engaging in oral discussions with the teacher when the teacher was present. When the teacher was not immediately present, on-task behaviors included changing library books, engaging in specified art or craft activities, and reading and writing in one's place. Off-task behaviors included leaving the room, arguing, shouting, walking aimlessly about the room, and playing with the toys. Following several phases of treatment designed to assess the effects of externally administered reinforcement on subjects' behavior, the self-control strategies were employed.

The behavioral self-control treatment was comprised of partial self-assessment, self-recording, partial self-determination of reinforcement, and self-administration of reinforcement. Briefly, subjects were instructed to assess their own performance following the sound of the tape-recorded signals. This procedure was used to enable subjects to decide for themselves whether they had earned reinforcement (self-determination of reinforcement). Subjects were also instructed to record their own behavior by placing a check on a recording sheet if (and only if) they were on-task at the sound of the "beep." Access to reinforcement was individually permitted, with free time and back-up reinforcers contingent upon individual on-task behavior, unlike the previous phases, in which reinforcement was administered in a group fashion.

The results of this study, as represented by the group's behavior, are depicted in Figure 6. These data indicate that during the self-control phases the subjects maintained the high rates of on-task behavior previously established by externally administered reinforcement techniques. The decline in variability of on-task behavior while the self-control procedures were in effect suggests that these techniques may lead to more stable rates of desired behavior than do external reinforcement procedures. Notwithstanding several shortcomings resulting from unavailability of observers, inability to isolate the effects of self-reinforcement procedures independent of the mode of reinforcement (individual versus group), and lack of long-term follow-up data, this study attests to the potential effectiveness of the self-control procedure in enhancing desired behavior.

Of the various self-control components elucidated at the beginning

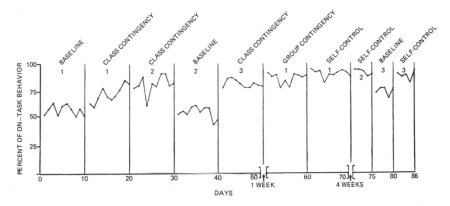

Figure 6. Mean daily on-task behavior (all subjects). From Glynn, Thomas, & Shee (1973); reprinted with permission.

of this section, self-reinforcement, as employed in the behavioral literature, has been shown to be one of the most effective techniques for altering behavior. That is, allowing children to self-determine and self-administer their reinforcement appears to have a desirable effect on subsequent performance. More specifically, a considerable body of literature demonstrates the effectiveness of self-reinforcement procedures in increasing academic performance (see Jones, Nelson, & Kazdin, 1977 and Masters & Mokros, 1974, for reviews). For example, Lovitt and Curtiss (1969) found that a 12-year-old boy's daily academic response rate was increased when he, rather than his teacher, arranged the contingency requirements. That is, based upon a calculated figure which represented performance in all subjects, it was shown that self-imposed contingencies increased the number of responses which this student gave per minute.

Teachers and other change-agents should, however, be aware of the recent speculation which has been focused upon the hypothesized role of racial and socioeconomic factors in self-reinforcement patterns. That is, in attempting to ascertain reasons for poor achievement on the part of black students, investigators have studied both social situation and disposition, including motivation, and, consequently, a growing concern about "intrinsic" versus "extrinsic" motivational orientations has arisen (Banks, McQuater, & Hubbard, 1978). Much of this concern has grown as a result of studies which suggest that children from low socioeconomic status homes administer self-reward at a higher rate than children from high socioeconomic status homes (Masters & Peskay, 1972) and that black children administer self-reward at a higher rate than white children (Hayes, 1978).

However, as Katz has pointed out (1967), in order to adequately assess the numerous hypotheses regarding various "motivational diffi-culties" of disadvantaged children, examination of the self-regulatory process with respect to environment is necessary. Indeed, recent data suggest that variables in addition to race should be considered when attempting to determine children's patterns of self-reinforcement. For example, Banks, McQuater, and Hubbard (1977) point out the need to assess the importance of task-liking, and Jones and Evans (1980) and Jones and Ollendick (1979) emphasize the need to attend to instructions. These findings are indicative of the influence which external variables may have upon the patterns of reinforcement observed in black children and children of low socioeconomic status.

Thus, the investigations designed to determine the relative influence of external variables in self-control procedures suggest that teachers may have to monitor children's self-control behavior in order to ensure that effortful behavior is enhanced (Jones, 1979, 1980). Indeed, studies in the self-control area do employ various degrees of external influence to ensure that behavior is developed and maintained. It should be remem-bered that self-control in applied settings should be "considered a matter of degree where external control is minimal or intermittent" (Kazdin, 1975, p. 207). Careful inspection of external variables may enable teach-ers to determine what components of the self-reinforcement procedure are most likely to produce behavior change.

In spite of the uncertainty of the issue concerning patterns of self-reinforcement and the role of external factors in the self-reinforcement process, self-control procedures have been found to be useful in the management of classroom behavior. As stated earlier, a benefit of the self-control procedure is that it may be employed with relatively little assistance from the classroom teacher. Also, given the fact that, in many environments, positive reinforcement is either relatively nonexistent or totally externally administered, allowing children to play a role in the determination and administration of reinforcement may be particularly useful. Although the relative role of external influence is yet to be as-certained clearly, self-reinforcement techniques (i.e., techniques in which the teacher exerts a large degree of external control) have been shown to enhance academic performance across a number of academic tasks and seem to afford the individual some control over his behavior.

GROUP CONTINGENCIES

A procedure which similarly allows participants to take an active part in the modification of their own behavior is that of group contin-gencies. Although several forms of group contingencies have been de-scribed (see Hayes, 1976, and Litow & Purmoy, 1975, for reviews), group reinforcement or punishment is typically determined by the performance of the collective members, with each individual contributing the final consequence (Medland & Stachnik, 1972). Several authors have shown that group contingencies have been successful in accelerating academic achievement (Alden, Pettigrew, & Skiba, 1970; DeVries & Edwards, 1973; Evans & Oswalt, 1968; Hamblin, Hathaway, & Wodarski, 1974; Wilson & Williams, 1973).

Two types of group contingencies that have been found to be quite effective in enhancing academic behavior are (a) the average group consequence, which involves the averaging of group members' scores to determine when reinforcement is administered, and (b) low group contingencies, when the behavior of a few group members, typically selected for their low level of academic performance, determines the reinforcement for the entire group. Although the first procedure, the average group consequence, has been employed successfully in enhancing cooperation among group members (DeVries & Edwards, 1973), the second, low group contingencies, was found to be successful in enhancing the academic achievement of black children in one study.

Hamblin and colleagues (1974), for example, had 38 black inner-city school children participate in one of five experimental groups in a study designed to assess the ability of different contingencies to enhance performance on spelling, math, and reading tasks. The five experimental contingencies to which each group was subjected are described below:

1. Average performance group contingency. All group members' responses were averaged, and reinforcement was determined by the group average.
2. High performance group contingency. All group members were reinforced on the basis of the highest performances produced by members of the group.
3. Low performance group contingency. All group members were reinforced on the basis of the lowest performances of members of the group.
4. Individual performance contingency. A subject's reinforcement was determined solely on his own performance.
5. Individual attendance contingency. Subjects were reinforced for simply being present.

Subjects were placed in each of the five experimental phases for a three-week period. Gains on academic achievement were assessed by gain scores on weekly tests. That is, scores obtained on the first test during the week were subtracted from scores on the second test, taken later in the week. Gain scores were calculated for each student and were used to assess the degree of change in math, reading, and spelling performance. During the course of this study, subjects were reminded that they were free to interact with group members in preparation for tests. Subjects were also reminded of the consequences of their performance under each contingency at the same time they were given the assignment. Reinforcement consisted of points, food, sundries, and toys.

The results showed that overall improvement, as measured by average standard gain scores in spelling, mathematics, and reading, was most notable under the low performance group contingency condition (1.5) and the high performance group contingency condition (1.4). Improvement in the average group contingency condition (1.0) and individual performance contingency condition (1.0) was average, whereas the individual attendance contingency condition (.5) resulted in the worst performance. These results provide important implications for poorly performing students who are placed in a low group contingency. The low group contingency not only increased the level of performance of both slower students (which the high group contingency did not) and gifted students but also resulted in a marked increase in cooperation toward lower achieving students. The authors hypothesized that poor students did three times better under the low group contingency than they did under both the high performance and individual attendance groups due to a type of "egalitarian excellence" fostered by the low performance group contingency.

These types of group contingency programs may well offer alternate ways of designing the classroom learning environment to accelerate rates of academic achievement. The numerous advantages of group contingencies—including the relative ease with which many programs may be implemented, the benefits of group monitoring and reinforcement delivery, and (in some programs) the increased cooperation among students, the use of peer tutoring, and the often competitive nature of groups—accelerate its attractiveness as an intervention strategy. In addition to these advantages, research has shown that group procedures are at least as effective as individual procedures (Axelrod, 1973; Brown, Reschly, & Sabers, 1974; Hamblin et al., 1974). Although a number of potential problems become evident when employing some types of group contingencies, including the need for individualized curricula, the need for self-pacing of teacher procedures, and the need for increased cooperation from teachers, their potential benefits certainly make them likely candidates for application in the classroom environment.

PUNISHMENT

To this point we have discussed techniques in which some form of positive reinforcement was administered to enhance desired response rates. Attention will now be given to punishment procedures, which have been found to contribute to academic attainment by controlling deviant and nonproductive behavior. Four widely used techniques which are often placed under the rubric of classroom punishment procedures will be discussed: time-out, response cost, overcorrection, and reprimands.

TIME-OUT FROM REINFORCEMENT

Time-out from reinforcement is perhaps the most extensively used classroom punishment procedure of behaviorally-oriented teachers and technicians (MacDonough & Forehand, 1973). The technique commonly referred to as time-out (Kazdin, 1975) or contingent social isolation (Drabman & Spitalnik, 1973) typically consists of a child's removal from a situation in which undesired behavior has occurred. Following an occurrence of off-task behavior, for example, a child may be placed in an isolated corner of the classroom for a specified period of time. In some cases, the child is required to emit appropriate behavior in order to return to the situation in which deviant behavior was emitted (O'Leary, O'Leary, & Becker, 1967). Once the child is placed into time-out, there is no access to positive reinforcers. Due to lack of total control over many classroom environments, however, the requirement of no access to positive reinforcers during the time-out interval is often not achieved. This situation may be remedied by a recent variation in the time-out procedure which allows the child to remain in the social situation but removes the opportunity to earn reinforcers (Foxx & Shapiro, 1978). The effectiveness of the time-out procedure in both decreasing disruptive, resistant, and aggressive behavior and increasing appropriate social behavior (Sibley, Abbott, & Cooper, 1969; White, Nielsen, & Johnson, 1972) and in increasing appropriate classroom behavior (Wasik, Senn, Welch, & Cooper, 1969) has been demonstrated, attesting to the usefulness of this technique in modifying a number of significant problem behaviors.

Contingent social isolation was investigated by Drabman and Spitalnik (1973), who selected five emotionally disturbed children ranging in age from 9 to 11 as subjects, based upon the amount of disruptive behavior which they exhibited during classroom periods. Three phases were employed to assess the effects of social isolation. They consisted of Baseline I, Contingent Social Isolation, and Baseline II. Target behaviors were out-of-seat (defined as observable, undesired movement of the child from his chair), aggression (defined as an intense movement directed at another person and resulting in contact with the other person), and vocalization (defined as any "audible" behavior emanating from the mouth and not allowed by the teacher). Each of these behaviors was observed and recorded during daily 55-minute class periods.

Following an 11-day baseline, the contingent social isolation phase was initiated. While inappropriate vocalization was not punished, occurrences of aggression and out-of-seat behavior now resulted in subjects being given the following instructions: "[name of child], you have misbehaved. You must leave the class" (p. 242). The subject was immediately escorted by the teaching assistant to a small music practice room which was empty, dimly lit, and sound-resistant. To ensure the subject's safety, the teaching assistant remained in close proximity. The subject stayed in the isolation room for a 10-minute period. Following 16 days of this procedure, a second baseline was implemented and observation of disruptive behavior continued.

Group results indicated a percentage drop in out-of-seat behavior from a mean of 34% (during Baseline I) to a mean of 11% (during the Social Isolation phase). Following the withdrawal of social isolation, a slight increase in this behavior was noted ($M = 15\%$). Similarly, aggression, which averaged 2.8% during Baseline, plummeted to 0.7% during the treatment phase. A comparison of the unpunished behavior (vocalization) and the other two behaviors was carried out within a multiple baseline design. The pattern of vocalizations remained relatively the same throughout each of the three phases, with a Baseline I mean of 32%, a treatment mean of 28% and a mean of 27% during Baseline II. This study demonstrates the relative effectiveness of the social isolation procedure in modifying disruptive classroom behavior.

RESPONSE COST

A technique which is similar to time-out is response cost, most frequently defined as the withdrawal of previously administered reinforcement following an undesired response (cf. Kazdin, 1972). Although these two techniques share the element of reinforcer withdrawal, there is no time requirement in response cost as there is in time-out (Weiner, 1962). Also, the time-out procedure requires no withdrawal of previously acquired reinforcers, whereas such removal is an essential element of the response cost procedure. Although response cost always involves the loss of free time, tokens, toys or other reinforcers, in classroom environments it usually involves the removal of tokens following inappropriate behavior (Broden, Hall, Dunlap, & Clark, 1970; Repp & Deitz, 1974; Schmidt & Ulrich, 1969). Among academic behaviors which have been altered by response cost in conjunction with other techniques are rate and percentage of correct responses in spelling and reading tasks (Sulzer, Hunt, Ashby, Koniarski, & Krams, 1971) and rule violation and off-task behavior (Iwata & Bailey, 1974). A typical example of the response cost procedure is provided in an investigation by Hall, Axelrod, Foundopoulos, Shellman, Campbell, and Cranston (1971), in which children lost the opportunity to engage in play time or free time as a result of whining, crying, or complaining.

OVERCORRECTION

A recently devised punishment technique, referred to as overcorrection, has been provided by Foxx and Azrin (1972, 1973). The procedure is characterized by two components: (a) positive-practice overcorrection, which requires that the individual repeatedly practice a positive act (e.g., after writing on a wall, the individual is required to clean that wall as well as other walls in the classroom), and (b) restitutional overcorrection, which requires that the individual restore the environment to a state much better than existed prior to an act of disruption (e.g., polishing furniture as well as restoring it to its original position after disrupting it). For example, Foxx and Azrin (1973) employed positive-practice overcorrection in a situation in which no environmental disruption had been created by an inappropriate act in order to decrease one subject's nonfunctional self-stimulatory behavior. An 8-year-old girl who had difficulty learning as a result of inappropriate head-moving served as this subject. Following a 20-day baseline in which the frequency of head-weaving behavior was observed and recorded, a positive practice overcorrection procedure was implemented. During this treatment, the occurrence of inappropriate head movement resulted in five minutes of functional movement training. The training began with the teacher using her hands to restrain the child's head and instructing her to move her head in various positions. When desired responses were not emitted, the teacher manually guided the child's head. After each instruction and response (or guided response), the child was required to hold her head stationary for 15 seconds. As the child began to follow directions, the teacher's manual guidance was faded out. A verbal warning procedure, in which the occurrence of head-weaving resulted in the child being told to stop the head-weaving, was also initiated. If the child failed to stop engaging in the undesired behavior after the warning or engaged in it a second time during the session, the overcorrection period was reinstated.

By employing two baseline conditions, two overcorrection conditions, and a verbal warning condition, the effects of overcorrection were demonstrated. During both overcorrection conditions the frequency of head-weaving behavior was found to plummet significantly. Maintenance of desired behavior was noted during the warning condition. Additionally, the elimination of the self-stimulatory behavior resulted in a dramatic increase in the child's attention to teaching materials and in an increase in test performance which permitted placement in a class for the higher-functioning, trainable mentally retarded.

VERBAL REPRIMANDS

The verbal reprimand, in the form of disapproving statements such as "sit down," "wait your turn," and "be quiet," is probably one of the most frequently employed modes of behavior control in the classroom. Indeed, disapproving responses have been found to be employed more frequently than even the more effective procedure of positive social reinforcement. Empirical findings supporting this fact are provided by Madsen, Becker, Thomas, Koser, and Plager (1970), who reported that 77% of the teachers' interactions with their students were negative, whereas only 23% of the interactions were positive.

When inappropriately used, verbal reprimands have been shown to be totally ineffective in changing undesired behavior (Madsen *et al.*, 1970). That is, reprimands which are employed unsystematically are not only insufficient in modifying deviant behavior, but often increase and maintain the very behavior they were to decrease. In spite of this lack of effectiveness, reprimands continue to be employed frequently in an unsystematic fashion.

Appropriately employed verbal reprimands, on the other hand, may lead to desired changes in behavior. Throughout the behavioral literature several illustrations of verbal reprimands which have been systematically and contingently employed and which have resulted in decreases in undesired responses have been provided (O'Leary, Kaufman, Kass, & Drabman, 1970; O'Leary & O'Leary, 1976). In the O'Leary *et al.* (1970) study, for example, soft reprimands were found to decrease disruptive behaviors when they were audible only to the subject who was emitting the disruptive behavior. However, notwithstanding the apparent effectiveness of appropriately employed verbal reprimands in modifying behavior, teachers should be acutely aware of the high correlation between disapproval rates and increases in disruptive behavior (Thomas, Becker, & Armstrong, 1968).

In summary, although the techniques described above have been found to modify undesired behavior, either alone or in conjunction with other procedures (e.g., token reinforcement), a number of considerations are of paramount importance. First, punishment procedures should be used only after positive means have been exhausted and should always be administered in conjunction with positive reinforcement procedures. It should be remembered that these procedures often teach children what not to do but do not teach them appropriate responses which can produce positive outcomes. A second concern of which change-agents should be aware is the probability of undesired side effects. Undesired emotional effects, such as negative self-statements, negative generalization, peer reactions, rebellion, and avoidance of the individual who administers punishment, may be noted following the implementation of some punishment procedures. Side effects such as social disruption or escape have been found to occur when response cost is employed (Boren & Colman, 1970). Procedures to mitigate such undesired behaviors should be engaged when possible (e.g., providing the child with opportunities to gain reinforcement for some alternative response). A third consideration is the age of children for whom these procedures are being implemented. Younger children, for example, may be found to have more undesirable emotional reactions following a time-out procedure than older children. As a fourth precaution, it is important that individuals employing punishment techniques stay abreast of the relevant literature, which points out guidelines for the usage of such procedures with children. A keen awareness and a working knowledge of procedures should be prerequisites for any application of these techniques. Given the relative ease of application and the convenience of these procedures, misuse may often occur. That is, individuals may employ punishment procedures where positive behavior change techniques are called for. Lastly, when using these procedures, the academic, social, and emotional welfare of the child should be of primary importance; not the convenience of the teacher.

TEACHER TRAINING

No discussion elucidating procedures to enhance academic performance is complete without mention of teacher training. To ensure maximum benefit from the various behavior change techniques previously discussed, teachers must be adequately trained to administer each procedure. The success of many classroom programs is determined by the teacher's understanding of behavioral principles and his ability to apply them. Thus, in designing a behavioral program for students with teachers as change-agents, the role of teacher training becomes an area of paramount importance.

A major type of teacher training is instructional methods in the form of in-service training, workshops, discussions, and lectures. Although administrators frequently assume that the "one-shot" lectures or workshop presentations are sufficient to equip teachers with the necessary weaponry with which to produce behavior changes, the results of such interventions have not shown them to be very effective in enabling teachers to implement newly learned behaviors (Sloat, Tharp, & Gallimore, 1977). That is, teachers may not be able to apply their knowledge to the alteration of student behavior. A major shortcoming of many of these methods is that they are seldom accompanied by practical training. During a "canned" lecture, for example, teachers may be told how to administer reinforcement to students for appropriate behavior, but the needed training in the application of the procedure may not be provided. Therefore, when the teacher returns to his classroom, he is faced with the dilemma of not being able to implement the suggested procedure. To overcome this problem, techniques which combine various instructional methods with training in situations where the procedure will actually be employed have been developed. For example, responsive teaching (Hall, 1972; Hall & Copeland, 1972), which combines two instructional methods, lectures and discussion, with practical training, has been shown to be relatively effective. During a course in which responsive teaching is implemented, behavior modification principles and techniques of classroom management are spelled out and each student is required to carry out a project in which behavior modification principles are employed and evaluated.

Although procedures have been developed and carried out to assess the effectiveness of several other techniques, including feedback, in training teachers, relatively few positive findings have resulted. For example, feedback alone has been found to have positive effects on teacher behavior in some programs (Cooper, Thompson, & Baer, 1970; Thomas, 1971), but the majority of these effects tend to be minimal or inconsistent (Breyer & Allen, 1975; Cossairt, Hall, & Hopkins, 1973). Instructions accompanied by feedback, in most instances, have also been found to be ineffective (Rule, 1972; Saudargas, 1972).

On the other hand, one procedure which has been found to be successful in training teachers to modify students' behavior is praise. Praise, one of the most powerful teacher-training procedures, has been shown to be effective both when combined with graphical feedback (Cossairt et al., 1973) and when used alone (McDonald, 1973). Praise is typically administered in the form of positive comments made in reference to the teacher's performance, and it appears to be of significant benefit when systematically applied (McDonald, 1973).

Other techniques which have been found to enhance teacher effectiveness in the use of behavioral principles include modeling (Ringer, 1973; Speidel & Tharp, 1978), role playing (Jones & Eimers, 1975), and token reinforcement (McNamara, 1971). Detailed descriptions of these techniques have been spelled out elsewhere (Kazdin & Moyer, 1975).

It is suggested that effective teacher training techniques do exist. Although concerted research attention has not been given to this area, preliminary findings attest to the potential of several techniques, including programs which combine praise and feedback. Before more definitive conclusions can be drawn on this topic, however, more extensive research endeavors must be undertaken.

When implementing behavioral training programs in which the teacher is the major change-agent, attention should be paid to teachers' needs and concerns to ensure their participation in the program. Incentives, including course credit, positive feedback from principals and parents, and monetary stipends (when available), should be systematically provided to enhance the likelihood of desired teacher performance. It should also be remembered that maintenance of desired teacher behavior is necessary to ensure its continuance. Unless procedures are implemented to maintain teacher behavior (following the removal of extrinsic consequences), the desired behavior often plummets to previous baseline levels (Brown, Montgomery, & Barclay, 1969; Cooper *et al.*, 1970). The teacher's role in behavior-change programs is of essential importance and should be of continual concern to school administrators.

THE PROBLEM OF GENERALIZATION

Perhaps one of the most obvious difficulties confronting behavior-change programs in classroom settings is the lack of generalization of target behavior to situations in which treatment has been withdrawn or to settings other than that in which the program was implemented. Often teachers raise questions concerning the effect of treatment withdrawal upon acquired responses and the extent to which behaviors taught in a classroom will be observed in a setting other than the one where they were originally taught. That these two questions are raised points to the need for researchers to pay close attention to the problem of generalization.

The issue which stems from these questions concerns the extent to which changes in behavior extend across stimulus conditions—commonly referred to as stimulus generalization. Stimulus generalization may exist in one of two different forms (Kazdin, 1977). The first of these two forms of stimulus generalization is referred to as response maintenance, or resistance to extinction. A problem in this type of stimulus generalization is the change in behavior which often follows the removal of the contingencies that were in operation during treatment. Typically, this change involves a return of the frequency or rate of behavior to initial baseline levels. The desired rates of appropriate behavior which were exhibited during a token program, for example, may sharply decline following the termination of the token program. Thus, the maintenance of behavior can be conceptualized as generalization across stimulus conditions. That is, behavior change in one situation (e.g., a classroom in which a behavioral program is in effect) may generalize to a different situation (e.g., the same classroom following the withdrawal of the behavioral program).

Transfer of training is the second form of stimulus generalization. Problems resulting from this type of generalization center around the lack of carry-over of treatment effects from the setting in which the behavior was taught to a setting in which training did not occur. For example, appropriate on-task behavior taught in a math classroom may not be observed in a reading classroom.

Several factors have been cited as plausible explanations for the lack of generalization. Perhaps the most plausible is simply failure to implement procedures which are designed to enhance generalization. This problem is highlighted by the assertion of Baer, Wolf, and Risley (1968) that generalization must be programmed rather than assumed to occur.

Although additional research attention is needed to provide more satisfactory answers to questions surrounding the issue of stimulus generalization, several investigations have been carried out in an attempt to develop strategies which enhance the probability of generalization. These procedures include substitution of one program for another (Walker, Hops, & Johnson, 1975), expansion of stimulus control (Emshoff, Redd, & Davidson, 1976), fading of contingencies (Turkewitz, O'Leary, & Ironsmith, 1975), delay of reinforcer delivery (Greenwood, Hops, Delquadri, & Guild, 1974), and implementation of self-control techniques (Bolstad & Johnson, 1972). These techniques have been found to be relatively effective in accomplishing the goals of response maintenance and transfer of training, both independently and in combination.

Jones and Kazdin (1975), for example, developed a treatment in which a number of separate procedures were combined to develop response maintenance of appropriate classroom behavior following the withdrawal of token reinforcement. Kazdin (1976) described these procedures as follows:

> After tokens had improved the students' behavior, these reinforcements were gradually phased out. To keep the children working at their new level, we encouraged them to reward each other at the close of the day by applauding each of the students who had done especially well. We also instituted special classroom activities, such as movies, ice cream, or extra recesses, that rewarded the whole class on the basis of each student's performance. We had shifted from the artificial reinforcement of tokens to natural events such as attention and class activities. By making the shift gradually, the gains in student behavior remained. Twelve weeks later, when the term ended, the children were still performing as well as they had under the token economy. (p. 105)

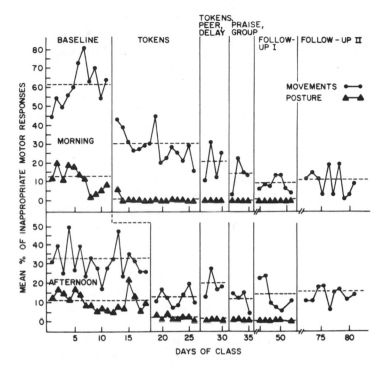

Figure 7. Percentage of inappropriate motor movements and posture behavior for all subjects (*R* = 4). From Jones & Kazdin (1975); reprinted with permission.

Although these findings are preliminary, inasmuch as each component is yet to be extensively evaluated, this investigation demonstrates the effectiveness of a combination of techniques in maintaining desired behavior.

In classroom situations both forms of stimulus generalization problems are likely to occur. For example, transfer of training may be especially improbable if children live in environments in which behaviors necessary for academic attainment are seldom reinforced in situations other than the classroom. Thus, teachers, parents, and other change-agents should be acutely aware of the problems of stimulus generalization. Knowledge of procedures with which to enhance generalization is an essential tool which each should possess. Although many of the previously mentioned procedures for enhancing response maintenance and transfer of training have not been thoroughly evaluated, preliminary results strongly argue for their employment.

Summary

In summary, the worth of the aforementioned techniques is attested to by their wide applicability and effectiveness in the enhancement of academic behavior as well as their ability to modify those behaviors which are incompatible with effective learning. Teacher attention, token reinforcement, self-control, group contingencies, time-out, response cost, and overcorrection are all techniques that have been found to be facilitative in fostering desired classroom behavior. Academic improvement (by both black and white students), ranging from increased performance on arithmetic tasks to increased performance on IQ tests, demonstrates the ability of behavioral techniques to produce desired change in the academic setting. Thus, these techniques appear to be beneficial in increasing the number of positive classroom experiences which students, black as well as white, encounter.

Although problems often arise in the employment of these techniques (e.g., the lack of generalization and maintenance), they do provide needed assistance to current educational systems. It should be remembered, however, that change-agents who are attempting to institute behavioral procedures should, in addition to receiving training in behavioral management, stay in close contact with professionals who have a firm understanding of the principles of behavior as well as the application of these principles to problem behavior. Far too often, school personnel assume that the proper application of these procedures requires simply a one-shot seminar or a small number of short training sessions to ensure their proper application. Research findings strongly suggest the need for extended training as well as continuous monitoring by individuals trained in behavior modification. Given this training and monitoring, behavioral techniques should continue to be used to develop and maintain an array of academic skills in classroom settings.

References

Alden, S. E., Pettigrew, L. E., & Skiba, E. A. The effect of individual-contingent group reinforcement on popularity. *Child Development,* 1970, *4,* 1191–1196.

Axelrod, S. Comparison of individual and group contingencies in two special classes. *Behavior Therapy,* 1973, *4,* 83–90.

Ayllon, T., & Kelly, K. Effects of reinforcement on standardized test performance. *Journal of Applied Behavior Analysis,* 1972, *5,* 477–484.

Ayllon, T., & Roberts, M. D. Eliminating discipline problems by strengthening academic performance. *Journal of Applied Behavior Analysis,* 1974, *7,* 71–76.

Baer, D. M., Wolf, M. M., & Risley, T. R. Some current dimensions of applied behavior analysis. *Journal of Applied Behavior Analysis,* 1968, *1,* 91–97.

Bandura, A. The self-system in reciprocal determinism. *American Psychologist*, 1978, *4*, 349–358.

Banks, W. C., McQuater, G., & Hubbard, J. L. Task-liking and intrinsic-extrinsic achievement orientations in black adolescents. *Journal of Black Psychology*, 1977, *3*, 61–71.

Banks, W. C., McQuater, G. V., & Hubbard, J. L. Toward a reconceptualization of the social-cognitive bases of achievement orientations in Blacks. *Review of Educational Research*, 1978, *48*, 381–397.

Birnbrauer, J. S., & Lawler, J. Token reinforcement for learning. *Mental Retardation*, 1964, *2*, 275–279.

Bolstad, O. D., & Johnson, S. M. Self-regulation in the modification of disruptive behavior. *Journal of Applied Behavior Analysis*, 1972, *5*, 443–454.

Boren, J. J., & Colman, A. D. Some experiments on reinforcement principles within a psychiatric ward for delinquent soldiers. *Journal of Applied Behavior Analysis*, 1970, *3*, 29–37.

Breyer, M. L., & Allen, G. J. Effects of implementing a token economy on teacher attending behavior. *Journal of Applied Behavior Analysis*, 1975, *8*, 373–380.

Broden, M., Bruce, C., Mitchell, M. A., Carter, V., & Hall, R. V. Effects of teacher attention on attending behavior of two boys at adjacent desks. *Journal of Applied Behavior Analysis*, 1970, *3*, 199–203.

Broden, M., Hall, R. V., Dunlap, A., & Clark, R. Effects of teacher attention and a token reinforcement system in a junior high school special education class. *Exceptional Children*, 1970, *36*, 341–349.

Brown, D., Reschly, D., & Sabers, D. Using group contingencies with punishment and positive reinforcement to modify aggressive behaviors in a Head Start Classroom. *Psychological Record*, 1974, *24*, 491–496.

Brown, J., Montgomery, R., & Barclay, J. An example of psychologist management of teacher reinforcement procedures in the elementary classroom. *Psychology in the Schools*, 1969, *6*, 336–340.

Bushell, D. The design of classroom contingencies. In F. S. Keller & E. Ribes-Inesta (Eds.), *Behavior modification: Applications to education*. New York: Academic Press, 1974.

Chadwick, B. A., & Day, R. C. Systematic reinforcement. Academic performance of un derachieving students. *Journal of Applied Behavior Analysis*, 1971, *4*, 311–319.

Cooper, M. L., Thompson, C. L., & Baer, D. M. The experimental modification of teacher attending behavior. *Journal of Applied Behavior Analysis*, 1970, *3*, 153–157.

Cossairt, A., Hall, R. V., & Hopkins, B. L. The effects of experimenter's instructions, feedback, and praise on teacher praise and student attending behavior. *Journal of Applied Behavior Analysis*, 1973, *6*, 89–100.

DeVries, D. L., & Edwards, K. J. Learning games and student teams: Their effects on classroom process. *American Educational Research Journal*, 1973, *10*, 307–318.

Drabman, R., & Spitalnik, R. Social isolation as a punishment procedure: A controlled study. *Journal of Experimental Child Psychology*, 1973, *16*, 236–249.

Emshoff, J. G., Redd, W. H., & Davidson, W. S. Generalization training and the transfer of treatment effects with delinquent adolescents. *Journal of Behavior Therapy and Experimental Psychiatry*, 1976, *7*, 141–144.

Evans, G. W., & Oswalt, G. L. Acceleration of academic progress through the manipulation of peer influence. *Behaviour Research and Therapy*, 1968, *6*, 189–195.

Foxx, R. M., & Azrin, N. H. Restitution: A method of eliminating aggressive-disruptive behavior of retarded and brain damaged patients. *Behaviour Research and Therapy*, 1972, *10*, 15–27.

Foxx, R. M., & Azrin, N. H. The elimination of autistic self-stimulation behavior by overcorrection. *Journal of Applied Behavior Analysis*, 1973, *6*, 1–14.

Foxx, R. M., & Shapiro, S. T. The timeout ribbon: A nonexclusionary timeout procedure. *Journal of Applied Behavior Analysis*, 1978, *11*, 125–136.

Glynn, E. L. Classroom applications of self-determined reinforcement. *Journal of Applied Behavior Analysis*, 1970, *3*, 123–132.

Glynn, E. L., Thomas, J. D., & Shee, S. M. Behavioral self-control of on-task behavior in an elementary classroom. *Journal of Applied Behavior Analysis*, 1973, *6*, 105–113.

Greenwood, C. R., Hops, H., Delquadri, J., & Guild, J. Group contingencies for group consequences in classroom management: A further analysis. *Journal of Applied Behavior Analysis*, 1974, *7*, 413–425.

Hall, R. V. Responsive teaching: Focus on measurement and research in the classroom and the home. In E. L. Meyen, G. A. Vergason, & R. J. Whelan (Eds.), *Strategies for teaching exceptional children*. Denver: Love, 1972.

Hall, R. V., & Copeland, R. E. The responsive teaching model: A first step in shaping school personnel as behavior modification specialists. In F. W. Clark, D. R. Evans, & L. A. Hammerlynk (Eds.), *Implementing behavioral programs for schools and clinics*. Champaign, Ill.: Research Press, 1972.

Hall, R. V., Axelrod, S., Foundopoulos, M., Shellman, J., Campbell, R. A., & Cranston, S. S. The effective use of punishment to modify behavior in the classroom. In K. D. O'Leary & S. G. O'Leary (Eds.), *Classroom management: The successful use of behavior modification*. New York: Pergamon Press, 1971.

Hall, R. V., Lund, D., & Jackson, D. Effects of teacher attention on study behavior. *Journal of Applied Behavior Analysis*, 1968, *1*, 1–12.

Hamblin, R. L., Hathaway, C., & Wodarski, J. Group contingencies, peer tutoring, and accelerating academic achievement. In R. Ulrich, T. Stachnik, & J. Mabry (Eds.), *Control of human behavior* (Vol. 3). Glenview, Ill.: Scott, Foresman, 1974.

Hawkins, R., McArthur, M., Rinaldi, P., Gray, D., & Schaftenaur, L. Results of operant conditioning techniques in modifying the behavior of emotionally disturbed children. Paper presented at the 45th Annual International Council for Exceptional Children, St. Louis, 1967.

Hayes, C. S. Effects of race, success, and failure on children's self-reward. *The Journal of Genetic Psychology*, 1978, *133*, 301–302.

Hayes, J. R. It's the thought that counts: New approaches to educational theory. In D. Klahr (Ed.), *Cognition and instruction*. Hillsdale, N.J.: Lawrence Erlbaum Associates, 1976.

Iwata, B. A., & Bailey, J. S. Reward versus cost token systems: An analysis of the effects on students and teacher. *Journal of Applied Behavior Analysis*, 1974, *7*, 567–576.

Jones, F. H., & Eimers, R. C. Role playing to train elementary teachers to use a classroom management "skill package." *Journal of Applied Behavior Analysis*, 1975, *8*, 421–433.

Jones, R. T. *The role of external variables in the self-reinforcement procedure*. Paper presented at the Fifth Annual Convention of the Association of Behavior Analysis, Dearborn, Michigan, June, 1979.

Jones, R. T. The role of external variables in self-reinforcement. *American Psychologist*, 1980, *35*, 1002–1004.

Jones, R. T., & Evans, H. Self-reinforcement: A continuum of external cues. *Journal of Educational Psychology*, 1980, 72(5), 625–635.

Jones, R. T., & Kazdin, A. E. Programming response maintenance after withdrawing token reinforcement. *Behavior Therapy*, 1975, *6*, 153–164.

Jones, R. T., & Kazdin, A. E. Childhood behavior problems in the school. In S. M. Turner, K. Calhoun, & H. E. Adams (Eds.), *Handbook of clinical behavior therapy*. New York: Wiley, 1981.

Jones R. T., Nelson, R. E., & Kazdin, A. E. The role of external variables in self-reinforcement: A review. *Behavior Modification*, 1977, *1*, 147–178.

Jones, R. T., & Ollendick, T. H. Self-reinforcement: An assessment of external influences. *Journal of Behavioral Assessment*, 1979, *1*, 289–303.

Kanfer, F. H. Self-management methods. In F. H. Kanfer & A. P. Goldstein (Eds.), *Helping people change*. New York: Pergamon Press, 1975.

Kanfer, F. H. The many faces of self-control, or behavior modification changes its focus. Paper presented at Eighth International Banff Conference, Banff, Alberta, 1976.

Karoly, P. Behavioral self-management in children: Concepts, methods, issues, and directions. In M. Hersen, R. M. Eisler, & P. Miller (Eds.), *Progress in behavior modification*. New York: Academic Press, 1977, *5*,197–262.

Katz, I. The socialization of academic motivation in minority group children. In D. Levine (Ed.), *Nebraska Symposium on Motivation*. Lincoln: University of Nebraska Press, 1967.

Kaufman, K. F., & O'Leary, K. D. Reward, cost and self-evaluation procedures for disruptive adolescents in a psychiatric hospital. *Journal of Applied Behavior Analysis*, 1972, *5*, 293–309.

Kazdin, A. E. Response cost: The removal of conditioned reinforcers for therapeutic change. *Behavior Therapy*, 1972, *3*, 533–546.

Kazdin, A. E. *Behavior modification in applied settings*. Homewood, Ill.: Dorsey, 1975.

Kazdin, A. E. Token economies: The rich rewards of rewards. *Psychology Today*, November, 1976, pp. 98; 101–102; 105; 114.

Kazdin, A. E. *The token economy: A review and evaluation*. New York: Plenum Press, 1977.

Kazdin, A. E., & Bootzin, R. R. The token economy: Evaluative review. *Journal of Applied Behavior Analysis*, 1972, *5*, 343–372.

Kazdin, A. F., & Moyer, W. Training teachers to use behavior modification. In S. Yen & R. McIntire (Eds.), *Teaching behavior modification*. Kalamazoo, Michigan: Behaviordelia, 1975.

Lahey, B. B., & Drabman, R. S. Facilitation of the acquisition and retention of sight–word vocabulary through token reinforcement. *Journal of Applied Behavior Analysis*, 1974, *7*, 307–312.

Litow, L., & Purmoy, D. K. A brief review of classroom group-oriented contingencies. *Journal of Applied Behavior Analysis*, 1975, *8*, 341–347.

Lovitt, T. C., & Curtiss, K. Academic response rate as a function of teacher-and self-imposed contingencies. *Journal of Applied Behavior Analysis*, 1969, *2*, 49–53.

MacDonough, T. S., & Forehand, R. Response contingent time-out. Important parameters in behavior modifications with children. *Journal of Behavior Therapy and Experimental Psychiatry*, 1973, *4*, 231–236.

Madsen, C. H., Becker, W. C., Thomas, D. R., Koser, L., & Plager, E. An analysis of the reinforcing function of "sitdown" commands. In R. K. Parker (Ed.), *Readings in educational psychology*. Boston: Allyn & Bacon, 1970.

Madsen, C. H., Madsen, C. K., Saudargas, R. A., Hammond, W. R., & Egar, D. E. Classroom RAID (Rules, Approval, Ignore, Disapproval): A cooperative approach for professionals and volunteers. Unpublished manuscript, University of Florida, Tallahassee, Florida, 1970.

Mahoney, M. J., & Thoresen, C. E. *Self-control: Power to the person*. Monterey, California: Brooks/Cole, 1974.

Masters, J. C., & Mokros, J. R. Self-reinforcement processes in children. In H. Reese (Ed.), *Advances in child development and behavior* (Vol. 9). New York: Academic Press, 1974.

Masters, J. C., & Peskay, J. Effects of race, socioeconomic status, and success or failure upon contingent and noncontingent self-reinforcement in children. *Developmental Psychology*, 1972, *7*, 139–145.

McDonald, S. The kibitz dimension in teacher consultation. In R. D. Klein, W. G. Hapkiewicz, & A. H. Roden (Eds.), *Behavior modification in educational settings*. Springfield, Ill.: Charles C Thomas, 1973.

148   RUSSELL T. JONES

McLaughlin, T. F. The applicability of token reinforcement systems in public school systems. *Psychology in the Schools,* 1975, *12,* 84–89.

McNamara, J. R. Teacher and students as a source for behavior modification in the classroom. *Behavior Therapy,* 1971, *2,* 205–213.

Medland, B., & Stachnik, J. Good behavior game: A replication and systematic analysis. *Journal of Applied Behavior Analysis,* 1972, *5,* 45–51.

Miller, L. K., & Schneider, R. The use of a token system in project Head Start. *Journal of Applied Behavior Analysis,* 1970, *3,* 213–220.

O'Leary, K. D., & Drabman, R. Token reinforcement programs in the classroom: A review. *Psychological Bulletin,* 1971, *75,* 379–398.

O'Leary, S. G., & Dubey, D. R. Applications of self-control procedures by children: A review. *Journal of Applied Behavior Analysis,* 1979, *12,* 449–465.

O'Leary, K. D., Kaufman, K. F., Kass, R. E., & Drabman, R. S. The effects of loud and soft reprimands on the behavior of disruptive students. *Exceptional Children,* 1970, *37,* 145–155.

O'Leary, S. G., & O'Leary, K. D. Behavior modification in the school. In H. Leitenberg (Ed.), *Handbook of behavior modification and behavior therapy.* Englewood Cliffs, N.J.: Prentice-Hall, 1976.

O'Leary, K. D., O'Leary, S., & Becker, W. C. Modification of a deviant sibling interaction pattern in the home. *Behaviour Research and Therapy,* 1967, *5,* 113–120.

Repp, A. C., & Deitz, S. M. Reducing aggressive and self-injurious behavior of institutionalized retarded children through reinforcement of other behaviors. *Journal of Applied Behavior Analysis,* 1974, *7,* 313–325.

Ringer, V. M. The use of a "token helper" in the management of classroom behavior problems and in teacher training. *Journal of Applied Behavior Analysis,* 1973, *6,* 671–677.

Rollins, H. A., McCandless, B. R., Thompson, M., & Brassell, W. R. Project success environment: An extended application of contingency management in inner-city schools. *Journal of Educational Psychology,* 1974, *66,* 167–178.

Rosenbaum, M. S., & Drabman, R. S. Self-control training in the classroom: A review and critique. *Journal of Applied Behavior Analysis,* 1979, *12,* 467–485.

Rule, S. A. Comparison of three types of feedback on teachers' performance. In G. Semb (Ed.), *Behavior analysis and education.* Lawrence: University of Kansas, 1972.

Saudargas, R. A. Setting criterion rates of teacher praise: The effects of video tape feedback in a behavior analysis Follow-Through classroom. In G. Semb (Ed.), *Behavior analysis and education.* Lawrence, Kansas: University of Kansas Support and Development Center for Follow-Through, 1972.

Schmidt, G. W., & Ulrich, R. E. Effects of group contingent events upon classroom noise. *Journal of Applied Behavior Analysis,* 1969, *2,* 171–179.

Sibley, S., Abbott, M., & Cooper, B. Modification of the classroom behavior of a "disadvantaged" kindergarten boy by social reinforcement and isolation. *Journal of Experimental and Child Psychology,* 1969, *7,* 203–219.

Silberman, C. E. *Crisis in the classroom: The remaking of American education.* New York: Random House, 1970.

Sloat, K. C. M., Tharp, R. G., & Gallimore, R. The incremental effectiveness of classroom-based teacher-training techniques. *Behavior Therapy,* 1977, *8,* 810–818.

Smith, B. Humanism and behavior modification: Is there conflict? *The Elementary School Journal,* 1973, *62,* 59–67.

Speidel, G. E., & Tharp, R. G. Teacher-training workshop strategy: Instructions, discrimination training, modeling, guided practice, and video feedback. *Behavior Therapy,* 1978, *9,* 735–739.

Staats, A. W., Minke, K. A., Finley, J. R., Wolf, M., & Brooks, L. O. A reinforcer system and experimental procedure for the laboratory study of reading acquisition. *Child Development,* 1964, *35,* 209–231.

Sulzer, B., Hunt, S., Ashby, E., Koniarski, S., & Krams, M. Increasing rate and percentage correct in reading and spelling in a fifth grade public school class of slow readers by means of a token system. In E. A. Ramp and B. L. Hopkins (Eds.), *A new direction for education: Behavior analysis.* Lawrence: University of Kansas, 1971.

Surratt, P. R., Ulrich, R. E., & Hawkins, R. P. An elementary student as a behavioral engineer. *Journal of Applied Behavior Analysis,* 1969, *2,* 85–92.

Thomas, D. A., Becker, W. C., & Armstrong, M. Production and elimination of disruptive classroom behavior by systematically varying teacher's behavior. *Journal of Applied Behavior Analysis,* 1968, *1,* 35–45.

Thomas, D. R. Preliminary findings on self-monitoring for modifying teaching behaviors. In E. A. Ramp & B. L. Hopkins (Eds.), *A new direction for education: Behavior analysis* (Vol. 1). Lawrence, Kansas: University of Kansas Support and Development Center for Follow Through, 1971.

Thomas, S. D., Presland, I. E., Grant, M. D., & Glynn, T. Natural rates of teacher approval and disapproval in grade-7 classrooms. *Journal of Applied Behavior Analysis,* 1978, *11,* 91–94.

Turkewitz, H., O'Leary, K. D., & Ironsmith, M. Generalization and maintenance of appropriate behavior through self-control. *Journal of Consulting and Clinical Psychology,* 1975, *43,* 577–583.

Walker, H. M., Hops, H., & Johnson, S. M. Generalization and maintenance of classroom treatment effects. *Behavior Therapy,* 1975, *6,* 188–200.

Ward, M. H., & Baker, B. L. Reinforcement therapy in the classroom. *Journal of Applied Behavior Analysis,* 1968, *1,* 323–328.

Wasik, B. H., Senn, K., Welch, R. H., & Cooper, B. R. Behavior modification with culturally deprived children: Two case studies. *Journal of Applied Behavior Analysis,* 1969, *2,* 181–194.

Weiner, H. Some effects of response cost upon human operant behavior. *Journal of Experimental Analysis of Behavior,* 1962, *5,* 201–208.

White, G. D., Nielsen, G., & Johnson, S. M. Time-out duration and the suppression of deviant behavior in children. *Journal of Applied Behavior Analysis,* 1972, *5,* 111–120.

Wilson, M. D., & McReynolds, L. U. A procedure for increasing oral reading rate in hard of hearing children. *Journal of Applied Behavior Analysis,* 1973, *6,* 231–239.

Wilson, S. H., & Williams, R. L. The effects of group contingencies on first graders' academic and social behaviors. *Journal of School Psychology,* 1973, *11,* 110–117.

Witmer, J. M., Bornstein, A. V., & Dunham, R. M. The effects of verbal approval and disapproval upon the performance of third and fourth grade children on four subtests of the Wechsler Intelligence Scale for Children. *Journal of School Psychology,* 1971, *9,* 347–356.

8

Rational Behavior Therapy

MAXIE C. MAULTSBY, JR.

INTRODUCTION

Rational behavior therapy (RBT) is a comprehensive, culture-free, short-term, cognitive-behavior therapy. It is comprehensive because it deals directly with all three groups of learned behaviors: the cognitive, the emotive, and the physical. An ever increasing body of research indicates that RBT is helpful to people regardless of race, cultural values, or life-style (Brandsma, Maultsby, & Welsh, 1979; Maultsby, 1975a; Maultsby, Costello, & Carpenter, 1976; Maultsby & Graham, 1974; Maultsby, Winkler, & Norton, 1975; Patton, 1976; Ross, 1978; Ruhnow, 1977; Schwager, 1975). In Chapter 3, I attempted to show why culture-free psychotherapy is essential for efficient, effective psychotherapy for black Americans.

Rational behavior therapy is a short-term psychotherapy that produces long-term results because it includes systematic instruction in the emotional self-help method called *rational self-counseling* (Maultsby, 1975a). Therefore, when adequately treated, patients terminate RBT and their skill in rational self-counseling enables them to handle future emotional problems either by themselves or with less professional help than they would otherwise need. In my experience, most clinically distressed blacks are poor. The short-term efficiency and long-term effectiveness of RBT make it doubly appealing to them, as well as to most other economy-minded patients regardless of their race (Maultsby, 1975a; Maultsby et al. 1976; Maultsby & Graham, 1974; Schwager, 1975).

BRIEF HISTORY OF RBT

Rational behavior therapy is the outgrowth of four major influences in my professional career: my experience as a physician, the neuro-

---

MAXIE C. MAULTSBY, JR. • Director, Rational Behavior Therapy Center, Department of Psychiatry, University of Kentucky College of Medicine, Lexington, Kentucky 40506.

psychology of Luria (1960, 1966a, 1966b, 1973), the behavioral learning theory of Skinner (Holland & Skinner, 1961; Mowrer, 1960; Skinner, 1957), and rational emotive therapy (Ellis, 1962). It was Ellis who had the single most important influence on the evolution of RBT as a technique of psychotherapy (Maultsby, 1977b). However, unlike Ellis' technique (Ellis, 1977a, 1977b, 1978), RBT leaves philosophical issues to the individual preferences of patients. In addition, RBT eschews technical eclecticism in favor of therapeutic techniques derived exclusively from basic RBT theory (Maultsby, 1968).

Basic Assumptions in RBT

The ten basic theoretical assumptions in RBT theory are listed below:

1. The brain is the main site of learning and control of both healthy and unhealthy cognitive, emotive, and physical habits (Beritoff, 1965; DiCara, 1970; Luria, 1960, 1966a, 1966b, 1973; Miller, 1969; Olds, 1969).
2. There are no significant differences between the brains of members of the different human races (Tobias, 1970).[1]
3. The human brain can be divided into three major anatomically distinct but interconnected functional units. The first regulates cortical tone, general awareness, and the orienting reflexes; the second processes and stores information from the outside worlds; and the third regulates and verifies mental activity (Luria, 1966a, 1966b, 1973).
4. The neuropsychological activities of the three major functional units of the brain form the RBT concept of the mind. The brain coordinates the activities of the autonomic nervous system with those of the peripheral nervous system and thereby controls the processes of learning (Luria, 1966a, 1966b, 1973).
5. In physically healthy people, words (especially nouns, verbs, and adjectives) are the most common learned stimuli for the neuropsychological activities that produce healthy and unhealthy emotional and physical habits (Hudgins, 1933; Luria, 1960; Mowrer, 1966a; Staats & Staats, 1957, 1958; Watzlawick, 1978).

---

[1] The contrary belief still has such a strong hold on the minds of educators (Jensen, 1969), mental health professionals, sociologists, and anthropologists that its scientific repudiation is still periodically necessary (Thomas and Sillen, 1972).

6. Human emotions are inner urges (i.e., specific motivations) for actions created by learned emotive (i.e., visceral) responses that are elicited and controlled by semi-permanent neuropsychological units called attitudes and beliefs (Adams & Victor, 1977; Grace & Graham, 1952; Maultsby, 1975a, 1978a).

7. The neuropsychological mechanisms of learning are the same for healthy and unhealthy emotional and physical habits (DiCara, 1970; Miller, 1969; Olds, 1969; Rotter, 1954, 1966, 1971).

8. There are two worlds: the world of objective reality outside human minds and the world of subjective reality, created and recorded by people's minds. Subjective reality is the only reality people can experience directly. But emotionally healthy living most consistently occurs when a person's world of subjective reality accurately reflects the world of objective reality (Eaton, Peterson, & Davis, 1976; Watzlawick, 1978).

9. Learned (as opposed to organically caused) behavioral problems are due to quantitative disturbance of limbic system control of emotive and physical behaviors secondary to unhealthy learning and conditioning (Smythies, 1966).

10. Psychotherapy without drugs or electric shock means a corrective educational experience in which people learn the most emotionally healthy use of their brains. Since corrective learning is solely a patient's activity, the most effective psychotherapy will include self-help constructs and techniques. In addition, to achieve permanent psychotherapeutic change, patients must practice the self-application of those self-help constructs and techniques at least as diligently as they would practice the maneuvers required to learn any new habits, for example, speaking a foreign language, driving a car, or typing.

THREE BASIC THEORETICAL CONSTRUCTS IN RBT

There are three basic theoretical constructs in RBT. The most basic is the ABCs of new human emotions. Second is the RBT concept of rational thinking and third is the concept of rational bibliotherapy. These concepts are discussed below.

THE ABC'S OF NEW HUMAN EMOTIONS

Immediately after completing the intake evaluation, rational behavior therapists teach patients the research-derived (Ellis, 1962; Grace

Figure 1

& Graham, 1952; Graham, Stern, & Winokur, 1958; Graham, Kabler, & Graham, 1962) model of new human emotions used in RBT. While summarizing their understanding of patients' problems, therapists simply state that they understand that it often appears as if external events caused human emotional feelings. But that is merely an unhealthy illusion. The psychosomatic fact is:[2]

Psychosomatic Fact 1: People cause their own emotional feelings by the way they manage their cognitive apparatus. At first, many people object to Psychosomatic Fact 1. It does not seem right to them to think that they cause their own emotional pain. Their objection is both normal and understandable. New facts usually feel wrong when they disagree with old beliefs. For example, most people laughed when the first person said that the world was round (Figure 1). But the only people who laugh now are naive children and babbling idiots. This fact brings me to:

Emotional Insight 1: Much of what everybody knows is just not worth knowing. Before people have a new emotion, they notice something; they

---

[2] The following discussion was taken from Booklet 1 in the illustrated bibliotherapeutic series entitled "Freedom from Alcohol and Tranquilizers." Because bibliotherapy is a basic construct in RBT, that excerpt serves the dual purposed of describing the ABC model of emotions used in RBT and of showing the reader a typical example of rational bibliotherapy.

Table 1. The ABC Model of New Human Emotions

A.	Perceptions, or what people notice
	plus
B.	People's sincere thoughts about their perceptions
	plus
C.	The "gut" or emotional feelings, triggered and maintained by the evaluative thoughts at B.

perceive some real event or they imagine or remember one. Second, they have sincere evaluative thoughts about what their perceptions mean to them or about them.

There are only three major types of evaluative thoughts: relatively positive, relatively negative, and relatively neutral. These evaluative thoughts trigger and control relatively positive, relatively negative, and relatively neutral emotional feelings. Those psychosomatic facts are the basis of both the ABC model of new human emotions and the rational self-help techniques used in RBT, which are presented in Table 1.

Next is evidence against the popular myth that *IT*—the outside world—causes human emotions. Imagine the scene in Figure 2. There were three people looking at the same bottle of whiskey, but each person had different emotional feelings about it. Why? Because each was thinking different types of thoughts about it. The man on the left was thinking about how nice a tall, cool cocktail would taste. The man in the middle

POSITIVE FEELINGS   NEGATIVE FEELINGS   NEUTRAL FEELINGS

Figure 2

Figure 3

was remembering his drunken driving conviction. Because the woman did not drink, her thoughts were neutral about the bottle but positive about the prospects of getting a check cashed inside the store.

Now imagine what would have happened if each of those people had taken a drink of coffee while it was still too hot to drink (Figure 3). Each person's mouth would have felt the same type of physical pain. That is because physical feelings do not always work like emotional feelings. *It*, a stimulus from the outside world, can and will cause physical feelings. But only the person can cause his emotional feelings. After learning their emotional ABCs, most people incredulously ask: "Are human emotions really that simple?" "Isn't there more to them than that?" The answer to both questions is yes. Before human emotions become habits, they are just that simple. But there is more to human emotions than just A,B,C. There are the important habitual emotions of everyday life that are listed in Table 2.

The key concept here is *Habit*. People most often react the way they are in the habit of reacting. Because A–C and B–C emotions are habits, they are the most common type of emotions that people normally have. But because these are concepts in advanced RBT theory, it would be inappropriate to include them in this brief introductory summary of theory and practice.[3]

---

[3] For a detailed discussion of RBT theory and models of habitual emotions, see Chapters 3 and 4 in Maultsby (1975a) or Chapters 4 and 5 in Maultsby (1978b).

Table 2.   Habitual Emotions of Everyday Life

A–C	Habitual emotions	*and*	B–C	Habitual emotions
A.	Their external perception and		B.	Their evaluative thoughts and
C.	Their emotive reactions	*or*	C.	Their emotive reactions

The same principles of learning apply, and the same results occur, to learning physical as well as emotional habits (DiCara, 1970; Miller, 1968; Olds, 1969; Rotter, 1966). Consequently, to replace emotionally unhealthy habits with emotionally healthy ones, people first must develop the habit of emotionally healthy thinking.

Emotionally healthy thinking means rational thinking, the second most basic theoretical construct in rational behavior therapy. The following five rules both describe and identify it (Maultsby, 1975a, 1978a).

THE FIVE RULES FOR RATIONAL THINKING

1. Rational thinking is based on obvious fact.
2. Rational thinking helps you protect yourself from probable harm.
3. Rational thinking helps you achieve your short-term and long-term goals.
4. Rational thinking helps you avoid your most undesirable interactions with other people.
5. Rational thinking helps you feel the emotions you want to feel.

Thinking has to obey at least three of those rules at the same time to deserve to be called rational. The following two facts show why rational behavior therapists believe that the rules for rational thinking are also the rules for the most emotionally healthy thinking. First, consistent, significant deviation from the established healthy norm for any one of the rules is almost always a sign of major psychiatric disorder. Second, the thinking emotionally healthy people do consistently obeys three or more of these five rules. Irrational thinking simultaneously disobeys three or more of the five rules for rational thinking. In addition, irrational thinking is the most common cause of nonorganic behavioral problems.

RATIONAL BIBLIOTHERAPY

Rational bibliotherapy is the third basic construct in RBT. Rational bibliotherapy means systematic reading by patients of easy-to-understand self-help reading materials that are based on RBT theory. This is a simple, yet highly effective way to get patients quickly involved in analyzing and solving their emotional and behavioral problems rationally. But as with any self-help maneuver, the therapeutic results tend to vary directly with the degree of structured, goal-oriented instructions patients receive. In my experience, the most effective instructions for bibliotherapy include daily reading goals. My standard routine includes a number of reading assignments.

Immediately after the intake evaluation, patients are instructed to read *You and Your Emotions* (Maultsby & Hendricks, 1975) once per day, every day until the next appointment.[4] Even if patients read slowly, they can probably read the chapter in 20 minutes. If they are not willing to invest 20 minutes per day in solving their problem, they are dooming themselves to slow therapeutic progress. I end by reminding them that they have the right to decide how rapidly they progress.

The reading on the first day merely serves to give patients a clear understanding of the material. The second day's reading is to help them discover ideas with which they disagree. I tell them to write those ideas down and bring them to the next session for discussion. At first, most patients disagree with almost anything that will require them to change their habitual behavior; thus, showing immediate interest in their possible disagreement is an important treatment strategy. It quickly gets those potential therapeutic barriers out in the open where they can be eliminated.

The third day's reading is for patients to find and briefly write down the ideas with which they agree and why they agree with them. Having patients record why they agree with insights gained from bibliotherapy aids therapeutic progress in two ways. First, it increases the probability that patients will put those insights to daily use. Second, it increases the probability that patients will avoid the antitherapeutic game of "fool-the-therapist."

For the fourth day's reading, I tell patients to look for and write down notes about events described in the book which they have seen in the daily lives of others. This exercise helps them quickly to get over the self-defeating idea that their lives are uniquely complicated or difficult.

For the fifth day's reading, I have patients look for examples of events in their daily lives in which they could have applied the self-help insights gained from their reading, but did not do so. Again, I remind them to write brief notes for therapeutic discussion.

For the sixth day's reading, I have patients look for and make written descriptions of events from their daily lives in which they applied the

[4] *You and Your Emotions* (Maultsby & Hendricks, 1974) is the single most popular example of rational bibliotherapy used in rational behavior therapy.

insights gained from their reading and the results they achieved. Since repetition is usually the royal road to the most rapid learning, for the seventh day's reading, I tell patients to review their notes as preparation for discussing them in their next therapy session.

After those instructions, 80 to 90% of patients will return to therapy having read their assignment at least once; of those, 40 to 60% will have read it twice; between 10 and 30% will have read the assignment three to five times; and about 0.1% will have read it six or more times. Many of these latter patients will have moderate to severe problems with obsessive-compulsive behavior. You can expect them to be the most worrisome and difficult patients to treat. But calm persistence will usually yield good therapeutic results.

Two Primary Self-Help Techniques in RBT

Only after patients have learned their emotional ABCs and the five rules for rational thinking are they ready to learn written rational self-analysis and rational emotive imagery (Maultsby, 1975a, 1978b). These procedures are the two primary emotional self-help techniques used in RBT.

RATIONAL SELF ANALYSIS (RSA)

Written rational self-analysis is the technique used by patients to analyze, solve, and prevent personal problems or to analyze personal successes to increase the probability of maintaining such behavior. An RSA consists of two basic parts (see Table 3). On the left side is a written example of an undesirable habit. On the right side are the corresponding changes in the habit that must be made to effect the desired self-change.

Table 3. Standard RSA Format

A.	Activating event	Da.	Camera check of A
B.	Your beliefs or self-talk	Db.	Rational debate of B
	B–1		Db–1
	B–2		Db–2
	Etc.		Etc.
C.	Consequence of B	E.	Expected new behavior
	1. Emotions		1. New emotions
	a.		a.
	2. Actions		2. New actions
	a.		a.

Each half of the RSA consists of three sections labeled and written in the following order: A, B, and C on the left and Da, Db, and E on the right. Immediately below the C section the patient writes each of the five rules for rational thinking in the form of a question.

In Table 4 there is a complete RSA written by a problem drinker. The RSA describes an example of the self-defeating anger that triggers this patient's alcohol abuse, plus the rational self-changes he decided to make to eliminate that self-defeating habit.

Following is an explanation of the therapeutic function of each section of the RSA.

The standard order for writing RSAs is: first the A section, followed by the B section, the C section, the Five Rational Questions, the Da section, the Db sections, and finally the E section.[5] The A section is a simple description of the person's experience of the event being analyzed. For example, the problem drinker wrote: A. Activating event: As soon as I got home my wife started accusing me of being drunk.

The B section contains all the thoughts the person had about A. The problem drinker wrote: B. My beliefs: B–1. She is a nosy wench. B–2. I can't stand her. B–3. Since she thinks I've been drinking, I may as well get drunk and prove it. B–4. It's crazy to start drinking to try to make her silly mistake into a fact; so I refuse to do it.

The C section simply lists the undesirable emotional feelings and physical actions the person usually has and now wants to replace with more desirable ones. This person wrote: C. Consequences of B: 1. Emotions: anger. 2. Actions: started to get drunk, but did an RSA instead.

The Da section (camera check of A) describes only what a video tape or movie camera of the A section event would have recorded. Doing the camera check helps people to separate the obvious facts from their opinions and feelings about them. The logic of the camera check is the idea that if a camera would not have recorded the A section description, that description is probably more opinion or feeling than obvious fact. In the Da section, patients are to correct their A sections to what a camera would have recorded. See Table 5 for an example.

If an A section passes the camera check (i.e., is completely factual) simply write: "All facts" in the Da section.[6] The camera check applies only to external events. When an A section contains a statement of feeling (e.g., "I feel depressed"), merely write, "That's a fact" in the Da section and "Depressed" in the C section.

---

[5] Many patients write the E section immediately after they write the C section. That is all right too.

[6] For detailed case examples of the clinical use of the camera check, see *Help Yourself to Happiness* (Maultsby, 1975a).

Table 4. An Example of an RSA

A.	Activating events As soon as I got home my wife started accusing me of being drunk.	Da.	Camera check of A She didn't accuse me of being drunk; she asked me if I had been drinking.
B.	My beliefs B–1. She is a nosy wench.	Db. Db–1.	Rational debate of B My thinking here disobeys all five of the rules for rational thinking. A more rational way to think would be: She's not a wench; she is just my concerned wife. I don't like being questioned about my drinking, but I don't have to make myself angry and call her names about it. I can calmly answer and/or ignore her.
	B–2. I can't stand her.		Db–2. My thinking here disobeys all five of the rational rules. More rational thinking would be that I am standing her; I'm just doing it miserably. But since I don't like that miserable feeling and I don't want to divorce her, I'll stop irrationally upsetting myself.
	B–3. Since she thinks I've been drinking, I may as well get drunk and prove it.	Db–3.	My thinking here disobeys all five of the rules for rational thinking. More rational thinking would be: My getting drunk can't prove what I haven't done. But since getting drunk is not good for me, I refuse to do it.
	B–4. It's crazy to start drinking to try to make her silly mistake into a fact; so I refuse to do it.	Db–4.	That's rational thinking.

C.	Consequence of B.
	1. Emotions
	  a. Anger
	2. Actions
	  a. Started to get drunk, but did an RSA instead.
		E.	Expected new behavior
			1. New emotions
			  a. Calmly talk to wife.
			2. New actions
			  a. Refuse to consider getting drunk.

The five rational questions
1. Is my thinking here based on obvious fact?
2. Will my thinking here help me protect myself from probable harm?
3. Will my thinking here help me achieve my short-term and long-term goals?
4. Will my thinking here help me avoid my most undesirable interactions with others?
5. Will my thinking here help me feel the emotions I want to feel?

Table 5. Standard Order for Writing RSAs

A.	Activating event	Da.	Camera check of A
	As soon as I got home, my wife started accusing me of being drunk.		She didn't accuse me of being drunk, she asked me if I had been drinking.

The Db section (rational debate of B) contains patients' opinions about whether their corresponding thoughts in the B section were rational. Rational thoughts will deserve three or more honest "Yes" answers to the five rational questions. In those cases, patients simply write: "That's rational" in the appropriate Db space, then debate the next thought in B. But if a thought in section B does not merit at least three honest "yes" answers, patients are to replace the thought with a personally acceptable one that does. Table 6 presents a typical example.

Normally it takes about six times as much space to debate an irrational idea rationally as it takes to describe the idea in the B section. Patients should be advised to leave about six times as many blank lines under each B section idea as was required to write it. Thus, there will usually be enough space on the right side of the page for an adequate rational debate. Of course, patients are free to use the back of each page if they need extra space.

In the E section (expected new behavior), patients simply list the more desirable behaviors with which they plan to replace the undesirable behaviors described in the C section (Table 7).

Well-done RSAs are mental guides for learning desirable new emotional and physical habits. But because they are only guides, they aid therapeutic progress only if people use them as bases for emotional practice. Unfortunately, emotionally distressed people rarely know how to do healthy emotional practice. Therefore, as soon as possible after patients complete a well-done RSA, RBT therapists teach them the rational technique for healthy emotional practice.

Table 6. RSA from a Problem Drinker

B.	My beliefs	Db.	Rational debate of B
	B–1. She is a nosy wench.		Db–1. My thinking here disobeys all five of the rules for rational thinking. A more rational way to think would be: She's not a wench; she is just my concerned wife. I don't like being questioned about my drinking, but I don't have to make myself angry and call her names about it. I can calmly answer her, and/or ignore her.

Table 7.   Expected New Behaviors

C. Consequences of B.	E. Expected new behavior

1. Emotions
    a. Anger
2. Actions
    a. Started to get
    drunk, but did an RSA
    instead.
	1. New emotions
	    a. Calmly talk to my wife.
	2. New actions
	    a. Refuse to consider getting
	    drunk.

RATIONAL EMOTIVE IMAGERY (REI)

Rational emotive imagery (REI) is the rational technique for healthy emotional practice. This technique of emotional reeducation is based on the neuropsychological fact that imagining (i.e., mentally practicing emotional or physical reactions) produces the same quality of rapid learning that real-life experience produces (Beritoff, 1965; Eccles, 1955; Luria, 1966a, 1966b, 1973; Mowrer, 1966a; Razran, 1961). Consequently, every time people mentally picture themselves thinking, emotionally feeling, and physically acting the way they want to, they are using REI, the most efficient form of emotional practice. REI can also be helpful for physical practice. When patients practice REI daily, they teach themselves new emotional habits in the safest and fastest way possible. Table 8 gives some standarized instruction for REI.

This material is very important. Patients should be told not to expect an emotional miracle after just two or three REI sessions. It takes both time and repeated practice to replace emotional habits. Patients should be advised to practice REI using the same RSA everyday until they habitually get the type of C section responses they want in everyday life.

Table 8.   Standardized Instructions for REI

1. Read the Da, Db, and E section of a well-done RSA.
2. Get relaxed using the instant better feeling maneuver (IBFM) (Maultsby, 1975a, 1978).
3. When you are noticeably relaxed, mentally picture yourself as vividly as possible back in the Da situation described in your RSA.
4. As you vividly picture yourself back in the Da situation, thinking your rational Db thoughts, imagine yourself having your E section emotional feelings and physical behavior. Make the experience as vivid and realistic as possible.
5. Maintain that image and rethink your rational Db thoughts. If B section thoughts pop into your mind, calmly challenge them with your Db thoughts, and calmly ignore all non-RSA thoughts.
6. Repeat step 5 over and over for ten minutes. If you have two RSAs for practice, spend five minutes on each. But do not do REI on more than two RSAs during one ten-minute REI session.

Table 9. Suggestions for Conducting REI

---

1. Put yourself to sleep every night with REI. It is cheaper, safer, and quicker than most sleeping pills.

2. Ten minutes before you get out of bed each morning, do morning REI. It will help you start your day with the pleasantly powerful emotional feelings associated with confidence of success.

3. Ten minutes before lunch or instead of a cigarette break, do REI. Then you will be fighting irrational emotions, lung cancer, heart disease, and bad breath all at the same time.

4. Ten minutes before your first afternoon cocktail, do REI. That way you are most likely to stop after only two cocktails, remember eating, and enjoy your dinner.

Also, there is a practice effect such that the more frequent the practice, the earlier therapeutic progress will be achieved. Table 9 lists several suggestions for REI.

Patients can also do REI with their eyes open: while driving or riding to work, waiting in lines, waiting in traffic jams, or waiting for someone who is late. At those times REI might help keep blood pressure down or prevent other stress-related difficulties such as tension headaches. Engaging in a daily practice schedule, patients will gain control of their cognitions for their new, more rational behavior in the shortest time possible. Experience reinforces patients' self-help efforts and increases their commitment to therapeutic change.[7]

Guidelines for Illiterate Patients in RBT

Bibliotherapy and written rational self-analyses are not essential for therapeutic progress. Those techniques merely make RBT most efficient. As many as 20% of all patients may refuse to do bibliotherapy and/or written RSAs, but if they keep regular appointments they still can benefit from RBT. Therefore, well-motivated illiterate patients are as appropriate as anyone for RBT. The following two therapeutic maneuvers usually will compensate adequately for either illiteracy or unwillingness to do bibliotherapy and RSAs.

1. Routinely record each session on audiotape. Then schedule a tape-listening session in which the patient listens alone to the tape of his last individual session at least once before the next

---

[7] For a detailed discussion of potential problems with REI and their solutions, read Chapter 7 in *Help Yourself to Happiness* (Maultsby, 1975a).

session. This maneuver is standard practice with all patients in the RBT Center, regardless of their level of affluence, education, or willingness to do bibliotherapy and RSAs.

2. Frequently describe concrete examples of possible applications in patients' lives of each rational self-help concept and technique. This excellent therapeutic maneuver is also routine in the RBT Center, regardless of patients' level of affluence or willingness to do bibliotherapy and RSAs.

RBT continually focuses on increasing patients' skills in coping with their lives in a personally satisfying manner. In my clinical experience, relatively uneducated white and black people usually accept that focus as willingly as more highly educated patients.

Two-year Follow-up Data on RBT

Two years post-therapy, fifty-five (82% of sixty-seven) of the former RBT patients treated in our program returned completed follow-up forms. When these patients had begun RBT, all 67 met the DSM-III classification for either generalized anxiety disorder or atypical anxiety disorder. The patients were white university students, with an average age of 23.5 years. There were 43 females and 24 males. They had an average of 27 half-hour RBT sessions once per week (or an average total of 13½ hours of RBT) over an average period of eight months. When these patients terminated RBT, their therapeutic improvement was estimated according to the criteria listed in Table 10 (Maultsby, 1971).

Those data indicated that the self-help skills learned in RBT enabled both groups of patients to maintain their therapeutic gains as well as to improve their emotional health without additional professional help (see Table 11). In addition, two years after RBT, the large majority of patients in both improvement groups were satisfied with their adjustment. Of course, these data suffer from several methological difficulties, not the least of which is that therapists rated their own patients using an ill-defined rating scale. Nonetheless, the data suggest that RBT is an effective treatment modality for the types of patients treated.

RBT and Black Patients

There are no comparative outcome studies (to my knowledge) of the effectiveness of RBT and other techniques with solely black patient groups. However, most of the RBT studies cited on page 151 included

Table 10. Basis of Therapist's Estimate of Patient Improvement[a]

| | Degree of improvement | | |
Criteria	Excellent	Moderate	None
Clear-cut improvement of presenting complaint	Yes	Yes	No
New problems or exacerbations of old problems appeared	No	No	Yes
Improvement appeared permanent	Yes	Yes	No
Improvement was noted by significant others	Yes	Not required	No
Minimum of 10 RBT sessions	Yes	Not required	No
Pre-RBT TMA score 21[8]	Must have dropped 10 points	Must not have increased	No requirement
Post-RBT TMA score 20	Must have decreased	Must not have increased	No requirement

[a]At discharge, the 55 patients described here were distributed in the following groups: 3 patients were in the NO IMPROVEMENT group, 17 were in the MODERATE IMPROVEMENT group, and 35 were in the EXCELLENT IMPROVEMENT group. Table 2 summarizes their follow-up data.

Table 11. Comparison of Excellent Improvement Group and Moderate Improvement Group on Follow-up Results

	Degree of improvement	
	Excellent	Moderate
1. Satisfied with current emotional control	94%	88%
2. Has needed further psychotherapy	0%	0%
3. Has maintained therapeutic improvement	91%	71%
4. Has improved on therapeutic progress by continued use of rational techniques of emotional self-help learned in RBT	71%	41%
5. Is continuing to think rationally	91%	88%

black patients. Those studies plus my clinical experience with black patients, together with reports of other black and white rational behavior therapists (Ellis, 1962; Wolfe & Brand, 1977), indicate that blacks readily accept RBT and seem to benefit more from it than from psychoanalytically based psychotherapy and counseling. In addition, the same seems true for economically deprived whites (Schwager, 1975) and middle- and upper-class whites (Maultsby, 1975). Granted, there is a paucity of controlled clinical studies of RBT with black populations. But RBT has the features that make it ideally suited to meet the little noted, but highly important culturally conditioned, psychological needs which American blacks seem to have for culture-free and self-help approaches to psychotherapy and counseling (see Chapter 3.)

One of the barriers to testing the effectiveness of RBT for black Americans in controlled studies is the relatively small number of RBT therapists. Of course, the best long-term approach to improving emotional health care for blacks will be making courses in rational behavior therapy and other self-help oriented, culture-free psychotherapies a routine part of the curricula for students in the mental health professions in graduate and professional schools. However, recent research at the Rational Behavior Therapy Center of the University of Kentucky Medical Center (Maultsby, 1977a, 1978a, 1978b) indicates that one and two-week intensive training courses are beneficial in acquainting mental health professionals (regardless of race) with RBT theory.

Some Words of Caution

As with any therapeutic technique, RBT can be misused to the disadvantage of patients. The three most common misuses of RBT that I have noted are:

1. The use of RBT as a means of decreasing direct patient contact, or the refusal to take a personal interest in patients. In reality, no therapeutic technique can alleviate the necessity for the relationship aspects of the therapeutic process.
2. The use of RBT to hide therapist incompetence. Of course, this problem is not unique to RBT but is a pervasive problem throughout the mental health professions. If one feels uncomfortable or ill-equipped to deal with a particular patient, one is ethically bound to refer that patient elsewhere.
3. The use of RBT by unskilled therapists as a form of punishment when patients fail to progress with other therapeutic techniques. Again, if one is unable to help a given patient, one must refer that patient to another therapist.

The above mentioned cautions are not unique to RBT. However, there are some therapeutic techniques which have a higher abuse potential. Of course, many of the behavioral therapies (e.g., aversion therapy) have such potential and require close professional scrutiny.

In summary, I have given a brief history of RBT as a therapeutic technique, summarized the basic assumptions of RBT, listed the three basic theoretical constructs, explained the ABC model of emotions, explained the two primary self-help techniques in RBT, described its applicability to a variety of patient populations, and presented some clinical data in support of its efficacy. For a more detailed discussion, the interested reader is referred to Maultsby (1975a, 1977).

References

Adams, R. D., & Victor, M. *Principles of neurology.* New York: McGraw-Hill, 1977.

Beritoff, J. S. *Neural mechanism of higher vertebrate behavior* (translated by W. T. Liberson). Boston: Little, Brown, 1965.

Brandsma, J. M., Maultsby, M. C., & Welsh, R. *Outpatient treatment of alcoholism: A review and comparative study.* Baltimore: University Park Press, 1979.

DiCara, L. V. Learning in the autonomic nervous system. *Scientific American,* 1970, *222,* 31–39.

Eaton, M. T., Peterson, M. H., & Davis, J. A. *Psychiatry flushing.* New York: Medical Examination Publishing Company, 1976.

Ellis, A. *Reason and emotion in psychotherapy.* New York: Lyle Stewart, 1962.

Ellis, A. RET as a personality theory, therapy approach, and philosophy of life. In J. L. Wolfe and E. Brand (Eds.), *Twenty years of rational therapy*. New York: Institute for Rational Living, 1977, 16–30. (a)

Ellis, A. Similarities and differences between RET and RBT. Personal communication, 1977. (b)

Ellis, A. The problem of achieving scientific cognitive-behavior therapy. *Counseling Psychologist*, 1978, *3*, 21–23.

Grace, W. J., & Graham, D. T. Relationship of specific attitudes and emotions to certain bodily diseases, *Psychosomatic Medicine*, 1952, *14*, 243–251.

Graham, D. T., Stern, J. A., & Winokur, G. Experimental investigation of the specificity of attitude hypothesis in psychosomatic disease. *Psychosomatic Medicine*, 1958, *20*, 446–457.

Graham, D. T., Kabler, J. D., & Graham, F. K. Physiological response to the suggestion of attitudes specific for hives and hypertension. *Psychosomatic Medicine*, 1962, 24, 159–169.

Holland, J. G., & Skinner, B. F. *The analysis of behavior*. New York: McGraw-Hill, 1961.

Hudgins, C. V. Conditioning and voluntary control of the pupillary light reflex. *Journal of General Psychology*, 1933, *8*, 38–48.

Luria, A. R. The role of speech in the regulation of normal and abnormal behavior. Bethesda, Md.: U.S. Department of Health, Education, and Welfare, Russian Scientific Translation Program, 1960.

Luria, A. R. *Human brain and psychological processes*. New York: Harper & Row, 1966. (a)

Luria, A. R. *Higher cortical functions in man*. New York: Basic Books, 1966. (b)

Luria, A. R. *The working brain*. New York: Basic Books, 1973.

Maultsby, M. C. Against technical eclecticism. *Psychological Reports*, 1968, *22*, 926–928.

Maultsby, M. C. Systematic written homework in psychotherapy. *Psychotherapy: Theory, Research, and Practice*, 1971, *8*, 195–198.

Maultsby, M. C. Help yourself to happiness through rational self-counseling. New York: Institute for Rational Living, 1975. (a)

Maultsby, M. C. Patients' opinions of the therapeutic relationship in rational behavior psychotherapy. *Psychological Reports*, 1975, *37*, 195–198. (b)

Maultsby, M. C. *S.A.F.E. Sex therapy for the office practice—The rational behavioral approach*. Terminal training grant report, H.E.W. Grant 04-A-001112-01-0, Atlanta, 1977. (a)

Maultsby, M. C. The evolution of rational behavior therapy. In J. L. Wolfe and E. Brand (Eds.), *Twenty years of rational therapy*. New York: Institute for Rational Living, 1977, 88–94. (b)

Maultsby, M. C. Rational management of alcohol addiction, Terminal Training Grant Report, H.E.W. Grant 05-A00126-01-0, Atlanta, 1978. (a)

Maultsby, M. C. *A million dollars for your hangover*. Lexington, Ky.: Rational Self-Help Books, 1978. (b)

Maultsby, M. C., & Graham, D. J. Controlled study of the effects on self-reported maladaptive traits, anxiety scores and psychosomatic disease attitudes. *Journal of Psychiatric Research*, 1974, *10*, 121–132.

Maultsby, M. C., & Hendricks, A. *You and your emotions*. Lexington, Kentucky: Rational Self-Help Books, 1975.

Maultsby, M. C., Winkler, P. J., & Norton, J. C. Semi-automated psychotherapy with preventative features. *Journal of Preventative Medicine*, 1975, Fall, 27–37.

Maultsby, M. C., Costello, R. T., & Carpenter, L. C. Classroom emotional education and optimum health. *Journal of the International Academy of Preventative Medicine*, December 1976, 24–31.

Miller, N. E. Learning of visceral and glandular responses. *Science*, 1969, *163*, 436–445.

Mowrer, O. H. *Learning theory and behavior*. New York: Wiley, 1960.

Mowrer, O. H. *Learning theory and the symbolic process.* New York: Wiley, 1966. (a)

Mowrer, O. H. The psychologist looks at language. *American Psychologist,* 1966, *9,* 660–694. (b)

Olds, J. The central nervous system and the reinforcement of behavior. *American Psychologist,* 1969, 24, 114–132.

Patton, L. P. *The effects of rational behavior training on emotionally disturbed adolescents in alternative school settings.* Doctoral dissertation, North Texas State University, 1976.

Razran, G. H. S. Conditioned responses. *Archives of Psychology,* 1935, *28,* 110–120.

Razran, G. H. S. Some psychological conditioning to verbal stimuli. *American Journal of Psychology,* 1949, *62,* 247–256.

Ross, C. Reducing irrational personal traits, trait anxiety and intra-interpersonal needs in high school students. *Jouranl of Measurement and Evaluation in Guidance,* 1978, *11,* 44–50.

Rotter, J. B. Social learning and clinical psychology. New York: Prentice-Hall, 1954.

Rotter, J. B. Generalized expectancies for internal versus external control of reinforcement. *Psychological Monographs,* 1966, *80,* 1–28.

Rotter, J. B. External control and internal control. *Psychology Today,* June, 1971, 37–59.

Ruhnow, M., Federal probation officer, North District of Texas. *Personal communication,* 1977.

Schwager, H. A. Effects of applying rational behavior training in a group counseling situation with disadvantaged adults. Counseling Services report 22. Glassgo AFB, Montana: Mountain-Plains Education, Economic Development Program, 1975.

Skinner, B. F. *Verbal behavior.* New York: Appleton-Century-Crofts, 1957.

Smythies, J. R. *The neurological foundations of psychiatry: An outline of the mechanisms of emotions, memory, learning and the organization of behavior with particular regard to the limbic system.* New York: Academic Press, 1966.

Staats, A. W., & Staats, C. K. Attitudes established by classical conditioning. *Journal of Abnormal and Social Psychology,* 1958, *57,* 187–191.

Staats, C. K., & Staats, A. W. Meaning established by classical conditioning. *Journal of Experimental Psychology,* 1957, *54,* 74–80.

Taylor, J. A. A personality scale of manifest anxiety. *Journal of Abnormal and Social Psychology,* 1953, *48,* 285–290.

Thomas, A., & Sillen, S. *Racism and psychiatry.* New York: Brunner/Mazel, 1972.

Tobias, P. V. Brain size, grey matter and race—Fact or fiction? *American Journal of Physical Anthropology,* 1970, *32,* 3–26.

Watzlawick, P. *The language of change.* New York: Basic Books, 1978.

Wolf, J. L., & Brand, E. *Twenty years of rational therapy.* New York: Institute for Rational Living, 1977.

9

Modification of Interpersonal Behavior

A. TOY CALDWELL-COLBERT AND JACK O. JENKINS

INTRODUCTION

Researchers in diverse disciplines (e.g., medicine, organizational behavior, business, politics, industry) have found interpersonal behavior to be one of the differentiating factors between success and failure within their professions. Psychological research (e.g., Libet & Lewinsohn, 1973; Zigler & Phillips, 1960) reveals that interpersonal behavior and the development of proficient patterns of communication have earnest implications for an individual's adjustment within a social milieu.

Harry Stack Sullivan (1953), a forerunner in the area, was the first to attribute interpersonal relationships to the development and maintenance of psychopathology. Sullivan defined the interpersonal relationship as the person behaving in relation to one or more individuals either real or illusory (e.g., reading of a fictional character like Anna Karenina). His theory proposed that alternate forms of behavior are developed as a result of anxiety acquired through interpersonal influences which pose threats to one's security. Thus, to protect oneself in interpersonal encounters, modes of behavior and communication patterns are formed to decrease anxiety and maintain some level of self-esteem.

Since Sullivan's work, the area of interpersonal behavior has been further developed and expanded, but the term *social skills* is more frequently used. The literature (see Argyle, 1967; Argyris, 1965; Lewinsohn, Weinstein, & Alper, 1970; Weiss, 1968), cites an omnibus of definitions for social skill, but it has generally been used in reference to the complex abilities necessary for effective interpersonal functioning.

Social skills are those behaviors that an individual uses to respond

A. TOY CALDWELL-COLBERT ● Center For Personal Growth, Department of Psychology, Emporia State University, Emporia, Kansas 66801.   JACK O. JENKINS ● Department of Psychology, University of Georgia, Athens, Georgia 30601.

171

in social situations; they encompass both verbal and nonverbal responses. The term *social skills deficits* has been used in reference to a diverse number of groups felt to be deficient in interpersonal behavior. Among those groups are persons suffering from social anxiety, shyness, and any low-frequency styles. With respect to social skills deficits, numerous assessment and treatment techniques have been developed to provide effective treatment for these groups. Assertion training has been the dominant focus in social skills development. In his early work, Wolpe (1958, 1969) conceptualized skills deficits in unassertive individuals as a result of their experiencing "unadaptive anxiety" that prevented them from functioning effectively in social situations.

A modified generic definition of assertive behavior has emerged from the literature which focuses away from anxiety as a function of social skills deficits. Hersen and Bellack (1976) recognized that some individuals are nonassertive as a function of anxiety, but others experience difficulty in social situations because of limited repertoires of learned social behaviors or faulty social learning histories. Libet and Lewinsohn (1973) further suggest that adaptive behavioral responses may have been punished or may have received no positive reinforcement; therefore, they are absent in the individual's response repertoire.

By focusing on unassertive behavior as a result of faulty social learning history, a single global definition of social skills is limited. Eisler, Hersen, Miller, and Blanchard (1975) and Hersen and Bellack (1977) suggest a situation-specific concept of social skills which focuses on one's effectiveness in specific social interactions. All of these various conceptualizations, therefore, demonstrate the behavioral complexity of assertiveness.

In considering social skill, of paramount interest is establishing interpersonal contact, carrying on conversations, terminating conversations, and establishing deeply meaningful relationships. However, it might be stated that the individual who cannot express his true feelings in these situations is simply nonassertive. This idea coincides with Rimm and Masters's (1979) definition that assertive behavior involves honest, straightforward expression of feelings, socially appropriate responses, and consideration of the welfare of others. They have also pointed out that a client benefits in two significant ways as a result of increased social skill (i.e., assertiveness):

> First . . . the client has a greater feeling of well being . . . (and) second . . . the client will be better able to achieve significant social (as well as material) rewards, and thus obtain more satisfaction from life. (Rimm & Masters, 1979, p. 63)

Assertiveness has also been defined as the ability to make appropriate requests and to refuse unreasonable requests (Lazarus, 1973). Which definition of social skill is most useful is debatable; nonetheless, most of the work done in social skills–assertiveness has been concentrated on the refusal of unreasonable requests and in making appropriate requests.

In this chapter, the term *social skill* will refer to all interpersonal behavior, both verbal and nonverbal. The term *social competence* is often used interchangeably with social skills, as well as the term *assertiveness*. For our purposes, *social competence* will be used in reference to interpersonal behavior and psychopathology as defined by social maturity or social effectiveness in meeting the tasks society sets (Zigler & Phillips, 1960). The area of assertiveness refers to a subcategory of social skills and is considered a primary component in overcoming social skills deficits (Bornstein, Bellack, & Hersen, 1976; Eisler, Hersen, & Miller, 1973; Hersen & Bellack, 1977).

Given some understanding of social skills, the reader will, we hope, perceive through this chapter the importance of social effectiveness in daily interactions with others. Available opportunities for whites to exercise and develop social skills have been adequately provided, but such opportunities have frequently been denied many blacks. A dearth of information exists regarding both the adequate application of social skills by blacks and their felt need for altered social behavior when interacting in this culture.

We will review the concept of social skills and its relationship to psychopathology and black populations. The focus will be directed toward cultural issues, suggestions for future areas of attention, and precautions to take when working with black populations. Assessment, the key in differentiating the socially skilled from the socially deficient, will provide a discussion on issues of assessment, review of present assessment strategies, implications for black populations, and suggestions for improved procedures. We will address issues in treatment and end the chapter with a section on problems of generalization, a summary, and conclusions.

SOCIAL SKILLS AND PSYCHOPATHOLOGY

Since Sullivan's early focus on interpersonal relations and psychopathology, more recent studies have systematically studied the role of social competence as it relates to patient populations. Among these studies is one by Zigler and Phillips (1960) that investigated social effectiveness and symptomatic behavior of hospitalized men and women. Their findings demonstrated that a systematic relationship does exist between measures of effectiveness and particular groups of symptoms. Symptoms were grouped under the following three categories: self-deprivation and turning against the self, self-indulgence and turning against others, and avoidance of others. The variables of intelligence, age, education, occupation, employment history, and marital status were the indicants of social effectiveness. Results showed that the most socially effective hospitalized persons evidenced symptoms categorized as self-deprivation and turning against the self, whereas the less socially effective patients manifested symptoms of the latter two categories. Hospitalized women, when compared to hospitalized men, were considered to be even more socially adept as evidenced by the increased frequency of occurrence of symptoms categorized under self-deprivation and turning against the self.

Zigler and Phillips (1962) further studied social competence as an aid in differentiating process vs. reactive schizophrenia, an ambiguous area when considering differences in symptom manifestations. By utilizing the three categories mentioned in the previous study, they demonstrated that the level of premorbid social competence could be characterized by the reactive vs. process dichotomy (i.e., symptomatology of the reactive is more frequently characterized by turning against the self). The authors concluded that the process–reactive distinction is reducible to a social competence dimension applicable to all psychopathology and not just schizophrenia. Thus, prognosis is directly linked to the level of premorbid social competence.

Further, to substantiate the role of competence in interpersonal behavior, Lewinsohn and his colleagues (Lewinsohn & Graf, 1973; Lewinsohn & MacPhillamy, 1974; Libet & Lewinsohn, 1973; MacPhillamy & Lewinsohn, 1974) investigated the association between the use of social skills and depression. One behavioral formulation of depression assumes that a low rate of response-contingent positive reinforcement establishes the critical preconditions for the occurrence of depression; thus, the intensity of the depression covaries with the rate of positive reinforcement (Lewinsohn, 1973).

An early study by Libet & Lewinsohn (1973) found that depressed individuals carried out substantially fewer actions than did nondepressed persons and that as a group the depressed were less socially skilled. This low level of social interchange has been further operationalized by the concept of reciprocity. These authors found that depressed individuals performed only half as many actions as did nondepressed persons and thus received less social reinforcement. The occurrence of reciprocated attention is considered to be positively reinforcing, but depressed individuals fail to make the instrumental responses leading to reciprocated attention and positive social reinforcement.

Pleasant activities, considered to be a major subset of positive reinforcement, were found to be associated with mood and depression.

The depressed are found to engage in a smaller number of pleasant activities. Lewinsohn and Graf (1973) concluded that decreased occurrence of pleasant events was synonymous with decreased response-contingent positive reinforcement. Their results showed that activities associated with mood were indicative of three categories: activities involving positive social interaction, incompatible affects, and ego-supportive activities. These results are consistent with previous clinical and laboratory data (Lewinsohn, 1973; Lewinsohn & Libet, 1972; Libet & Lewinsohn, 1973). Although these findings do not clarify the direction of cause, they further indicate the social deficiencies of the depressed and support the usefulness of social skills training for these individuals.

Activity level and subjective enjoyability of pleasant events are also considered to be related. In the literature are found several similarities between the behavior of depressed individuals and that of elderly persons. Lewinsohn and MacPhillamy (1974) took these two groups and compared activity level and subjective enjoyability of pleasant events. Both depressed individuals and the elderly were found to have a decreased level of pleasant events. Yet, the subjective enjoyability of potentially pleasant events was found to be uniquely associated with being depressed. For depressed individuals, these findings are in accordance with the behavioral position on depression and point to a major difference between patient and nonpatient populations. The authors felt that the decreased activity levels of the elderly were a result of systematic changes in their social skills (i.e., they emit fewer behaviors that elicit social reinforcement) and/or limited availability of reinforcing stimuli in the environment. Consequently, the response-contingent positive reinforcement is decreased and their social interchanges become affected, leading to problems similar to those found in depression (i.e., decreased activity level).

However, studies focusing on elderly patient populations cannot be carried on in a vacuum because serious problems in later life are often a result of inadequate socialization during childhood. Viewing Zigler and Phillip's (1960, 1962) conclusions of psychopathology in a developmental context, it seems social skills deficits evidenced during early school years may set the stage for inappropriate social functioning during the adult years. O'Connor (1969) pointed out that a child lacking social skills will be handicapped in acquiring the complex behavioral repertoire necessary for effective social functioning. Bornstein, Bellack, and Hersen (1977) demonstrated that a social skills program could train socially deficient children to express both positive and negative feelings and not to fear the loss of social reinforcement. Although no longitudinal studies on long-term effects of treatment have been performed to date, this additional focus on appropriate social skills and on children further indicates the dominant role social competence plays in level of adjustment.

Although these studies are not exhaustive, they do give an adequate background. Investigation in the domain of social competence has illustrated significant relationships to the level of adjustment within various populations as well as the fact that patient prognosis is heavily influenced by interpersonal development. Process vs. reactive schizophrenia was shown to be differentiated according to the level of social competence. Social skills training was also found to be effective in working with depressed and elderly populations. Both of these groups showed a decrease in activity level which was a result of changes in their social skills. The preceding studies suggest that social competence and skills play an important role in adjustment.

Social Skills and Black Populations

The literature repeatedly emphasizes the use of social skills training as an effective treatment approach and aid in channeling institutionalized clients back into the community to improve their resistance to environmental stresses (Gladwin, 1967; Goldsmith & McFall, 1975; Hersen & Bellack, 1976, 1977; Hersen & Eisler, 1976). Unfortunately, it has not been until recently that professionals have begun focusing on the role of social skills in the adjustment levels of blacks. Even with the increased focus, there are only a few articles attempting to catalogue differences in black-black and black-white interpersonal relationships. Many of these articles that are limited in scope take a sociological approach and provide the reader with no systematic investigation or data collection from which conclusions can be drawn. Certainly, in only a few instances (e.g., Frederiksen, Jenkins, Foy, & Eisler, 1976) has *any* attention been paid to racial differences in behavioral assessment or in the treatment of social skill difficulties.

CULTURAL ISSUES

In discussing what constitutes appropriate social skills for blacks, it becomes necessary to review the aspects of the culture which have influenced the present interpersonal patterns of this group. Since the colonization of America, the black man has found himself in an inauspicious position. From the lynchings of the past to the present-day high unemployment, ghetto cultures, and de facto segregation, a black person who is deficient in assertive social skills stands to lose a great deal (including his life).

Black individuals show a history of having abstained from expression of their true attitudes and beliefs in fear of fatal consequences that have tended to foster a withdrawn behavior style when interacting with whites. On the other hand, social pressure and built-up hostility perpetuated aggressive behavior in the form of physical and verbal outbursts which sometimes caused fear and uneasiness in interpersonal situations. These two situations typify the passive-aggressive behavior style of black interpersonal behavior (Cheek, 1976; Minor, 1978). This pattern of interaction appears to be serving as a stereotype and a bias interfering with the communication patterns both for black individuals themselves and for others who are involved in social interaction.

These stereotypes developed as a result of the limited communication patterns of blacks (Cheek, 1976; Minor, 1978; Porter, 1974). An excellent example of options available for blacks in interpersonal situations during and after slavery has been sighted by Pugh (1972). He suggests two forms of responses: "anxiety conditioned to blackness" and "adaptive inferiority." The latter refers to the tendency of blacks to take on an inferior posture during stressful encounters because there was no early precedent for equality on which to model coping styles. "Anxiety conditioned to blackness" suggested the tendency to be deprecatory in responding to one's blackness or to the economic pursuits of other blacks. Even though these responses cannot be generalized to all blacks, it is exemplary of the response styles that enable blacks to cope with oppression. On the part of recipients in a biracial interaction, the communication channel is blocked and messages are thus misinterpreted due to held biases and stereotypes of blacks (Minor, 1978; Porter, 1974).

Blacks acquired a response style necessary for their survival in this society (Cheek, 1976). In the past, a black individual who asserted himself was accused of stepping out of line, was punished or in some other way negatively reinforced (e.g., passed over for promotion, loss of job, or lost privileges) which tended to foster a passive response style (i.e., lack of direct eye contact and increased personal space). Along with these experiences occurred development of anxiety and threats to self-esteem. To reduce anxiety, blacks were forced to develop alternative behaviors and communication patterns to decrease anxiety and sustain some form of security.

Even though there exists in the literature a wide variety of studies on interaction patterns, there is a limited application for interracial or intrasocial interaction patterns. Most of these studies date back to the late 1950s and are virtually obsolete in view of the major cultural changes which have occurred since the 1960s. The establishment of equal rights for minorities was a major accomplishment with great significance for blacks as well as other minority groups. This change broadened the scope of interpersonal relationships and the possibility of alternative lifestyles. The scope of interpersonal relationships was broadened in two significant ways. First, opportunities for biracial interactions were increased—especially through multiplying job opportunities, education, housing, entertainment, and alternate social opportunities. Secondly, personal relationships themselves became more highly valued, fostering enhanced self-esteem and improvement in the quality of personal life. Bound by past socialization patterns, blacks have had to overcome many barriers in developing interpersonal skills to enable them to interact effectively in our society.

Linguistic differences also function as a negative factor in biracial interpersonal situations (Cheek, 1976; Dubner, 1972; Kochman, 1969). Williams, Whitehead, and Miller (1971) described this problem well when they suggested the "Pygmalion effect—that is, the attitudes which language characteristics may elicit in listeners" (p. 166). What happens repeatedly is that blacks who use nonstandard English are stringently appraised according to standard English modes of speech. A nonstandard English response by a black may be labeled passive and thus ignored, may be labeled aggressive and perceived as a threat, or may result in social stereotyping and misinterpretation of the message. Consequently, problems are further complicated by listeners (e.g., whites) attending less to *what* was said and more to *how* it was said.

Linguistically, blacks have learned how to survive within the black community. Kochman (1969) feels that the forms of black verbal behavior that have developed are those which most successfully manipulate and control people and situations. "Rapping," "shucking and jiving," "running it down," "copping a plea," and "signifying" are illustrations of different black ghetto idioms, each having its own form, style, and function. Kochman (1969) refers to their directiveness as an "instrument to manipulate and control people to get them to give up or do something . . . and expressive . . . to project his personality . . . or to evoke a generally favorable response" (p. 28). He concludes that these language forms are used to "assert oneself" and to acquire something which is of benefit to the speaker.

These language forms serve as a series of transactions enabling constant readiness to achieve personal gain from the individual or situation or a defense against being victimized. Blacks have therefore conditioned themselves to keep their guard up to prevent fellow blacks from "getting over" on them (Kochman, 1969). Unfortunately, when these same forms of verbal intercourse are utilized in interracial situations, they are ineffective.

Different socialization processes of blacks and whites result in failure or barriers in communication. What may qualify, therefore, as assertive in the black community minimally generalizes to the broadened scope of black–white interpersonal relationships. It should be noted that these present communication patterns can serve as a basis for effective intraracial communication and, with appropriate training, black interaction styles can be channeled into assertive skills relevant to the black perspective.

RESEARCH ON CULTURAL DIFFERENCES

A study focusing on increased racial understanding was conducted through the United States Army Institute for the Behavioral and Social Sciences (Landis, Day, McGrew, Thomas, & Miller, 1976). This systematic approach, while not an exact parallel to social competence studies, addresses some relevant recurring themes of black–white interpersonal behavior. Underlying the approach of Landis and his colleagues was the assumption that cultural groups should learn about the norms and lifestyles of other cultures as well as "unlearn" misperceptions about them. Through the development of a "cultural assimilator," junior grade officers were trained to "become sensitized to subtle cues important in social interaction with representatives of another culture" (p. 171).

The procedure involved a large number of short episodes which described interpersonal situations often encountered in interracial situations along with alternative explanations for the events presented. The trainee chose one explanation and then was given immediate feedback about his choice and relevant information about events within the episode to increase his understanding of the other culture. Empirical investigation and use of the critical incident technique led to a valid and effective culture assimilator that depicted those areas of cultural contrast which had the largest impact on social behavior within the culture being studied (i.e., interactions between white officers and black enlisted men). A sample item, with options and rationales, follows:

> The white CO of a racially integrated unit tried to recommend promotions on the basis of his men's work and proficiency scores. After the list of promotions was posted, a black Spec 4 entered his office and asked why he had not been promoted. The Spec 4 claimed that he had fairly good scores and asked the CO to review his decision. The CO was surprised at this behavior, but promised to give some attention to the complaint. Upon reflection, the CO noted that promotion reviews were requested much more frequently by

blacks in his unit than by whites. The CO was puzzled and surprised by this realization.

Why did more blacks than whites request reviews of promotion decision?

Option 1. Blacks feel they won't be given a promotion unless they ask for one. (Yes)

Rationale: Many blacks feel that a good mark record alone is not sufficient for a promotion. They feel that unless they call attention to their case, it will not be acted upon. This action is not to be taken as disrespectful, but rather as an action which is assumed to be necessary for promotion.

Option 2. The CO was prejudiced and promoted more whites than blacks. (No)

Rationale: There is no evidence to support this. Reread the incident and select another response.

Option 3. Blacks are troublemakers more often than whites are. (No)

Rationale: There is nothing in the incident to suggest that the blacks were troublemakers. Try again.

Option 4. Many blacks hope to get promotions they don't deserve by intimidating their CO's and getting them to give in to avoid being called "prejudiced." (No)

Rationale: The black's behavior was not intimidating. There were no threats or insinuations. You're reading too much into this incident. Reread the incident and try again (Landis *et al.*, 1976, p. 174–175).

The results of the study, as hypothesized, found blacks to be significantly more familiar with the items than were whites; blacks also received higher scores for appropriate option choices. In regard to training or learning, white officers showed steady learning as they worked through episodes indicating significant changes and increased understanding with the use of the cultural assimilator.

Although this study (Landis *et al.*, 1976) was not directed at social skills training for blacks, it points to a realistic problem that blacks encounter in asserting themselves. This study showed that blacks display the same behavior as whites in identical situations, but their behavior is not equivalently perceived. Whites will perceive blacks as aggressive but perceive other whites displaying the same behavior as appropriately assertive. This finding is consistent with current clinical data (Hazzard, 1979; Kirchner, Kennedy, & Draguns, 1979) which support the idea that black assertive responses, more often than not, are labeled as aggressive or inappropriate. The proposed cultural assimilator in the above study (Landis *et al.*, 1976) would help improve white understanding of blacks and give a more realistic perspective toward black social competence and assertiveness. It also indicates the awareness and vital importance of cultural differences in interpersonal development.

Researchers, however, have identified salient differences in verbal and nonverbal behavior. Dubner (1972) reported that a mutually understood language does not exist between blacks and whites. He asserts that black interpersonal communication patterns are a distinctive phenomenon and examines in detail their nonverbal communication patterns. Young children of black communities are taught that meeting an older person's gaze is a sign of hostility or defiance. In the classroom, these children will refrain from looking directly at the teacher; this behavior is often misinterpreted by the teacher as a sign of disrespect and arrogance (Dubner, 1972). Research has shown eye contact to be a relevant component of social behavior (Eisler, Hersen, & Miller, 1973) and the development of social competence in childhood (i.e., appropriate eye contact or facial gaze) is crucial to interpersonal functioning in adult life (O'Connor, 1969).

Another example related to nonverbal behavior is well represented in job interview situations. It was suggested that black Job Corps applicants must have different ways of communicating attention to the interviewer (Hall, 1974). Blacks often fail to engage in headnods or minimal encouragements such as "uh-huh" to promote the conversation, but instead adopt a fixed stare that whites assume is indicative of disinterest in the interaction.

Timing is also a critical factor in nonverbal behavior. Two systematic observational studies by LaFrance and Mayo (1976, 1978) investigated patterns of gaze direction in communications between black–black and black–white conversants. The major finding of these studies was that there were subcultural differences in patterns of conversational behavior. Looking while listening was an important focus of subcultural differences. For instance, when the white listener encountered a pause with sustained gaze from a black speaker, the white was cued to speak, and both found themselves talking at once (LaFrance & Mayo, 1976). The results of these studies showed that blacks used a gaze pattern the reverse of the gaze patterns of whites. While interacting with whites, blacks gazed directly at others while speaking and gazed away while listening. These different gaze patterns of conversants in interracial dyads created misperceptions and awkwardness that are not found in black dyads.

In these studies of interracial dyads, it was concluded that differences are not perceived as cultural differences but instead result in negative evaluations and stereotypic interpersonal judgments that create further tension in black–white relations. For example, intensity of sustained gazes is often experienced or labeled as aggressive and intrusive (LaFrance & Mayo, 1978). Since no more than 35% of the social meaning is carried in the actual verbal message (Harrison, 1965), this is of major importance.

SUMMARY

Up to this point, the discussion has addressed the effects of social-ization and diverse cultural experiences on the development of social skills in black persons. Blacks have tended to lean toward two types of interpersonal style: (a) passive-withdrawn and (b) aggressive. Histori-cally, this passive form of behavior appears to have been fostered by the negative consequences (e.g., loss of jobs, physical abuse, lynchings) which many blacks experienced as a result of expressing themselves during and after slavery. Incidences of aggressive behavior in blacks resulted from built-up pressure and hostility due to oppression. But the aggres-sive behavior styles seem more a result of misperceptions and stereotypic judgments by whites as they interacted with blacks. Blacks are perceived as aggressive by whites when they express their feelings, raise questions, or are assertive.

Research has shown that blacks have developed their own verbal and nonverbal patterns of interpersonal behavior. "Rapping," "shuck-ing," and "jiving" were developed as effective verbal patterns in the black community. The effectiveness of these verbal behaviors has failed to generalize to interracial situations. A scrutiny of the nonverbal behavior of facial gaze has shown that blacks do not look when listening, which represents the exact opposite of white facial gaze patterns. This behavior no doubt has resulted in failure or barriers in interracial interactions. Adequate and appropriate eye contact, facial expression, and gestures are all a part of effective communication and must match the receptive capabilities of the larger population.

FUTURE SUGGESTIONS AND PRECAUTIONS

Knowing that differences exist in social skills patterns, one must understand that each group (i.e., black, white, Chicano) interprets the behavior within his own system of communication and responds ac-cordingly. Therefore, it is necessary to acquire an understanding of these cultural differences when establishing appropriate social skills for blacks. A clear conceptualization would reduce significantly stereotypic judg-ments and miscommunications. It is absolutely essential that therapists be familiar with these cultural differences.

The following suggestions and precautions can be useful in working with all cultural differences in social skills for black persons:

1. It is often assumed that a common socialization pattern exists between blacks and whites. Since this is not true in many cases, blacks use different methods of coping with threats and other forms of interpersonal distress. Therefore, it is essential that those persons working with blacks have a clear understanding of those cultural differences.

2. There should be a very broad definition of what constitutes appropriate social skills so that options for appropriate behavior will not be socially biased. For example, use of black dialect should be as effective and acceptable as standard English. Differences across social classes would also be minimized.

3. Closely related to the above suggestion is the idea that blacks should be made aware of the fact that they are often incorrectly perceived as aggressive but must continue to assert and clarify themselves by explaining the intent of their message.

4. An understanding of the nonverbal behaviors of blacks should be firmly established, followed by training or a relay system that would enable them to learn about how their nonverbal cues are perceived.

5. Changes within our system have resulted in an increase of social situations requiring greater social adaptiveness. Thus, specific situations which have generally been difficult for blacks to handle should be identified so they can be addressed directly (i.e., job interviews, tenant concerns, pay raises).

6. An early focus on social skills development in children is a must. By establishing appropriate skills in children, one may eliminate problems that might otherwise occur in adult life. It would also make skills such as assertive behavior much more natural and part of the social repertoire. Present social skills programs have ignored these issues. Donald Cheek's (1976) book, *Assertive Black . . . Puzzled White,* is the only book which addresses similar topics and issues. Although it is not based on systematic observation and research, it does address the development of social competence through assertiveness.

Establishing social skill patterns in blacks could increase their ability to cope with various environmental demands. It would also lessen their vulnerability to more severe problems such as depression (e.g., Zigler & Phillips, 1961, 1962). Blacks are faced with a large number of environmental stresses (i.e., housing, tenant problems, education, jobs) and social pressures that demand social competence. Because the role of social competence is also crucial in prognosis, it has far-reaching implications for other areas such as mental health. Social skills training could be a viable factor for rehabilitation of black criminals, for blacks who exhibit antisocial behavior and violent outbursts, and could further assist in the remedy of the vast array of other socially perpetrated problems that seem to infiltrate the black community. The development of appropriate social skills is critical and of unequivocal relevance for the present span of black interpersonal relationships.

Assessment of Social Skills: A Black Perspective

The preceding discussion is only a step toward establishing the proper perspective for understanding development of social skills in blacks. However, it is our hope that the reader now (if he did not before) has some insight into the area of social skills development. The ensuing discussion will focus on those aspects of behavioral assessment and social skills training which are important for the treatment of black clients.

SELF-REPORT MEASURES

In the extant literature, a total of 11 assertion inventories can be found (Heimberg, Montgomery, Madsen, & Heimberg, 1977). The use of these self-report measures varies, but basically they serve as an aid in determining the need for assertion training, identifying specific problem areas, and assessing assertion training effectiveness. Instructions for these inventories are similar in that persons are told to indicate the likelihood of their engaging in a given act and their anticipated level of anxiety in that situation.

The first of these subjective scales is the Wolpe–Lazarus Assertiveness Questionnaire, which consists of 30 questions of common interpersonal situations (Wolpe & Lazarus, 1966). Some of the other earlier scales focused on hostile responses or negative assertion (Bates & Zimmerman, 1971; McFall & Lillesand, 1971). None of these scales has been well validated but the reliability estimates have yielded coefficients of .76 or above.

A more global measure of assertiveness can be obtained on the Rathus Assertiveness Schedule (Rathus, 1973). This scale also consists of 30 items but samples a wider range of assertive behavior, persons, and situations. Some examples are:

Item 2:   I have hesitated to make or accept dates because of "shyness."

Item 12: I will hesitate to make phone calls to business establishments and institutions.

Item 16: I have avoided asking questions for fear of sounding stupid.

Item 26: When I am given a compliment, I sometimes just don't know what to say. (Rathus, 1973 p. 400)

Based on measures of male and female college students, a .78 test–retest reliability was obtained over a two-month period and a .77 split-half reliability based on odd-even item scores was obtained.

A better validated measure of assertiveness is the College Self-Expression Scale (Galassi, Delo, Galassi, & Basten, 1974; Galassi & Galassi, 1974). It measures social skill in positive, negative, and self-denial interpersonal contexts. However, this test is limited in that it only handles situation-specific incidents or problem areas within the natural environment of the college population. Galassi and some of his other colleagues (Gay, Hollandsworth, & Galassi, 1975) have since developed an assertion inventory for adults which helps to accommodate this problem. For a detailed listing of other self-report measures see Heimberg *et al.*, 1977.

Even though there is a great emphasis placed on the development of self-report measures, those presently utilized have been designed without any recognition of cultural differences which may affect responding. Therefore, the rendered instrument is invalid for certain groups. This is not to say that tests such as the Rathus Assertiveness Schedule (Rathus, 1973), the Assertion Inventory (Gambrill & Richey, 1975), the College Self-Expression Scale (Galassi *et al.*, 1974) are not useful in assessing assertiveness across cultures. For example, an item like "avoiding asking questions" from the Rathus Assertiveness Schedule should certainly elicit some useful information regarding the assertiveness of the respondent. However, Check (1976) has pointed out the fact that the race of the responder is ignored during assessment of assertive behavior and suggests that one may not be adequately assessing the assertive behavior of blacks or other ethnic groups. Obviously, this responder–respondent situation could be reversed; whites may evaluate themselves on self-report measures as they imagine other whites in that situation and not as if imagining a black or a person of another minority in that situation. We have already addressed the results of different socialization processes upon the development of black social skills patterns; thus, in assessment, the race of the responder becomes even more important. It is the personal experiences of the authors that a dear penalty can be imposed upon blacks for being outspoken and assertive.

A dissertation recently completed by Hazzard (1979) at the University of Georgia supports some of our assumptions about black assertive behavior. Using the Rathus Assertiveness Schedule (Rathus, 1973), the Assertion Inventory (Gambrill & Richey, 1975), and several paper-and-pencil inventories (Caldwell, 1977; Hazzard, 1979) requiring assertive responses to some 24 situations, Hazzard compared black and white levels of assertiveness. On her paper-and-pencil inventories, she asked subjects to write their responses to the situations according to whether the person in the situation was white or black.

Hazzard's (1979) systematic investigation indicated that the blacks employed in her study generally were more aggressive on level and overall assertiveness measures, even though mean scores on the Rathus Assertiveness Schedule scored the level of assertiveness as higher for blacks than for whites. She supported the finding (i.e., the use of black aggressive reponses) reported in Lange and Jakubowski's (1976) study that certain cognitive, affective, and behavioral patterns lead to aggressive behavior. Examples of these are: powerlessness and threat, overreaction resulting from past stressful situations, oppression and reinforcement, and skill deficits (Hazzard, 1979). All of these examples are very much in keeping with the cultural differences and factors mentioned in the early portion of this chapter. Her investigation also indicated that blacks were perceived as being more aggressive when responding assertively than were whites.

Other significant findings in the Hazzard study indicated that blacks modified a higher percentage of their responses in interracial situations when compared to whites. It was reported that the modifications of blacks were more aggressive, whereas, whites modified their responses as appeals to authority. Also, 90% of the black modified responses used black English vernacular. Such findings indicate that linguistic differences are evident in both verbal and written communication patterns of blacks. Although the blacks in Hazzard's study were rated as being more aggressive, they did report a positive attitude about assertion and could distinguish assertive responses from aggressive and nonassertive responses. It was concluded that faulty learning histories, negative reinforcement of appropriate assertive responses (Hersen & Bellack, 1976; Libet & Lewinsohn, 1973), and cultural differences in the tolerance of assertive or aggressive responses influenced the degree of assertion in black subjects.

Hazzard's (1979) study can be criticized in terms of: (a) total reliance on self-report measures, and (b) the demands of the experimental situation. However, the results are at least suggestive of the fact that self-report measures which do not take the race of the responder into account may not adequately assess black or white assertiveness (not to mention that of Chicanos, native Americans, Chinese, Japanese, etc.).

The question one must ask when utilizing self-report and other measures of assertiveness is whether or not black assertive behavior is in and of itself different. Hazzard (1979) found the responses of blacks to be more aggressive than those of whites on the self-report measures; this fact suggests that there may be a difference in assertive behavior.

Yet, the lack of data on responses other than those assessed by self-report measures limits the conclusions that can be made. One must also ask whether the blacks in Hazzard's study were inappropriately assertive or if they simply manifested an assertive style unique to blacks. It would appear that when blacks are appropriately assertive, they are actually perceived as being aggressive by whites. One explanation for this finding is that the behavior used by blacks to refuse or make a request is perceived as being aggressive for whites. Thus, response styles are culturally different such that responses used appropriately by blacks are judged as aggressive by whites. It would then follow that different assertive response styles must be taken into consideration when assessing assertive responses to prevent therapists from making erroneous conclusions regarding the level of assertiveness in black clients.

Although self-report measures are potentially useful in gathering information, users are cautioned that they provide only an indication that some type of response or behavior will occur in a situation; they in no way guarantee that a given response will be appropriate or assertive (Rimm & Masters, 1979). This point becomes even more relevant for blacks in the face of the following example. If a black person were going to a party consisting primarily of whites, would he act differently than he would if it were a party of all blacks? The answer is probably yes. Even if it were a group of high-status black professionals, the use of language, verbal gestures, and so forth, would vary to a degree. The implication of this for self-report measures is that unless one is very specific in terms of the situations and the race of those involved in assessing responses, some relevant information may be missed entirely.

Other points of caution and suggestions when using self-report inventories are:

1. Look carefully at the verbal content of situations on the inventory before administering it. Most of the inventories are geared toward the college student and may fluster a black person who has only a high school education and limited reading skills. If this is the case, the test may have to be given verbally.
2. Review the context of the situations found in the inventory. Present inventories may not be covering situations relevant to what the majority of black clients consider difficult interpersonal situations. We suggest developing an inventory which summarizes the types of interpersonal situations salient to black experiences.
3. Develop norms and standardizations on a black population to enable more accurate test interpretations. Current inventories are standardized on results from a white middle-class population. Test–retest reliability and validity measures should be examined using a diverse black population.

BEHAVIORAL INTERVIEWING

Many of the points which have been developed thus far support the usefulness of a behavioral interview in assessment of black clients to acquire information that an assertiveness inventory might not provide. We strongly encourage this in light of the limitations of self-report—measures for black clients. Such an interview would probably further structure the client's problems into a situation-specific context which could enhance the components of the treatment program.

Although the behavioral interview is clearly the most heavily utilized assessment instrument, still a number of client and therapist variables may interact to produce inaccurate information. As a caution to white therapists who may be working with black clients, Cheek (1976) articulated a number of factors that could affect the client–therapist relationship. They are: (a) differences in the language style of the black client and the therapist; (b) different uses of gestures, eye contact, and other nonverbal behavior; and (c) misunderstandings on the part of the therapist of blacks' patterns of social interaction. Although not based on systematic investigation, these factors may interact to cause miscommunication between the therapist and client and therefore lead to inaccurate assessment.

We suggest that the preceding factors be taken into consideration for both black and white therapists. As Cheek asserts, there are black therapists who may be as different from some black clients as some white therapists. There are also some white therapists who have a very good understanding of black communication. The point to be made here is that therapists should assess their own knowledge of the culture of ethnically different clients and then if it is deficient, take appropriate action to correct the problem. The therapist might also let that client know of his concern about the cultural differences and ask for the client's assistance in increasing his (the therapist's) level of knowledge.

BEHAVIORAL ASSESSMENT

The distinguishing feature of behavior therapy is its emphasis on observable and measurable events. In the area of social skills, this implies naturalistic or contrived observation of the client's behavior in situations requiring certain types of social skill. Many different behavioral measures assessing assertive behavior in analog social situations have been developed (see Heimberg et al., 1977). The general purpose of these behavioral measures has been to assess further self-reported levels of assertion as a guide in selecting specific components for training, as a generalization tool for clinical situations, and for situations encountered in the natural environment. All of these uses of behavioral role-playing tests have been stringently criticized and raise some pertinent questions about their applicability to black persons.

The most widely used behavioral assessment is the Behavioral Role Playing Test, originally developed by McFall and Marston (1970) and revised by Eisler et al., (1975). The formats of these analog situations are all similar: A subject is presented with a brief narrative followed by a verbal prompt given by a role player; then the verbal prompt serves as a cue or signal for the subject or client to respond. An example of such a situation is:

> *Narrator:* You are in a crowded grocery store and are in a hurry. You pick up one small item and get in line to pay for it. You are really trying to hurry because you are already late for an appointment. Then a woman with a shopping cart full of groceries cuts in line right in front of you. *Role player's prompt:* "You don't mind if I cut in line here, do you?" (Eisler *et al.*, 1975, Appendix H)

The subject's responses are usually recorded on audiotape or videotape for later scoring by independent raters. Early ratings of analog situations consisted of one overall assertiveness score or global rating. Since that time, other studies (Eisler, Hersen, & Agras, 1973; Eisler, Miller, & Hersen, 1973; Eisler, Hersen, Miller, & Blanchard, 1975), have delineated several specific behaviors seen to be related to judgments of assertiveness by using a five- to seven-point Likert scale. They are: (a) duration of looking at target person; (b) frequency of smiles; (c) duration of reply; (d) latency of reply; (e) voice inflection; (f) compliance; (g) requests that target person change his behavior; (h) affect; and (i) overall ratings of assertiveness. A factor analytic study by Pachman, Foy, Massey, & Eisler (1978) found eye contact, response duration, requests for change, and compliance to be significantly correlated with global ratings of assertion. These findings support the use of such behavior components in assessing assertive behavior.

As we stated earlier, the nonverbal styles of blacks, when compared with those of whites, were found to be different (LaFrance & Mayo, 1976). If such differences are not accounted for, components such as eye contact and response latency duration will lead to considerable error in judgment when assessing a black individual's level of assertiveness. All of the studies thus far are based on what is appropriate for the larger middle-class white population and have failed to consider any cultural variations. Obviously, a large number of people are making inaccurate generalizations if they interpret these components as being characteristic of all people.

The use of behavioral role-playing tests has been found to be a poor measure for extremely anxious individuals (Hersen, Eisler, & Miller, 1973). The socially anxious person will usually experience inhibitory or disruptive effects when faced with a role-player in the interpersonal situation, an observation which points out another limitation of this type of assessment. Although this is a general limitation for this type of assessment, it leads to another point, which is probably even more relevant to blacks. Individuals using behavioral role-playing tests may assume that role-playing comes naturally. It cannot be assumed that all people can or will play roles effectively (Bellack, Hersen, & Turner, 1978). Such an experience may be quite foreign and unrealistic for a black man who lives in the ghetto. Therefore, we are talking about a behavioral measure which may have realistic limitations if introduced into a predominantly lower-income black community mental health environment.

With respect to the significance of situational themes portrayed in behavioral role-playing tests, the situations should be carefully studied to find out whether they are relevant to the client and his interpersonal problems. This point was also brought out in considering self-report inventories for blacks. Since the behavioral measure is an extension of the self-report measure, the situational themes of both should coincide.

While not an investigation of racial parameters of behavioral role-playing tests, a study by one of the authors of this chapter (Jenkins, 1976) compared the parameters of personal investment on behavioral role-playing tests and self-report measures (i.e., Rathus Assertiveness Schedule). Jenkins found that the Rathus was a limited screening device when the parameters of behavioral role-playing tests were varied. His final conclusions suggested that the Rathus was an appropriate screening device only for high and low assertive subjects under conditions of low investment (e.g., borrowing $2.00 vs. $10.00 or waiting 10 minutes vs. 25 minutes). If changes in parameters of personal investment seem to influence the validity of self-report measures and responses to role-played situations, it would seem to follow that racial or cultural differences could also exert some influence.

Heimberg et al. (1977) pointed out that there is a lack of test–retest reliability, concurrent validity, and construct validity of behavioral role-playing tests, especially when related to self-report inventories. A group of very recent studies by Bellack and his colleagues (Bellack, Hersen, & Turner, 1976, 1978, 1979) examined the validity of role-playing tests. Their results revealed a poor correlation between those behaviors displayed during a behavioral role-playing test and the same behaviors in other social situations. The brief format is idiosyncratic; thus, the subject's focus is narrowed and the range of response alternatives becomes limited. The present components of behavioral role-playing tests only assess the skill of assertiveness and ignore the broader range of interpersonal cues which a person is required to attend to in the natural environment (Bellack *et al.*, 1978, 1979). This factor obviously has a direct bearing on generalization and the external validity of role-playing tests. In terms of the adequate assessment of the social skills of blacks and other culturally distinct groups, the use of present role-playing tests are affected by demand characteristics which limit its use as a global measure of interpersonal behavior.

In general, these results are in keeping with the stimulus-specific theory of assertiveness (i.e., an individual who is assertive in one interpersonal context may not be assertive in a different interpersonal environment). Changes in the specific parameters of the role-played scenes have a direct effect on a person's responses. Thus, subsequent research must address itself to a detailed evaluation of situation specificity of black asserters and assertees so we will have an indication of what these differences in responses really are and not make *a priori* assumptions.

Throughout the development of this chapter, aggression has been repeatedly addressed as a problem in appropriate assertion as well as a factor in perceiving, describing, and interpreting black interpersonal behavior. Hazzard's study (1979) is clearly a beginning in depicting the role of aggression in black assertive behavior, but precise conclusions and generalizations are limited because of the employment of self-report measures only. With the use of self-report measures, behavioral role-playing tests, and a scale which assessed the level of aggression, Kirchner *et al.* (1979) were able to explore race vs. offender and nonoffender differences in the use of aggressive and assertive behavior. Kirchner and her colleagues used the Adult Self-Expression Scale (Gay *et al.*, 1975) and two other self-report measures: the Buss–Durkee Hostility Inventory (Buss & Durkee, 1957), and the Social Anxiety and Distress Scale (Hollandsworth, 1976). The nine component measures of the behavioral role-playing test as indicated by Eisler *et al.* (1975), as well as a rating of assertion, aggression, and degree of noncompliance, were also employed. Results of this study indicated: (a) offenders assert themselves in conflict situations in a more aggressive manner than do nonoffenders; (b) self-reported aggression was higher for black offenders than for black nonoffenders, while there was no significant difference among whites; (c) black offenders reported higher assertiveness for themselves, but this was not reflected in their role-playing behavior; (d) behavioral and self-report measures of assertiveness were significantly related for only white nonoffenders; and (e) significant relationships between behavioral and self-report measures of aggression were found in black offenders.

The generalizability of this study may be limited by its restricted population, but it does reveal some interesting findings. The authors of this study (Kirchner *et al.*, 1979) pointed out that "higher behavioral aggression among offenders may not be a surprising finding; it is, after all, merely concordant with sociological definitions of criminals as persons who violate others' rights" (p. 468). Although no overall racial differences were found, this study suggests that the relationship between self-report and behavioral measures may be specific to the measures employed and the population being assessed. Since there were some differences for offenders and nonoffenders on both self-report and behavioral measures of aggression, it does indicate the usefulness of self-report measures of assertiveness in adequately assessing the aggressive aspect of one's behavior. For rating assertion and aggression, use of such a scale may serve as a tool in clearing up lay beliefs about the aggressive aspect of anyone's responses, especially blacks', since they are so often wrongly perceived as being aggressive. Although this point will be addressed in the following section, we should mention that assertion scales serve a useful purpose in training to see whether the newly acquired assertive style is in actuality assertive with no aggressive manner.

Having developed the role of assessment in social skills, we offer the following salient variables relevant to black individuals. First, the relative importance (quantitatively and qualitatively) of various social skills has not been fully investigated in the *available* social skills literature. The importance, then, of certain skills for different cultural groups has received even less attention. The point being made here should be clear. How can a therapist adequately assess the social skills of a culturally distinct group if it is not clear exactly what should be assessed?

Secondly, the systematic variation of the race of the role-player has only rarely been done. Hazzard's (1979) results certainly suggest that variation of the race of the responder may affect an individual's social skills. Whether a person's response to an individual of a different race during a behavioral role-playing test is a valid indication of his or her *actual* response is open to empirical investigation. But race should definitely be taken into account when assessing social behavior.

The behavioral role-playing test appears to be a useful instrument for the assessment of social skills. However, the cultural milieu of the client should be taken into account as much as possible. This may be done as indicated above by carefully questioning the client about his culture. Asking persons with social skills difficulties how people interact in their cultures may appear awkward. However, it is our opinion that persons with social skills difficulties can very often tell you what they would like to do and how someone they know does it, even when they simply cannot do it themselves. Information of this sort could then be utilized both to construct valid scenes for the behavioral role-playing test and to decide which behaviors are most important and which should be evaluated.

PHYSIOLOGICAL MEASUREMENT

While physiological measurement has not been utilized nearly as often as self-report and behavioral role-playing tests, it is nonetheless a valid sphere of assessment. The utility of physiological measurement is dependent on several factors. Kallman and Feuerstein (1977) suggest that, due to the complexity and expense of physiological equipment, it should be used only to provide a reliable measure which cannot be obtained by other means; there must be a relationship to a psychological variable to allow a measure useful in predicting and modifying behavior and selecting and evaluating treatment programs; and it must have an adequate degree of reliability and validity of measures across time, situations, and individuals. While these are the major points to consider in making physiological measures, a much more common concern centers around the expense of the equipment and special knowledge of physiology and electronics required for accurate assessment.

Considering these factors, two early studies by McFall and Marston (1970) and Twentyman and McFall (1975) utilized pulse rate as a dependent measure to investigate the effects of assertive training. Their findings revealed pulse rate to be the most sensitive of all the measures used in assessing assertive behavior. However, considering the difficulty and expense of physiological assessment, this does not appear to be a feasible way of assessing assertiveness in the clinical setting. Moreover, Eisler (1976) cautioned that any study employing physiological measures to assess assertiveness should be interpreted with caution because such procedures are intrusive even when investigators take great strides to create as natural a situation as possible.

More recently, Hersen, Bellack, and Turner (1978) assessed assertiveness in female psychiatric patients using heart rate and finger pulse. These results were somewhat more promising in that there was a significant interaction obtained in the analysis of physiological data and responding to behavioral role-playing tests. Physiological measurement might be used to identify specific stimuli that are, for instance, threatening, anger-provoking, or anxiety-reducing, to clients. For example, one might systematically vary the race of role-players as certain physiological measures are taken to help decide whether race is a significant factor in a person's social skills difficulties.

Considering the possibilities as well as the limitations of physiological measures for blacks, it is safe to say that most therapists do not have the benefit of such equipment. Community mental health facilities where a large majority of black clients would be seen certainly lack physiological recording devices. Black clients might also become inhibited or negatively affected by being "wired up" or being in the presence of physiological equipment. These and other factors may influence and detract from the naturalistic features of other assessment procedures.

In summary, the assessment strategies of self-report, behavioral interviews, behavioral assessments, and physiological measures have all been presented. The relevant aspects for assessing black social skills were addressed for each of these assessment techniques. Suggestions for improvements and consideration with black individuals were also presented.

TREATMENT OF SOCIAL SKILLS FOR BLACK POPULATIONS

All behavioral interventions characteristically imply a close relationship between assessment and treatment; this close relationship is of particular importance in the social skills area (Hersen and Bellack, 1977). Considering that assessment of the three major response areas (self-report, behavioral, physiological) has depicted some skill deficits, the training program focuses on these specific deficits. The goal of treatment, then, is to develop new skills and/or modify present patterns of behavior, with assessment being an ongoing process which evaluates the effects of treatment during treatment as well as after treatment. The most well-developed social skills treatment package has focused on assertion training and encompasses modeling, behavioral rehearsal, response feedback, and reinforcement.

MODELING

Modeling consists of showing the client what is to be done. It is most often used in combination with the above list of approaches, basically because studies show that modeling alone has not enhanced assertiveness (McFall & Twentyman, 1973). A replication study by Voss, Arrick, and Rimm (1976) does support the use of modeling in complex situations (e.g., requests made to authority figures). To implement modeling for *any* client, the therapist should have a general knowledge of what is the most effective response(s) to model. If the client is of a different culture, this implies that the therapist should be aware of which responses will be most culturally correct. A black person's response to another black person *may* vary from his response to a white person in the same situation. Some of these varied dimensions might be: (a) type of language used, (b) type of nonverbal communication used, (c) topics of conversation, and (d) meaning of various language and gestures.

In terms of the type of language, one may observe (as certainly many blacks, Chicano, and other minorities have while reading this chapter) stylistic differences in communication. A conversation between a white person and a black person about NBC's Today Show host, Bryant Gumbel, may be initiated by the black person remarking, "Don't you think Mr. Gumbel adds a refreshing new dimension to the 'Today Show'? He is very talented." While the very same question asked by a black of a black might sound more like this: "Say, don't you think that brother Bryant Gumbel really has his act together?"

One should keep in mind that blacks as well as whites are individuals. The statements above are only suggestive and may never have been used by blacks or whites. The point is, there are differences in how persons from different cultures express themselves. If the response to be modeled does not follow the cultural style of the individual, it will probably be ignored or deemed useless and not be adopted into the individual's response repertoire.

Other considerations for enhancing the effects of modeling might be the use of cotherapists, one black and one white. This pairing might help in the assimilation of cultural differences with a black client and ease the therapeutic situation itself. Occasionally, it may even be as effective to bring in another person to serve as the model. In any case, these suggestions must be viewed in light of the fact that modeling itself is seriously limited and for the best results, should be combined with one or more of the following treatment strategies.

BEHAVIOR REHEARSAL

Behavior rehearsal is the most commonly used technique in assertion training. It consists basically of the client's practicing the desired behavior. Within the context of behavior rehearsal, the therapist acts as model and also assumes the role of the respondent in the interpersonal situation. In the social skills training literature, the role-playing task is used as the vehicle for behavioral rehearsal. The situation is presented and discussed; the therapist then provides a verbal prompt which signals the client to rehearse the assertive statement. Throughout the behavioral rehearsal, the therapist will provide feedback and coaching to assure proper social skills development. In some instances, the effectiveness of behavioral rehearsal alone has been shown to enhance assertiveness (McFall & Marston, 1970; McFall & Twentyman, 1973).

Rimm and Masters (1979) note that the therapist must realistically portray the role of the other person. Such a portrayal requires the client to describe the person the therapist is to portray. If the therapist is white and the client is black, this will provide the opportunity for cultural differences to be explained and clarified, enabling the therapist to adequately portray his role.

As we pointed out in the section on modeling, the therapist must address himself to the verbal or nonverbal style of the black client in giving examples of the assertive response which he is expected to rehearse. Behaviors which are practiced and developed may involve initiating, continuing, and terminating conversations; expressing positive feelings, expressing negative feelings; asking questions to obtain information; and refusing unreasonable requests. While the same general classes of behavior are probably required across cultures, the exact ways in which they are manifested may vary. The therapist should be sensitive to the richness of these cultural differences, the meanings of words, and the subtle uses of nonverbal behavior. If he is not, he may find himself exhorting the client to behave in ways which might cause him to appear odd and/or ineffective in his own culture. The therapist should be alert to signs that he is off-target in training certain types of responses.

Obviously, there are many instances in which the therapist must train the client in behavior more typical of another culture to enable effective communication across ethnic groups. A black man, for example, may simply not be able to communicate with his white peers at work or be effective with a white job interviewer. Present response alternatives for the larger black population have been rather limited (i.e., passive or aggressive). The development of an understanding about assertive behaviors would provide another response alternative and application of this response style in a variety of situations.

As we have previously pointed out, blacks who are responding assertively often are perceived as being aggressive by whites. Cheek (1976) states that it is the intent of the message which differentiates a response as either aggressive or assertive. Behavior rehearsal could be very useful in preparing the black client for interracial situations. Some specific treatment suggestions for black clients which can be applied during behavior rehearsal focus on *message-matching* and *backup assertion*.

Cheek (1976) describes *message-matching* (for black clients) as a useful practice in being effective and communicating with various audiences. Several general audiences are identified based on race (black vs. white) and economic status (middle-class vs. the masses) and conventional versus nonconventional. He suggests that each group's expectation or perception of a response by a black varies. Realizing these differences, a black delivering an assertive message must "match" or "fit" that assertive message to its respective group to produce the right effect. Cheek (1976) concludes that assertive training for blacks should enable them "to intentionally and consciously select the most appropriate assertive message considering the different types of people to be dealt with" (p. 61).

Backup assertion (Minor, 1978), on the other hand, deals much more directly with the perceived aggression of black–white assertive encounters. In proposing backup assertion, Minor (1978) first points out the importance of choosing to be assertive. The development of assertive skills can have a great impact and positive change on anyone's interpersonal relationships. Considering that this may be a new-found response style for many blacks, they should be prepared to go beyond honest and open assertions of their findings. Backup assertion is an honest and open inquiry directed toward the respondent "to check out the message received and to provide clarification if a discrepancy exists" (Minor, 1978, p. 69). If there is a communication breakdown (i.e., that statement was not assertive but felt to be aggressive), backup assertion enables the individual to restate and clarify his response to ensure correct interpretation. Although backup assertion does not guarantee a solution to this problem, it does provide an avenue for maintaining a level of assertion even in the face of perceived aggression. Unfortunately, neither of these techniques has been investigated systematically; still, they do present logical resolutions and answers to some of the problems which blacks may experience with the development and use of assertive responses.

RESPONSE FEEDBACK

Rimm and Masters (1979) discussed several studies that implemented different varieties of feedback. They concluded that the value of feedback was clearly dependent on the nature of the feedback. Obviously, for any group the types of feedback which enhance behavior change are varied. Therefore, we will briefly discuss those two types of feedback most frequently implemented with no specific conclusions regarding the value of one type over another for black individuals.

Feedback in the form of verbal praise is almost always used. During behavior rehearsal, this type of feedback occurs spontaneously. Outcome studies suggest that greater generalization has been reported in groups that do not utilize feedback (cf. Rimm & Masters, 1979). Another frequently used feedback measure is audiotape or videotape. Such feedback can enhance the effects of modeling and behavioral rehearsal when training clients. Tapes provide immediate feedback and an accurate portrayal of the client's behavior. Used in combination with other treatment components, they can augment a training program.

Modeling, behavior rehearsal and feedback are three of the most

effective treatment approaches. Although we did not differentiate between individual treatment and group treatment, we feel our conclusions
and guidelines can serve a useful purpose in either situation. The only
recommendation along these lines that we should like to make is that
the results of the initial assessment should determine the client's effectiveness and opportunities for learning in a group setting versus a one-
on-one setting. It may be that the group will be too overpowering (especially in the earlier stages of social skill development) and inhibit responses rather than develop them. On the other hand, a subject may
have a repertoire of skills but need the development and practice in a
controlled group situation. In either case, ongoing assessment throughout treatment will be the key in answering many questions and providing
guidelines for the thrust of the training program.

OUTCOME STUDIES IN SOCIAL SKILLS

Social skills and assertion training have been implemented with a
variety of clinical cases (e.g., obsessive-compulsive clients) and in combination with other behavioral treatment strategies (e.g., systematic desensitization). Its most common application has been with nondating-shy
college students, juvenile delinquents, and nonassertive psychiatric patients. Several researchers have concluded that assertion training universally helps dysfunctional individuals acquire a response repertoire
which enables them to interact more effectively in interpersonal situations (Goldsmith & McFall, 1975; Hersen & Bellack, 1976).

A clinical case study (Edwards, 1972) of a forty-year-old homosexual
pedophiliac was successfully treated with assertion training. Edwards
concluded that enhanced assertion allowed the client's normal heterosexual tendencies to occur. Patterson (1972) used time-out and assertion
training to reduce frequent crying in a nine-year-old boy. Similarly, an
aggressive housewife was trained through behavioral rehearsal to be
more appropriately assertive with her mother and husband (McPherson,
1972). A two-year followup assessed her as still being assertive and symp-
tom-free. This study represents generalization of treatment to the natural environment, since the situation-specificity of her problem enabled
the development of a treatment package unique to her immediate concerns.

Although the literature reveals an array of other case studies, for
our purposes we will let these citations depict the general positive trend
of social skills training. Unfortunately, only a few black case studies have
been reported. These studies also report positive outcome as a result of
social skills training. A twenty-year-old black college freshman showing
under-controlled aggression was trained in assertive behavior (Rimm,

1977). Up until the assertion training, the client would handle conflict situations by becoming physically abusive. His treatment consisted of coaching, behavioral rehearsal, and feedback. The therapist would present an assertive statement to a situation which was then followed by the client's reiterating that same idea in his own words (i.e., use of black verbal expression) until he felt comfortable with the new response. No follow-up data were reported.

Frederiksen *et al.* (1976) successfully trained two black adult psychiatric patients hospitalized for antisocial abusive behavior. Their social skills program consisted of behavioral rehearsal with modeling, focused instructions, and feedback. Five target behaviors—looking, irrelevant comments, hostile comments, inappropriate requests, and appropriate requests—were trained through a multiple-baseline design. Behavioral assessment was based on several role-played scenes. Three of these scenes were specific to each individual's interpersonal situation and the remaining four were general scenes requiring an assertive response. Training improved all of the target behaviors. These effects also generalized to novel role-played scenes, scenes with a different respondent (i.e., different as to race) and to interpersonal situations on the hospital ward. Although this study does evidence generalization within the therapeutic setting, the lack of follow-up in the patients' natural environment limits any firm conclusions about skill usage under stress of actual encounters. It does, however, support the use of social skills training for black clients.

Several controlled group experiments have also evaluated the effects of assertion training paradigms. A fairly recent study implementing both black and white psychiatric inpatients reported positive results with interpersonal skill training. Goldsmith and McFall (1975) compared an assertion training group with an assessment-only control and pseudotherapy control groups. The subjects were divided to include equal numbers of black and white patients as well as diagnostic classifications of character disorders, neurotics, and schizophrenics. Subjects were interviewed to obtain information concerning interpersonal difficulty. Scenes were then developed from this empirical investigation to include training content relevant to that population and their target problems. Appropriate responses and rating procedures were also empirically investigated and developed using both black and white staff and doctors. Training for the treatment group consisted of three one-hour sessions, including coaching, modeling, recorded response playback, and corrective feedback. A post-assessment was given to each group and consisted of conversation with a confederate and retest on a battery of global self-report measures. Results showed that the skill training group was superior to the control groups on all measures. The rate of improvement for the treatment group on treated situations was three times greater than the rate of improvement on nontreated situations on the behavioral measures. An eight-month follow-up based on 72% of the original sample showed a decreased readmission rate for skill-training subjects when compared with the control groups.

This study is one of the first to examine empirically constructed training content for a specific population. Considering the diversity of the group (i.e., racial differences and diagnostic classification), this study does show that adequate assessment and appropriate training procedures can benefit a variety of groups. It also indicates the outcome of mixed group intervention and racially focused content scenes during training. Even though the generalization results within the therapeutic setting were not overwhelming, data on readmission rate suggest a positive transfer to real-life situations for the skill-training group. Goldsmith & McFall (and the present authors) feel that the relevance of the content situations was major in producing the positive outcomes of this study.

GENERALIZATION OF TREATMENT

A major problem with social skills research centers around the lack of adequate data documenting generalization of newly developed social skills to the nontherapeutic environment. Hersen and Bellack (1977) reported several types of behavioral measures developed to assess generalization of training. These methods vary according to the treatment population (i.e., college students vs. psychiatric patients), but three of these behavioral measures have been used to assess generalization with both groups.

The first measure involved a pretest–posttest evaluation of situations on a behavioral role-playing test which were not selected as the specific training situations (e.g., Kazdin, 1974; McFall & Marston, 1970; McFall & Twentyman, 1973). Such an evaluation would reveal a client's level prior to training, assess changes, and measure skill development after training. Considering the idiosyncratic format of role-playing tests (Bellack et al., 1978), one would predict, within the context of the tests, a fairly high degree of generalization. It is only in contrast to skill usage in the natural environment that adequate generalization will be hampered. A derivative of the above-mentioned method is the Extended Interaction Test (McFall & Lillesand, 1971). This method assesses generalization by creating a scene in which the client is challenged to persist in his assertive refusal while interacting with a pleading antagonist. Reports on this method of assessing generalization are limited but may be a helpful measure when combined with other methods.

The second major method of assessing generalization consists of changing the stimulus person to whom the client is to respond. (Edelstein

& Eisler, 1976; Frederiksen *et al.*, 1976). Most programs will utilize the same model-role player throughout training. Requiring the client to address a new person would give a good indication of generalization of treatment. This method does appear to hold promise, yet does not really assure greater generalization to the natural environment.

The final major strategy employed uses deception. By making unobtrusive naturalistic observations of clients outside the therapeutic setting, it is felt that a good assessment of generalization can be obtained. The most frequently reported assessment of this nature is the use of telephone calls made to the subject which are tape-recorded and scored. The situation usually requires the subject to respond to a magazine salesman or volunteer worker, for instance, who persists in making unreasonable requests (Kazdin, 1974; McFall & Lillesand, 1971; McFall & Marston, 1970). Other methods reported have been: being shortchanged (Friedman, 1971; Hersen, Eisler, & Miller, 1973) and making unrealistic requests of patients while on the ward (Bellack *et al.*, 1979). Although all of these methods may be very useful as measures of generalization, the ethical issues of deception cannot be overlooked. McFall and Twentyman (1973) made the following suggestion to eliminate deceptive approaches to generalization: Acquiring informed consent from clients, which lets them know that they will be unobtrusively observed at an unspecified time, would enable such an assessment to take place in the natural environment. Ethical guidelines limit many of the measurement possibilities which could be implemented for the assessment of treatment generalization. We are, however, in agreement with Hersen and Bellack (1977) in preferring the use of naturalistic observation (with consent) over the analog situations presented in the behavioral role-playing tests.

The importance of assessing generalization of treatment for black clients appears to us to be threefold. First, the attention paid to cultural variables in social skills assessment and training has been limited. Therefore, there is no way to report exactly how much generalization of social skills training has occurred (if any) for blacks, native Americans, Mexicans, Chicanos, or any minority group. Secondly, present treatment programs for black clients may have failed to generalize to the natural environment because they did not focus on training the appropriate cues. In other words, the treatment program itself may have been adequate. However, the actual behaviors trained did not meet the needs of black clients or were found to be inappropriate and awkward in the client's milieu. Thirdly, training by a black therapist, instead of a white therapist, even one who is cognizant of cultural factors, may enhance skill generalization to the natural environment of the black client. Actual research in the area of social skills has not addressed the race of the trainer in treatment outcome. Studies in other areas do stress the importance of the same sex and same race of the therapist in enhancing the therapeutic process (Garcia, 1971; Mizio, 1972, 1973; National Association of Black Social Workers, 1973). Considering the use of modeling and behavior rehearsal in treatment, a black therapist could serve as a role model and representative of the client's natural environment, thus enhancing generalization.

The lack of a detailed analysis of social skills differences in different ethnic groups has limited our ability to answer many of the questions which must be addressed in assessment, treatment, and generalization. In any case, the systematic investigation and utilization of cultural variables in social skills training should lead to a greater use of newly acquired social skills by blacks and other ethnic groups. It simply makes common sense to practice and develop those responses which are most effective and most likely to be reinforced in the natural environment.

SUMMARY AND CONCLUSIONS

This chapter has been concerned with the importance of social skills and social skills training for blacks and other culturally distinct groups. Although it has been in no way exhaustive of the literature on treatment studies which implement social skills training, it has reviewed some of the relevant studies concerning black interpersonal behavior.

A review of the literature reveals that very little attention has been given to the importance of different cultural styles as they affect assessment of social skills and social skills training. This dearth of systematically investigated variables is reflected in our discussion of the three spheres of assessment and training approaches. However, the reader is referred to Cheek's (1976) book, *Assertive Black . . . Puzzled White,* for continued discussion of some of the issues in black social skill development.

Several specific conclusions, guidelines, and suggestions have been given to facilitate social skills training for black clients. Many of our conclusions are based on our awareness of cultural differences which influence us as black therapists, while other guidelines stem from social skills training we have conducted with black clients. Perhaps we cannot clearly say *what* changes (if any) are called for when a black person talks to a white person; however, we do know that the cultural experiences of blacks and whites have been different enough to warrant further investigation of social skills development. We recommend that future research should focus upon:

1. The systematic delineation of cultural differences in social skills.

There is limited information in the behavioral literature which looks at cultural differences or stylistic differences in social skills. For example, are black dating behaviors different from white dating behaviors? How aggressive are black clients, or are they really aggressive at all? These and other similar questions can be only addressed as they relate to a detailed analysis of social skills differences of ethnic groups.

2. A more adequate description of subject characteristics in reported studies, especially those using a different race of subject. More often than not, studies do not speak of the subject's race. Group studies may not have reported race because subjects were not equally represented; this omission could lead to confounding results, whereas single case studies may have ignored race because of the individual-oriented approach to therapy. In each of these cases, lack of clear subject characteristics prevented a full understanding of what the actual treatment consisted of, what contributed to generalization, or why the particular treatment may *not* have been effective for that particular subject.

3. A more adequate description of the client's cultural milieu. This point bears closely on subject characteristics. Certain sociocultural factors may either support or have a negative effect on therapy; therefore, these factors must be presented if one is to develop a complete portrait of the client.

4. Utilization of cultural variables to enhance treatment effectiveness and generalization. In selecting content situations and responses to train black clients, the following question must be addressed: Is this going to be an effective assertive response when the client is in his natural environment? If this question cannot be answered with a yes, it should become obvious that cultural variables have probably been overlooked. One should take time to assess the effectiveness of the treatment program by discussing with the client whether or not social skills training is having any effect at all on his interpersonal relationships.

5. Attention to the race of the responder in social skill assessment and training. We have reported the only two authors (Cheek, 1976; Hazzard, 1979) who have discussed the importance of race in skill development. Hazzard's study in particular has shown that blacks have learned two ways to deal with two different groups of people. An adequate assessment to determine the best treatment package must include both black and white role-players or stimulus persons.

6. Attention to an adequate sample of blacks, Chicanos, and other ethnic groups in inventories designed to assess assertiveness. Like several of the intelligence measures, assertiveness tests have failed to include minorities in the standardized group results. For any one to interpret accurately the raw scores of a self-report measure, it is essential to have sampled that group from which one is generalizing. The failure of pres-

ent assertion inventories to include minorities in their samples has limited the tests' application and conclusive interpretation with black clients. We strongly encourage this final focus as a primary research endeavor.

REFERENCES

Argyle M. *The psychology of interpersonal behavior*. Baltimore: Penguin, 1967.

Argyris, C. Explorations in interpersonal competence—I. *Journal of Applied Behavioral Science*, 1965, *1*, 58–83.

Bates, H. D., & Zimmerman, S. F. Toward the development of a screening scale for assertive training. *Psychological Reports*, 1971, *28*, 99–107.

Bellack, A. S., Hersen, M., & Turner, S. M. Generalization effects of social skills training in chronic schizophrenics: An experimental analysis. *Behaviour Research and Therapy*, 1976, *14*, 391–398.

Bellack, A. S., Hersen, M., & Turner, S. M. Role-play tests for assessing social skills: Are they valid? *Behavior Therapy*, 1978, *9*, 448–461.

Bellack, A. S., Hersen, & Turner, S. M. Relationship of role-playing and knowledge of appropriate behavior to assertion in the natural environment. *Journal of Consulting and Clinical Psychology*, 1979, *47*, 670–678.

Bornstein, M. R., Bellack, A. S., & Hersen, M. Social skills training for unassertive children: A multiple-baseline analysis. *Journal of Applied Behavior Analysis*, 1977, *10*, 183–195.

Buss, A. H., & Durkee, A. An inventory for assessing different kinds of hostility. *Journal of Consulting Psychology*, 1957, *21*, 343–384.

Caldwell, A. T. A comparison of assessment modes with low assertive men and women. Unpublished doctoral dissertation, University of Georgia, 1977.

Cheek, D. K. *Assertive black . . . Puzzled white*. San Luis Obispo, Calif.: Impact, 1976.

Dubner, F. S. Nonverbal aspects of black English. *The Southern Speech Communication Journal*, 1972, *37*, 361–374.

Edelstein, B. A., & Eisler, R. M. Effects of modeling and modeling with instructions and feedback on the behavioral components of social skills. *Behavior Therapy*, 1976, *7*, 382–389.

Edwards, N. B. Case conference: Assertive training in a case of homosexual pedophilia. *Journal of Behavior Therapy and Experimental Psychiatry*, 1972, *3*, 55–63.

Eisler, R. M. The behavioral assessment of social skills. In M. Hersen and A. S. Bellack (Eds.), *Behavioral assessment: A practical handbook*. New York: Pergamon Press, 1976.

Eisler, R. M., Hersen, M., & Agras, W. S. Videotape: A method for the controlled observation of nonverbal interpersonal behavior. *Behavior Therapy*, 1973, *4*, 420–425.

Eisler, R. M., Hersen, M., & Miller, P. M. Effects of modeling on components of assertive behavior. *Journal of Behavior Therapy and Experimental Psychiatry*, 1973, *4*, 1–6.

Eisler, R. M., Hersen M., Miller, P. M., & Blanchard, E. B. Situational determinants of assertive behaviors. *Journal of Consulting and Clinical Psychology*, 1975, *43*, 330–340.

Eisler, R. M., Miller, P. M., & Hersen, M. Components of assertive behavior. *Journal of Clinical Psychology*, 1973, *4*, 1–6.

Fredericksen, L. W., Jenkins, J. O., Foy, D. W., & Eisler, R. M. The modification of inappropriate verbal outbursts in adults using social skills training. *Journal of Applied Behavior Analysis*. 1976, *9*, 117–125.

Friedman, P. H. The effects of modeling and role-playing on assertive behavior. In R. D. Rubin, H. Fensterheim, A. A. Lazarus, & C. M. Franks (Eds.), *Advances in behavior therapy*. New York: Academic Press, 1971.

Galassi, J. P., & Galassi, M. D. Validity of a measure of assertiveness. *Journal of Counseling Psychology*, 1974, *21*, 248–250.

Galassi, J. P., Delo, J. S., Galassi, M. D., & Basten, O. S. The college self-expression scale: A measure of assertiveness. *Behavior Therapy*, 1974, *5*, 165–171.

Gambrill, E. D., & Richey, C. A. An assertion inventory for use in assessment and research. *Behavior Therapy*, 1975, *6*, 550–561.

Garcia, A. The Chicano and social work. *Social Casework*, 1971, *52*, 274–278.

Gay, M. L., Hollandsworth, J. G., & Galassi, J. P. An assertiveness inventory for adults. *Journal of Counseling Psychology*, 1975, *22*, 340–344.

Gladwin, T. Social competence and clinical practice. *Psychiatry*, 1967, *30*, 30–43.

Goldsmith, J. B., & McFall, R. M. Development and evaluation of an interpersonal skill training program for psychiatric inpatients. *Journal of Abnormal Psychology*, 1975, *84*, 51–58.

Hall, E. T. *Handbook for proxemic research.* Washington, D.C.: Society for the Anthropology of Visual Communication, 1974.

Harrison, R. Nonverbal communication: Explorations into time, space, action, and object. In J. H. Campbell & H. W. Hepler (Eds.), *Dimensions in communication: Readings.* Belmont, Calif.: Wadsworth, 1965.

Hazzard, M. *An assessment of assertive behavior: A black–white comparison.* Unpublished doctoral dissertation, University of Georgia, 1979.

Heimberg, R. C., Montgomery, D., Madsen, C. H., Jr., & Heimberg, J. S. Assertion training: A review of the literature. *Behavior Therapy*, 1977, *8*, 953–971.

Hersen, M., & Bellack, A. S. Social skills training for chronic psychiatric patients: Rationale, research findings, and future directions. *Comprehensive Psychiatry*, 1976, *17*, 559–580.

Hersen, M., & Bellack, A. S. Assessment of social skills. In A. R. Cimminero, K. S. Calhoun, & H. E. Adams (Eds.), *Handbook for behavioral assessment.* New York: Wiley, 1977.

Hersen, M., Bellack, A. S., & Turner, S. M. Assessment of assertiveness in female psychiatric patients: Motor and autonomic measures. *Journal of Behavior Therapy and Experimental Psychiatry*, 1978, *9*, 11–16.

Hersen, M., & Eisler, R. M. Social skills training. In W. E. Craighead, A. E. Kazdin, & M. J. Mahoney (Eds.), *Behavior modification: Principles, issues and applications.* Boston: Houghton Mifflin, 1976.

Hersen, M., Eisler, R. M., & Miller, P. M. Development of assertive responses: Clinical, measurement, and research considerations. *Behaviour Research and Therapy*, 1973, *11*, 505–521.

Hollandsworth, J. G. Further investigation of the relationship between expressed social fear and assertiveness. *Behaviour Research and Therapy*, 1976, *14*, 85–87.

Jenkins, J. O. *An investigation of personal investment in behavioral role-playing tasks used to assess assertiveness.* Unpublished doctoral dissertation, University of Georgia, 1976.

Kallman, W. M., & Feuerstein, M. Psychophysiological procedures. In A. R. Cimminero, K. S. Calhoun, & H. E. Adams (Eds.), *Handbook for behavioral assessment.* New York: Wiley, 1977.

Kazdin, A. E. Effects of covert modeling and model reinforcement on assertive behavior. *Journal of Abnormal Psychology*, 1974, *88*, 240–252.

Kirchner, E. P., Kennedy, R. E., & Draguns, J. G. Assertion and aggression in adult offenders. *Behavior Therapy*, 1979, *10*, 452–471.

Kochman, T. Rapping in the black ghetto. *Transaction*, 1969, *6*, 26–34.

La France, M., & Mayo, C. Racial differences in gaze behavior during conversations: Two systematic observational studies. *Journal of Personality and Social Psychology*, 1976, *33*, 547–552.

La France, M., & Mayo C. Gaze direction in interracial dyadic communication. *Ethnicity*, 1978, *5*, 167–173.

Landis, D., Day, H. R., McGrew, P. L., Thomas, J. A., & Miller, A. B. Can a black "culture assimilator" increase racial understanding? *Journal of Social Issues*, 1976, *32*, 169–183.

Lange, A., & Jakubowski, P. *Responsible assertive behavior: Cognitive/behavioral procedures for trainers*. Champaign, Ill.: Research Press, 1976.

Lazarus, A. A. An assertive behavior: A brief note. *Behavior Therapy*, 1973, *4*, 697–699.

Lewinsohn, P. M. Clinical and theoretical aspects of depression. In K. S. Calhoun, H. E. Adams, & K. M. Mitchell (Eds.), *Innovative treatment methods in psychotherapy*. New York: Wiley, 1973.

Lewinsohn, P. M. & Graf, M. Pleasant activities and depression. *Journal of Consulting and Clinical Psychology*, 1973, *41*, 261–268.

Lewinsohn, P. M., & Libet, J. Pleasant events, activity schedules, and depression. *Journal of Abnormal Psychology*, 1972, *79*, 291–295.

Lewinsohn, P. M., & MacPhillamy, D. J. The relationship between age and engagement in pleasant activities. *Journal of Gerontology*, 1974, *29*, 290–294.

Lewinsohn, P. M., Weinstein, M. S., & Alper T. A behaviorally oriented approach to the group treatment of depressed persons: A methodological contribution. *Journal of Clinical Psychology*, 1970, *4*, 525–532.

Libet, J. M., & Lewinsohn, P. M. Concept of social skill with special reference to the behavior of depressed persons. *Journal of Consulting and Clinical Psychology*, 1973, *40*, 304–312.

MacPhillamy, D. J., & Lewinsohn, P. M. Depression as a function of levels of desired and obtained pleasure. *Journal of Abnormal Psychology*, 1974, *83*, 651–657.

McFall, R. M., & Lillesand, D. B. Behavior rehearsal with modeling and coaching in assertive training. *Journal of Abnormal Psychology*, 1971, 77, 313–323.

McFall, R. M., & Marston, A. R. An experimental investigation of behavior rehearsal in assertion training. *Journal of Abnormal Psychology*, 1970, *76*, 295–303.

McFall, R. M., & Twentyman, C. T. Four experiments on the relative contributions of rehearsal, modeling, and coaching to assertion training. *Journal of Abnormal Psychology*, 1973, *81*, 199–218.

McPherson, E. L. R. Selective operant conditioning and deconditioning of assertive modes of behavior. *Journal of Behavior Therapy and Experimental Psychiatry*, 1972, *3*, 99–102.

Minor, B. J. A perspective for assertiveness training for blacks. *Journal of Non-White Concerns*, 1978, 63–70.

Mischel, W. *Personality and assessment*. New York: Wiley, 1968.

Mizio, E. White worker—minority client. *Social Work*, 1972, *17*, 82–86.

Mizio, E. Puerto Rican social workers and racism. *Social Casework*, 1973, *53*, 267–272.

National Association of Black Social Workers. *Diversity, cohesion or chaos—mobilization for survival*. Nashville: Fisk University, 1973.

O'Connor, R. D. Modification of social withdrawal through symbolic modeling. *Journal of Applied Behavior Analysis*, 1969, *2*, 15–22.

Pachman, J. S., Foy, D. W., Massey, F., & Eisler, R. M. A factor analysis of assertive behaviors. *Journal of Consulting and Clinical Psychology*, 1978, *46*, 347–348.

Patterson, R. L. Time-out and assertive training for a dependent child. *Behavior Therapy*, 1972, *3*, 466–468.

Porter, L. W. Communication: Structure and process. In H. L. Fromkin & J. J. Sherwood (Eds.), *Integrating the organization: A social psychological analysis*. New York: Free Press, 1974.

Pugh, R. *Psychology of the black experience*. Monterey, Calif.: Brooke/Cole, 1972.

Rathus, S. A. A thirty-item schedule for assessing assertive behavior. *Behaviour Research and Therapy*, 1973, *11*, 57–65.

Rimm, D. C. Assertive training and the expression of anger. In R. E. Alberti (Ed.), *Assertiveness: Innovations, applications, issues*. San Luis Obispo, Calif.: Impact, 1977.

Rimm, D. C., & Masters, J. C. *Behavior therapy: Techniques and empirical findings* (2nd ed.). New York: Academic Press, 1979.

Sullivan, H. S. *Interpersonal theory of psychiatry.* New York: Norton, 1953.

Twentyman, C. T., & McFall, R. M. Behavioral training of social skills in shy males. *Journal of Consulting and Clinical Psychology*, 1975, *43*, 384–395.

Voss, J., Arrick, C., & Rimm, D. C. The role of task difficulty and modeling in assertive training. Unpublished master's thesis, Southern Illinois University, 1976. (*Dissertation Abstracts International*, 1976.)

Weiss, R. L. Operant conditioning techniques in psychological assessment. In P. McReynolds (Ed.), *Advances in psychological assessment.* Palo Alto, Calif.: Science & Behavior, 1968.

Williams, F., Whitehead, J. L., & Miller, L. M. Ethnic stereotyping and judgments of children's speech. *Speech Monographs*, 1971, *63*, 264–271.

Wolpe, J. *Psychotherapy by reciprocal inhibition.* Stanford: Stanford University Press, 1958.

Wolpe, J. *The practice of behavior therapy.* New York: Pergamon, 1969.

Wolpe, J., & Lazarus, A. A. *Behavior therapy techniques.* Oxford: Pergamon, 1966.

Zigler, E., & Phillips, L. Social effectiveness and symptomatic behaviors. *Journal of Abnormal and Social Psychology*, 1960, *61*, 231–238.

Zigler, E., & Phillips. L. Social competence and outcome in psychiatric disorders. *Journal of Abnormal and Social Psychology*, 1961, *62*, 264–271.

Zigler, E., & Phillips, L. Social competence and the process-reactive distinction in psychopathology. *Journal of Abnormal and Social Psychology*, 1962, *63*, 215–238.

10

Substance Abuse

JACK O. JENKINS, SARA RAHAIM, LILY M. KELLY, AND DOUGLAS PAYNE

INTRODUCTION

The phenomenon of drug abuse is no longer regarded as a problem restricted to populated urban areas or to certain economic, social, educational, or ethnic groups. Alcoholism, representing the major form of drug abuse in America, is responsible for a tremendous amount of human misery. In addition, a large expenditure of funds is required to deal with the social problems associated with drug abuse. The increasing awareness of the problem by all social strata has led to increased demands for a solution. The purpose of this chapter is to review behavioral change strategies used to treat drug abuse, with particular emphasis on their application to and effectiveness with black populations. Attention will also be directed toward explicating modification of treatment techniques which might enhance their effectiveness with black clients. Initially, we will discuss alcoholism and then treat other forms of drug abuse in a separate section.

THE PROBLEM OF ALCOHOL ABUSE

Alcoholism represents a major health problem in the United States and other countries for all people, regardless of race. Over nine million Americans are currently alcoholic. However, few well controlled studies on drinking patterns and the effects of alcoholism on blacks are to be found in the literature. Harper and Dawkins (1976) found that out of 16,000 articles listed and abstracted in the classified *Abstract Archives* of the alcohol literature over a 30-year period ending in 1974, only 77 contained any significant references to alcohol and blacks. This, of course, does not mean that there are not male and female black alco-

JACK O. JENKINS, LILY M. KELLY, AND DOUGLAS PAYNE • Department of Psychology, University of Georgia, Athens, Georgia 30601.   SARA RAHAIM • Veterans Administration Hospital, Kansas City, Missouri 64128.

holics. Rather, it reflects less interest on the part of researchers with this particular population. To some extent, it also no doubt reflects the absence of a significant number of black mental health professionals, particularly in the alcoholism area.

Recently, however, there has been an increase in literature on alcoholism in blacks. After examining this literature, Harper (1978) reached several conclusions. He found that rates of heavy drinking among black men and white men tended to be similar, with some reports favoring slightly higher rates of heavy drinkers among black men. Black women tended to have a higher rate of both abstention and heavy drinking when compared to white women. Harper also found some differences in the drinking behavior of blacks and whites. He reported that blacks in general were more likely to be weekend drinkers. Middle- and lower-class blacks preferred to impress others with prestigious brand names. However, Vitols (1968) found this only among middle-class blacks. He found also that on the basis of admissions to hospitals, black alcoholics were younger and experienced the onset of alcoholism at a younger age. Another finding reported by Harper (1978) was that blacks were more likely than whites to be victims of their own alcoholism and heavy drinking in terms of physical illness, assaults, homicides, accidents, early mortality, and trouble with the law. He further noted that Viamontes and Powell (1974) had reported findings indicating no differences between blacks and whites in this regard. A final conclusion of this extensive report involved the accessibility of treatment facilities to blacks. According to Harper, blacks have more limited access to treatment facilities than whites. However, black alcoholics admitted to treatment evidence stronger motivation, are more cooperative during treatment, and express fewer complaints. The author further concluded that some treatment modalities which succeed for white alcoholics may not be appropriate for blacks.

Brunswick and Tarica (1974) presented empirical data consistent with many of Harper's (1978) conclusions. In a sample of 659 black adolescents (ages 12–17) living in Harlem, these researchers found that approximately 24% of the youths reported drinking alcohol. Using interview data to investigate the relationship between drinking and health, these investigators found that these adolescents recognized alcohol consumption as a major health threat. Results also indicated that drinkers were more likely to have 16 of 51 health problems which were investigated and that psychosomatic complaints were heavily represented among the reported health difficulties. On measures of mental health, although drinkers evidenced higher self-regard than nondrinkers, older drinkers experienced more sleep disturbance than their nondrinking peers. Drinking was related to other life-style behaviors and attitudes such as anticipation of death by violent means, smoking (especially among boys), and early pregnancy among girls. Finally, results of step-wise multiple regression analyses indicated that a combination of life-style behaviors, psychosomatic problems, and worries explained nearly 40% of the variance in boys' drinking and 30% in that of the girls.

Employing a modification of the Thematic Apperception Test (TAT) and an interview schedule, Maddox and Allen (1961) explored social characteristics of black and white college students, as well as their attitudes toward and experience with alcohol. Whites were classified socioeconomically as representative of the middle class, and blacks were described as "black bourgeoisie," a term often used to describe the black middle class. With regard to TAT stories, whites were more likely to indicate that their fantasy characters were drinking in a social situation rather than in isolation. On the other hand, blacks' fantasy characters evaluated drinking as inappropriate and immoral. Blacks also evidenced greater ambivalence toward drinking. The greater ambivalence and more prominent negative emphasis on drinking by blacks was not par-alleled by significant differences in abstinence for these subjects. This finding was interpreted as stemming from black students' ambiguous social position and their attempt to identify with perceived moral codes of middle-class whites. In addition, one plausible speculation is that ex-cessive drinking for black students represents an attempt at insulation from a frustrating existence, whereas whites tend to view drinking as a socially necessary and desirable behavior. Also, it is not clear what utility the TAT has in this type of investigation. Hence, the findings may be meaningless.

Because of the relatively few studies investigating factors associated with alcoholism among blacks, the above findings should be considered with appropriate skepticism. Most of the existing studies suffer from numerous methodological inadequacies. However, these studies do sug-gest that there are cultural differences in alcohol patterns. As those differences may have profound implications for treatment, they do de-serve further consideration. However, this theory is inconsistent with studies demonstrating the effectiveness of various behavioral strategies applied to sober alcoholics, particularly those treatments directed toward controlled drinking.

A BEHAVIORAL DEFINITION OF ALCOHOLISM

Behavioral definitions of alcoholism have generally emphasized the fact that alcohol is a potent reinforcer. Rather than conceptualizing al-coholism as the manifestation of disease process (Jellinek, 1960), most view the disorder as a learned behavior and hence subject to modification by learning-based strategies. Several definitions, not radically different from each other, have been proposed.

Blake (1965) defined alcoholism as a learned habit of uncontrollable drinking instrumental in the individual's attempts to reduce a disturbance in psychological homeostasis. He proposed that a variety of emotional conditions may lead to a disturbance in psychological homeostasis, including "fear, anger, anxiety, the lack of assertive behavior, even states of intense happiness, elation, and the like" (p. 75). The emergence of uncontrollable drinking as the dominant response is explained by the notion that an immediate reduction in a strong drive acts as a reinforcer of the behavior resulting in drive reduction.

Storm and Smart (1965) formulated a theory of alcoholism which has extensive implications for treatment. According to this theory, the loss of control seen in alcoholics can be accounted for by a chain of responses: one drink serves as a discriminative stimulus for the next one. The alcoholic is unable to stop this loss of control by thinking of or experiencing aversive consequences because of the lack of transfer of learning from an intoxicated to a sober state. Treatment implications that ensue from this theory would involve treating the alcoholic while he is intoxicated rather than sober, since little transfer from the sober state to the intoxicated state would occur. However, this theory is inconsistent with studies demonstrating the effectiveness of various behavioral strategies applied to sober alcoholics, particularly those treatments directed toward controlled drinking.

Sobell and Sobell (1973) have proposed a behavioral account of alcoholism which emphasizes the drive-reduction concept but is somewhat broader than other similar theories. Problem drinking is postulated to have been acquired because the drinker has been rewarded, consciously or unconsciously, for such behavior. In addition to the negative reinforcement resulting from avoiding or escaping stressful situations, drinking may be associated with many powerful positive reinforcers such as attention or money.

Davidson (1974), integrating drive-reduction concepts and models of positive reinforcement, has provided one of the most comprehensive behavioral accounts of alcoholism. Reviewing the literature, he concluded that both positive and negative reinforcement, as well as complex combinations of these and other learning variables, may be involved in the development and maintenance of excessive drinking behavior. A potential alcoholic may initially drink under the primary control of either positive or negative reinforcement (e.g., he drinks because he likes the taste or the experience or to escape or avoid aversive states). Some may drink because "it is the thing to do" (modeling). Certain stimuli may set the occasion for drinking, and these stimuli may subsequently become discriminants for the drinking response. According to this formulation, the frequency of drinking should increase in the presence of such discriminant stimuli (SDs) and decrease in their absence. For example, a party setting and social reinforcement may be important factors in the learning to drink sequence. Avoidance of aversive states may be learned in a similar fashion. Stimuli previously associated with such states may become SDs for drinking.

> "Even when such symptoms have not been forthcoming, drinking may be maintained on a superstitious basis (the individual now drinks to avoid symptoms that might not have occurred in the absence of drinking). This extends the stimulus control over the behavior and increases the number and range of situations in which drinking might occur." (Davidson, 1974, p. 157)

While the behavioral definitions described above vary in emphasis, one common thread is the notion that inappropriate drinking behavior has been learned; consequently, perhaps it can be unlearned and appropriate drinking patterns established. These definitions are in sharp contrast to the predominant view that excessive drinking represents a progressive disease which can be arrested but is irreversible (e.g., Jellinek, 1960). One of the major implications of the break with the disease model of alcoholism is the feasibility of a change of focus in regard to goals of treatment. While most workers in the field have emphasized total abstinence because alcoholics were believed to be incapable of returning to social drinking, a behavioral interpretation leads to different conclusions. If alcoholism is acquired through conditioning and learning mechanisms, it should be possible to *modify* drinking behavior by the same or similar learning processes. Hence, one should be able to learn to drink in a socially appropriate fashion.

It should be noted that many of the studies to be reviewed in this chapter have concentrated on total abstinence as the goal of treatment. However, in only a few cases was this goal achieved. A large number of subjects simply improved their drinking behavior, providing some evidence for the contention that new, more adaptive drinking behavior may be acquired by alcoholics without the inevitable loss of control postulated by the disease concept. Additionally, several studies with social drinking as the goal of treatment demonstrate promising results.

For the purpose of this chapter, alcoholism will be defined as a learned behavior resulting in physiological dependency and often complicated by deteriorating health and other problems in living. This definition, consistent with Davidson's (1974) account of the etiology and consequences of alcoholism, is held to be viable for all races, with group and idiosyncratic variations in patterns of drinking behavior.

SOME COMMENTS ON CULTURAL ISSUES

Throughout this chapter the term *cultural factors* will repeatedly be used. Therefore, some comments concerning what we mean are in order. Chapter 2 in this book and several other sources (e.g., Jones, 1974, 1979) discuss this issue in detail. Hence, we will be brief in our discussion here.

In describing black culture in America, it should be noted that although there are general patterns of behavior that can be described in general as characteristic of blacks, it must be recognized that there are differences among various black populations just as there are among white populations. Such variables as socioeconomic status, urban or rural setting, and region of the country must be given some consideration. Some of the characteristic black behavior patterns are described by Jackson in Chapter 2.

With the above *caveat* in mind, it is true that the oppression experienced by black Americans has undoubtedly influenced the development of coping skills and methods for dealing with stress. Segregation, legal as well as social and religious, has forced blacks to live in their own neighborhoods and attend their own churches, schools, and social events. This pattern of separatism has fostered the development of distinct black language patterns and distinct patterns of negotiating with the environment. Similarly, the development of distinct value systems in black populations has been observed.

REVIEW OF THE LITERATURE

Several behavioral strategies have been employed in the treatment of maladaptive drinking patterns. This literature review will be organized around a brief description of each technique, the presentation of some information regarding its effectiveness, and implications for the use of each strategy with black clients. The first technique considered will be aversive conditioning (chemical and electrical), followed by covert sensitization, controlled drinking, community-based approaches, and combined techniques.

Before we begin our review, it should be noted that, although black alcoholics have served as subjects in many experiments in the modification of alcoholism by behavior therapists, only rarely is race mentioned in the description of subject characteristics. Since the characteristics of a particular subject (such as race) may act solely or in conjunction with other factors to influence the results, this oversight could lead to the inappropriate utilization of some procedures to treat black alcoholics. The reason for this lack of information concerning black subject characteristics reflects the cavalier attitude of psychology in general, and behavior therapy in particular, toward such issues. The fact that behavior therapy has heavily relied on single-case designs should argue positively for a more complete description of subject characteristics as well as of the environment in which the subject lives. Yet, rarely is cultural information given any import. This is surprising in light of the theoretical emphasis placed on precise assessment of the individual and his environment.

Obviously, if a behavioral strategy results in reduced drinking, then it should be considered successful regardless of racial factors. However, one must wonder whether in some instances the behavioral strategy employed could have been more effective if cultural factors had been taken into account. Although behavior therapy generally has a higher rate of effectiveness than other therapies in this area, as can be seen in the following review, the number of alcoholics who improve is not 100%. Certainly, to enhance generalization of treatment effects, cultural factors and individual differences must be considered. Lunde and Voegler (1970) reported that in many studies certain subject characteristics were more predictive of successful outcome than the type of treatment administered. McCance and McCance (1969), in a study of aversive conditioning, also found that certain social and behavioral attributes were highly related to the outcome of treatment with alcoholics. They found that poor outcomes were more prevalent in lower-class patients, in those from a heavy drinking subculture, and in those who were continual rather than binge drinkers. Of all the factors studied, marital stability was the most positive prognostic feature. Another interesting finding was that among patients who were cooperative in the hospital a number failed to maintain their improvement. In contrast, the "rebels" against treatment who *did* do well initially, generally continued to do so. Rathod, Gregory, Blows, and Theodore (1966) also noted that "conforming" patients did not do well. It is possible that such individuals passively comply in the hospital but gradually relapse after their discharge, unable to take an independent line in a drinking environment. This type of patient might benefit from continued contact with the therapist, from direct environmental interventions, and from such treatment strategies as assertiveness training.

McCance and McCance (1969) reviewed the scanty literature on the relationship between behavioral and social attributes of alcoholics and their response to treatment and concluded that the most consistent finding was that individuals who maintained stable interpersonal relationships, persisted in their employment, and did not behave antisocially were more successful in modifying their drinking behavior. Voegtlin and Broz (1949) reported similar findings. In addition, they found age to be an important factor in maintaining abstinence, with clients under the age of 25 showing the lowest rates. Motivational factors have also been found to be important in the generalization of treatment effects (Voegtlin, Lemere, Broz, & O'Hollaren, 1941).

While far from definitive, there is evidence to suggest that cultural and behavioral characteristics do affect the treatment outcomes of alcoholics. This argues strongly for increased emphasis on a thorough behavioral assessment prior to treatment. For black, as well as other clients, this behavioral assessment should include cultural variables which may affect treatment. A typical assessment of cultural factors by a therapist might include questions like:

1. How much like this patient am I? Do we dress alike, talk alike, live in the same area of town?
2. How does he view me?
3. Where does he live and where do I live?
4. With whom does he live and associate?
5. How much do I know about his culture?
6. Have I ever been in a bar in his particular section of town?
7. How does knowledge about his culture and behavioral patterns alter my procedures (e.g., assertive training)?
8. How does he view treatment?
9. Have I developed sufficient rapport with him to trust the information he will give me about his drinking?

Exactly how answers to these questions affect or do not affect treatment depends on the individual case. A black alcoholic who operates primarily in a white middle-class culture both in employment and social involvement may simply need the standard treatment package. A black from Harlem who is on welfare and only interacts with the white landlord or white grocery store owner may be another story.

AVERSION CONDITIONING

Punishment procedures involve the withdrawal of a positive reinforcer or the administration of an aversive stimulus contingent upon the occurrence of an undesirable behavior. Punishment techniques are most often identified as appropriate for the treatment of behavioral disorders in which a powerfully evocative stimulus is an important component of the maladaptive behavior (Rimm & Masters, 1979). Certainly, alcoholism represents a good example of such a behavioral disorder. In the case of alcoholism, punishment procedures have sometimes involved the association of aversive stimuli with the entire sequence of drinking (from urges to actual consumption), as well as with the environmental cues that elicit drinking.

The most widely accepted theoretical account of the effectiveness of punishment techniques is the two-factor theory advanced by Mowrer (1960) and Solomon (1964). Punishment is postulated to involve two processes. The first process involves classical conditioning, in that an association is formed between the unconditioned aversive stimulus, including the internal aversive states, such as anxiety and unpleasantness, which are evoked by the aversive stimulus. For example, the treatment of alcoholism with an aversive stimulus (e.g., shock) might be paired with the client's taking a sip of alcohol. With repeated pairings, alcohol should theoretically lose its positive valence as it becomes associated with feelings of anxiety or discomfort, even in the absence of shock. The second process involves operant conditioning. Any behavior (e.g., abstinence) that is instrumental in avoiding the aversively conditioned stimuli (e.g., alcohol consumption) will decrease anxiety and will be negatively reinforced.

An aversive stimulus may be delivered in several ways. Punishment may be administered following the completion of the problematic behavior. For example, an electric shock might be delivered immediately after the alcoholic client ingests a jigger of alcohol. An aversive stimulus might also be delivered during the occurrence of the maladaptive behavior, image of the behavior, or problematic stimulus. An example of this procedure is inducing nausea as the client takes a sip of his favorite alcoholic beverage.

Another strategy involves the administration of an aversive stimulus concurrently with the client's initiation of a problematic behavior, but allowing for the termination of the aversive stimulus contingent upon the client's engaging in more adaptive behavior. For example, an alcoholic could terminate a shock by switching from a glass of alcohol to a glass of soda. Finally, punishment may involve the removal of a positive reinforcer contingent upon the occurrence of the maladaptive behavior. For example, an alcoholic might forfeit $10 each time he pours a drink. (For a more thorough discussion of these punishment techniques and the underlying theoretical issues, the reader is referred to Rimm & Masters, 1979).

Aversive conditioning for the treatment of alcoholism has taken three general forms: (1) the use of chemical aversive stimuli, (2) the use of electrical aversive stimuli, and (3) the use of imaginal aversive stimuli (e.g. covert sensitization). Each type of treatment will be reviewed below.

CHEMICAL AVERSION.   During chemical aversion a drug is utilized to produce an aversive state, and this aversive state is paired with a maladaptive behavior such as drinking. The most commonly used drugs are emetics, such as apomorphine hydrochloride or emetine hydrochloride, which produce nausea and vomiting. Rimm and Masters (1979) note that emetine is generally favored over apomorphine because the latter drug is a central nervous system (CNS) depressant, and some reports indicate that CNS depressants retard conditioning, thereby diminishing the effectiveness of aversive procedures. For this reason, stimulants are frequently given simultaneously with emetics to counteract the CNS depressant effects.

Curare-type, short-term paralytic drugs, which cause a temporary inability to breathe, have occasionally been employed. The most common drug of this type is succinylcholine chloride, injected directly into the blood stream. The paralysis and associated feelings of panic and fear of death are apparently intensely aversive.

The use of chemical conditioning methods has fallen into some disfavor among clinicians for a variety of reasons: (1) the difficulty in controlling the onset and offset of the aversive stimulus, notably with the emetics; (2) the medical complications which may ensue from the introduction of drugs into the body; and (3) the extremely aversive nature of the procedures.

Rimm and Masters (1979) describe a typical chemical aversive conditioning procedure. The treatment room is usually sound-proofed and darkened, with the alcohol clearly lighted and salient. The client is given a description of the procedures. When emetic drugs are employed, the client is initially given two large glasses of warm salt water containing 1½ grains of emetine and 1 gram of salt. Subsequently, he is given an injection of both emetine hydrochloride and 1½ grams of ephedrine sulphate (a nausea-inducing drug). As nausea begins, the client is given several ounces of alcohol in a glass and instructed to smell, taste, swirl around in his mouth, and then (in some procedures) swallow the alcohol. Vomiting usually occurs immediately afterward. Some therapists prolong nausea at this point. Subsequent sessions (typically ranging from four to seven) may involve increased dosages of emetine, lengthened treatment sessions, and a diversity of alcoholic beverages to enhance generalization.

When a paralytic drug is used, the client is connected to a polygraph which monitors his galvanic skin response, respiration, heart rate, and muscle tension. A respirator is always available. Prior to the intravenous injection of the drug, the client is given alcohol and instructed to look at it, smell it, taste it, and return it to the therapist. These procedures are repeated several times, approximately once a minute. Subsequently, succinylcholine is injected. When the polygraph indicates that the drug's effect is imminent, the therapist gives the client the bottle. The drug typically takes effect just as the bottle is put to the lips. Subsequently, the therapist holds the bottle to the clients lips and places a few drops of the alcohol into the client's mouth. When signs of normal respiration appear, the bottle is taken away.

Results of empirical investigations of the effectiveness of chemical aversive therapy with alcoholics are equivocal. Holzinger, Mortimer, and Van Dusen (1967) utilized 23 male subjects in a study designed to assess the effectiveness of succinylcholine-induced paralysis on drinking behavior. After the subjects had sniffed and tasted their favorite drinks for five brief trials, succinylcholine was injected. Paralysis occurred approximately 16 seconds after injection, at which time a few drops of the subject's favorite drink was placed in his mouth. A follow-up, conducted after an unspecified period of time, indicated that of the 21 subjects contacted, 81% continued to drink. One possible explanation for the poor results achieved with the procedure in this study is that the procedure was actually a backward conditioning (presentation of the unconditioned stimulus prior to the conditioned stimulus) paradigm rather than the usual classical conditioning procedure.

Clancy, Vanderhoff, and Campbell (1967) compared a succinylcholine-induced apnea group with the following groups: (a) a pseudoconditioning group that underwent the same procedure but did not receive a drug, (b) a group that received standard inpatient treatment, and (c) a group of subjects who refused treatment. Results indicated that the succinylcholine treatment resulted in significantly longer periods of abstinence than the standard hospital treatment and no treatment. However, there was no significant difference between the pseudoconditioning and succinylcholine groups. Other investigators also report disappointing results (Madill, Campbell, Laverty, Sanderson, Vandewater, 1966; Quin & Henbest, 1967).

Results of studies employing emetine appear more promising. Lemere and Voegtlin (1950) report a 51% abstinence rate after a 1–10 year follow-up. Miller, Duorak, and Turner (1960) reported that 80% of their subjects had maintained abstinence at an eight-month follow-up. Shanahan and Hornick (1946) reported a 70% abstinence rate. After reviewing the literature, Rimm and Masters (1979) tentatively concluded that nausea-producing drugs are superior to succinylcholine and electric shock in the treatment of alcoholism through aversive conditioning. Their conclusion is consistent with Wilson and Davison's (1969) argument that aversion techniques are most effective when the therapist uses a type of aversion related to the target behavior. Certainly, nausea appears more relevant to alcoholism than paralysis or the pain of electric shock.

ELECTRICAL AVERSION. In electrical aversion therapy, painful shocks are associated with drinking behavior. Electrical aversion has been applied with the goal of total abstinence and with the goal of social drinking. In the latter instance, individuals receive painful shocks contingent on inappropriate drinking. The use of electrical aversive stimuli offers a number of useful advantages. The electrical stimulus can have an altogether discrete onset and offset, intensity can be controlled, very little equipment is required, and there are fewer possible side-effects in comparison to chemical agents.

Several methods of electrical aversive conditioning for alcoholics have been employed. Blake (1965) supplemented escape-conditioning procedures with progressive relaxation and motivation arousal. In the first phase of treatment, subjects were taught to relax via the Jacobson (1938) procedure. The second phase consisted of motivational arousal during which subjects were asked to relax and then to consider the consequences of their drinking behavior. The third phase consisted of electrical aversion. The subject was asked to mix his favorite drink (if available) and then to sip but not swallow it. A shock in increasing intensity, beginning above the threshold reported by the subject in a preaversion test to be unpleasant, was delivered continuously with his sip on reinforced trials. Shocks were administered by means of electrodes attached to the subject's forearm and were delivered on a schedule randomized around a 50% ratio. Subjects were instructed to spit the alcohol in a bowl as a means of terminating the shock.

Blake also included a group which received aversion therapy only. At six-month follow-up, the two treatment groups did not significantly differ. It is noteworthy that a combined total of 56% of all subjects were either abstinent or improved after relaxation–aversion or aversion alone. Although this percentage represents a much better than average response to treatment by alcoholics, the fact that only about half of the subjects improved is not impressive. In a 12-month follow-up, Blake (1967) found that 48% of the subjects in the three-phase treatment program maintained abstinence, whereas merely 23% of the group on aversion therapy only maintained abstinence. These results cast further doubt upon the effectiveness of electrical aversion techniques as an effective treatment strategy for alcoholism.

Hsu (1964) used a combination of punishment and avoidance-conditioning to treat alcoholism. Electric shocks applied to the head of the client was used as the aversive stimulus. The client was presented with a tray containing six cups filled with beer, wine, whiskey, milk, water, and fruit juice. The client was instructed to drink them in any order he chose until all six were finished. The client was shocked only after he had swallowed one of the alcoholic beverages. Treatment was given daily for five days. On the fourth day, the client was allowed to take only five out of the six drinks and on the fifth day to take four of the six. This procedure was designed to allow the client to develop an avoidance response. Booster sessions were conducted at one and six months. At the time the study was published, less than half of the clients were abstinent at follow-up visits conducted at varying intervals (two to six months).

Wilson, Leaf, and Nathan (1975) utilized a different kind of behavioral test to assess drinking in a series of experiments concerned with the aversive control of excessive drinking. In this investigation, subjects were allowed to consume alcoholic beverages *ad libitum* over a twenty-four-hour period. In the first experiment, two white male alcoholics received aversive conditioning therapy in a crossover experimental design. After a three-day baseline period and a fourth day of recovery, one subject received electrical escape conditioning and the other subject a control procedure. After a second three-day *ad libitum* drinking period and fourth day of recovery, the treatment procedures for each subject were reversed. Electrical aversion conditioning did not lead to a suppression of drinking when subjects were administered the *ad libitum* drinking test after escape conditioning. No differences were found between control and experimental procedures. A second experiment with four subjects replicated the results of the first. In a third experiment, subjects were shocked contingently upon taking a drink and were allowed to self-administer shock in the latter part of the study. Results indicated a suppression of drinking behavior during experimenter-administered shock with a fairly quick return to baseline drinking levels for all subjects. Self-administered punishment reduced drinking during the procedure, at a baseline administered after the procedure, and again as the procedure was reinstituted. The lone black subject in this series of experiments was a widower aged 40, a high school graduate who worked as a sheet metal layout man. He participated with three white subjects in this third experiment. In a fourth experiment designed to rule out some rival hypotheses which could be used to weaken the results of the third experiment, four subjects received contingent and noncontingent shock and experimenter-administered and self-administered punishment. Results of this study revealed that contingent shock suppressed drinking, whereas noncontingent shock did not. The results for experimenter-administered vs. self-administered shock were mixed, with two subjects drinking less under experimenter-administered shock than under self-administered shock (which they administered very sparingly). Both procedures suppressed drinking in the other two subjects. Wilson *et al.* concluded that their series of experiments demonstrated that an alcoholic's drinking can be controlled by environmental events occurring after drinking. These authors also concluded that their data were consistent with other data that challenge the loss-of-control disease model postulated by Jellinek (1960).

MacCulloch, Feldman, Oxford, and MacCulloch (1966) utilized an anticipatory avoidance procedure in the treatment of several alcoholics. Of one male and three female alcoholics, all resumed or were presumed to have resumed drinking after leaving the alcoholic unit. The race of the subjects involved was not indicated.

Vogler, Lunde, Johnson, and Martin (1970) randomly assigned 73 male alcoholics to booster, conditioning only, pseudoconditioning, and sham conditioning groups. Booster group subjects received booster sessions of conditioning after their initial treatment. Conditioning-only subjects did not receive booster sessions. Pseudoconditioning subjects received shocks on a random schedule and sham-conditioning subjects underwent the same treatment as the booster and conditioning-only subjects but did not receive any shocks. Another group undergoing regular hospital routines was added later.

The aversive conditioning procedure of Vogler *et al.* consisted of having subjects take a sip of liquor and (on reinforced trials) terminate a shock to the fingers by spitting the drink into a bucket. On nonreinforced trials the subjects simply spat out the drink. Since most subjects failed to return initially for booster sessions, the conditioning-only group consisted primarily of subjects who had failed to return for booster sessions. Of 73 subjects who began the study, 51 completed it. Results indicated that booster session subjects had a significantly longer time before relapse than conditioning-only subjects and pooled control groups. However, these results must be interpreted with caution because of the selection of conditioning-only subjects. Conditioning-only subjects took significantly longer to relapse than pooled control subjects. Vogler *et al.* reported that the sobriety rate of their subjects was much lower than that reported by Blake (1965). However, these authors make the point that Blake's subjects were upper-class fee-paying patients, whereas their patients were lower-class non-fee-paying patients. No data on the racial composition of their subject sample are mentioned.

Hallam, Rachman, and Falkowski (1972) attempted to treat 10 alcoholics with aversive conditioning. The aversive conditioning produced no clear psychological effects (indicative of conditioning) during treatment and apparently had little effect on the modification of the subject's attitudes toward drinking or actual drinking behavior. When compared to a control group of eight subjects at a four-month follow-up, six of the experimental group subjects were reported to have abstained or to have had no heavy drinking bouts or frequent drinking, while only two of the control group met the same criteria. Hallam *et al.* determined through recording of heart rate and skin response data that the major factor predictive of success or failure for all successfully treated subjects was the increase in heart responsivity to neutral and alcoholic stimuli before and after treatment. Aversion therapy produced no significant differences in heart rate responding to alcoholic stimuli pre- to post.

Miller and Hersen (1972) treated a 41-year-old college-educated black male alcoholic in an inpatient setting. This subject reported a nine-year history of heavy drinking, with a consumption of one fifth of bourbon or vodka each day. His drinking had resulted in marital and employment difficulties. In this study a novel "taste test" was administered. The client was asked to rate several alcoholic and nonalcoholic beverages for seven days prior to the institution of treatment. The "taste test" was actually an indication of pretreatment drinking behavior. Treatment consisted of electrical aversive conditioning. Shocks were administered to the subject's forearm and ranged from three to four milliamps. During this procedure the subject drank a mixture of 50% bourbon and 50% water. He would take a sip of alcohol and avoid swallowing it. Shock was then administered and terminated as soon as the subject spat the alcohol and water into a pan. Results of the Miller and Hersen (1972) investigation indicated that shock was effective in suppression of this black subject's drinking of alcoholic beverages. A "taste test" conducted at a six-month follow-up revealed that the treatment gains had been maintained. The patient and his relatives also reported that the subject had been abstinent since his discharge from the hospital.

Although no cultural factors were apparently taken into account in the treatment of this patient's alcoholism, complete abstinence was achieved. While one might certainly point out that these results argue for the unimportance of cultural factors in a conditioning procedure such as aversive conditioning, it should be noted that this was an N = 1 design. Therefore, it is a rather large step to generalize these results to any particular population. Additionally, a six-month follow-up is probably too brief to determine whether treatment gains were maintained. It may be that due to lack of attention to these factors, the patient resumed drinking not long after the six-month follow-up. Nonetheless, the results of this experiment speak for themselves.

Miller, Hersen, Eisler, and Hemphill (1973) compared electrical escape conditioning to two control groups. The first control group received barely noticeable electrical shocks. The second control group received confrontation therapy. The previously mentioned "taste test" was utilized to assess the rate of drinking among the alcoholics on a pre-post basis. Results of this study revealed that all three procedures led to decreases in drinking (of about 30%) at posttest. Miller et al. concluded that effects of electrical-aversion conditioning with alcoholics may be due more to nonspecific treatment effects than to the electrical aversion conditioning itself.

COMMENTS AND IMPLICATIONS FOR BLACKS. Electrical aversion conditioning has been effective in reducing the rate of drinking in some alcoholics. However the "cure" rate is not 100% for most of the subjects in most studies. Electrical aversion offers some advantages over chemical aversion, such as better control of the aversive stimulus, fewer side effects, and ease of administration. However, results from studies employing such procedures indicate that other factors which have not been taken into account may exert a significant influence on the outcome of therapy. Several factors could influence the effectiveness of any aversive conditioning with a black alcoholic. First, how does the black patient perceive being shocked by a white clinician? If a good, trusting relationship does not exist between the patient and his white or black middle-class therapist, the patient may see the therapist as deriving some type of pleasure from the encounter. His cognitive apparatus may then link the shock he receives to the punisher rather than to the drinking behavior. One could certainly argue that the association between the shock and the alcohol would be made anyway; however, the likelihood that the patient would continue in therapy would certainly decrease, as well as the likelihood that he would be totally cooperative with the remainder of the therapeutic regime. Secondly, the bar setting in which the aversive conditioning takes place might be made more realistic by paying attention to "atmosphere" differences typically found in a black bar (such as soul music and black language). Prompting to consume more alcohol should be in both black language and standard English.

COVERT SENSITIZATION

Covert sensitization consists of the pairing of imagined appetitive stimuli with imagined aversive consequences. Cautela (1967) first described this procedure and its potential as a therapeutic technique for alcoholism. The procedure typically involves having the individual imagine preparing to engage in the target behavior, engaging in the target behavior, the introduction of an aversive stimulus, and the sensation of relief upon escaping from the setting in which the problem behavior is performed (Cautela, 1966). Nausea is typically used; however, any stimulus which is strongly aversive to the client is appropriate (Steinfeld, 1970). The client is first taught progressive relaxation techniques. When able to relax completely, he is reminded that he is unable to stop excessive drinking because it is a strong learned habit which gives a great deal of pleasure. The client is then informed that he can eliminate the habit by associating unpleasantness with alcohol.

While relaxed, the client is told to imagine or visualize clearly a glass of alcohol. When he signals, by raising his index finger, that the image is clear, he is told to visualize a sequence of events leading up to consuming the alcohol, including holding the glass, bringing it up to the lips, and having the glass touch the lips. When the client imagines this latter scene, he is told to imagine feeling sick to his stomach. Preliminary preparation is required to develop a scene which is sufficiently aversive to the client and to determine the client's ability to imagine the scene. Typically, the client is given a nauseating scene that involves vomit, wine, feces, bodily harm, or humiliation. A feeling of relief is provided in pleasurable scenes when the client turns away from or refuses the alcoholic beverage. The client is told that the feeling of nausea will go away whenever he refuses a drink.

Cautela (1970) employed a procedure to treat alcoholism involving systematic desensitization (if needed) to treat maladaptive anxiety which leads to drinking, thought-stopping to control covert responses which may be precursors to drinking, and covert sensitization. Twenty covert sensitization scenes were presented to patients during each therapy session. Ten scenes paired drinking with nausea and vomiting. The alternative scenes had the patients imagine experiencing an urge to drink, feeling mildly uncomfortable, and then deciding not to drink and losing the discomfort. Patients were then told to practice the twenty scenes at home or on the (hospital) ward twice a day. Patients were told that when an urge to take a drink was felt they were immediately to relax, shout "stop" to themselves and then imagine themselves becoming nauseated and vomit all over the drink and the host. No results were given by Cautela for this procedure. However, he referred to other studies (Ashem & Donner, 1968; Anant, 1967) as proof of the effectiveness of this strategy.

COMMENTS AND IMPLICATIONS FOR BLACKS.   Due to the paucity of research on the use of covert sensitization with alcoholics, conclusions regarding its effectiveness are difficult to make at this time. However, this strategy has been effective in the treatment of sexual disorders and is intuitively appealing for the treatment of alcoholism (Barlow, Leitenberg, & Agras, 1969; Brownell, Hayes, & Barlow, 1977). With regard to black alcoholics, we might speculate that the effectiveness of the procedure might be enhanced by giving some attention to the development of scenes which take into account the fact that the black client comes from a different culture.

As with any client, the clinician should identify those stimuli that are especially aversive to the patient. The fact that little or no attention has been given to cultural factors influencing scene aversiveness means that, quite possibly, some black and other ethnic group alcoholics may be failures of alcoholic treatment programs when they might have been successes. Future research should involve attention to factors which make the black client different and the utilization of such factors to improve the technique.

CONTROLLED DRINKING

One assumption emanating from the disease conception of alcoholism is that the subject not only has lost the ability to control his drinking but can never return to social drinking. The goal of treatment, therefore, must be total abstention. Any return to drinking most assuredly means a return to excessive consumption. Challenges to this assumption have generally been the target of much criticism by groups such as Alcoholics Anonymous and established centers for the treatment of drinking problems.

Yet, evidence remains that challenges the assumption of permanent loss of control in the disease model (Sobell and Sobell, 1973). Arguments for controlled drinking include: (a) our society reinforces a pattern of moderate drinking; (b) many alcoholics who know that total abstention would be the goal of therapy may have not entered therapy for that reason (Sobell & Sobell, 1973); (c) there are experiments which point to the efficacy of controlled drinking procedures (Cohen, Liebson, Faillace, & Speers, 1971; Mills, Sobel, & Schaefer, 1971; Schaefer, 1972; Sobell & Sobell, 1973; Sobell & Sobell, 1976).

The study by Mills *et al.* (1971) provides a good example of experiments designed to teach alcoholics to drink socially. Thirteen male subjects who had been voluntarily admitted served as subjects for the study. As with most studies, the race of the subjects was not mentioned. In a bar setting subjects were required to engage in appropriate drinking behavior (i.e., ordering mixed drinks, sipping drinks, and consuming a maximum equivalent of three fluid ounces of 86 proof liquor) or to receive painful electric shocks contingent upon maladaptive drinking behavior (beer and wine were considered to be mixed drinks). With the nine subjects who completed this study, results indicated that the procedures utilized by Mills *et al.* were effective in altering the drinking behavior of alcoholics into more socially acceptable patterns. Six-week follow-up data indicated that two of the experimental subjects and none of the subjects from a control group could be classified as social drinkers. When the categories of abstinence and social drinking were combined, the experimental group had over twice as many subjects ($N = 5$) reporting a favorable change in drinking behavior than the control group.

COMMENTS AND IMPLICATIONS FOR BLACKS. Rimm and Masters (1979), reviewing the literature, concluded that there is clear evidence that alcoholics can learn to moderate their drinking through contingent punishment techniques, or through contingent positive reinforcement and discrimination training. Social drinking approaches appear for some alcoholics to be the best choice between alcoholism and total abstinence. For the black alcoholic, as with all alcoholics, the decision to pursue a goal of social drinking is dependent upon the individual case.

The aversive conditioning portion of social drinking procedures might take into account some variables we have already mentioned. Other changes in the social drinking procedures might involve an emphasis on cultural differences in assertion training. For example, having a black alcoholic practice an assertive response of "No, no more tonight" is probably all right and will probably be effective if used. On the other hand, some other culturally biased response should be practiced by the patient as well. Such a response might be "You can sit around here getting drunk and talking trash if you want to; I've got to go and do something else." It is probably in the social drinking procedures that cultural factors play the most critical role.

COMMUNITY-BASED APPROACHES

The majority of studies referred to above have involved treating alcoholics in a hospital setting with follow-up procedures to determine if the in-hospital treatment was effective. Certainly, the fact that many alcoholics suffer from a variety of physical disorders including nutritional deficiences argues for vigorous in-hospital assessment of their physiological state. In-hospital treatment also allows for enforced abstinence, more frequent treatment sessions, and longer periods of continuous treatment.

Yet, there may be some disadvantages in the in-hospital treatment of alcoholics. Some alcoholics do manage to hold some sort of job and go to work regularly enough so that they are seen as fairly dependable employees. They may not want to take the time off from work to go into the hospital. On the other hand, they may not be able to afford in-hospital treatment unless they are veterans. The alcoholic may not want to admit to others that he has a drinking problem although he does desire help for it. Two weeks to a month away from family and friends is rather hard to explain. Therefore, some advantages of outpatient treatment for alcoholism may be: (a) the alcoholic can live at home and encounter daily life stresses, his alcoholic friends, for instance, and practice strategies designed to resolve his problems; (b) while in treatment, the alcoholic does not have to leave his friends and family for a long period of time; (c) if already working, the alcoholic can continue to work; (d) milder or early forms of alcoholism can be identified and prevented from developing further; and (e) this is probably the treatment of choice for relatively intact problem drinkers. Indeed it may be speculated that placing some problem drinkers in the hospital may be more harmful than helpful. Many more alcoholics may be reached in a community setting and assisted effectively than could possibly be helped by in-hospital treatment facilities. It is our impression that most beds in most hospitals could be filled with just alcoholics alone. Perhaps hospitals should be utilized for only the most chronic alcoholics, with significant medical problems.

An example of a behavioral community-based approach is a study conducted by Vogler, Weissbach, Compton, and Martin (1977). Eighty problem drinkers eventually served as subjects in this study. In contrast to most subjects in the other studies we have reviewed here, subjects in this study were believed to be persons whose lives were relatively intact in such areas as job, marriage, health, and self-respect. One group of subjects received the full treatment procedure consisting of videotaped self-confrontation of intoxicated behavior, alcohol education, discrimination training for blood alcohol level, aversion training for over-consumption, behavior counseling, and alternatives training. Three other groups received some of the components of the full treatment procedure. Results from this investigation indicated that 66% of the subjects (53 of 80 subjects) could be considered successes over a 12-month follow-up period as measured by reduction and/or redistribution of alcohol-intake. There were no statistically significant advantages of one combination of treatments over another.

Community-based approaches would appear to be a quite viable method for the treatment of alcoholics for the reasons alluded to above. For years groups such as Alcoholics Anonymous have utilized an out-of-hospital approach with some success. The power of the behavioral strategies and the advantages of treating an alcoholic in a community setting are intuitively appealing. For black alcoholics, treatment through this modality may offer other advantages as well. First, there is the possibility that more black alcoholics could be served in this manner than in an in-hospital setting. Although too often community mental health centers do not serve the people they are designed to serve, the potential is there. Second, because of the emphasis of community mental health programs on maintaining and treating individuals in their own environment, the recognition that cultural factors may be important in the treatment of alcoholism may be more readily understood and utilized. It remains, however, for behavior therapists employed in such mental health settings to do the research in which cultural factors are taken into account.

OTHER TECHNIQUES

It suffices to say that the number of different behavioral strategies useful or potentially useful in the treatment of problem drinking have not been exhausted here. A few other techniques will be mentioned briefly and the reader is referred to other sources for more thorough description.

Miller (1972) used behavioral contracting to treat a 44-year-old married male alcoholic. During a two-week baseline period, the subject recorded the number of alcoholic beverages he consumed daily, with his wife's corroboration. After the baseline period, a behavioral contract was arranged whereby the subject could drink three drinks at a specified time but would have to give his wife twenty dollars if he drank more than that. The wife also agreed to refrain from making critical comments about drinking and to be fined twenty dollars if she did. In addition, both partners agreed to increase positive attention toward each other contingent upon appropriate behavior (as opposed to the contingent withdrawal of positive attention along with the fines for maladaptive behavior). Results indicated that after an initial period of overdrinking (and fines), drinking remained at an acceptable level at six-month follow-up and marital relations improved.

A behavioral technique used to modify alcohol abuse is systematic desensitization (Kraft, 1967), which is consistent with a behavioral definition of alcoholism emphasizing the role that drinking plays in anxiety reduction. Still another technique is covert modeling (Cautela, Flannery, and Hanley, 1974). Cautela used this technique to treat a 48-year-old male with a 30-year history of excessive alcohol abuse. The procedure consisted of having the subject imagine himself in high-probability drinking situations and coping with those situations. The subject reported only one three-day stint of drinking during the 11 months after his hospitalization period and abstinence the rest of the time.

A more or less supportive strategy that is directly concerned with continued abstinence or controlled drinking on the part of the alcoholic is that of assertiveness training. Several studies reviewed above that used multiple component packages utilized some sort of assertive training procedure. Simply, the alcoholic practices refusing drinks (or refuses invitations to go places where he will drink). This procedure should probably be part of any adequate treatment program for alcoholics.

Stricker, Bigelow, Lawrence, and Liebson (1976) utilized a procedure consisting of abstinence and instructions, supervised drinking practice, blood alcohol concentration regulation, and part situations. To summarize briefly these phases: (a) subjects remained abstinent by taking disulfuram or being monitored by breathalyzer tests as drinking patterns were analyzed; (b) subjects practiced moderate drinking with no contingencies attached to drinking behavior; (c) subjects practiced self-regulation of intake in response to discriminated blood alcohol level concentration; (d) subjects were exposed to a part situation of long duration. Results indicated that, of three subjects, two manifested significantly decreased drinking when compared to pretreatment levels at a six-month follow-up. The third subject drank more than the other two subjects during treatment and more than they did after treatment, displaying no real change in level of drinking.

SUMMARY AND CONCLUSIONS

Even a cursory examination of the studies reviewed above reveals that little or no attention has been given to cultural differences affecting outcome. While it is important to note that subjects may have benefited from behavior change methods, few studies report that 100% of their subjects have improved and/or remained abstinent. Some of the black patients (those identified in studies and those unidentified) undergoing behavior change methods for alcoholism have benefited as well. However, one must wonder whether a more individually oriented treatment approach which takes the culture of the patient into consideration might improve the results obtained so far.

The kinds of procedures reviewed here may not need to be altered *per se* in terms of their general procedural application. The principles of learning appear to be applicable to black Americans and other ethnic groups just as they are applicable to whites. However, cultural variables probably quantitatively and/or qualitatively enhance the effectiveness of behavior therapy procedures.

RESEARCH DIRECTIONS FOR ALCOHOLISM

If the above discussion of cultural factors seems overly populated by *maybe, should,* and *could,* it is because of the scarcity of research on these factors and their possible effects on behavioral treatment strategies for alcoholism. This deficit has probably resulted from a belief that cultural factors are unimportant in the behavior modification of drinking behavior.

This line of thinking may be due to several influences. First, many studies have been concerned only with in-hospital treatment of the alcoholic, and specific factors affecting generalization have not been taken into account. Second, most studies have been conducted by white researchers who may have felt they knew all of the relevant cultural variables. Third, for a time the identification of race was unpopular and considered improperly discriminatory. All subjects were to be treated exactly the same way because there were no differences. Obviously that is not true. One must be careful not to generalize about black patients from only a few in a particular study. But a systematic compilation of factors improving the successful treatment of black patients by behavioral strategies is a legitimate thrust of behavioral research.

Future behavioral studies dealing with alcoholics should follow these guidelines:

1. An adequate description of all subject characteristics including race;
2. Attention and description of the patient's cultural milieu;
3. Use of cultural variables to improve the low cure rate of alcoholics.

OTHER DRUG ABUSE

While alcohol abuse represents the major problem of drug abuse in America, it is far from the only drug problem. The problems of narcotic, barbituate, stimulant, and hallucinogenic abuse have been with us for some time. Besides the problems that the drugs cause directly (physiological addiction, accidental drug overdose, suicide), the indirect costs of drug abuse in terms of crime and human suffering are enormous.

For years drug abuse was seen primarily as a problem of ghetto youth rather than society at large. However, since the 1960s and the adoption of hallucinogenic and other mind-altering drugs by middle- and upper-class whites, the problem is now recognized as affecting all levels of society. In addition to illicit drug use, the middle-class housewife who must have barbiturates daily is no less a drug addict than the ghetto youth who is a heroin addict.

A number of theories have been advanced concerning individuals' motivations to abuse drugs. Among them are reduction of anxiety and sensation seeking (cf. Kilpatrick, Sutker, and Smith, 1976), social conformity (Gonsuch and Butler, 1976), the opponent process theory of acquired motivation (Solomon, 1977) and reinforcement for drug seeking behavior (Wikler, 1969, 1971).

The drug abuse problem for blacks is probably due to a number of complex factors which include but are probably not limited to the aforementioned reasons.

BEHAVIORAL APPROACHES TO DRUG ABUSE

Whether physical or psychological addiction to drugs has been present, the goal of behavioral strategies has been viewed most parsimoniously as the reduction in the frequency of drug-taking behavior. Several different procedures have been utilized, including chemical and electrical aversive conditioning, covert sensitization, and behavioral contracting.

Since most of these strategies have been described above, only a brief description of each technique in relation to drug abuse will be made below. Techniques, rather than treatment of each specific type of drug abuse, will be reviewed because of space limitations. Please note that each addiction may have some idiosyncratic characteristic which might make some behavioral procedures more useful in its treatment than others.

Hardy and Cull (1973), for example, argue that black male narcotic-users seem to come from the worst conditions of the urban ghetto:

> Negro male narcotic users seem to be products of the worst conditions of the urban ghetto. Various researchers (Bates, 1968; Chambers et al, 1968; Robins and Murphy, 1967) have suggested that these conditions can be directly related to their narcotic use. The majority of black male addicts come from broken, fatherless homes, a condition which has been related to their subsequent narcotic use. Negro male addicts themselves have little success with marriage as indicated by the statistic that over half of them have experienced at least one broken marriage. Black addicts are educationally deprived. Only a little more than a third of them complete high school, a factor undoubtedly related to later drug experimentation. If such drop-outs also have delinquency records, the chances of their becoming addicted to heroin are further enhanced. Additionally, it has been found that the younger the age at which these youth experiment with drugs, the greater the possibility they will eventually become addicted to heroin. These addicts also present very poor work histories both prior to and after their initial drug use. Nearly two-thirds had never started steady employment before their drug use and of those that had, three-fourths had a mediocre work performance record. In summary, the aforementioned conditions of the ghetto undoubtedly contribute to certain Negro adolescents' subsequent use of heroin. (p. 79)

The black female addict emerges from the same deprived and deviant ghetto background. According to these authors, she usually comes from the northern ghettos. She is often the product of a broken home which was financially supported by the mother. She most frequently initiates drug use in a peer-oriented social group. Her heroin is obtained from pushers and is paid for largely with funds obtained through illegal means—chiefly the sale of drugs or prostitution.

While much has been written concerning the black heroin addict, very little can be found concerning the presumed etiology of other types of drug use for black youth. Certainly, the same ghetto pressures which contribute to the abuse of narcotics can serve as an etiological bases for other types of drug abuse as well.

Since we are dealing with a multitude of drugs and drug-related problems, we cannot explore the causes, patterns, physiological effects, and other factors associated with drug abuse in much detail. However, a few of the problems associated with drug abuse will be considered briefly. First, certain types of drug abuse, especially opiate abuse, are highly correlated with crime. Simpson, Curtis, and Butler (1975) reported that 31% of their sample of several different types of drug abusers supported themselves by illegal means and that 40% were on probation or parole or were awaiting trial proceedings. They also found that prior to entering treatment, over 60% had spent at least one month in jail, and for almost one third of those patients, the time in jail was over three years. Almost one half of the patients in this study were black. Another problem associated with drug abuse is related to increased risk of health problems and death. Heroin addicts, for example, tend to have very poor and scanty diets and thus tend to suffer from malnutrition and lowered resistance to disease (Calhoun, Acocella, and Goodstein, 1977). Heroin addicts also die from accidental overdoses and occasionally die during withdrawal. Barbiturate withdrawal without medical supervision is more dangerous than withdrawal from heroin and quite often may result in death. A third problem associated with the abuse of some drugs is clinically related significant changes in the addicted individual's behavior occurring as a result of his drug abuse. Heavy amphetamine usage, for example, results in delusions of persecution and an emotional condition similar to that seen in the paranoid schizophrenic (Bell, 1973). Sudden termination of extended high-level use of amphetamine or cocaine results in the physical and psychological symptoms of depression (Calhoun, Acocella, and Goodstein, 1977). While the problems associated with drug abuse have certainly not been discussed in an exhaustive fashion, it should be clear that drug abuse represents a clear and present danger to black and other citizens in this country.

A DEFINITION OF DRUG ABUSE

The definition of drug abuse that will be used here is one offered by the World Health Organization:

> Drug addiction is a state of periodic or chronic intoxication detrimental to the individual and to society, produced by the repeated consumption of a drug (natural or synthetic). Its characteristics include: 1) an overpowering desire or need (compulsion) to continue taking the drug and to obtain it by any means, 2) a tendency to increase the dosage, and 3) a psychic (psychological) and sometimes physical dependence on the effects of drug. (Eddy, 1965, p. 722)

This definition, while not necessarily behavioral in origin, aptly describes what most would call drug abuse. It should be noted that a large number of researchers in this field tend to separate physical addiction in which the individual needs the drug to maintain internal physiological homeostasis from psychological addiction. In psychological addiction, the individual does not need the drug to satisfy a physical need. However, it should be noted that one would find very few differences in the behavior of someone who is physically addicted to a drug and one who is psychologically addicted to a drug. In both cases, the overpowering need to have the drug would result in changes in life-styles designed to satisfy the need.

REVIEW OF THE LITERATURE

Several behavioral strategies have been employed in the treatment of drug abuse. The strategies that will be reviewed here are chemical and electrical aversive conditioning paradigms, covert sensitization, covert extinction, modeling, contingency contracting, and systematic desensitization. A number of blacks have served as subjects in studies employing these techniques, but as with the behavioral treatment of alcoholism, there has been very little in the way of utilization of cultural factors to improve the effects of treatment. Although a variety of drug addictions have been treated in the studies reviewed below, the reader should note that only those studies which have dealt with abuse of illegal drugs were included and that studies dealing with the modification of habits such as smoking (nicotine addiction) were not.

AVERSIVE CONDITIONING PROCEDURES

Aversive conditioning procedures would seem a logical behavior therapy approach to the amelioration of drug abuse. Since the properties of the drugs are highly reinforcing, it would be difficult to find a number of other reinforcers that are powerful enough to compete with the drug. Hence, the systematic application of negative reinforcers in both punishment and aversive counterconditioning paradigms is certainly intuitively appealing.

CHEMICAL METHODS.   It is interesting that one would employ one drug to treat addiction to another drug. However, whereas the use of one drug generally involves the avoidance of the noxious state of being without the drug, chemical methods involve associating the use of a drug with the relatively immediate onset of an aversive condition. If the association is made between taking a particular drug and the onset of anxiety, then the frequency of drug-taking behavior should decrease, and with this reduction the physiological and/or psychological craving should diminish over time due to nonadministration of the drug.

Raymond (1964) reported the successful treatment of a 30-year-old married woman, who for six years had been addicted to physeptone, an addictive stimulant originally prescribed for headaches. Treatment occurred in an in-patient setting. Seven minutes after being given a 1/40 gram injection of apomorphine, she was told to inject herself with physeptone (which was diluted without her knowledge over the course of treatment). Five minutes later she became nauseated. After eight days, aversion therapy was discontinued and electroconvulsive therapy instituted because of depression. She received no physeptone during this period, the length of which was not specified. When the depression improved, the client reported that she still craved physeptone and aversion therapy was resumed. This period of treatment lasted for nine days. Seven weeks later, the subject was discharged from the hospital. She was seen as an out-patient for six months. No further aversion therapy sessions occurred. Two and one half years after discharge she reported that she was drug free.

Liberman (1968) treated two heroin addicts with apomorphine aversion therapy. One patient was a 24-year-old married laborer who had used heroin since he was 16 years old and had been jailed several times for burglary. The patient terminated treatment some time after the 25th session, following an injection with saline solution instead of apomorphine. He returned to drug use and was arrested for auto theft. The other patient was a 38-year-old divorcee who had been a high-dose addict for five years. She became addicted through an attachment with a man who was addicted. She received booster sessions and supportive therapy for a one-year period, after which she was reported drug free.

COMMENTS AND IMPLICATIONS FOR BLACKS. It is not clear whether chemical conditioning procedures are effective in the treatment of drug abuse. First, there are a number of problems with chemical aversive procedure which have already been mentioned. In terms of drug abuse, this strategy has not been applied on a large scale for any of the addictions. It is possible that the procedures could be effective for such behaviors but this has not been demonstrated. Given that drug abuse has been a large problem in the ghetto for years, any technique which could prove effective should be investigated.

ELECTRICAL METHODS. Electrical aversive stimuli can be utilized either in punishment or aversive counterconditioning paradigms. The goal of treatment is to eliminate drug-taking behavior by either directly consequating the behavior or urges or altering the valence (from positive to negative) to the drug which elicits the behavior. Electrical aversion offers a number of advantages over chemical methods which have already been mentioned (e.g., strict control of onset, offset, duration, intensity).

The application of shock administered contingently upon the occurrence of urges to engage in drug-consuming behavior was used by Wolpe (1965). The client was a physician who had been addicted to Demerol for three years and had been in psychoanalysis about the same amount of time. His usual dosage was 1,000 to 1,500 mg of the drug per day. The patient was given a portable shock apparatus and instructed to shock himself when he craved an injection of Demerol. On three different occasions he gave himself 4, 3, and 2 brief shocks, which he reported as dispelling the craving. The apparatus then broke down. The client remained drug-free for 12 weeks, but resumed drug usage at a later time. He then came under the care of another psychiatrist, who did not continue the aversive procedure.

It has been assumed that if one could classically condition an aversive property to stimuli associated with a target behavior, then that behavior would decrease in frequency. This procedure is called aversive counterconditioning (Rimm & Masters, 1979). Shock has also been used to countercondition stimuli associated with the taking of drugs, (e.g., one's friends, the paraphernalia for drug use, and one's pleasurable anticipations (Lesser, 1967; Copemann, 1976). Copemann treated 13 males and 17 female black heroin addicts. The clients' drug-taking behavior was separated into three phases: a) the events leading up to the decision to consume the drug; b) the events between the time the decision was made and the drugs were available; and c) the preparation and use of the substance, including the "high." The clients were then asked to imagine the entire sequence and describe it in present tense. The result of this exercise was that the clients subjectively experienced a "high." The clients were then told that the treatment would change from feeling good about drug-taking to feeling bad. They then received 15 electrical aversive conditioning sessions, in which all three phases of drug use were counterconditioned. At a two-year follow-up, 80% of the clients were drug-free on the basis of urinalysis. This is an extremely high success rate and was attributed to the structuring of clients' expectations regarding therapy (Kanfer & Goldstein, 1976). This was manifested in showing the clients how powerful their imaginations were in making them feel "high" and explaining to them that this would be a therapeutic tool used to make drug-taking feel bad.

COMMENTS AND IMPLICATIONS FOR BLACKS.   The results of electrical aversion with drug abuse to date are inconclusive. However, the Copeman (1976) results are quite encouraging, given the high failure rate of most treatment approaches with heroin addiction. As with other addictions, this treatment has not been applied on a large scale with a number of the addictions, nor have factors related most closely to black clients been taken into account.

COVERT SENSITIZATION

Covert sensitization, as we indicated earlier, was introduced by Cautela (1966, 1967) and consists of pairing aversive images with images of the target response and the stimuli associated with it. It has been used effectively in the treatment of behavioral excesses such as drug addiction (Rimm & Masters, 1979).

Steinfeld (1970) treated two addicts individually and one group of seven addicts with covert sensitization. The specific drugs used were given only for one of the clients treated individually. This client, a 36-year-old divorced male, used alcohol, hallucinogens, amphetamines, barbiturates, and heroin. He was given four sessions of relaxation training and told that the way to eliminate his problem would be to associate the pleasurable drug with an unpleasant experience. A scene using specifics from the client's drug-taking environment was constructed. In the scene, taking drugs was followed by nausea and vomiting. This was followed by a description of feeling relieved when he left the drug-taking stimuli. This scene was imagined twice a session during two sessions a week for four weeks. At the fifth week, the client was asked to imagine a respected friend seeing him about to take heroin. This was then changed to imagining bees and wasps swarming on him as he attempted to take heroin. This scene was utilized for three weeks. The client did not return for more treatment during a five-month follow-up. The other client was a male in his mid-twenties. His treatment was similar to that for the other subjects except that covert sensitization lasted for only two weeks, at which time he checked out of the hospital. No additional information was available. No specific demographic characteristics are given for the seven clients treated with group covert sensitization. Only five of the seven addicts were still in treatment at the time the article was written. These five had received three weeks of relaxation training. A group covert sensitization scene was then constructed in which situations that made each client anxious were woven into a scene involving taking drugs. No outcome for these five clients was reported, as they were still in treatment.

One ingredient in covert sensitization is the adequate description of the covert sensitization scene. In covert sensitization, the use of cultural factors in scene content may facilitate treatment. Copemann (1977) offers an excellent example of a covert sensitization scene which makes use of the client's own language:

You're cooking up some smoking stuff you copped that day. You draw it up in the nipple, tie it up, check the spike, and stick it in your arm. You get a rise and begin to squeeze it in slowly. After it's all in, you boot a couple of times to bring on a faster rush. As the rush comes on you begin to feel nice and warm and very relaxed, and you say to yourself, "man, this feels good!" All of a sudden, you get a queasy feeling in your stomach, but you don't pay it any mind because you're digging on the high. All of a sudden, your stomach starts to churn and you break into a cold sweat with chills. You still want to dig on the high but now you're scared. Then you start foaming at the mouth. You're beginning to feel that maybe being high has something to do with the way you feel. You can still feel the high, but now you begin to puke, a stinking greenish-yellow puke, and it splatters all over the dope fiends in the room. The puke runs down your chin, all over your clothes, and you can taste the sickening taste of it in your mouth. You got a hot shot, somebody slipped you battery acid instead of dope. Now you begin to feel hot all over as your skin begins to burn up. The acid is eating away your blood vessels and the blood begins to flow in your body like boiling hot water. Then the blood starts coming through your pores, your skin, your eyes, your ears, and your mouth. The blood mixes with the puke in your mouth. By this time you're bleeding all over your body, you're like one mass of raw flesh. You try to get up, but you slip in the shit and the puke and the blood. You ask for help, but instead, your dope fiend friends take you and dump you in an alley, and leave you to die in your own misery. (p. 20)

Another important factor in treatment is to assess the individual's own fears that may be used as an aversive event. Steinfeld (1970), for example, used a client's fears of bees and wasps.

Occasionally, clients may have some difficulty imagining the scene clearly enough for it to be sufficiently aversive (Copemann, 1977). Maletsky (1974) reported a treatment method he called "assisted" covert sensitization. The client is treated within a normal covert sensitization paradigm. However, at selected times during the covert sensitization scene, the client holds a bottle of valeric acid under his nose and inhales. The smell of valeric acid is extremely nauseating and reportedly increases the aversiveness of the imagined scene. The client can carry the valeric acid into the environment and apply it to himself whenever or wherever he experiences a desire for drugs. A group receiving assisted covert sensitization improved significantly and maintained that improvement better than did a normal treatment control group. This technique would seem to be effective for two reasons: a) the application of valeric acid increases the aversiveness of the imagined scene, and b) carrying the bottle of valeric acid should serve as an additional stimulus for the application of covert sensitization in a number of different situations.

When treating clients with covert sensitization, one occasionally finds that the initial scene presentations are especially aversive, but then this aversiveness declines with repetition (Copemann, 1977). In response to this drawback, Copemann introduced hypnosis to replace relaxation in the covert sensitization paradigm. Several benefits of hypnosis were reported. The clients indicated that the scenes were more vivid and actually led to the behaviors suggested by the therapist (retching, cold sweat, etc.). Also, several trials could be presented in each session without client fatigue or loss of vividness of the image. Three successful cases were reported using hypnosis with covert sensitization.

COMMENTS AND IMPLICATIONS FOR BLACKS. Covert procedures have been successfully applied to the treatment of drug abuse problems, though not on a grand scale. This technique requires the ingenuity of the therapist in tailoring the treatment to the client, who is frequently from a lower social class and a different ethnic or racial background. The therapist should be able to use and understand the client's language and adopt his language for the aversive scene and the presentation of the rationale. The few equipment requirements and speed of treatment recommend covert procedures to social agencies that usually serve the drug abuser.

COVERT EXTINCTION

Covert extinction was introduced by Cautela (1971). The treatment is based upon operant learning principles in which responses that are not reinforced decline in frequency and are extinguished. In covert extinction, the client imagines the behaviors engaged in while taking the drug. However, he does not imagine the pleasurable effects that usually result from taking the drug. The drug-taking behavior goes unreinforced in imagination, leading to a reduction in drug-taking behavior. This procedure has been applied to amphetamine addiction (Gotestam & Melin, 1974). Four female amphetamine addicts, who maintained 100–200 mg three to five times a day, served as subjects. During the procedure the client imagined all of the consuming responses leading up to and including amphetamine injection and then imagined not receiving the reinforcing effects of the drug. Eight to fifteen trials per day were conducted for each subject. One subject was a 30-year-old woman who had taken amphetamines for eight years, for six of them intravenously. After 100 covert extinction trials, she left the hospital and injected herself with amphetamine. This produced no feeling, according to her self-report. She returned for 100 more trials and at a nine-month follow-up did not report the use of amphetamines. A second subject was a 47-year-old housewife who had used amphetamines for 18 months. She underwent the extinction treatment for 10 days, then left the hospital and injected herself with amphetamine 17 times in one week. She returned for treatment but was discharged before therapy was completed. She did not report the use of amphetamines during a nine-month follow-up period. A third subject was a 16-year-old school girl who had injected amphetamines for six months. After 12 covert extinction trials she left the hospital and injected herself three times in one day. She returned for three weeks of relaxation training and the covert extinction therapy. She did not report the use of amphetamines at nine-month follow-up. The last subject was a 27-year-old woman who had used amphetamines for seven years. After one week of treatment, she left the hospital and injected herself but reportedly did not experience a flash. She relapsed into amphetamine use after 2½ months.

COMMENTS AND IMPLICATIONS FOR BLACKS.   Covert extinction for the treatment of drug abuse is not well researched (Rimm & Masters, 1979). The four case studies above are only suggestive. The technique, however, is worthy of further investigation.

MODELING

Most simply, modeling involves exposing the client to one or more individuals actually present (live), filmed (symbolic), or even imagined who demonstrate behaviors to be adopted by the client (Bandura, 1969). Modeling may also result in the vicarious acquisition or extinction of emotional responses, as well as information regarding the nature of stimulus situations in which certain behaviors are exhibited. While the use of modeling procedures in behavior therapy is a relatively recent development (Rimm & Masters, 1979), the effectiveness of modeling procedures has been demonstrated, especially in the area of assertive training (Kazdin, 1975; Frederiksen, Jenkins, Foy, & Eisler, 1978). The major argument for its application with drug addicts may be that it is a powerful way to teach complex new behaviors.

Reeder and Kunce (1976) treated 19 male and 3 female black heroin addicts in a residential drug-abuse treatment program. The mean age was 29 years, and both voluntarily committed and incarcerated addicts served as subjects. Six problem areas which the subjects most often encountered following treatment were delineated. These problem areas were (a) accepting help from others, (b) capitalizing on street skills, (c) job interviewing, (d) employer relations, (e) free-time management, and (f) new life-style adjustment. Video tapes were made for each problem area. The model was initially pessimistic and ineffective. He then discussed the problem and attempted new solutions. Gradually the model became more independent, relying less upon the advice of others. The addicts who received the video model treatment had significantly better vocational outcomes than a comparable group, who watched video lectures on the same problem areas.

COMMENTS AND IMPLICATIONS FOR BLACKS.   Video modeling would seem to be an effective adjunct to any drug treatment program, particularly in facilitating the acquisition of interpersonal skills, in general social skills necessary for the acquisition of a job, and in teaching the drug addict to cope with stress. Cultural variables should be taken into account so that appropriate and not inappropriate behaviors for a particular individual in terms of his or her culture is modeled.

CONTINGENCY CONTRACTING

Generally speaking, contingency contracting consists of a written agreement specifying what behaviors will be engaged in and what the individual will obtain for engaging in a given behavior; Kanfer and Goldstein (1976) emphasize several basic elements in contingency contracting: (a) the clear and detailed description of the behavior required for reinforcement, (b) the specification of the criteria for termination, (c) the specification of the positive reinforcers to be used, (d) a clause for the provisions made for the aversive consequation of nonfulfillment, (e) the specification of a bonus clause, (f) the specification of the procedures for measuring results, and (g) the timing for reinforcement delivery. The basic procedure for contingency contracting in terms of drug abuse is to reinforce behaviors which are incompatible with drug-taking.

Polakow and Doctor (1973) treated a 20-year-old man and his 23-year-old wife. Both were on a three-year grant of probation for possession of marijuana. The husband had an extensive record of arrests for drug possession and sales and was the heavier drug abuser, using narcotics and marijuana each night, while the wife's drug use was minimal. A behavioral contract was arranged in which the clients were to engage in one non-drug-related activity a week (this was eventually increased to seven such activities a week). Completion of the activity resulted in a matching week off the total probationary period. The wife agreed to provide praise for verbalizations from the husband indicative of a desire to stop drug abuse, and the husband agreed to start looking for a job on a four-week contractual sequence involving development of job acquisition behaviors. Job-hunting activities were reinforced in small successive approximations. The clients were taught to negotiate their own contracts by the end of the 20th week of therapy. Results indicated that the contingency contracting procedure was successful, with the couple being dismissed from probation since no new violations or arrests had occurred for the nine-month contract period. The husband had also maintained regular employment for approximately seven months. Follow-up contacts made at 3, 6, and 12 months revealed that, although the contract was no longer in use, neither reported any instance of drug use and the husband was still employed at the same job. Neither had been arrested or was suspected of being involved in drug activities from the time they were dismissed from probation.

COMMENTS AND IMPLICATIONS FOR BLACKS.   The major advantage of behavioral contracts for black drug users is that the technique allows the clients (once certain basic principles are understood) to establish their own contracts and hence their own reinforcers, punishers, and so forth. This built-in flexibility allows the black client capable of such activity to tailor a contract to his or her own culture and thus enhance its potential for success.

SYSTEMATIC DESENSITIZATION

Systematic desensitization was introduced by Wolpe (1958). It involves the imagined exposure of the client to anxiety-arousing stimuli while the client is relaxed. It has been suggested that systematic desensitization could be used to inhibit the conditioned stimuli surrounding drug use (Droppa, 1973). In this procedure, the client would be desensitized to stimuli preceding and associated with drug use. In an interesting treatment approach, Panyard and Wolf (1974) conceptualized the fear of withdrawal from methadone as a phobia and treated their client with systematic desensitization. The initial hierarchy was changed from fear of symptoms of withdrawal to the fear of being without medication for increasing periods of time. The client was drug-free at a one-year follow-up.

COMMENTS AND IMPLICATIONS FOR BLACKS.   Attention to cultural variables in the development of scenes to be utilized in a systematic desensitization hierarchy may be important. Since the technique is predicated on the evocation of anxiety through imagery, the use of culturally specific language in scene description and the inclusion of certain culturally specific variables in scene content may evoke more anxiety than scenes without such content.

METHADONE MAINTENANCE

Methadone maintenance as a treatment for drug abuse has been practiced since the 1950s. The primary action of methadone is one of substitution, eliminating the craving for heroin and setting up a blockade to its effect so that the "highs" are not experienced should heroin be taken. It will not eliminate addiction, for methadone itself is addicting (Davison & Neale, 1978).

Methadone maintenance programs have received both positive (Dole, Nyswander, & Warner, 1968) and negative reviews (Larra, 1970; Dobbs, 1971). Positive side effects for treatment have included reduction in the administration of heroin and a reduction in criminal activity (Dale & Nyswander, 1968). However, it has been questioned whether methadone maintenance is effective for all addicts (Luria, 1970), given the high dropout rates from methadone programs. Other studies (e.g., Dobbs, 1971) have found that most of the heroin addicts continued to use heroin during methadone maintenance. Methadone maintenance programs have also been criticized in terms of merely substituting one drug for another. However, it should be noted that heroin abuse is an extremely difficult problem to treat and any legitimate treatment with some reported effectiveness should be thoroughly investigated.

SUMMARY OF DRUG ABUSE TREATMENT

Although a number of different strategies have been used successfully to treat drug abuse, only methadone maintenance has been applied on a large scale. The problems causing and maintaining drug abuse are so numerous and diverse that the programs which take the most comprehensive approach utilizing several behavioral strategies rather than any single one will probably be the most successful. It is noteworthy that in the drug abuse literature race of the subject is mentioned more often. This is not surprising, since it has long been known that a number of drug abusers, notably heroin abusers, were black and the literature has simply continued to document this fact. However, the cultural milieu in which the black or white subjects lived was generally not investigated nor taken into account in a systematic fashion to enhance the effects of treatment. More time and effort should be spent on the assessment of such cultural factors and how they might be used to increase the success rate of therapy.

General Summary and Conclusions

The behavioral literature presents many innovative treatment procedures for the treatment of alcohol and drug abuse. However, cultural factors have largely been ignored. Even when the race of the subjects is mentioned, this information was more incidental than useful. Future studies in behavior modification should take into account cultural variables and employ them systematically to enhance the effects of treatment for culturally diverse populations. In our opinion, behavior modification strategies offer the greatest promise for the treatment of alcoholism and drug abuse. However, such strategies will not reach their full potential until the full range of subject variables are explored and utilized in treatment.

REFERENCES

Anant, S. S. A note on the treatment of alcoholics by a verbal aversion technique. *Canadian Psychologist*, 1967, *1*, 19–22.

Ashem, B., & Donner, L. Covert sensitization with alcoholics: A controlled replication. *Behavior Research and Therapy*, 1968, *6*, 7–12.

Bandura, A. *Principles of Behavior Modification*. New York: Holt, Rinehart & Winston, 1969.

Barlow, D. H., Leintenberg, H. & Agrag, W. S. Experimental control of sexual deviation through manipulation of noxious scene in covert sensitization. *Journal of Abnormal Psychology*, 1969, *74*, 596–601.

Bell, D. S. The experimental reproduction of amphetamine psychosis. *Archives of General Psychiatry*, 1973, *29*, (1), 35–40.

Blake B. The application of behavior therapy to the treatment of alcoholism. *Behavior Research and Therapy*, 1965, *3*, 75–85.

Brownell, K. D., Hayes, S. C. and Barlow, D. H. Patterns of appropriate and deviant sexual arousal. The behavioral treatment of multiple sexual deviation. *Journal of Consulting and Clinical Psychology*, 1977, *45*, 1144–1155.

Brunswick, A., & Tarica, C. Drinking and health: A study of urban black adolescence. *Addictive Diseases: An International Journal*, 1974, *10*, 21–42.

Buss, A. M. *Psychopathology*, New York: Wiley, 1966.

Calhoun, J. F., Acocella, J. R. and Goodstein, L. D. *Abnormal Psychology: Current Perspectives*, New York: Random House, 1977.

Cautela, J. R. Covert extinction. *Behavior Therapy*, 1971, *2*, 192–200.

Cautela, J. R., Flannery, R., Jr. and Hanley, S. Covert modeling: An experimental test. *Behavior Therapy*, 1974, *5*, 494–502.

Cautela, J. The treatment of alcoholism by covert sensitization. *Psychotherapy: Theory, Research and Practice*, 1970, 7 86–90.

Clancy, J., Vanderhoff, E., & Campbell P. Evaluation of an aversion technique as a treatment of alcoholism: Controlled trial with succinylcholine-induced apnea. *Quarterly Journal of Studies on Alcoholism*, 1967, *28*, 476–485.

Cohen, J., Liebson, L., Faillace, A., & Speers, W. Alcoholism: Controlled drinking and incentives for abstinence. *Psychological Reports*, 1971, *28*, 575–580.

Copemann, C. Drug addiction: II. An aversive counterconditioning technique for treatment. *Psychological Reports*, 1976, *38*, 1271–1281.

Copemann, C. D. Treatment of polydrug abuse and addiction by covert sensitization: Some contraindication. *The International Journal of the Addictions*, 1977, *12*, (1) 17–23.

Dole, V. P., Nyswander, M. E., and Warner, A. Successful treatment of 750 criminal addicts. JAMA: *Journal of the American Medical Association*, 1968, *206*, (12), 2708–2711.

Davidson, R. S. Alcoholism: Experimental analysis of etiology and modification. In K. S. Calhoun, H. E. Adams, and K. M. Mitchell (Eds.), *Innovative treatment methods in psychopathology*. New York: Wiley, 1974.

Davison, C. C. And Neale, J. M. *Abnormal Psychology: An experimental clinical approach*. New York: Wiley, 1978.

Dobbs, W. Methadone treatment of heroin addicts. *Journal of the American Medical Association*, 1971, *218*, 1536–1541.

Droppa, D. Behavioral treatment of drug addiction: A review and analysis. *The International Journal of the Addictions*, 1973, *8*, 143–161.

Eddy, N. B., Halback, H., Isbell, H., & Seevas, N. H. Drug dependence. Its significance and characteristics. *WHO Bulletin*, 1965, *32*, 721–733.

Frederiksen, L. W., Jenkins, J. O., Foy, D. W., & Eisler, R. M. Social–skills training to modify abusive verbal outbursts in adults. *Journal of Applied Behavior Analysis*, 1976, *9*, 117–125.

Gorsuch, R. G. and Butler, M. C. Initial drug abuse: A review of predisposing social. Psychological factors. *Psychological Bulletin*, 1976, *83*, 120–137.

Gotestam, K., & Melin, L. Covert extinction of amphetamine addiction. *Behavior Therapy*, 1974, *5*, 90–92.

Hallam, R. Rachman, S. and Falkowski, W. Subjective, attitudinal and physiological effects of electrical aversion therapy. *Behavior Research and Therapy*, 1972, *10*, 1–13.

Hardy, R. E. and Cull, J. G. *Alcohol abuse and rehabilitation approaches*. Springfield, Ill.: Thomas, 1974.

Harper, F. D. Alcohol use among North American blacks. In Y. Israel, F. B. Glaser, H. Kalant, R. E. Popham, W. Schmidt, and R. G. Smart (Eds.), *Research advances in alcohol and drug problems* (Vol. 4), New York: Plenum, 1978.

Harper, F. D., & Dawkins, M. P. Alcohol and blacks: Survey of the periodical literature. *British Journal of the Addictions*, 1976, *71*, 29–36.

Holzinger, R., Mortimer, R., & Van Dusen, W. Aversion conditioning treatment of alcoholism. *American Journal of Psychiatry*, 1967, *124*, 246–247.

Hsu, J. Electroconditioning therapy of alcoholics: A preliminary report. *Quarterly Journal of Studies on Alcoholism*, 1965, *27*, 449–459.

Jacobson, E. *Progressive relaxation*. Chicago: University of Chicago Press, 1938.

Jellinek, E. *The Disease Concept of Alcoholism* New Haven: College and University Press, 1960.

Jones, R. L. *Black Psychology*, New York: Harper and Row, 1974.

Jones, R. L. *Black Psychology*, New York: Harper and Row, 1979.

Kanfer, F. H. and Goldstein, A. P. *Helping People and Change: a textbook of methods*. New York: Pergamon Press, 1975.

Kraft. T. Alcoholism treated by desensitization *Research and Therapy*, 1967, *5*, 69–70.

Kazdin, A. E. Covert modeling, imagery assessment, and assertive behavior. *Journal of Consulting and Clinical Psychology*, 1975, *43*, 716–724.

Lemere, F., & Voegtlin, W. An evaluation of aversive treatment of alcoholism. *Quarterly Journal of Studies on Alcoholism*, 1950, *11*, 199–204.

Lesser, E. Behavior therapy with a narcotic user: A case report. *Behavior Research and Therapy*, 1967, *5*, 251–252.

Lunde, S., & Vogler, R. Generalization of results in studies of aversive conditioning with alcoholics. *Behaviour Research and Therapy*, 1970, *8*, 313–314.

Luria, D. *Overcoming drugs: Program of action*. New York: McGraw-Hill, 1970.

McCance, C., & McCance, P. F. Alcoholism in North-East Scotland: Its treatment and outcome. *British Journal of Psychiatry*, 1969, *115*, 189–198.

MacCulloch, M. J., Feldman, M. P., Oxford, J. F., & MacCulloch, M. L. Anticipatory avoidance learning in the treatment of alcoholism: A record of therapeutic failure. *Behaviour Research and Therapy*, 1966, *4*, 187–196.

Maddox, G., & Allen, B. A comparative study of social definitions of alcohol and its uses among selected male negro and white undergraduates. *Quarterly Journal of Study on Alcoholism*, 1961, *22*, 418–427.

Madill, M., Campbell, D., Laverty, S., Sanderson, R., & Vanderwater, S. Aversion treatment of alcoholics of succinyl-chlorine–induced apneic paralysis. *Quarterly Journal of Studies on Alcoholism*, 1966, *27*, 483–509.

Maletzky, B. Assisted covert sensitization for drug abuse. *The International Journal of the Addictions*, 1974, *9*, 411–429.

Miller, E. C., Duorak, A., & Turner, P. W. A method of creating aversion to alcohol by reflex conditioning in a group setting. *Quarterly Journal of Studies on Alcohol*, 1960, *21*, 424–431.

Miller, P. The use of behavioral contracting in the treatment of alcoholism: A case report. *Behavior Therapy*, 1972, *3*, 593–596.

Miller, P., & Hersen, M. Quantitative changes in alcohol consumption as a function of electrical aversion conditioning. *Journal of Clinical Psychology,* 1972, *28,* 590–593.

Miller, P., Hersen, M., Eisler, R., & Hemphill, D. Electrical aversion therapy with alcoholics: An analogue study. *Behaviour Research and Therapy,* 1973, *11,* 491–497.

Mills, K., Sobell, M., & Schaefer, H. Training social drinking as an alternative to abstinence for alcoholics. *Behavior Therapy,* 1971, *25,* 18–27.

Mownen, O. M. Learning theory and the symbolic processes. New York, Wiley, 1960.

Panyard, C., & Wolf, K. The use of systematic desensitization in an outpatient drug treatment center. *Psychotherapy: Theory, Research and Practice,* 1974, *11,* 329–330.

Polakow, R., & Doctor, R. Treatment of marijuana and barbiturate dependency by contingency contracting. *Journal of Behavior Therapy and Experimental Psychiatry,* 1973, *4,* 375–377.

Quinn, J., & Henbest, R. Partial failure of generalization in alcoholics following aversion therapy. *Quarterly Journal of Studies on Alcoholism,* 1967, *28,* 70–75.

Rathod, N. M., Gregory, E., Blows, D., & Theodore, G. H. A two-year follow-up study of alcoholic patients. *British Journal of Psychiatry, 112,* 683–692.

Raymond, M. The treatment of addiction by aversion conditioning with apomorphine. *Behaviour Research and Therapy,* 1964, *1,* 287–291.

Reeder, C., & Kunce, J. Modeling techniques, drug abstinence behavior, and heroin addicts: A pilot study. *Journal of Counseling Psychology,* 1976, *23,* 560–562.

Rimm, D. C., & Masters, J. C. *Behavior Therapy: Technique and empirical findings.* New York: Academic Press, 1974.

Rimm, D. C., & Masters, J. G. Behavior therapy: *Techniques and empirical findings (2nd Ed.),* New York: Academic Press, 1979.

Schaffer, H. Twelve-month follow-up of behaviorally trained ex-alcoholic social drinkers. *Behavior Therapy,* 1972, *3,* 286–289.

Shanahan, W. M., & Hornick, E. J. Aversion treatment of alcoholism. *Hawaii Medical Journal,* 1946, *6,* 19–21.

Simpson, D. Curtis, B., and Butler, M. Description of drug users in treatment: 1971–1972. DARP admission. *American Journal of Drug and Alcohol Abuse,* 1975, *2,* 15–28.

Sobell, M., & Sobell, L. Individual behavior therapy for alcoholics. *Behavior Therapy,* 1973, *4,* 49–72.

Sobell, M., & Sobell, L. Second year treatment outcome of alcoholics treated by individualized behavior therapy: Results. *Behaviour Research and Therapy,* 1976, *14,* 195–215.

Solomon, R. C. Punishment. *American Psychologist,* 1964, *19,* 239–253.

Solomon, R. C. An opponent-process theory of acquired motivation: The affective dynamics of addiction. In J. D. Moser and M. E. P. Seligman (Eds.) *Psychopathology: Experimental models.* San Francisco: W. H. Freeman, 1977.

Steinfeld, G. The use of covert sensitization with institutionalized narcotic addicts. *The International Journal of the Addictions,* 1970, *5,* 232–235.

Storm, T. and Smart, R. G. Dissociation: A possible explanation of some feature of alcoholism, and implication for its treatment. *Quarterly Journal of Studies on Alcoholism,* 1965, *26,* 111–115.

Strickter, D., Bigelow, G., Lawrence, C., & Liebson, I. Moderate drinking as an alternative to alcohol abuse: A non-aversive procedure. *Behaviour Research and Therapy,* 1976, *14,* 279–288.

Viamontes, J. A., & Powell, B. J. Demographic characteristics of black and white male alcoholics. *The International Journal of the Addictions,* 1974, *9,* 489–494.

Vitols, M. M. Culture patterns of drinking in negro and white alcoholics. *Diseases of the Nervous System,* 1968, *29,* 291–394.

Voegtlin, W. L., & Broz, W. R. The conditioned reflex treatment of chronic alcoholism: An analysis of 3125 admissions over a period of ten and a half years. *Annals of Internal Medicine*, 1949, *30*, 480–597.

Voegtlin, W. L., Lemere, F., Broz, W. R., & O'Hollaren, R. Conditioned reflex therapy of chronic alcoholism IV: A preliminary report on the value of reinforcement. *Quarterly Journal of Studies on Alcoholism*, 1941, *2*, 505–511.

Vogler, R., Lunde, S., Johnson, G., & Martin, P. Electrical aversion conditioning with chronic alcoholics. *Journal of Consulting and Clinical Psychology*, 1970, *34*, 302–307.

Wilson, G., & Davison, G. Aversion techniques in behavior therapy: Some theoretical and metatheoretical considerations. *Journal of Consulting and Clinical Psychology*, 1969, *33*, 327–329.

Wilson, G., Leaf, R., Nathan, P. The aversive control of excessive alcohol consumption by chronic alcoholics in the laboratory setting. *Journal of Applied Behavior Analysis*, 1975, *8*, 13–26.

Wolpe, J. Conditioned inhibition of craving in drug addiction: A pilot experiment. *Behaviour Research and Therapy*, 1965, *2*, 285–288.

Wolpe, J. *Psychotherapy by reciprocal inhibition.* Stanford: Stanford University Press, 1958.

Wikley, A. Conditioning factors in opiate addiction and relapse. In I. M. Wilson and G. C. Kasselbaum (Eds.) *Narcotics.* New York: McGraw-Hill, 1965.

Wikler, A. Some implication of conditioning theory for problems of drug abuse. *Behavioral Science*, 1971, *16*, 92–97.

11

Sexual Disorders

CAROLYN M. TUCKER

INTRODUCTION

The "sexual revolution" which American society is experiencing has not only resulted in more liberal sexual attitudes and behaviors but also in more open discussion and concern about sexual disorders. It is increasingly acceptable in recent years to acknowledge disorders that inhibit or disrupt enjoyment of new sexual freedoms. Behavioral researchers and clinicians have been foremost in developing approaches for successful treatment of sexual disorders and thus in popularizing sex research (Kaplan, 1974; Lobitz & LoPiccolo, 1972; Masters & Johnson, 1970; Obler, 1973).

Contrary to myths about the super-sexuality of blacks, they too experience sexual disorders. However, the incidence, prevalence, and specific nature of these disorders have not been determined as they have been among whites. The recent seeking of therapy for a variety of sexual disorders by blacks in Los Angeles and in other urban areas evidence the existence of sexual concerns among blacks and their need to have these concerns addressed. Yet, treatment of sexual disorders among blacks remains a relatively unresearched area (Wyatt, Strayer, & Lobitz, 1976).

IDENTIFICATION OF SEXUAL DISORDERS

Sexual disorders include both sexual dysfunctions and sexual deviations or variations. Sexual dysfunctions are disruptions in the sexual response cycle which obstruct optimum enjoyment of the sexual experience. Such dysfunctions make sexual intercourse impossible or very unsatisfactory. In males the common sexual dysfunctions are premature ejaculation, primary and secondary impotence, and ejaculatory incompetence. Common female sexual dysfunctions include primary and se-

CAROLYN M. TUCKER ● Department of Psychology, University of Florida, Gainesville, Florida 32611.

condary orgasmic dysfunction, vaginismus, and dyspareunia. The sexual dysfunctions are usually psychological and can be overcome or much improved with therapy. The new sex therapies have been specifically designed to treat these types of sexual disorders (Kaplan, 1974; Masters & Johnson, 1970).

Identification of the sexual deviations is not as easy as specifying the dysfunctions. This is because of the willingness of too many people to label any sexual activity that deviates from their own behavior as deviant or perverted. Yet, sexual practices and ethics vary within and between cultures (McCary, 1978). Thus, normal sexual behaviors exist in every culture that would be considered deviant by another culture. However, there is agreement across American cultures that certain sexual behaviors are indeed deviant or perverted. The more common among these are sadism, masochism, exhibitionism, voyeurism, transvestism, fetishism, pedophilia, and homosexuality (McCary, 1978). The identifying characteristic of these widely recognized sexual deviances is that they occur with low frequency in the population (Ullmann & Krasner, 1975). Homosexuality, however, is becoming an exception in that it is recently being viewed as an alternative, healthy, sexual life-style that is accepted by a minority. As with dysfunctions, behavior therapists have demonstrated effective treatment of sexual deviances through the use of several behavioral strategies including aversion conditioning procedures (Barlow & Agras, 1973; Brownell & Barlow, 1976; Curran & Gilbert, 1975; Green, Newman, & Stoller, 1972; Marks & Gelder, 1967; Obler, 1973; Rachman & Teasdale, 1969).

PREVALENCE OF SEXUAL DISORDERS: A SPECIAL FOCUS ON BLACKS

Psychiatrists, psychologists, and social workers report that as many as 75% of their patients have sexual problems (Wiener, 1969). Masters and Johnson (1970) estimated that one out of every two marriages is a sexual disaster area.

Information about sexual dysfunctions among blacks in particular is limited. Rainwater (1966), in one of the few sex research studies including a significant number of blacks, found that 14% of middle-class women, 31% of upper-lower-class women, and 54% of lower-lower-class women have negative feelings toward sex or reject it. Athanasiou, Shaver, and Tavris (1970) reported similar findings and concluded that sexual dissatisfaction becomes increasingly prevalent as level of social class declines. Since blacks are concentrated in the lower social classes, it is implied that sexual dysfunctions and dissatisfactions are quite prevalent among blacks.

Very little is known about sexual deviance among blacks. However, it is because their culture is prone to deviance from middle-class values. Among the hypotheses about deviance among blacks are that (1) there are more black than white male homosexuals due to lack of male role models in female-headed households, (2) blacks are more likely to be bisexual than exclusively homosexual, (3) black lesbians are increasing in number due to a shortage of black males, and (4) homosexuality and other sexual deviations occur less frequently among blacks than among whites because of strong group sanctions against it in black communities. Unfortunately, no research evidence exists to support these hypotheses (Staples, 1971).

Research data concerning sexual dysfunctions and sexual deviations among whites are available (Masters & Johnson, 1970; McCary, 1978). The absence of such data on blacks can be understood in part by looking at the type of individuals who seek sex therapy from research programs. Masters and Johnson (1970) report that 53.5 percent of their sex therapy clients had a history of prior or continuing exposure to psychotherapy and that one or both partners, in 17.5% of their client couples, had medical training. The social structuring of their clinical research group has been middle class. It thus appears that therapy experience, desensitization to medical professionals, and financial stability are conducive to seeking needed sex counseling in a therapy research program. These motivating conditions do not exist for the majority of black Americans, who tend not to get involved in sex therapy or research. Consequently, numerous unsubstantiated assumptions about sexual disorders among blacks are rampant.

SEXUAL DYSFUNCTIONS

GENERAL CAUSATIVE FACTORS

Sexual dysfunctions may be caused by physical conditions or illnesses, psychological stressors, or some combination of both. Physical causes are rare but include such conditions as diabetes, prostatic surgery, drug and alcohol abuse, aging, lumbar disc disease, neurological diseases, fatigue, and stress. The psychological stressors linked to sexual dysfunctions are: (1) past anxiety-producing teachings about sex (e.g., that sex is sinful and painful), (2) traumatic experiences such as rape, (3) relationship problems (e.g., loss of love), (4) limited sexual communication and/or sex education, (5) lack of interpersonal relationship skills, (6) sexual identity problems, and (7) performance anxiety from inexperience, low self-esteem, or personal insecurity. In some cases, the psychological stress involved in a sexual dysfunction is a reaction to a physical condition which may or may not actually be a causal factor in the dysfunction. For example, impotence may be due to performance anxiety resulting from loss of an arm or from awareness of lumbar disc problems that may actually cause impotence. The latter example is one of a sexual dysfunction being caused by a combination of physical and psychological factors.

When the primary cause of a sexual dysfunction is not physical, learning theorists assert that it is usually the result of some combination of performance-related anxiety, the lack of social skills, not having a sexually reinforcing partner, and/or ignorance of the physiology of sexual functioning (Kaplan, 1974; Masters & Johnson, 1970; O'Leary & Wilson, 1975). Additionally, religious orthodoxy and negative sexual conditioning during the formative years are responsible for a significant percent of sexual dysfunctions (Lehrman, 1970). A single sexual failure can lead to future failure, and fear of future failure often becomes a self-fulfilling prophecy (McCary, 1978). These identified causes of sexual dysfunctions have led to the frequent use of direct behavioral treatment strategies. These include structured learning of some new, non-anxiety-producing sexual behaviors, social skills training, sex education, and facilitation of sexual and nonsexual communication between partners (Lobitz & LoPiccolo, 1973; Masters & Johnson, 1970; O'Leary & Wilson, 1975).

HISTORICAL, CULTURAL, AND SOCIOECONOMIC FACTORS IN SEXUAL DYSFUNCTIONS OF BLACKS

The sexual behavior, attitudes, and values of blacks and any other racial group may only be understood by studying them in relation to the social and cultural past where their shaping began (Frazier, 1966). That past for black Americans was an enslaved one, in which sex was the major instrument of power and status among black males and premarital sex was the forced norm among black women (Bernard, 1966). Sex and religion were not closely linked to each other (Johnson, 1941). However, the American culture into which blacks have had to assimilate instead values monetary and social status, virginity, and adherence to religious teaching about sex.

The antagonistic sexual values of the white majority are believed to have contributed to feelings of guilt and anxiety among some black women about sex. It has also been hypothesized that many black males have experienced demasculinization and feelings of inadequacy as a result of the relatively low importance white Americans attach to sexual adequacy as a measure of masculinity (Staples, 1973).

Stereotypes and myths about black sexuality have seemingly contributed to sexual dysfunctions among blacks by creating unrealistic norms and performance standards for them. For example, the myth that black men and women do not require sexual foreplay before intercourse (Wyatt *et al.*, 1976) is a basis for orgasmic dysfunction among black women. Lack of foreplay decreases the probability of arousal necessary for orgasm. Blacks do not differ from whites in the need to experience the excitement phase (which involves foreplay) of the physiological sexual response cycle.

Some myths about black sexuality seem to have negatively influenced the sexual functioning of whites as well as blacks. The myth that black males have huge penises has made penis size a source of performance anxiety among males (Wyatt *et al.*, 1976), which is sometimes causal in male sexual dysfunctions (Kaplan, 1974). Research comparing penile size of black and white males, however, revealed no significant difference in the length of the erect penis regardless of race (Bell, 1968). This finding and other facts have been used by behavior therapists to facilitate sex therapy success.

Other common sexual myths about blacks include the belief that black males are naturally sensual lovers. Acceptance of this myth may inhibit sexual communication and teaching among partners. Initiation of different kinds of sexual activities to keep sex exciting may also be subject to inhibition by a myth—that black women can only be satisfied through intercourse. Couples focus on orgasm through intercourse and do not engage in activities which produce satisfying orgams for many women even more easily than intercourse (i.e., masturbation and oral sex) (LoPicollo & Lobitz, 1973).

Stereotypes about blacks have been detrimental to their sexual functioning. These stereotypes are often unquestioned generalizations based on a single case study (Rosen & Frank, 1962; Shane, 1960; Vontress, 1970). These generalizations, however, become norms against which many blacks compare themselves. When their sexual experiences differ from these norms, blacks are likely to feel inadequate. For example, the popular press stereotypes the black woman as sexually aggressive with unrestrained sexual urges. Yet, many black women are restrained and traditional in sexual expression (Staples, 1972). Unawareness of the variance among black women could cause a black female to experience needless stress about her normality which could in fact lead to a dysfunction.

Certain conditions of black relationships today are also probable factors in the development of sexual dysfunctions among partners. The competition for a black male creates a situation in which a black woman allows sexual exploitation resulting in guilt and frustration which can inhibit her sexual responsiveness (Staples, 1972). The problematic sexual functioning of some black males seems to be due, in part, to feelings of lessened power and masculinity in relation to their more assertive and independent black female partners. Black males do not have available to them social, economic, and political power, as do their white counterparts, to make them feel masculine (Derbyshire, 1967).

A clearly influential factor in the occurrence of sexual dysfunctions among blacks is the low socioeconomic status environment in which most of them are reared. Poverty conditions often encourage sexual experimentation before sexual maturity. Knowledge about sex tends to come from the peer group and thus is often inaccurate or incomplete. Coital contact often takes place in uncomfortable conditions (e.g., a bedroom shared with the children) or anxiety-producing conditions (e.g., parked cars, the girl's house) because of overcrowding or the need to be secretive. Contraceptives are frequently not used, thus creating a fear of pregnancy. It should be noted, however, that fear, anxiety, and inaccurate sexual information are repeatedly identified factors in sexual dysfunctions regardless of race (Kaplan, 1974; Lobitz & LoPiccolo, 1972; Masters & Johnson, 1970; McCary, 1978).

GENERAL TREATMENT APPROACHES

Treatment of sexual dysfunctions generally aims to help a person or couple overcome difficulties that obstruct natural sexual functioning. The prognosis for such treatment has been unfavorable until the development of programs using various behavioral strategies and techniques (Coleman, 1964; Hastings, 1967). Masters and Johnson (1970) developed the first of such programs. It is a multifaceted treatment package incorporating many fundamental behavioral principles. Emphasis is on both teaching clients new behaviors that are important for sexual functioning, and correction of irrational attitudes and beliefs. The treatment approach is directive and many of the treatment procedures are amplifications of the general anxiety-reduction approach common to behavior therapy. There is frequent utilization of informed instruction and referral to non-moralistic and authoritative literature. Such practices are necessary elements of behavior therapy. Other major treatment programs have followed the Masters and Johnson approach (Kaplan, 1974; Lobitz & LoPiccolo, 1972; LoPiccolo & Lobitz, 1973).

All of these major sex therapies follow the behavioral model which emphasizes the individual's conscious control of his own behavior and minimizes the role of the unconscious. The most salient dynamics exist between the therapist(s) and client(s). The therapist's role is based on the technician/educator model rather than on the analytic model (Wyatt et al., 1976).

The behavioral model employs behavioral techniques based on the principles of learning (e.g., reinforcement and conditioning principles). Behavior therapists, like learning theorists, view sexual symptoms as learned behaviors. Thus, sex therapy usually involves assessment of symptoms to be modified in terms of their reinforcement or extinction contingencies and then formulation of treatment plans accordingly. Strategies are used (1) to remove reinforcers of the sexual symptom in order to punish undesired sexual responses and (2) to extinguish the fear impairing desired sexual responses. Antagonistic sexual responses to the destructive ones are taught and reinforced (Kaplan, 1974).

The popular sex therapies for treatment of sexual dysfunctions differ from traditional psychotherapeutic treatments in which the emphasis is on verbal therapy within the office setting. The new therapies actually fit well into a behavioral framework, even though this is not acknowledged by some of their proponents (e.g., Kaplan, 1974; Masters & Johnson, 1970). Like the more traditional behavior therapies, the new sex therapies are action-oriented, incorporating significant others (e.g., husbands, wives) in home-based treatment procedures. The therapist functions much as a coach in teaching partners to reinforce each other's desirable behavior and to extinguish sexually inappropriate responses. It is the couple who actually does the work for problem resolution.

General features of the major sex therapy approaches include frequent use of dual-sex co-therapists, ongoing assessment, and assignment of homework activities that are highly structured, graduated, and geared toward extinction of performance anxiety. Identification of sexual likes and dislikes through sensual body exploration (sensate focus) and communication and resolution of personal and relationship problems effecting sexual adequacy are usually included as sex therapy goals.

In the following section the causes and more specific features of treatment for each of the common sexual dysfunctions will be discussed briefly. The sexual dysfunction identification, treatment approaches, and success rates of Masters and Johnson (1970) were chosen for discussion because they have provided the most dramatic demonstration of the efficacy of direct behavioral treatment of sexual problems having a psychological basis. The other major behavioral treatment approaches not discussed are variations of those developed by these researchers.

MALE SEXUAL DYSFUNCTIONS

PREMATURE EJACULATION

Premature ejaculation is the inability to delay ejaculation long enough for an orgasmic woman to experience orgasm 50% of the time of intercourse (Masters & Johnson, 1970). It is often the result of hurried sex and performance anxiety, but it may result from infrequent sex due to the withdrawal method of birth control. Treatment involves a procedure called the "squeeze technique" which involves the woman's manually stimulating the penis to full erection and then, just prior to ejaculation, firmly squeezing the penis on each side of the coronal ridge using the thumb and first two fingers of the same hand. The pressure stops the urge to ejaculate. The squeeze procedure is repeated after about 30 seconds. The progression then moves from the woman straddling the man and inserting his penis into her vagina while remaining motionless, to gradually building up to vigorous pelvic thrusting. If at any time the urge for quick ejaculation occurs, the woman elevates her body, repeats the squeeze technique, and then reinserts the penis. Fairly quickly the goal of intercourse for fifteen minutes or longer is reached. About 98% of treated cases using this procedure in the Masters and Johnson program were successful at a five-year follow-up.

IMPOTENCE

Two types of impotence are described by Masters and Johnson. One type is primary impotence, which means that a man has never had an erection in a sexual encounter with a female. The other is secondary impotence, which means that a man has successfully engaged in intercourse on at least one occasion but at present does not have this capacity. Impotence often results from traumatic failures at initial attempts at intercourse, homosexual interests, restrictive religious beliefs, an extremely passive or aggressive female partner, and premature ejaculation. Treatment focuses first on relationship adjustment, education geared to correcting faulty attitudes and misconceptions about sex, and dispelling religion-related guilt. Then the couple practices sensate focus exercises (body touching for pleasure) until an erection spontaneously occurs. Next, the female partner employs the "teasing technique," in which she manipulates the penis to erection, and then relaxes with her male partner until the erection disappears. This is repeated several times to extinguish the man's fear of losing an erection and not getting it back during the sexual encounter. The woman then facilitates nondemanding intromission followed by more vigorous thrusting until orgasm occurs involuntarily. Of the primary impotent males treated, 59.4% regained sexual functioning, which was maintained at a five-year follow-up. Of the secondary impotent males followed in the same study, 73.8% were successfully treated, but 11% had remitted to erectile inadequacy at follow-up.

EJACULATORY INCOMPETENCE

Ejaculatory incompetence is the inability to ejaculate intravaginally. It usually is associated with painful intercourse, infidelity of partner, being caught masturbating, and fear of the partner's pregnancy. Therapy is similar to that for impotence, with emphasis on first achieving ejaculation by the female's manual stimulation, gradually leading up to orgasm during vaginal intercourse. Focusing away from ejaculation is stressed. Ejaculatory incompetence is rare, but treatment has been quite successful. Masters and Johnson restored ejaculatory ability, which was maintained at five-year follow-up, in 82.4% of 17 treated cases.

FEMALE SEXUAL DYSFUNCTIONS

ORGASMIC DYSFUNCTION

Orgasmic difficulties are the most common female sexual dysfunctions. Masters and Johnson (1970) have identified two types of orgasmic dysfunctions—primary and secondary. A primary orgasmic dysfunction is a condition in which a woman has never experienced orgasm. A secondary or situational orgasmic dysfunction is a condition in which a woman experiences orgasm but only in very limited circumstances (e.g., through masturbation but not during intercourse). The most common causes of orgasmic dysfunctions are religious prohibitions, negative feelings toward one's mate, and being married to a sexually inadequate man. Treatment involves helping the female to develop positive feelings toward her partner and to become aware of what is sexually arousing for her. The female then teaches her partner how to stimulate her. Next, the couple proceeds to intercourse in which the woman assumes the superior position and is in control of the rate and type of thrusting. Kaplan (1974) suggests additional manual stimulation of the clitoris while the penis is inserted. Orgasmic dysfunctioning was overcome by 80.3% of the women whom Masters and Johnson treated. These effects were maintained at a five-year follow-up.

As part of a program modeled after that of Masters and Johnson, Lobitz and LoPiccolo (1972) incorporated some additional techniques and reported their treatment outcome for 13 cases of primary orgasmic dysfunction to be 100% successful. One of these additional techniques involves having the woman play the role of experiencing an orgasm to overcome embarrassment about sexual expression. In primary orgasmic dysfunction cases, a graduated masturbation program is employed in which the woman is taught how to masturbate to orgasm and then teaches her partner how to do this through observing her masturbation.

VAGINISMUS

Masters and Johnson define vaginismus as an involuntary tightening or spasm of the outer third of the vagina such that the penis cannot enter it. This condition often develops following experiences of rape, painful intercourse, or being taught that first coital experiences are painful. Vaginismus is treated by having the male partner insert progressively larger dilators into the vagina. An IN VIVO desensitization procedure under the woman's guidance is used until the woman can comfortably accommodate fairly prolonged insertion. Treatment outcome with this procedure was 100% successful. The effects of this treatment were maintained at a five-year follow-up.

DYSPAREUNIA

Dyspareunia is a condition in which intercourse is painful. It sometimes occurs in men but more often occurs in women. In men, it is usually the result of congestion in the prostate, seminal vesicles, or ejaculatory ducts. Eighty-five percent of the cases of dyspareunia in women have a physical cause such as lesions or scar tissue. In other cases, its inception is often in tension, fear, or anxiety over initial sexual intercourse. Poor lubrication due to lack of arousal is also a common factor contributing to the occurrence of this dysfunction. When there is no physical basis for the pain, treatment involves discrediting myths about intercourse and relaxation training. Relationship counseling is conducted in cases where poor lubrication is due to lack of interest in the sexual partner. Specific outcome data for this dysfunction are not reported by the major sex therapy programs, probably because of the few cases which are psychological in origin.

Behavioral Intervention Strategies Uniquely Important in Sexual Dysfunction Counseling with Blacks

STRATEGY I: ALLEVIATION OF THE COUPLE'S ANXIETY ABOUT THERAPY AND THE THERAPIST

The anxiety that blacks have about therapy is often the result of a lack of information about what therapy generally involves and the stigmatization of professional counseling by many in the black community. Anticipation of difficulty in relating to a white therapist or middle-class black therapist with whom they cannot identify also generates much anxiety about seeking help for a problem (Grantham, 1973). This anxiety interferes with concentration on problem resolution and establishment of a trusting, comfortable client–therapist relationship which is important for candid discussion of one's personal sex life.

A discussion of the client's feelings about being in therapy, during which the therapist anticipates some probable feelings of discomfort for the client, will help to overcome therapy anxiety (Adams, 1970; Vontress, 1970). In this discussion, it is important for the therapist to be empathetic, concerned about the client's feelings, and expressive of his own feelings about working with them. He should point out to the client that seeking professional help for personal problems is common, normal, and healthy. The therapist should also assure clients that therapy sessions will not be discussed with others without their written consent. This assurance is particularly important for blacks in view of possible ridicule from community members and friends who may have misconceptions about the need for psychological counseling.

STRATEGY II: ALLEVIATION OF THE CLIENT'S EMBARRASSMENT ABOUT HAVING A SEXUAL PROBLEM

Because of poverty and a poor education, many blacks have little chance of achieving the high social status, monetary stability, and power which are valued in the American culture. To achieve a sense of power and status, many blacks try to live up to myths about their lovemaking skills (Bernard, 1966). They thus tend to have high expectations of themselves and their partners with regard to sexual performance. They take pride in and feel powerful from being able to execute a pleasurable, satisfying, sexual experience (Dye, 1975). A loss or lack of this ability may cause embarrassment, low self-esteem, withdrawal from partner, and limited discussion of sex. Consequently, sex therapy is further complicated.

Alleviation of black clients' embarrassment about a sexual problem mainly involves making them aware of the existence of sexual dissatisfactions and dysfunctions among blacks just as they exist among whites. Disclosure by the therapist about a close friend's or relative's having experienced a similar sexual problem is also effective (O'Leary & Wilson, 1975). This should, however, only occur after the therapist has established credibility with his clients. Simply addressing the client's embarrassment and acknowledging an understanding of it may also help to make the client feel less embarrassed. A somewhat informal conversational style and tone by the therapist, along with use of some of the client's colloquialisms, may also facilitate the client's comfort (Vontress, 1970).

STRATEGY III: MODIFICATION OF PROBLEMATIC SEXUAL ATTITUDES BASED ON MYTHS, MISCONCEPTIONS, AND STEREOTYPES

The belief that oral sex is nasty, that men are supposed to be the aggressors during sex, that sex only means intercourse, and many other such attitudes often contribute to sexual dissatisfaction among blacks (Rainwater, 1966). These attitudes may result in sex being routine, boring, and often a responsibility rather than a pleasure. Consequently, sex becomes dissatisfying for one or both partners, and sexual dysfunction often occurs. For example, the female may be inorgasmic because she does not initiate and aggressively participate in those sexual behaviors that generate sexual arousal and orgasm for her.

Careful assessment of attitudes toward different sexual behaviors throughout therapy is crucial in sexual counseling with blacks. Disruptive attitudes should be explored with the clients by the therapist, who must be careful not to make the clients defensive. It is important for the therapist to show interest in understanding client's attitudes and then to provide information conducive to attitude change. This information should be presented as something to think about that will hopefully change their attitudes. The objective is to motivate rather than force clients to change disruptive sexual attitudes. This nonauthoritarian empathic approach is especially important in counseling blacks, because they are likely to resent any demand to alter a sexual belief system which has contributed to positive self-esteem (Wyatt *et al.*, 1976).

STRATEGY IV: FACILITATION OF THE FEMALE'S AND ESPECIALLY THE
MALE'S EXPRESSION OF LOVING, NEUTRAL, AND NEGATIVE FEELINGS

It is quite typical to find very little expression of feelings within the
relationship among black couples who seek counseling for sexual problems. The black male tends to be less communicative about feelings than
black female partners (Balswick & Peek, 1971; Horowitz, 1977). This is
probably a function of the supermasculine identity society has ascribed
to the former, which does not allow the disclosure of vulnerability that
is often revealed along with feelings. Because enjoyable sex is usually
dependent upon communication of sexual likes and dislikes as well as
caring and complementary feelings, such communication is a target area
in counseling blacks with sexual problems. Their lack of practice neces-
sitates much role-play involving expression of loving and possession of
neutral and negative feelings. Daily homework assignments in expressing
a positive feeling(s) to the partner facilitates the regeneration of roman-
tic, caring feelings which tend to be instrumental to the resolution of
sexual problems (Kaplan, 1974). A distinction between a feeling and a
compliment must be drawn for the clients via role-play and feedback
about emotional expressiveness. It is important to warn clients that,
initially, expressing feelings to each other will seem mechanical and
maybe silly, but will become natural and enjoyable over time. The importance of postively acknowledging feelings expressed should also be
stressed. The therapist can be instrumental in helping clients become
comfortable in expressing and acknowledging feelings by praising this
behavior. Reinforcement of the less verbal partner's expression of feelings by the more verbal partner is also helpful.

Because expression of negative feelings may lead to relational dis-
cord, the therapist should train the couple in using problem-solving and
fair fighting techniques. The importance of conflict resolution should
be stressed as crucial to an emotional set conducive to enjoyable sex.

STRATEGY V: CONSISTENT BOOSTING OF THE MALE'S SELF-ESTEEM
THROUGHOUT THERAPY

Because many black males' self-esteem and pride are closely related
to their perceived sexual competence, experiencing sexual problems is
likely to threaten their sense of self and masculinity (Staples, 1971).
Consequently, black male clients with sexual problems often tend to be
resistant, defensive, and much less cooperative than female partners.
Thus, it is important for the therapist to be nondemanding and very

supportive of them for successful execution of homework exercises. The views of black male clients about therapy direction should particularly be sought and respected.

Discussion of the fact that having a sexual problem does not render one less masculine may be particularly helpful in boosting the black male client's self-esteem. Honest acknowledgment of his physical and personality attributes at appropriate times throughout therapy may also be helpful. Positive self-esteem can be conducive to making the attitudinal and behavioral changes which sex therapy involves.

SEXUAL DEVIANCE

COMMON DEVIANT SEXUAL BEHAVIOR IN AMERICAN SOCIETY

Homosexuality is the deviant behavior which has been of most interest to behavior therapists (O'Leary & Wilson, 1975). In recent years, there has been much controversy as to whether homosexuality is clearly opposite from "normal" heterosexuality. The heart of the controversy concerns whether homosexuality is just a variation of sexuality, which itself is on a continuum, having degrees of heterosexuality and homosexuality as earlier suggested by Kinsey, Pomeroy, Martin, and Gebhard (1953). Despite the controversy, homosexuality is usually defined as a sexual preference for members of one's own sex and is found across all socioeconomic classes and races. It and the other clearly perceived sexual deviances are punishable by fines and arrests in most places in the United States. However, this does not occur often; few homosexuals are identifiable because their public behavior and dress are usually consistent with their gender (O'Leary & Wilson, 1975). Thus, it is impossible to assess the exact prevalence of homosexuality.

Kinsey *et al.* (1953) reported that about two thirds of all males have a homosexual experience in childhood (prior to age 15) and that 13% of all females have at least one homosexual experience to orgasm in adulthood. About 2% of all males and slightly less than 1% of all females in their sample were exclusively homosexual. Approximately 63% of the males and 87% of the females were exclusively heterosexual. Hunt (1974) reported that approximately 20% to 25% of males have an overt homosexual experience in adulthood, as do about 10% of married women and 20% of single women. Hyde (1979) concluded on the basis of Hunt's and Kinsey's research that approximately 75% of men and 85% of women are exclusively heterosexual and that approximately 2% of men and slightly less than 1% of women are exclusively homosexual. The remaining 25% of men and 15% of women have had varying amounts of both heterosexual and homosexual experience.

It is important to note that Kinsey's sample included a total of 5,300 males and 5,940 females, who were interviewed for detailed sex histories. Though some blacks were interviewed, only interview findings of whites were published. His sample was not representative, but rather arbitrarily selected. There was an overrepresentation of college students, young people, well-educated people, Protestants, people living in cities, and people living in Indiana and the Northeast. To compensate for his sampling inadequacies, Kinsey used statistical methods to correct his sample so that it would agree with the United States Census.

Hunt's sample consisted of 982 males and 1,044 females; 90% were white, and 10% were black; 71% were married, 25% had never been married, and 4% had previously been married but were not married at that time. In terms of such characteristics as age, education, occupation, and urban-rural background, the sample was fairly similar to the American population aged 18 and over. Data were obtained via 2,000 questionnaire responses and 200 in-depth interviews. To obtain the sample, names were randomly selected from telephone directories of 24 cities throughout the United States. Selected persons were called and asked to participate in a panel discussion on American sexual behavior. Twenty percent of the selected sample agreed to participate in the research that was carried out in 1972.

In view of the sampling limitations (particularly in Kinsey's study), the generality of these findings is open to question, particularly as it relates to blacks and other minority populations. Gay liberation, which is gaining for homosexuality more tolerance or acceptance, is causing more and more homosexuals to reveal their sexual preference. A more accurate estimate of prevalance should be possible in the future.

Sadism and masochism are clearly defined as dichotomous sexual deviances. Sadism is the achievement of sexual pleasure through inflicting physical and/or psychological pain on a sexual partner. In contrast, masochism is the achievement of sexual gratification from being hurt, physically or mentally, by a sexual partner or oneself. It is important to note that sadists and masochists do not consistently find experiencing pain and giving pain sexually satisfying. Pain is arousing only as a part of some type of ritualistic behavior (Hyde, 1979). Hunt (1974) reported that 5% of the males and 2% of the females in his sample had engaged in sadistic behavior and that 2.5% of the males and 4.6% of the females had experienced masochistic behavior. The rate of deviance for both found among men and women under age 35 was double that for those over age 35 and five times greater among single men than among married men.

Kinsey *et al.* (1953) found that about 10% of males and 3% of females reported definite or frequent arousal responses to sadomasochistic stories. He also found that 26% of females and the same percentage of males had experienced definite or frequent erotic responses as a result of being bitten during sexual activity. According to Hyde (1979), sadistic and masochistic fantasies appeared to be considerably more common than real-life sadism and masochism. He also stated that there are more masochists than sadists. However, Hyde gave no basis for these conclusions.

Exhibitionism is a sexual deviance in which sexual gratification is obtained from public display of genitals, usually to members of the opposite sex. It is considered common in that it is involved in 35% of all arrests for sexual violations (Allen, 1961). Exhibitionism is far more common among men than women. Fifty percent of arrested exhibitionists had exhibited themselves repeatedly and thus are referred to as compulsive exhibitionists. Most of the other exhibitionists who have been arrested were either mentally deficient or drunk. In addition, most of them appeared to have had difficulty establishing social and sexual relationships (Hyde, 1979). Exhibitionism occurs mostly in the summer months and usually out-of-doors, in secluded places. Frequently, the exhibitionist displays his penis from the bedroom window of a house while he is cross-dressed (Randell, 1976). In a survey by Randell (1976), it was found that 60% of accused male exhibitionists were single and that those who were married often had marital problems. He concluded from all of his findings that the exhibitionist is typically a normal male and that exhibitionism occurs in younger males beginning at puberty and reaching a peak in late adolescence or early adult manhood.

Voyeurism, in contrast to exhibitionism, is a deviant behavior that is engaged in secretly with the hope of not being seen. It is the act of viewing sexual acts or other erotic stimuli to receive sexual pleasure. The viewing usually involves "Peeping Tom" behavior whereby the privacy of others is invaded. The viewing is consistently preferred to petting or intercourse, and it is often compulsive. About 89% of voyeurs are males. Viewing sexual acts and nudity for sexual pleasure is only considered deviant or abnormal when such acts replace sexual intercourse or when a crime is committed such as breaking and entering to observe others (Hyde, 1979). Voyeurs may use mirrors or periscopes to spy on their victims. They also sometimes cross-dress to gain access to women's bathrooms and other places where women gather. A common variation of voyeurism is scotophilia which involves observing sexual acts and the genitals (Randell, 1976). Voyeurs are generally not dangerous, but those who enter the confines of a building or other structure to view their victim, or make it known to their subject that she is being watched, are potentially dangerous (Yalom, 1960). The voyeur is noted to be typically shy, sexually inadequate, and unable to establish satisfying heterosexual relationships (Gebhard, Gagnon, Pomeroy & Christenson, 1965).

Transvestism and fetishism are somewhat related sexual deviances. The former involves obtaining sexual or emotional excitement or gratification from wearing the clothes of someone who is of the opposite sex. The latter involves obtaining excitement from clothes or other items of the opposite sex. Fetishism may also involve deriving sexual excitement from inanimate objects or from focusing on a particular part of the body. Estimates of transvestism vary because of the secrecy with which transvestites indulge in their cross-dressing behavior (Brown, 1961). The ease of keeping fetishes private also makes estimates of their prevalence difficult to determine. However, it has been estimated that more than a million males in the United States engage in transvestism, if all instances of men getting at least temporary arousal from wearing female clothing are counted (Pomeroy, 1975). The vast majority of transvestites are heterosexuals and most are married and have children (Prince & Butler, 1972).

Pedophilia is a very common form of sexual deviance in which one derives sexual pleasure from some form of child molestation. The types of molestation vary, as evidenced in a study by Jaffe (1976), who found that 85% of child molestation cases involved such behavior as indecent exposure, genital manipulation, obscene language, and physical advances. Vaginal intercourse, anal penetration, and rape were involved in the other cases. Approximately 30% of all sex offenders are pedophiles and are males between 30 and 40 years of age (Ellis & Bruncale, 1956). Their victims are usually family friends, relatives, or acquaintances and involve both male children and female children. There is a high incidence of psychotics, alcoholics, and asocial and mentally deficient persons among those who practice pedophilia (McCaghy, 1971).

Kinsey et al. (1953) found that 24% of the women in his sample had been approached between the ages of 4 and 13 by males at least 5 years older than they were. These males had attempted to make various types of sexual contacts. Twenty to twenty-five percent of middle-class and 33% to 40% of lower-class female children had experienced some molesting (Hyde, 1979). In a survey of 1,800 university students, 35% of the women and 30% of the men reported having had childhood experiences with sexual deviants (J.T. Landis, cited by McCaghy, 1971).

Transsexualism is the desire to become a member of the opposite sex. A transsexual believes that he or she is trapped in the body of the wrong gender. Transsexualism is a problem of gender identity, not of sexual behavior (Hyde, 1979). Most of these men and women seek sex change operations to make their sex organs consistent with their felt gender identity. Others manage to change their gender role without medical or social help.

Fear of being ridiculed frequently forces transsexuals not to reveal their orientation. Thus, the incidence of transsexualism is unknown and only those who come for a sex operation provide any kind of statistical information. It has been estimated that there are 30,000 male transsexuals in the United States (Randall, 1976). Male transsexuals outnumber female transsexuals, three to one (Green, 1975).

SEXUAL BEHAVIOR PERCEIVED AS DEVIANT AMONG MANY BLACKS

Lower-class black Americans have not been allowed to participate fully socially, economically, or politically in the mainstream of American culture. Thus, it is reasonable that they do not fully adhere to the middle-class sexual or nonsexual values of the American majority (Derbyshire, 1967). Several sexual practices generally accepted or engaged in by the majority of nonblacks are practiced infrequently, negatively perceived, and/or totally rejected as deviant by blacks. The particular sexual behaviors not fully accepted by blacks reflect their different traditions, values, and past experiences.

Masturbation and oral sex are two sexual practices which many blacks consider deviant sexual behaviors but which white Americans in general do not consider abnormal. In a study conducted by Staples (1972), these two sexual practices and homosexuality were reported by black women as being abnormal or repulsive. Whites, however, often substitute masturbation and oral sex for coitus (Bell, 1968). The Kinsey Institute reported that coital orgasm was the first source of orgasm for less than 1% of white females, but it was the first source of orgasm for more than a third of the black females interviewed (Kinsey, 1953). The traditional importance of performing intercourse and having children to affirm one's masculinity has made coitus the norm in the black culture and has made noncoital sex deviant or less frequently practiced among blacks than whites. However, middle-class blacks are likely to be similar to the majority of Americans in their practice of oral sex and other sexual behaviors because of their assimilation into the broader American culture.

Group sex is another sexual practice regularly or occasionally engaged in by middle-and upper-class Americans that is considered deviant by blacks. The rejection of group sex among blacks may derive from the fact that the black man does not want his wife to be promiscuous even though he may be willing to have different sex partners (Staples, 1971).

The expense of group sex parties or marathons is another factor that has probably kept this practice out of poor and black communities. Sexual practices to which one is not exposed are often labeled deviant (Krasner, 1969).

FORMULATION OF SEXUAL DEVIANCE WITHIN THE BEHAVIORAL MODEL

The behavioral model holds that all behavior is the product of learning and cultural influences. It postulates that gender and sex role behavior is learned and that man is shaped by his environment and experiences into being heterosexual, homosexual, or any one of the sexual variations. Sexual deviances are thus considered to be learned sexual behaviors.

The behavioral model does not define certain sexual behaviors as normal and others as abnormal or deviant. Behaviorists simply recognize that certain sexual behaviors occur with low frequency, are rarely sanctioned by society, and often prompt individuals to seek therapy (O'Leary & Wilson, 1975). The behavioral model provides a system of learning principles addressing the acquisition, development, and maintenance of sexual behavior. From these principles, intervention procedures are developed for modification of learned sexual behavior which an individual seeks to change. The behavioral model is not a system of ethics dictating which behaviors are acceptable and which should be changed (Bandura, 1969). The formulation of sexually deviant behavior within the behavioral model is no different from the formulation of normal sexual behavior (Ullman and Krasner, 1975). All sexual behaviors are the product of learning and conditioning, just as is the case with other types of behavior (Kinsey, 1953). The greater prevalence of some sexual behaviors, which society thus labels normal, is assumed by several adherants of the behavioral model to be due to the exposure of a majority of people to similar learning processes (Simon & Gagnon, 1970; Ullman & Krasner, 1975; Wilson & Davison, 1974).

Learning of sexual deviance has been demonstrated experimentally. For example, Rachman (1966) induced a mild fetish in a male using classical conditioning. He showed that penile erection resulting from exposure to slides of nude females could be produced by repeatedly pairing the picture of women's boots with the nude slides. Eventually, seeing the boots alone became sexually arousing and thus became a fetish. Similar studies have been done by McConaghy (1970) and Wood and Obrist (1968).

On the basis of naturalistic and clinical studies, Bandura (1969) reported indications of sexually deviant behavior being learned as a result of modeling and reinforcement of deviant behavior by parents.

Similarly, Stoller (1967) found in a study of transvestites that they had been initiated into transvestism by wives and mothers and heavily reinforced for dressing in feminine clothes. Thus, as predicted by behaviorists, it appears that one's early experiences and environment strongly influence one's sexual as well as nonsexual behavior.

BEHAVIORAL TREATMENT OF SEXUAL DEVIANCE

Behavioral approaches to sexual deviance have been more successful and popular than traditional psychotherapy in the treatment of sexual disorders (Bancroft, 1974; Barlow, 1973; Barlow & Abel, 1976; Marks, 1976). Behavioral intervention has recently focused on the modification of sexual behavior in the direction of choice requested by the client seeking a change in his sexual orientation. Treatment involves behavioral evaluation in all areas of sexual functioning and intervention in one or more of these areas. There are four such areas—sexual arousal, sexual responsiveness, heterosexual interactions, and gender role identity (Brownell & Barlow, 1980). Thus, treatment intervention may involve (1) extinction of deviant sexual arousal, (2) removal of deficiencies in appropriate sexual arousal, (3) improvement of heterosexual skills, and/or (4) alleviation of gender role deviation. Treatment in all areas of sexual functioning in which there are difficulties is extremely important. Failure to assess and treat problems in any one area could make the sexual deviation more problematic (Brownell & Barlow, 1980). Thus, treatment often involves the use of several intervention techniques.

Extinction of deviant arousal through the use of aversion therapy has been the most widely used approach in the treatment of sexual deviation. The general approach involves immediately administering an aversive stimulus (e.g., electric shock, pharmacologically created nausea, covert imagery, shame) in association with deviant sexual behavior or arousal from a deviant sexual fantasy. Such aversive conditioning has resulted in extinction of a deviant behavior as well as parallel attitude change such that deviant sexual stimuli lose their arousal eliciting value (Evans, 1970; Feldman & MacCulloch, 1971; McGuire & Vallance, 1964; Rachman & Teasdale, 1969). Feldman and MacCulloch (1971), using electrical aversion in the treatment of homosexual behavior, report improvement in 60% of their aversion conditioning subjects, whereas only 20% of their subjects treated by traditional psychotherapy improved. Electrical aversion has statistically yielded the best treatment results of all the aversive conditioning procedures.

According to Brownell and Barlow (1980), removal of deficiencies in heterosexual arousal as a treatment for sexual deviance has primarily involved one or more of the following techniques: (1) aversion relief in which presentation of a deviant stimulus is followed by an electric shock, the termination of which is paired with a heterosexual stimulus (Larson, 1970; McConaghy, 1969; Thorpe, Schmidt, Brown, & Castell, 1964); (2) systematic desensitization involving anxiety reduction during exposure to a series of imagined sexual situations that are increasingly more fearful (Bancroft, 1970; Obler, 1973); (3) orgasmic reconditioning involving masturbation to deviant imagery with substitution of a heterosexual image just prior to ejaculation (Marquis, 1970; Marshall, 1973; Wilson, 1973); (4) fading, pairing, and exposure which involve direct visual presentation of heterosexual stimuli in an effort to enhance heterosexual responsiveness (Barlow & Agras, 1973; Beech, Watts, & Poole, 1971; Herman, Barlow, & Argas, 1974).

The techniques to remedy a deficiency in heterosexual arousal have had little success in producing treatment effects. Barlow (1973) concluded from his review of these techniques that there is no evidence that aversion relief increases heterosexual responsiveness. In addition, he found little evidence that systematic desensitization increases heterosexual responsiveness. The usefulness of orgasmic reconditioning has not been reliably evaluated with controlled research. The treatment techniques involving direct visual presentation of heterosexual stimuli have been demonstrated to increase heterosexual arousal, but the scarcity of controlled research with these techniques makes their usefulness difficult to evaluate.

Behavioral treatment approaches to improve heterosexual skills have focused on reduction of interpersonal anxiety through systematic desensitization, and social skills training (Brownell & Barlow, 1980). Case studies have shown increased heterosexual responsiveness with the use of social skills training as a part of a broader treatment program in the treatment of male homosexuals (Hanson & Adesso, 1972) and a female homosexual (Blitch and Haynes, 1972). Stevenson and Wolpe (1960) increased heterosexual behavior and decreased deviant behavior in three subjects by assertiveness training. The lack of controlled studies employing techniques to improve heterosexual skills to modify sexually deviant behavior makes it difficult to assess their effectiveness as independent treatment procedures. However, such techniques seem to be useful and necessary from studies reporting that subjects have been unable to respond behaviorally to newly acquired sexual arousal due to a lack of social skills (Annon, 1974; Barlow and Agras, 1973; Herman, et al., 1974).

As we previously stated, treatment of sexual deviance may involve alleviation of gender identity deviation. Gender role deviation is a condition often labeled transsexualism in which opposite sex role behaviors are present and are preferred (Brownell & Barlow, 1980). Other than among transsexuals, opposite sex role behaviors occur among effeminate homosexuals and transvestites. Successful treatment to alter gender role identity to be consistent with biological genetic sex has until recent years involved surgically refitting the secondary sex characteristics in harmony with the preferred gender identity (Money & Erhardt, 1972; Stoller, 1968, 1969). More recent alternative treatments have involved behavior therapy. Rekers and Lovaas (1974) demonstrated reinforcement control over pronounced feminine behaviors in a male four-year-old child who was manifesting "childhood cross-gender identity." Masculine behaviors were reinforced and feminine behaviors were extinguished by using social reinforcement in the clinic and a token reinforcement procedure in the home. Follow-up data three years after treatment began suggested that sex-typed behaviors had normalized. Successful behavioral intervention in the treatment of gender identity deviation has also been reported by Barlow, Reynolds, and Agras (1973). They treated a 17-year-old transsexual male using a multifaceted approach involving teaching of masculine behaviors through modeling and videotape feedback, social skills training, use of the fading technique to increase heterosexual arousal (Barlow & Agras, 1973), and a combination of covert sensitization and electrical aversion to eliminate deviant arousal. In a follow-up study by Barlow, Abel, and Blanchard (1979), it was reported that after 6½ years appropriate gender identity was maintained in this case. These authors also reported two replications of their treatment package intervention which resulted in alleviation of transsexual identities but practice of homosexual life-styles. These findings should give impetus to more behavioral research in the area of sexual deviance in general and transsexualism in particular. Such research is especially important in view of the facts that not everyone is satisfied with surgery and that some tragic outcomes have been noted (Hore, Nicolle, & Calnan, 1975).

In addition to each of the treatment approaches and techniques discussed, several variables are important in the behavioral treatment of sexual deviance. These include conducting a thorough behavioral assessment of relevant variables, supportiveness from family members, maintaining a client/therapist relationship conducive to disclosure and cooperation by the patient, a comfortable treatment setting, and a strong desire for and commitment to sexual behavior change (Brownell & Barlow, 1980). The latter is particularly important and is facilitated by having the client formulate the therapy goal. If the therapist's own sex preference or morals interfere with the client's choice of sexual life style (e.g., to be an adjusted homosexual), then the client should be referred to another therapist who can counsel the client objectively (Feldman & McCullough, 1971).

When the therapy for sexual deviance involves a black client, two of the treatment procedures discussed may be inappropriate or at least difficult to implement with the client. These procedures are aversion therapy and orgasmic reconditioning. The use of aversion therapy in treating black sexual deviants may be inappropriate in view of the distrust of white therapists and the apprehensions that many black clients have about therapy (Bernard, 1972). Willingness to subject one's self to shock or nausea-evoking pharmaceuticals and acceptance of the rationale for aversive treatment methods require trust of the therapist and respect for his judgment.

Perhaps using aversive imagery as the aversive conditioning stimulus would be more appropriate than shock or nauseating drugs in aversion therapy with black clients. This technique, which is referred to as covert sensitization, was successfully used by Barlow, Leitenberg, and Agras (1969) in the treatment of one homosexual and one pedophile. Treatment involved pairing deviant images with noxious scenes of nausea and vomiting. Four homosexuals were treated in a similar manner by Barlow, Agras, Leitenberg, Callahan, and Moore (1972). Brownell and Barlow (1976) found covert sensitization to be useful in the treatment of multiple sexual deviations. Thus, covert sensitization seems to be an effective alternative to painful electrical aversion and nauseating chemical aversion. In fact, Callahan and Leitenberg (1973) found covert sensitization to be just as effective as electrical aversion in decreasing objectively measured deviant sexual arousal of two exhibitionists, one transvestite, two homosexuals, and one homosexual pedophile. On subjective measures of sexual arousal, covert sensitization was superior to electrical aversion. The additional facts that covert sensitization requires no expensive apparatus and can be self-administered seem to make it more useful and acceptable to black clients than other aversion procedures.

The use of orgasmic reconditioning may not be a treatment procedure of choice in working with black sexual deviants simply because it involves masturbation, which blacks often consider deviant behavior (Staples, 1972). However, for those blacks who do not perceive masturbation negatively and those who can be influenced to masturbate without guilt, this procedure may be a desirable treatment alternative. Since orgasmic reconditioning may be executed in the privacy and security of one's home, it seems quite appropriate for use with the black client who is already reluctant, anxious, and/or suspicious of therapy. Orgasmic reconditioning and other alternatives to widely used aversive conditioning, especially electrical aversion, should always be considered as treatment strategies in working with any sexually deviant client (Wilson & Davison, 1974).

POSITIVE ASPECTS OF BEHAVIORAL INTERVENTION FOR BLACKS WITH SEXUAL DISORDERS

The behavioral approach to sexual disorders appears to be especially suitable for black populations who generally need action-oriented counseling (Gunnings & Simpkins, 1972). Behavioral counseling for sexual dysfunctions employs sexual tasks to be performed by the couple at home. It involves couples in planning activities to improve their communication and relationship. The clients apply suggested behavioral techniques and share their feelings with each other. The therapist provides information about tools for problem resolution, but the clients themselves use the tools and actually resolve the problems. Thus, behavioral sexual dysfunction counseling allows the clients to feel adequate and positive about working out their own problems. The therapist only coaches in the problem resolution process (Wyatt et al., 1976).

The emphasis on short-term, immediate behavioral goals using the method of successive approximation approach is a particularly positive feature of behavioral sexual dysfunction therapy with blacks. It allows immediate observable changes that facilitate the credibility of the therapist, and it assures the client of the relevance and potential benefit of therapy. Such skepticism is frequently present in black clients.

The short-term nature of behavior therapy for both sexual dysfunctions and deviations makes it more appealing to blacks who may not be willing to commit themselves to an indefinite expenditure of time and money that analytic therapy modes often entail. The frequent use of cotherapy teams in behavioral treatment of sexual disorders is also advantageous in working with blacks because there is a need for such clients to have someone with whom they are able to identify. This is important because differences between the therapist and the black client create pessimism in the latter about the therapist's ability to understand him (Carkhuff & Pierce, 1967). Having a therapist of the same sex decreases these differences and thus is likely to facilitate a more positive attitude about therapy.

CONSIDERATIONS IN MAKING SEX THERAPY AVAILABLE TO BLACKS

One of the major considerations in making sex therapy available to black populations is that availability of counseling is not sufficient to generate many black clients. Black males are particularly likely to be reluctant to seek sex counseling, since sexual adequacy is stereotypically a source of strength; acknowledgment of a sexual inadequacy would expose a weakness to their white rivals, especially white male therapists (Wyatt *et al.*, 1976). Thus, sexual dysfunctions are often unexposed.

Studies have consistently shown that physicians who ask patients specifically about their sexual adjustment uncover far more sex problems than physicians who do not make inquiries in this area (Pauly & Goldstein, 1970). Psychiatrists, psychologists, and social workers report that as many as 75% of their patients have sexual problems which require help (Wiener, 1969).

The absence of blacks among sex therapy clientele must not be quickly misinterpreted to mean that they do not have sexual problems as myths about blacks might suggest. In training sex therapists, strong consideration should be given to the fact that being black does not naturally make the therapist better prepared to work with black clients. If the white therapist's training has not adequately prepared him for sex counseling with blacks, then the black therapist trained in the same white-oriented programs may find himself just as inadequately equipped (Bell, 1971; Grier & Cobbs, 1968; Griffith, 1972; Jones & Jones, 1970). This is especially likely when the therapist is from a middle-class background and the client is of low socioeconomic status. Thus, the black therapist must not be deluded into thinking that he can automatically make the transition from textbook cases to real life. For example, he may find that distrust of mental health professionals is not necessarily cast aside when the therapist is black (Griffith, 1977).

When the therapist is black, there is also danger that his assessment of the black client's problem will not be questioned. In addition, there is the possibility of the black therapist overly focusing on the black client's feelings about his blackness, poverty, and militance since the therapist strongly identifies with these feelings (Wyatt *et al.*, 1976).

Black and white therapists alike should consider the fact that existing paper-and-pencil sexual and marital adjustment assessment tests (e.g., the Sexual Interaction Inventory, LoPiccolo & Steger, 1974; the Locke–Wallace Marital Adjustment Inventory, Locke, 1959) may be inappropriate for blacks because they were not a representative sample in the standardization group. In addition, many low-income blacks may have reading and writing difficulties that make assignments requiring these skills impossible to execute as well as degrading and anxiety-producing. In making sexual counseling available to blacks, consideration must also be given to the fact that much of the sex information that the therapist is given to disseminate to clients may be inaccurate in reference to black populations. The absence of normative data handicaps black and white professionals who attempt to help sexually dysfunctioning black couples through reeducation (Wyatt *et al.*, 1976).

IMPLICATIONS FOR FUTURE TREATMENT
AND RESEARCH

Sexual counseling with black clients requires some additional strategies and approaches to those now used in sex therapy developed by white professionals for white clients. The development of sex therapy and research programs involving black client–subjects and black therapists and professionals involved in research about black relationships, families, and culture in general are needed. It is important that these programs focus on (1) training black and white sex therapists in counseling blacks; (2) acquiring normative data on sexual and marital adjustment of blacks; (3) development of written, verbal, and behavioral assessment measures appropriate for use in sex therapy with blacks; and (4) systematic outcome research comparing black, white, and interracial therapy teams.

Past reluctance of blacks to involve themselves in ongoing sex research and treatment programs suggests the need to actively encourage their participation in these programs. Facilitation of a positive attitude among blacks toward counseling is essential. Informing blacks of the occurrence of sexual problems among blacks and making treatment accessible and affordable would also be significant steps. Active recruitment of black clients and sex research participants is of paramount importance. Training of medical doctors and ministers in black communities to inquire appropriately about sexual problems in black families and to serve as referral agents for sex therapy and research programs seems possible.

Perhaps the most important implication of what is known about sexual disorders among blacks is that sex education is needed in both black and white schools and communities to dispel myths and stereotypes about black sexuality. Focus on sexual enrichment and prevention of sexual disorders is certainly a most important direction for professionals in the area of human sexuality.

REFERENCES

Adams, P. L. Dealing with racism in bi-racial psychiatry. *Journal of the American Academy of Child Psychiatry*, 1970, *9*, 33–43.

Allen, C. Perversions, sexual. In A. Ellis and A. Abarbanel (Eds.), *The Encyclopedia of Sexual Behavior* (Vol. 2). New York: Hawthorne Books, 1961.

Annon, J. S. *The behavioral treatment of sexual problems: Vol 1, Brief therapy*. Honolulu: Enabling Systems, 1974.

Athanasiou, R., Shaver, P., & Tavris, C. Sex. *Psychology Today*, 1970, *4*, 37–42.

Balswick, J. O., & Peek, C. W. The inexpressive mate: A tragedy of American society. *Family Coordinator*, 1971, *29*, 363–368.

Bancroft, J. A comparative study of aversion and desensitization in the treatment of homosexuality. In L. E. Burns, and J. L. Worsley (Eds.), *Behavior Therapy in the 1970's*. Bristol: John Wright, 1970.

Bancroft, J. H. *Deviant sexual behavior*. Oxford: Oxford University Press, 1974.

Bandura, A. *Principles of Behavior Modification*. New York: Holt, 1969.

Barlow, D. H. Increasing heterosexual responsiveness in the treatment of sexual deviation. *Behavior Therapy*, 1973, *4*, 655–671.

Barlow, D. H., & Abel, G. G. Recent developments in assessment and treatment of sexual deviation. In W. E. Craighead, A. E. Kazdin, and M. H. Mahoney (Eds.), *Behavior modification: Principles, issues, and applications*. Boston: Houghton Mifflin, 1976.

Barlow, D. H., & Agras, W. S. Fading to increase heterosexual responsiveness in homosexuals. *Journal of Applied Behavior Analysis*, 1973, *6*, 355–366.

Barlow, D. H., Abel, G. G., & Blanchard, E. B. Gender identity change in transsexuals. *Archives of General Psychiatry*, 1979, *36*, 1001–1007.

Barlow, D. H., Agras, W. S., Leitenberg, H., Callahan, E. J., & Moore, R. C. The contribution of therapeutic instructions to covert sensitization. *Behavior Research and Therapy*, 1972, *10*, 411–415.

Barlow, D. H., Leitenberg, H., & Agras, W. S. The experimental control of sexual deviation through manipulation of the noxious scenes in covert sensitization. *Journal of Abnormal Psychology*, 1969, *74*, 596–601.

Barlow, D. H., Reynolds, E. J., & Agras, W. S. Gender identity change in a transsexual. *Archives of General Psychiatry*, 1973, *28*, 569–576.

Beech, H. R., Watts, F., & Poole, A. D. Classical conditioning of sexual deviation: A preliminary note. *Behavior Therapy*, 1971, *2*, 400–402.

Bell, A. Black sexuality: Fact and fancy. Paper presented in *Focus: Black America Series*, Indiana University, Bloomington, Indiana, 1968.

Bell, R. L. The culturally deprived psychologist. *Counseling Psychology*, 1971, *2*, 104–107.

Bernard, J. Marital stability and patterns of status variables. *Journal of Marriage and the Family*, 1966, *28*, 421–439.

Bernard, V. W. Interracial practice in the midst of change. *American Journal of Psychiatry*, 1972, *128*, 92–98.

Blitch, J. W., & Haynes, S. N. Multiple behavioral techniques in a case of female homosexuality. *Journal of Behavior Therapy and Experimental Psychiatry*, 1972, *3*, 319–322.

Brown, D. C. Transvestism and sex-role inversion. In A. Ellis and A. Abarbanel (Eds.), *The encyclopedia of sexual behavior*. New York: Hawthorne Books, 1961.

Brownell, K., & Barlow, D. H. Measurement and treatment of two sexual deviations in one person. *Journal of Behavior Therapy and Experimental Psychiatry*, 1976, *7*, 349–354.

Brownell, K. D., & Barlow, D. H. The behavior treatment of sexual deviation. In E. Foa and A. Goldstein (Eds.), *The handbook of behavioral interventions*. New York: Wiley, 1980.

Callahan, E. A., & Leitenberg, H. Aversion therapy for sexual deviation: Contingent shock and covert sensitization. *Journal of Abnormal Psychology*, 1973, *81*, 60–73.

Carkhuff, R. R., & Pierce, R. Differential effects of therapist race and social class upon patient depth of self-exploration in the initial clinical interview. *Journal of Consulting Psychology*, 1967, *31*, 632–634.

Coleman, J. C. *Abnormal psychology and modern life*. Chicago: Scott, Foresman, 1964.

Curran, J. P., & Gilbert, F. S. A test of the relative effectiveness of a systematic desensitization program and interpersonal skills training with date anxious subjects. *Behavior Therapy*, 1975, *6*, 510–521.

Derbyshire, R. L. The uncompleted Negro family: Suggested research into the hypotheses regarding the effect of the Negro's outcast conditions upon his own and other American sexual attitudes and behavior. *Journal of Human Relations*, 1967, *15*, 458–468.

Dye, T. R. *Power and society: An introduction to the social sciences.* North Scituate, Mass.: Duxborg Press, 1975.

Ellis, A., and Bruncale, R. *The Psychology of Sex Offenders.* Springfield, Ill.: Charles C Thomas, 1956.

Evans, D. R. Subjective variables and treatment effects in aversive therapy. *Behaviour Research and Therapy*, 1970, *8*, 147–152.

Feldman, M. P., & MacCulloch, M. J. *Homosexual behavior: Therapy and assessment.* New York: Pergamon, 1971.

Frazier, E. F. *The Negro family in the United States.* Chicago: The University of Chicago Press, 1966.

Gebhard, P. H., Gagnon, J. H., Pomeroy, W. B., & Christenson, C. V. *Sex offenders: An analysis of types.* New York: Harper: Hoeber, 1965.

Grantham, R. Effects of counselor sex, race, and language style on black students in initial interviews. *Journal of Counseling Psychology*, 1973, *20*, 553–559.

Green, R. Adults who want to change sex; adolescents who cross-dress; and children called "sissy" and "tomboy." In R. Green (Ed.), *Human sexuality: A health practitioner's text.* Baltimore: Williams & Wilkins, 1975.

Green, R., Newman, L. E., & Stoller, R. J. Treatment of boyhood transsexualism. *Archives of General Psychiatry*, 1972, *26*, 213–217.

Grier, W. H., & Cobbs, P. M. *Black rage.* New York: Bantam, 1968.

Griffith, M. S. Some considerations for training in community psychology. *APA Division of Community Psychology Newsletter*, 1972, *5* (3), 7–9.

Griffith, M. S. The influence of race on the psychotherapeutic relationship. *Psychiatry*, 1977, *40:* 27–40.

Gunnings, T. S., & Simpkins, G. A. A systematic approach to counseling disadvantaged youth. *Journal of Non-White Concerns*, 1972, *1*, 4–8.

Hanson, R. W., & Adesso, V. J. A multiple behavioral approach to male homosexual behavior: A case study. *Journal of Behavior Therapy and Experimental Psychiatry*, 1972, *3*, 323–325.

Hastings, D. W. Sexual potency disorders of the male. In A. M. Freedman and H. I. Kaplan (Eds.), *Comprehensive textbook of psychiatry.* Baltimore: Williams & Wilkins, 1967.

Herman, S. H., Barlow, D. H., & Agras, W. S. An experimental analysis of classical conditioning as a method of increasing heterosexual arousal in homosexuals. *Behavior Therapy*, 1974, *5*, 33–47.

Hore, B. D., Nicolle, F. V., & Calnan, J. S. Male transsexualism in England: Sixteen cases with surgical intervention. *Archives of Sexual Behavior*, 1975, *4*, 81–89.

Horowitz, J. The relationships among marital adjustment, sexual satisfaction and adjustment, and communication. Unpublished dissertation, University of Florida, Gainesville, 1977.

Hunt, M. *Sexual behavior in the seventies.* Chicago: Playboy, 1974.

Hyde, J. S. *Understanding human sexuality.* New York: McGraw-Hill, 1979.

Jaffe, A. C. Child molestation. *Medical Aspects of Human Sexuality*, April, 1976, pp. 73, 96.

Johnson, C. S. *Growing up in the black belt.* Washington, D.C.: American Council on Education, 1941.

Jones, M. H., & Jones, M. C. The neglected client. *Black Scholar*, March 1970, 35–42.

Kaplan, H. S. *The new sex therapy.* New York: Brunner/Mazel, 1974.

Kinsey, A. C., Pomeroy, W. B., Martin, C. E., & Gebhard, P. H. *Sexual behavior in the human female*. Philadelphia: W. B. Saunders, 1953.

Krasner, L. Behavior modification: Values and training. In C. M. Franks (Ed.), *Assessment and status of the behavior therapies*. New York: McGraw-Hill, 1969.

Larson, D. An adaptation of the Feldman and MacCulloch approach to treatment of homosexuality by the application of anticipatory avoidance learning. *Behaviour Research and Therapy*, 1970, *8*, 209–210.

Lehrman, N. *Masters and Johnson explained*. Chicago: Playboy Press, 1970.

Lobitz, W. C., & LoPiccolo, J. New methods in the behavioral treatment of sexual dysfunction. *Journal of Behavior Therapy and Experimental Psychiatry*, 1972, *3*, 265–272.

Locke, H. J., & Wallace, K. M. Short marital adjustment and prediction tests: Their reliability and validity. *Marriage and Family Living*, 1959, *21*, 251–255.

LoPiccolo, J., & Lobitz, W. C. Behavior therapy of sexual dysfunction. In L. A. Hamerlynck, L. C. Handy, and E. J. Mash (Eds.), *Behavior change: Methodology concepts and practice*. Champaign, Ill: Research Press, 1973.

LoPiccolo, J., & Steger, J. C. The sexual interaction inventory: A new instrument for assessment of sexual dysfunction. *Archives of Sexual Behavior*, 1974, *3*, 585–595.

Marks, I. M., & Gelder, M. G. Transvestism and fetishism: Clinical and psychological changes during faradic aversion. *British Journal of Psychiatry*, 1967, *113*, 711–729.

Marks, J. Management of sexual disorder. In H. Leitenberg (Ed.), *Behavior modification and therapy*. Englewood Cliffs, New Jersey: Prentice-Hall, 1976.

Marquis, J. N. Orgasmic reconditioning: Changing sexual object choice through controlling masturbatory fantasies. *Journal of Behavior Therapy and Experimental Psychiatry*, 1970, *1*, 262–271.

Marshall, N. C. The modification of sexual fantasies: A combined treatment approach to the reduction of deviant sexual behavior. *Behaviour Research and Therapy*, 1973, *11*, 557–564.

Masters, W. H., & Johnson, V. E. *Human sexual inadequacy*. Boston: Little Brown, 1970.

McCaghy, C. H. Child molesting. *Sexual Behavior*, August, 1971, *1*, 16–24.

McCary, J. *McCary's human sexuality*. New York: Van Nostrand, 1978.

McConaghy, N. Subject and penile plethysmograph responses following aversion relief and apomorphine aversion therapy for homosexual impulses. *British Journal of Psychiatry*, 1969, *115*, 723–730.

McConaghy, N. Penile response conditioning and its relationship to aversion therapy in homosexuals. *Behavior Therapy*, 1970, *1*, 213–221.

McGuire, R. J., & Vallance, M. Aversion therapy by electric shock: A simple technique. *British Medical Journal*, 1964, *1*, 151–153.

Money, J., & Erhardt, A. N. *Man and woman, boy and girl*. Baltimore: Johns Hopkins, 1972.

Obler, M. Systematic desensitization in sexual disorders. *Journal of Behavior Therapy and Experimental Psychiatry*, 1973, *4*, 93–101.

O'Leary, K. D., & Wilson, G. T. *Behavior therapy: Application and outcome*. New Jersey: Prentice Hall, 1975.

Pauly, I. B., & Goldstein, S. G. Prevalence of significant sexual problems in medical practice. *Medical Aspects of Human Sexuality*, 1970, 46–63.

Pomeroy, W. B. The diagnosis and treatment of transvestites and transsexuals. *Journal of Sex and Marital Therapy*, 1975, *1*, 215–224.

Prince, V., & Butler, P. M. Survey of 504 cases of transvestism. *Psychological Reports*, 1972, *31*, 903–917.

Rachman, S. Sexual fetishism: An experimental analogue. *The Psychological Record*, 1966, *16*, 293–296.

Rachman, S., & Teasdale, J. *Aversion therapy and behavior disorders.* London: Routledge and Kegan Paul, 1969.

Rainwater, L. Some aspects of lower class sexual behavior. *Journal of Social Issues,* 1966, *22,* 96–109.

Randell, J. *Sexual variations.* London: Technomic, 1976.

Rekers, G. A., & Lovaas, O. I. Behavioral treatment of deviant sex role behaviors in a male child. *Journal of Applied Behavior Analysis,* 1974, *7,* 173–190.

Rosen, H., & Frank, J. D. Negroes in psychotherapy. *American Journal of Psychiatry,* 1962, *119,* 456–460.

Shane, M. Some subcultural considerations in the psychotherapy of a negro patient. *Psychiatric Quarterly,* 1960, *34,* 9–27.

Simon, W., and Gagnon, J. Psychosexual development. In J. H. Gagnon and W. Simon (Eds.), *The sexual scene.* New York: Transaction, 1970.

Staples, R. Sex life of the African and American Negro. In A. Ellis and A. Arbarbanel (Eds.), *Encyclopedia of Sexual Behavior.* New York: Hawthorn Books, 1961.

Staples, R. *The black family: Essays and studies.* Belmont, Calif.: Wadsworth, 1971.

Staples, R. The sexuality of black women. *Sexual Behavior,* June, 1972, 4–5.

Staples, R. *The black woman in america: Sex, marriage, and the family.* Chicago: Nelson Hall, 1973.

Stevenson, I., & Wolpe, J. Recovery from sexual deviation through overcoming of nonsexual neurotic responses. *American Journal of Psychiatry,* 1960, *116,* 737–742.

Stoller, R. J. Transvestites' women. *American Journal of Psychiatry,* 1967, *124,* 333–339.

Stoller, R. J. *Sex and gender.* New York: Science House, 1968.

Stoller, R. J. Parental influences in male transsexualism. In R. Green and J. Money (Eds.), *Transsexualism and sex reassignment.* Baltimore: John Hopkins, 1969.

Thorpe, J. G., Schmidt, E., Brown, P. T., & Castell, D. Aversion-relief therapy: A new method for general application. *Behaviour Research and Therapy,* 1964, *2,* 71–82.

Ullmann, L. P., & Krasner, L. *A psychological approach to abnormal behavior* (Ed. 2). Englewood Cliffs, N. J.: Prentice-Hall, 1975.

Vontress, C. E. Counseling blacks. *Personnel and Guidance Journal,* 1970, *48,* 713–719.

Weinberg, M. S., & Williams, C. *Male homosexuals: Their problems and adaptations.* New York: Oxford, 1974.

Wiener, D. N. Sexual problems in clinical experience. In C. B. Broderick and J. Bernard (Eds.), *The individual, sex and society.* Baltimore: Johns Hopkins, 1969.

Wilson, G. T. Innovations in the modification of phobic disorders in two clinical cases. *Behavior Therapy,* 1973, *4,* 426–430.

Wilson, G. T., & Davison, G. C. Behavior therapy and homosexuality: A critical perspective. *Behavior Therapy,* 1974, *5,* 16–28.

Wood, D., & Obrist, P. Minimal and maximal sensory intake and exercises as unconditioned stimuli in human heart-rate conditioning. *Journal of Experimental Psychology,* 1968, *76,* 254–262.

Wyatt, G. E., Strayer, R. G., & Lobitz, W. C. Issues in the treatment of sexually dysfunctioning couples of Afro-American descent. *Psychotherapy: Theory, Research and Practice,* 1976, *13,* 44–50.

Yalom, I. D. Aggression and forbiddenness in voyeurism. *Archives of General Psychiatry,* 1960, *3,* 317.

12

Stress Disorders

GERALD GROVES

INTRODUCTION

The word *stress* is a Latin derivative which has existed in the English language for centuries. Originally, it denoted hardship or adversity. Later, stress was used to denote a "force, pressure, strain or strong effort" applied to an object or person including his "organs or mental powers" (Hinkle, 1974b; Onions, 1933). In the biological sciences, the term *stress* has a connotative rather than a denotative function, suggesting, on the one hand, external stimulus characteristics which tend to upset the "milieu interieur" of the organism and, on the other, characteristics of the organism's response to such stimulus characteristics. Stressful stimuli include mechanical and chemical trauma, toxins, bacterial and viral pathogens, loud noises, monotonous work, and threats to or changes in social relationships. The general adaptation syndrome exemplifies organismic responses which qualify as stress (Selye, 1946, 1976). This syndrome refers to a sequence of nonspecific bodily reactions which occur in response to generalized noxious stimuli. The development of the syndrome depends on the functional integrity of the pituitary and adrenal glands and is characterized by the secretion of adrenalin, noroadrenalin, and adrenocortical hormones. These hormonal responses enhance resistance to stressors, but if such stressors are operative for too long, a stage of exhaustion will occur with the emergence of tissue damage, such as gastrointestinal ulcers, shock, and ultimately death.

Stress is relevant to disturbed function in a number of ways: (a) It may act as a nonspecific factor which heightens susceptibility to unrelated pathological processes; (b) it may act together with other predisposing or precipitating factors to initiate the onset of pathology; (c) once pathology is established, stress may operate to maintain or exacerbate it.

GERALD GROVES ● Department of Psychiatry, Boston University Medical School, Boston, Massachusetts and Edith Nourse Rogers Memorial Veterans Hospital, Bedford, Massachusetts 01730.

These factors represent plausible hypotheses, supported by some data but far from conclusively proven. Mechanic (1974) has drawn attention to another consequence of stress which is relevant to the consideration of illness, namely, the propensity for stress to give rise to increases in health-seeking behavior.

There are two assumptions that frequently underlie a consideration of the relationship between stress and disease. One is that stress acts as a nonspecific factor; the other is that stress acts with specificity and is especially implicated in certain diseases. The relationship between antecedent life changes and disease onset supports the nonspecific assumption and is exemplified in the work of Holmes and Rahe (1967) and Rahe, Romo, Bennett, and Siltanen (1974). The assumption of specificity has been applied to disease states such as hypertension, myocardial infarction, peptic ulcer, tension headaches, asthma, and ulcerative colitis. At the present time, both hypotheses are speculative rather than confirmed, since the evidence available is inconclusive, both in quality and quantity. The present chapter focuses on some of the major causes and results of stress, especially with reference to the black community. The treatment of disorders produced or influenced by stress will also be discussed.

INTERACTION OF PHYSIOLOGICAL AND PSYCHOLOGICAL SYSTEMS

The separation of responses to stress into psychological and physiological realms is artificial but convenient, since each conceptual convention must ultimately be definable in terms of the other. Psychological concepts describe the relationships between the environment and observed behavior and between observed behavior and inferred covert processes of behavior such as feelings, strategies, and tactics. Physiological concepts are concerned with the physical processes of the organism internally and in relation to its environment. Pavlov (1928), in his studies of conditioned reflexes, demonstrated the capacity of external stimuli to exert control over (exocrine) glandular functions such as salivation. This phenomenon may be termed exteroceptive conditioning in contrast to the establishment of similar conditioned reflexes in relation to stimuli arising from organs within the body which may be termed interoceptive conditioning. This latter phenomenon was established by Bykov (1942, 1954) in further experiments using methods of inquiry similar to those of Pavlov. These studies indicated that the highest centers of the nervous system regulate the organism's responses to its environment and to aspects of its own functioning including the endocrine glands and automatic nervous system, previously thought to be relatively independent of the central nervous system.

The kinds of stimulation which have been shown to produce stressful reactions in Pavlovian laboratories include: (a) intensely powerful stimuli; (b) frequent and finely differentiated inhibitory conditioned signals; (c) alternate positive and inhibitory stimuli without intervening intervals; and (d) simultaneously presented stimuli of radically different biological significance (alimentary, defense, sexual, herd). Some of these categories of stimuli encompass situations which would be predictably stressful in humans as well.

A unified theory regarding several aspects of the neural and endocrine responses to stress and their psychological correlates is now possible. It involves both the Pavlovian view that the reflex is the most frequent response in the life of complex organisms as well as Selye's description of the hormonal aspects of the general adaptation syndrome and Cannon's (1935) fight or flight principle, which is adrenalin-based.

In the Pavlovian view, the general adaptation syndrome would be a reflex originating in the cerebral cortex with efferent neural impulses to the hypothalamus, which by neuro-secretory processes would then activate the pituitary-adrenal system, which is primarily hormonal. The subjective sense of arousal, fear, or anger is the psychological correlate of adrenalin or nonadrenalin production by the adrenal medulla. The general adaptation syndrome is a nonspecific reaction to stress and is not shaped by specific characteristics of the stressor. The general-adaptation syndrome is described as proceeding through three phases: a) anxiety or shock, b) resistance, and c) exhaustion, which may result in death if the adaptation response is not successful.

The proportion of the wide range of adrenal hormones secreted is probably a function of the individual's constitution, as is the tissue damage or regulatory disturbance associated with them. For example, peptic ulcer is more likely to occur in persons with blood type O than other types. In a similar vein, the adaptation syndrome interacts with other factors such as diet, heat or cold, age, and previous trauma or concurrent pathology (e.g., the recurrence of a previously healed peptic ulcer). Stress also affects health-related behaviors which may interact with the factors mentioned above. Such behaviors include drug abuse, particularly alcohol and tobacco, dietary habits, and patterns of physical activity.

PSYCHOLOGICAL REACTION TO STRESS

The first reaction to an actual or potential stressor is perceptual and greatly influences the nature of subsequent psychological responses to the stressor. Whether an event is perceived as stressful depends on the individual's prior experience and acculturation, the individual's cognitive set, the individual's stimulus background for the stressor, and the individual's judgment regarding his or her ability to cope with the potential stressor.

In the case of catastrophe or calamitous events, the sequence of psychological reactions has been repeatedly observed: shock, denial, depression/rage/anxiety, acceptance, resolution. Engel (1971) has written on the giving-up/given-up response to severe stress and speculated on the significance of this for the physical health and even the existence of such individuals. Engel (1968) found that patients often become ill in settings in which they experience the following: a feeling of giving up, of hopelessness or helplessness; "a depreciated image of the self; a sense of loss of gratification from relationships or roles in life; a feeling of disruption of the sense of continuity between past, present and future; and a reactivation of memories of earlier periods of giving-up" (pp. 296–298). This complex of psychological reactions he termed the "giving-up/given-up complex" and hypothesized that through neural mechanisms it alters the organism's ability to cope with "concurrent pathogenic processes," thereby contributing to the development of disease and death.

Cannon (1935) elucidated the "fight–flight" response later incorporated into the general adaptation syndrome described by Selye (1946, 1976). The individual's awareness of his own physiological response may further modify psychological reactions, especially if such physiological responses themselves act as stressors. Some individuals have become sensitized to some of their own physiological responses such as palpitations, sweating, and sensations of lightheadedness. Such responses serve as signals that something catastrophic is imminent (e.g., heart attack or fainting) and cause predictable apprehension and autonomic arousal, even though the interpretation of these signals may be incorrect.

Complaints of anxiety and depression, vague or specific psychophysiological complaints, and psychiatric syndromes are frequently precipitated by stressful circumstances. These syndromes are not specific to the stressor. Stressors frequently have marked effects on the established behavioral repertoire of the individual, disrupting both operantly and classically conditioned behaviors. Beyond that, stressors may disturb the individual's capacity to acquire new conditioned responses. Pavlov (1928) described experiments in which dogs were made "neurotic." In that state, such animals not only lost established conditioned reflexes but were unable to acquire new ones for some time. Commenting on a natural disaster in Leningrad in 1924 which necessitated the difficult rescue of experimental dogs, Pavlov observed that "the conditioned re-flexes disappeared for sometime and only slowly reappeared." Skinner (1965) comments on the disruptive capacities of aversive and punishing stimuli, and of anxiety responses on operant repertoires. The abrupt loss of a reinforcer, as may be involved in job loss, may depress behaviors linked to the job in complex chains, including covert behaviors such as evaluations of self-worth and competence.

PSYCHOSOMATIC DISORDERS

Psychosomatic disorders are those in which psychological phenomena appear to play a prominent role in the pathogenesis and precipitation of clinically evident disturbance. The clinical syndromes described in this section are all psychosomatic according to the definition given above.

HYPERTENSION

Hypertension, or high blood pressure, may have multiple etiologies, the majority of which are not considered psychosomatic. However, the most prevalent syndrome of systemic hypertension, and consequently the most important, is primary or essential hypertension, which is considered to be a psychosomatic disorder. It is a tenet of both professional and nonprofessional belief that stressful circumstances play a role in the pathogenesis, maintenance, and exacerbation of essential hypertension, and aspects of its treatment are based on this belief.

Jenkins, Tuthill, Tannenbaum, and Kirby (1979) noted a definite statistical relationship between "social stressors and excess mortality from hypertensive diseases." Using a category called "hypertensive diseases" which included malignant hypertension, essential benign hypertension, hypertensive heart disease, and hypertensive renal disease, these workers showed that excessive deaths due to these causes were highly correlated with areas characterized by: (a) most males in low occupational status; (b) median years of schooling for adults very low; (c) percentage of families in poverty very high; and (d) percentage of disabled and hand-icapped persons high.

Ostfeld and D'Atri (1977) reviewed a large number of studies related to the hypothesis that rapid sociocultural change tends to elevate blood pressure. The evidence is inconclusive and typically does not explicate the mechanisms by which this might occur. However, Ostfeld and D'Atri suggest one mechanism that may be related to the higher blood pressures often noted in urban versus rural populations. Rapidly urbanized populations frequently increase their caloric intake and reduce their physical activity, thereby increasing their body weight, a factor often associated with elevated blood pressure both at individual and group levels.

Ostfeld and D'Atri (1975) also reviewed the relationship between crowding and elevated blood pressure in animals and man and concluded that there is a positive relationship.

Some animal experiments establish a link between hypertension and psychosocial stimuli. Henry, Meehan, and Stephens (1967) were able to produce hypertension in mice when they were "strangers" rather than littermates by placing them in interconnecting boxes linked to a common feeding place.

Other factors involved in hypertension are genetic and dietary. Inheritance is probably on a polygenic basis, that is, several genes rather than one gene are involved and the method of inheritance is more complex than with single-gene inheritance. High sodium intake or dietary factors which cause the retention of sodium predispose to hypertension. Retained sodium is associated with increased intravascular volume, which may contribute to elevated blood pressure. Prior to age 55, there is a consistent and direct correlation between hypertension and obesity.

In summary, the following factors probably contribute to essential hypertension:

1. Stressors such as overcrowding, poverty, chronic social conflict, and rapid sociocultural change. These stressors may be associated with chronic neuro-endocrine stimulation which leads to repeated acute elevations of blood pressure, which eventuate in permanent elevation of blood pressure either through vascular changes or resetting of regulatory mechanisms.
2. Genetic influences which predispose to the elevation of blood pressure under many prevalent sociocultural circumstances.
3. Dietary habits which result in obesity and high levels of retained sodium.

PEPTIC ULCER

Peptic ulcer is a term generally used to designate ulceration of the pyloric region of the stomach and the first part of the duodenum. There is a considerable degree of overlap between the gastric (stomach) and duodenal ulcer but some important differences as well. Duodenal ulcers are more prevalent in men and associated with increased gastric secretion of hydrochloric acid and the enzyme pepsin. In contrast, gastric ulcers occur with equal frequency in both sexes and are not associated with increased gastric secretion but are associated with higher incidence of gastric carcinoma (Yager and Weiner, 1971). Predisposing factors are believed to include genetic, dietary and psychosocial elements. Persons with blood group O who are nonsecretors of the blood–group antigens (ABH) into the saliva and gastric juice have a higher incidence of duodenal ulcer. Ectomorphy and phenylthiocarbamide sensitivity are also correlated with duodenal ulcer. Alcohol is a potent stimulus of gastric acid secretion, and peptic ulcer is believed to be more prevalent among chronic alcoholics than in the general population.

Clinically, emotional stress is correlated with precipitation and exacerbation of peptic ulcer. At one time corticosteroid hormones were believed to be implicated in peptic ulcer disease, but this view has since been discounted.

A number of animal experiments indicate a relationship between stress and peptic ulcer. Working with electric shock as a stressor, Weiss et al. (1976) showed that rats shocked in isolation develop more numerous and larger ulcers than rats shocked in the presence of another rat to whom they respond aggressively when shocked. This work suggests a protective psychosocial factor in the presence of another animal.

Brady, Porter, Conrad, and Mason (1958) demonstrated the "executive" monkey phenomenon in which only one animal of a pair could defer shock by its responses while the other animal received an identical amount of shock, independent of its own responses and dependent on the "executive" monkey. The latter animal repeatedly showed much greater ulceration than the former in this research paradigm. Because of its similarity to some human situations in which one individual is responsible for himself and others, this experimental finding created considerable interest. Since that time, Weiss (1972) has reinterpreted these findings in conjunction with his own experimental findings. In his view, the Brady findings represent an artifact produced by the manner of selection of the "executive" monkey by virtue of its response frequency characteristics, and the absence of "relevant" feedback consequent upon its avoidant responses. He has elaborated a hypothesis that degree of ulceration is a direct function of frequency of avoidance responses and an inverse function of "relevant" feedback produced by the same responses.

The meaning of these animal findings for humans is suggestive rather than conclusive. When men respond to aversive conditions and receive prompt feedback that their responses have reduced the probability of further aversive responses, the risk of ulcers is less than when there is no such feedback.

CORONARY HEART DISEASE

Coronary heart disease is related to both biological risk factors and psychological variables. It is a psychosomatic disorder which is a leading cause of death in America. Psychological factors are believed to be involved in recurrent myocardial infarctions and sudden death (Rosenmann, 1978). In an extensive review of the psychosomatic aspects of coronary heart disease (CHD), Jenkins (1977) noted that "the numbers of independent studies reporting consistent findings is greater for the Type A behavior pattern than for any of the other major categories of psychosocial variables."

CHD refers to two major clinical syndromes: angina pectoris (AP) and myocardial infarction (MI). AP refers to chest pain due to insufficient oxygenation of the heart muscle; MI refers to death of a portion of heart muscle because of an even greater and probably more sudden lack of oxygenation and is frequently fatal. Both conditions are related to pathological processes which compromise or obliterate the lumina of the coronary arteries.

Type A behavior is characterized by intense competitiveness, considerable job involvement, and impatience with a subjective sense of time urgency (Friedman & Rosenmann, 1974; Jenkins, 1971). The relationship between Type A behavior patterns and coronary disease (MI) is important because biological risk factors account for only 50% of the variation in CHD rates between different populations studied (Gordon, Garcia-Palmieri, Kagan, Kannel, and Schiffman, 1974). Such biological risk factors are elevated blood pressure, high serum cholesterol, cigarette smoking, and overweight.

Jenkins (1977) notes that "earlier reviews showed consensus that CHD risk was related to social mobility, both those changes occurring between generations and those within the lifetime of the group at risk." Similarly, CHD risk is related to status incongruity, a concept which describes discrepancies in an individual between different indices of social status such as education, occupation, income, organizational membership, and ethnicity. Medalie, Snyder, Groen, Neufeld, Goldbourt, and Riss (1973) found that problems in finances and family and work relationships were associated with increased risk of AP, but not MI, prospectively.

The mechanisms by which factors predictive of high risk for coronary heart disease exert their effects have not been completely elucidated. Speculation is that elevated blood pressure and obesity act by increasing strain on the heart. Further, elevated blood pressure and high serum cholesterol contribute to degenerative vascular changes in the coronary arteries. Type A behavior is associated with enhanced adrenergic output, higher levels of serum cholesterol, and more cigarette smoking, although its relationship to coronary heart disease is independent of the latter two factors.

OTHER DISORDERS

Other disorders in which stress has been recognized as an especially important contributing factor include bronchial asthma and headaches.

Bronchial asthma may be precipitated by biological factors such as allergens or respiratory infection, by stressful psychosocial stimuli, or by unknown factors. Allergens are identified as the predominant factors in one third of cases and as contributing factors in another third. Respiratory infections appear largely responsible in about 40% of cases. Psychogenic and conditioning factors are considered to be important in a significant number of cases and episodes of asthma. Episodes are characterized by the acute or insidious onset of paroxsyms of expiratory dysnea and wheezing, overinflation of the lungs, and cough. These features are due to bronchospasm, mucosal edema, and excessive bronchial secretions. In about one third of cases, asthma is present in immediate family members (Norman & Cluff, 1966).

Migraine headaches are characterized by episodes of vasoconstriction followed by vasodilation in cranial arteries supplying the brain and scalp. In the vasoconstrictive phase, prodromial symptoms may occur and are usually visual in nature. Vasodilation is the painful phase. The headache begins in the supra-orbital, retro-orbital, or fronto-temporal area on one side and spreads to involve the hemicranium. Dull initially, the pain increases in intensity to a pulsating crescendo which may last for several hours and is often accompanied by photophobia, nausea, and vomiting. There is a family history of this condition as an autosomal dominant or autosomal recessive trait. Attacks are precipitated by nonspecific stresses such as frustration, fatigue, mild hypoglycemia, and foods containing tyramine or monosodium glutamate. It is estimated to affect 5 to 10% of the population (Gilroy & Meyer, 1975).

Tension headaches are ubiquitous and are related to states of anxiety, tension, and depression. They are often exacerbated or precipitated by stressful circumstances and may become chronic. They result from sustained contraction of skeletal muscles in the scalp, face, neck, and shoulders. Faulty posture of the head and neck and shoulders may also play a role. Tension headaches are generalized and often accompanied by a constant tight, constricting quality. They may last for days, and some patients complain that they are never free of them (Gilroy & Meyer, 1975).

The psychosomatic disorders described in this section have nearly all been treated in part by behavioral methods, often with promising results. Behavioral methods (discussed below) show particular promise for secondary prevention and have advantages over drug treatments, which are frequently expensive and associated with unwanted, and, sometimes, dangerous side effects.

STRESS IN BLACK POPULATIONS

As a racially oppressed minority in America, blacks are presumably exposed to greater degrees of psychosocial and other stresses than white Americans (Arsenian & Arsenian, 1948). In many instances, the different types of stresses may interact with other variables in a synergistic manner (e.g., psychosocial stress, poor housing, poor nutrition, less-than-adequate medical care, and low education). The critical stressor for the majority of black Americans is economic. Many other stressors are spawned by it. The rough ratio of unemployment between blacks and whites is 2:1, although it is much higher in selective age ranges and geographical locations. When blacks are employed, their earnings are uniformly less than those of whites in similar occupations. In several unionized industries, blacks are generally the most recently hired and consequently the first to be laid off or fired when economic conditions deteriorate. These adverse economic conditions have powerful effects on family life and organization (Gutman, 1976), and on education and child-rearing (David, 1968). To add insult to injury, communal responses to economic adversity may be misinterpreted as "pathology" in the black community, thereby misdirecting problem-solving strategies as in the Moynihan Report (Rainwater & Yancey, 1967) and giving rise to demoralization. At higher socioeconomic levels, blacks may find themselves relatively isolated as they move into occupational settings formerly denied them. Typically, there are few other blacks who share their position, and they must face hazards such as institutional racism without the benefit of support systems which exist for blacks in other settings. Acts of individual and group violence against blacks continue to characterize American life, as do incidents of racially inspired verbal abuse and social discrimination. Such instances create a generally stressful ambience for blacks in all walks of life.

It is frequently asserted that in modern societies psychosocial stresses are the most important. Social stimuli which act, or are perceived to act, in such a way that they threaten the individual's status, prestige, or existing relationships are important in this regard. Rahe *et al.* (1974) have posited that important life changes, even when of an apparently positive nature, may be related to illness episodes. Moving to a new home which may be more desirable than the old may still involve stressful elements related to new economic responsibilities and the social adaptation to a new neighborhood which may be hostile to a black family. A promotion to a new job may involve greater demands, uncertainty about efficacy, and the need to relate to new and threatening co-workers.

Although stress and life-change may be related to illness episodes, not all individuals are subject to these influences. A number of investigators have been intrigued by this resistance to stress exhibited by both humans and animals and have attempted to explain it. Cobb (1976) has been impressed by the value of viable social networks in this regard and by the value of at least one friend in whom the stressed person may confide regularly. At the animal level, Weiss (1972) has studied the availability of coping responses to protect against ulcerogenic stimuli. A coping response is defined as one which enables the animal to avoid or escape a stressor, in this instance electric shock. A yoked animal which received as much shock as the one with a coping response at its command showed more gastric ulceration, suggesting the protective effect of the coping response.

Jenkins et al. (1977), in a paper entitled "Zones of excess mortality in Massachusetts," describe findings of grave importance for the black population with reference to several environmental stressors. They demonstrated that the rate of death in a certain Mental Health Catchment (MHC) Area 602 (one of 29 in the state) was 28% greater than that prevailing in the state as a whole and over 60% greater than that prevailing in an affluent suburban MHC Area only 16 kilometers away. MHC Area 602 was characterized by the following features: (a) very low median income; (b) a large proportion of families living in poverty; (c) high levels of unemployment, underemployment, and low-status employment; (d) large numbers of blacks, Hispanics and other nonwhites; (e) a large number of one-parent and one-person households.

A disproportionately large number of blacks, compared with the general population, live in circumstances similar to those described above. Such circumstances constitute stressors in themselves and offer little or no protection against many other stressors. For example, under generally adverse economic circumstances such as high rates of inflation and rising levels of unemployment, the black poor are disproportionately affected, as are those in marginal and low-status occupations. Many blacks are among the most recently hired employees in their workplace and among the first to be laid off when such action is taken. Job loss is a well-established stressor (Gore, 1973).

The factors described by Jenkins et al. (1977) are also associated with increased rates of death from a variety of causes including hypertension, combined respiratory diseases, some forms of heart disease, "fires and flames," and homicide, among others. It seems reasonable to assume that such circumstances are also associated with increased rates of morbidity from a variety of causes.

Within this century, black people have migrated in large numbers from the southern states where they lived predominantly in rural-agrarian communities, to the northern states, especially of the Northeast, where they live in predominantly urban-industrialized communities, often large cities and urban conglomerates. Such migration involves stressful circumstances for many blacks and may be associated with the rupture of family and other supportive networks and the pursuit of unattainable ambitions.

In many instances, "successful" blacks will have experienced upward social mobility and status incongruity. The latter term describes the possession of simultaneous identifying markings from different social classes. This is evidenced by discrepancies between occupation, level of education, housing, and, for blacks, ethnic membership itself. Social mobility and status incongruity have been associated with increased risks of heart disease (Kaplan, Cassel, & Gore, 1977; Syme, Hyman, & Enterline, 1965; Williams, 1968). Such sociocultural changes are important in both inter- and intra-generational movement.

Superimposed on the adverse material condition of the black population as a whole are the active and current stresses of racial prejudice and discrimination. The fact that discriminatory practices have recently been disavowed by the government adds a quality of ambiguity to the relationship between many blacks and the wider society, and this engenders internal psychological conflict, insecurity, and distrust regarding the wider society.

In the *Textbook of Black-Related Diseases* (1975), Saunders and Williams declared that "hypertension is the major medical problem affecting blacks today." The prevalence of hypertension is greater among blacks than whites, and hypertension results in fatality more frequently and at an earlier age among the former. In a paper entitled "Social Stressors and Excess Mortality from Hypertensive Diseases," Jenkins *et al.* (1979) concluded that, of a large number of sociodemographic factors positively correlated with high mortality from hypertension, poor education and low occupational status were the most significant statistically.

Hypertension is an established biological risk fact for cerebrovascular accident (stroke) and for coronary heart disease. Stroke occurs at an earlier age and with twice the frequency among blacks as among whites (Bates, 1975). The reasons for the greater prevalence of hypertension among blacks as compared to whites remain to be elucidated.

Certainly, differential levels of psychosocial and other stressors deserve further evaluation.

A thorough assessment of stress-related disorders in the black population in terms of incidence, prevalence, etiological factors, and optimal methods of treatment is impossible at the present time for several reasons, some general and some specific. General reasons include lack of information about the *actual* mechanisms by which various stressors act and the relationship of stress to other potential etiological factors. Chronic activation of the hypothalmic-pituitary-adrenal medullary system and of the hypothalamic-pituitary-adrenal cortical system *could* lead to stress-related disease in man but it is not yet known if it *does*. Accurate incidence and prevalence data are not available for the well-recognized stress-related disorders because their reporting is not mandatory. For blacks, such data are even more sparse. Longitudinal studies which have been informative such as the Framingham Study and the Western Collaborative Study (Brand, Rosenmann, Sholtz, & Friedman, 1976) included too few blacks or did not consider data for blacks specifically. Similarly, many types of information related to health and health care do not allow specific consideration of blacks. Jenkins *et al.* (1979) note that "race-specific mortality rates" could not be computed from the data at their disposal.

Kaplan, Cassel, and Gore (1977) reviewed the concept of social support and its relationship to health. They concluded that social support protects the individual against the health-eroding effects of stress. This would seem an especially important concept for blacks. It would seem important for blacks to exercise care in the creation and maintenance of social networks in which individual needs for intimacy, self-esteem, and predictability may be met and group membership affirmed. The black individual who is socioeconomically mobile can easily find himself isolated as a marginal member of work and neighborhood groups.

BEHAVIORAL APPROACHES TO STRESS

Many behavioral approaches to stress have emphasized the self-management of physiological variables like blood pressure, skeletal muscle tension, and local skin temperature, either for their direct or derivative value. Where certain behavioral characteristics are correlated with disease (e.g., type A personality with myocardial infarction), behavioral strategies have sought to alter these characteristics in the hope that their pathological correlates would also be altered (Rosenmann *et al.*, 1975; Rosenmann & Friedman, 1977).

The traditional risk factors for coronary artery heart disease are high serum cholesterol levels, elevated blood pressure (hypertension), and heavy cigarette smoking (Weiko, 1976). It has been hypothesized by many that the reduction of these risk factors in individuals in whom they exist would lead to a corresponding reduction in the frequency and severity of coronary heart disease. The Multiple Risk Factor Intervention Trial (MRFIT, 1976) is a six-year primary prevention program designed to lower the traditional risk factors in high risk males aged 40–59 and to assess the impact of this on coronary heart disease in this cohort. The MRFIT will attempt to modify smoking and dietary behavior and to increase compliance with medical regimens for the control of hypertension. The Hypertension Detection and Follow-up Program (1977) has demonstrated that compliance with medication regimens for the control of hypertension among males is a significant problem, especially among black males.

ADVANTAGES OF A BEHAVIORAL INTERPRETATION

A comprehensive behavioral approach involves (a) the accurate identification of stressors; (b) the accurate identification of the behavioral responses to stress—perceptual/cognitive, physiological, and operant; (c) coping strategies; (d) evaluation of effects; and (e) modification of coping strategies.

Compared to the purely medical model, with its emphasis on biological causes and effects and on interventions such as medication, a behavioral approach has the advantage of focusing on environmental variables and a wider range of responses, many of which are potentially modifiable. To the extent that certain stressors are embedded in the environment and are likely to be recurrent, behavioral approaches contemplate coping strategies which, once mastered, may be used as the necessity arises, without the obvious disadvantages of drugs: dependence, side effects, and a sense of personal inefficacy. Certain behavioral strategies might even be effective in reducing biological risk factors like cigarette-smoking, obesity, and hypercholesterolemia which are largely due to behavioral habits.

The behavioral emphasis on pinpointing stimuli and response, recording, and periodic review of the effects of intervention tends to generate highly specific data and hypotheses about clinical efficacy in a given case. In many instances, a behavioral approach cannot replace a medical approach but in tandem with it may greatly expand both the range of clinical intervention and the extent of therapeutic efficacy.

Specific Treatment Interventions

Because there is a vast literature attesting to the many behavioral intervention strategies for dealing with various stress-related disorders, this section will be limited to treatments aimed at major disorders.

HYPERTENSION

Benson, Kotch, and Crassweller (1978) reviewed the relaxation response as a behavioral treatment for hypertension. In this review, transcendental meditation and Yoga are considered cultist methods of eliciting the relaxation response and share four basic elements with all techniques designed for such elicitation: (a) a cognitive device in the form of a constant self-applied stimulus (e.g., a sound, phrase, or word repeated vocally or subvocally); (b) a passive attitude in which one is not concerned about one's performance; (c) a comfortable posture requiring a minimum of muscular effort; and (d) a quiet environment with a minimum of stimulation. These reviewers concluded that practice of the relaxation response for 10 to 20 minutes twice a day can lead to significant reductions of the systolic and diastolic pressures in hypertensives and reduce the amount of antihypertensive medication necessary for blood pressure control. Apparently, regular elicitation of the relaxation response for an indefinite period is required for the maintenance of its antihypertensive effect.

Frumkin, Nathan, Prout, and Cohen (1978) reviewed nonpharmacological control of essential hypertension in man and divided it into two main categories: biofeedback and relaxation. They concluded that biofeedback has not been demonstrated to lower blood pressure outside of laboratory sessions so that it is of limited, if any, clinical significance at this time. Relaxation techniques including Yoga, transcendental meditation, and progressive muscle relaxation have been associated with durable lowering of blood pressure outside of the laboratory.

Williamson and Blanchard (1979) reviewed the biofeedback literature on blood pressure, including four studies using hypertensives with reported peak decreases of 10 mm Hg or more. They noted that only a few workers chose diastolic blood pressure as the target response but that both systolic and diastolic pressures covaried. They also noted that knowledge of the correct response being modified is not essential for the development of blood pressure modification. Consequently, it is a moot point whether the biofeedback information is itself effective. Chennault (1980) conducted a controlled study designed to evaluate the effect of biofeedback training on hypertensive blacks. The control groups included an "EMG feedback" group and an "instructions with continued monitoring of blood pressure" group. The blood pressure biofeedback condition was no more effective than the others, none of which was demonstrably effective. This finding is consistent with the equivocal results of relevant biofeedback on blood pressure. It is the only such study known to the author which utilizes only black subjects.

Given the technical difficulties in blood pressure biofeedback and the equivocal findings to date, it may be worthwhile to utilize an alternative biological function which correlates well with blood pressure and which can be monitored continuously, for instance, pulse wave velocity (Williamson & Blanchard, 1979). The nonpharmacological control of blood pressure has such obvious potential advantages that every effort should be made toward attaining it. Such measures other than biofeedback may include quantitative and qualitative dietary control and exercise such as proposed by Leonard, Hofer, and Pritikin (1974).

CORONARY HEART DISEASE

Rosenman (1978) described the behavioral principles underlying attempts to modify the Type A personality. He identifies the three-part origin of this personality type as (a) personality traits, (b) environmental demands, and (c) interpretation of the quality of response to these demands. Rosenman utilizes this as a take-off point. Cognitive restructuring is utilized to alter the patient's basic attitude to experience for an overreliance on quantity. Specifically, the Type A patient is encouraged to pursue more humanistic avocations and to reduce contact with others who evoke hostility and competitiveness, to thin out the ranks of acquaintances and concentrate more on promoting meaningful friendships. Relaxation training and practice in motor deceleration are prescribed to reduce chronic overarousal and autonomic hyperstimulation. Reengineering of the work situation is encouraged, for instance, reducing desk clutter, which causes feelings of anxiety and urgency, and structuring open-ended appointments where necessary. Group therapy is utilized to assist processes of self-observation, self-control, and self-management. Rahe, O'Neill, Hogan, and Arthur (1975) have demonstrated the value of brief group therapy along these lines for secondary prevention of myocardial infarction.

Another approach to the treatment of coronary heart disease is the reduction of traditional risk factors.

SMOKING. In general, no methods for the cessation of smoking are consistently very effective. Nonetheless, a number of behavioral methods exist. Bernstein (1970) reviewed the methods that have been researched. A combination of discussion and hypnosis suggesting reduced pleasure from smoking was used with 75 subjects, usually for one session only.

Nine of 50 contacted for follow-up were abstinent 30 months later. Twenty-eight others initially improved but relapsed during the 30-month period. A combination of hypnosis and behavioral prescription to change to a less desirable brand and to cut out smoking for increased periods after meals and before retiring resulted in 96% abstinence for 4 to 13 months. Four treatments were administered over a period of three weeks. Aversive conditioning and systematic desensitization have been used with no demonstrable superiority over placebo or other treatments. Smoking to satiation, contingent cigarette smoke with hot air, and electric shock have all been used as aversive agents. Systematic desensitization has been used to overcome the urge to smoke in habitual smoking situations. Many treatments produce effects discernible by the end of treatment, but the restoration of smoking to pretreatment levels within varying periods following the cessation of treatment is the dominant pattern.

HIGH BLOOD CHOLESTEROL. Davis and Havlik (1977) reviewed a number of studies seeking to modify serum lipids or cholesterol by dietary methods. These have not shown significant results in terms of lowered frequency of myocardial infarction. These authors also reviewed efforts to lower serum cholesterol by long-term use of medication. The findings to date have been negative, but two major prospective studies are currently underway: the World Health Organization trial using clofibrate, and the Lipid Research Clinics and Type II Coronary Primary Prevention Trial utilizing cholestyramine. Results of these studies are not available at this time.

OBESITY. There is concurrence from many countries that obesity contributes to ischemic heart disease and to hypertension (James, 1976). Stuart and Davis (1972) described a program for weight control utilizing tracking of food intake, monitoring of daily weight, and restricted stimulus control of eating behavior. In addition, increased response cost for eating is introduced by the removal of preprepared and easy-to-prepare foods from the home so that eating must be preceded by lengthy preparation. Finally, coverants are used for favored binge items such as chocolates and ice cream where applicable. Coverants are imagined positive and negative reinforcers contingent upon imagined behavior involving the consumption of certain foods. Stuart (1977) compared the relative effectiveness of self-help and traditional professional services for weight reduction in the obese. He concluded that self-help services were superior to professional, in part because of the practical and behavioral focus of the self-help groups. Finally, he described a combination of behavior modification modules and the Weight Watchers program implemented through lay Weight Watchers group leaders and concluded that this combination produced statistically significant greater weight loss than the Weight Watchers program alone. Self-monitoring of eating and weight behavior appeared to be one of the effective components. Stunkard (1977) reviewed in detail four behavior modification studies including Stuart's (1967) landmark study which described unprecedented weight losses for outpatient therapy and which used behavior modification methods. Stunkard concluded that, although behavior modification is clearly superior to other therapies in producing weight loss, to date it suffers the limitation of other therapies in that maintaining weight loss is problematic.

BRONCHIAL ASTHMA

Knapp and Wells (1978) reviewed the literature on behavior therapy for asthma and concluded that classical conditioning approaches are far superior to operant conditioning approaches. Systematic desensitization appeared to be the most effective single intervention and to be more effective than relaxation alone (e.g., Moore, 1965). Hierarchies for desensitization include both exteroceptive and interoceptive stimuli related to asthmatic attacks. Mitchell and Mitchell (1971), in two controlled studies, concluded that a combination of relaxation, desensitization, and assertive training was superior to relaxation alone and no-treatment groups.

TENSION AND MIGRAINE HEADACHES

Tension headaches are generally believed to be due to excessive muscular tone in the muscles of the face, scalp, and back of the neck. Deep muscle relaxation alone and electromyographic feedback-assisted relaxation of the frontalis muscle are used in the treatment of tension headaches with good results (Budzynski & Stoyva, 1969; Budzynski & Stoyva, 1973; Budzynski, Stoyva & Adler, 1970). However, the designs used do not allow the contribution of biofeedback *per se* to be evaluated.

Migraine headaches have been successfully treated with two temperature biofeedback techniques. Turin and Johnson (1976) demonstrated that finger-warming assisted by a visual temperature display, but not finger-cooling similarly assisted, had a significant therapeutic effect. Subjects were instructed to use the finger-warming strategy when headache threatened outside the laboratory and to practice for 10 minutes twice daily at home. Feuerstein and Adams (1977) utilized the other technique, cephalic vasomotor response modification. In this instance, a photoelectric transducer is placed over the zygomatico-facial branch of the temporal artery. In this report, two subjects with migraine were treated first with cephalic vasomotor response feedback and subsequently with EMG feedback from the frontalis muscle. Two other subjects suffering from tension headaches had the sequence of treatments reversed. In all subjects, both the vascular and frontalis muscle responses were monitored simultaneously. One subject demonstrated concurrent changes with both treatments. The remainder demonstrated changes only in the target responses, with concurrent clinical improvement only when the relevant response was being addressed.

SUMMARY

Stress is a nonspecific concept which embraces a variety of environmental stimuli and organismic responses. It is being increasingly understood that a variety of environmental factors may predispose to, or precipitate, ill health, even when not impinging physically on an individual. Psychosocial factors are especially important in this regard since the social environment is preeminent in human affairs. The individual's response to the environment may be equally important in the development of ill health as when the stress response occurs inappropriately. It is assumed that the stress response may be conditioned to inherently innocuous stimuli and that such stimuli may be perceived as stressors due to idiosyncratic patterns of social development and experience.

Generally, much less is known about the health of blacks than of whites, and this is especially true of the stress-related disorders. The adverse material and social conditions which delimit the lives of many blacks constitute powerful stressors and are intimately related to the patterns of racial prejudice and discrimination which characterize American life. Blacks are particularly in need of ways to cope with stress and to combat ill health. A behavioral approach to stress and its health consequences seems especially advantageous in dealing with psychosocial stressors.

REFERENCES

Arsenian, J., & Arsenian, J. M. Tough and easy cultures: A conceptual analysis. *Psychiatry*, 1948, *11*, 377–385.

Bates, E. A. Neurology. In R. A. Williams (Ed.), *Textbook of black-related diseases*. New York: McGraw-Hill, 1975.

Benson, H. Kitch, J. B., & Crassweller, K. D. Stress and hypertension interrelations and management. In G. Onesti and A. N. Brest (Eds.), *Cardiovascular clinics, hypertension: Mechanisms, diagnosis and treatment*. F. A. Davis, 1978.

Bernstein, D. A. The modification of smoking behavior: An evaluation review. In W. A. Hunt (Ed.), *Learning mechanisms in smoking*. Chicago: Aldine, 1970.

Brady, J. V., Porter, R. W., Conrad, D. G., & Mason, J. W. Avoidance behavior and the development of gastro-duodenal ulcers. *Journal of Experimental Analysis of Behavior,* 1958, *1,* 69–72.

Brand, R. J., Rosenmann, R. H., Sholtz, R. I., & Friedman, M. Multivariate prediction of coronary heart disease in the Western Collaborative Group Study compared to the findings of the Framingham Study. *Circulation,* 1976, *53,* 348–355.

Budzynski, T. H., & Stoyva, J. M. An instrument for producing deep relaxation by means of analog information feedback. *Journal of Applied Behavior Analysis,* 1969, *2,* 231–237.

Budzynski, T. H., & Stoyva, J. M. EMG biofeedback and tension headache: A controlled-outcome study. *Psychosomatic Medicine,* 1973, *35,* 484–496.

Budzynski, T. H., Stoyva, J. M. & Adler, C. S. Feedback-induced muscle relaxation: Application to tension headache. *Journal of Behavior Therapy and Experimental Psychiatry,* 1970, *1,* 205–211.

Bykov, K. M. *The cerebral cortex and the viscera* (Vol. 2). Moscow: Izbran. Proizved, 1942, 1954, 5–415.

Cannon, W. B. Stresses and strains of homeostasis. *American Journal of Medicine,* 1935, *1,* 189.

Chennault, M. Personal communication, 1980.

Cobb, S. Social support as a moderator of life stress. *Psychosomatic Medicine,* 1976, *38,* 300–314.

David, J. (Ed.), *Growing up black.* New York: William Morrow, 1968.

Davis, C. E., & Havlik, R. J. Clinical trials of lipid lowering and coronary artery disease prevention. In B. M. Rifkind and R. I. Levy (Eds.), *Hyperlipidemia: diagnosis and therapy.* New York: Grune and Stratton, 1977.

Engel, G. L. A life setting conducive to illness. The giving-up—given-up complex. *Annals of Internal Medicine,* 1968, *69,* 293–300.

Engel, G. L. Sudden and rapid death during psychological stress. Folklore or folk wisdom? *Annals of Internal Medicine,* 1971, *74,* 771–782.

Feuerstein, M., & Adams, H. E. Cephalic vasomotor feedback in the modification of migraine headache. *Biofeedback and Self-Regulation,* 1977, *2,* 241–253.

Friedman, M. & Rosenmann, R. H. *Type A behavior and your heart.* New York: Knopf, 1974.

Frumkin, K., Nathan, R. J., Prout, M. F., & Cohen, M. C. Non-pharmacologic control of essential hypertension in man: A critical review of the experimental literature. *Psychosomatic Medicine,* 1978, *40,* 294–320.

Gilroy, J., & Meyer, J. S. *Medical neurology.* New York: Macmillan, 1975.

Gordon, T., Garcia-Palmieri, M. R., Kagan, A., Kannel, W. B., & Schiffman, J. Differences in coronary heart disease in Framingham, Honolulu and Puerto Rico. *Journal of Chronic Disease,* 1974, *27,* 329–337.

Gore, S. The influence of social support in ameliorating the consequences of job loss. Unpublished dissertation, Ann Arbor, University of Michigan, 1973.

Gutman, H. G. *The black family in slavery and freedom,* 1750–1925. New York: Vintage, 1976.

Henry, J. P., Meehan, J. P., & Stephens, P. M. The use of psychosocial stimuli to induce prolonged hypertension in mice. *Psychosomatic Medicine,* 1967, *29,* 408.

Hinkle, L. E., Jr. The concept of "stress" in the biological and social sciences. *International Journal of Psychiatric Medicine,* 1974, *5,* 335–357.

Holmes, T., & Rahe, R. The social readjustment rating scale. *Journal of Psychosomatic Research,* 1967, *11,* 213.

Hypertension detection and follow-up program cooperative group. Blood pressure studies in 14 communities. *Journal of American Medical Association,* 1977, *22,* 2385–2391.

James, W. P. T. Research on obesity, a report on the DHSS/MRC Group. London: Her Majesty's Stationery Office, 1976, pp. 22–24.

Jenkins, C. D. Psychologic and social precursors of coronary disease. *New England Journal of Medicine,* 1971, *284,* 307–317.

Jenkins, C. D. Epidemiological studies of the psychosomatic aspects of coronary heart disease: A review. In S. Kase & F. Reichsman (Eds.), *Advances in psychosomatic medicine,* 1977.

Jenkins, C. D., Tuthill, R. W., Tannenbaum, S. I., & Kirby, C. R. Zones of excess mortality in Massachusetts. *New England Journal of Medicine,* 1977, *296,* 1354–1356.

Jenkins, C. D., Tuthill, R. W., Tannenbaum, S. I., & Kirby, C. R. Social stressors and excess mortality from hypertensive diseases. *Journal of Human Stress,* 1979, 29–40.

Kaplan, B. H., Cassel, J. H., & Gore, S. Social support and health. *Medical Care,* May, 1977, *15,*(5), Supplement, 47–58.

Knapp, T. J., & Wells, L. A. Behavior therapy for asthma: A review. *Behaviour Research and Therapy,* 1978, *16,* 103–115.

Leonard, J. N., Hofer, J. L., & Pritikin, N. *Live longer now.* New York: Grosset and Dunlop, 1974.

Mechanic, David. Discussion of research programmes on relations between stressful life events and episodes of physical illness. In B. S. Dohrenwend and B. P. Dohrenwend (Eds.), *Stressful life events and episodes of physical illness.* New York: Wiley, 1974.

Medalie, J. H., Snyder, M., Groen, J. J. Neufeld, H. N., Goldbourt, U., & Riss, E. Angina pectoris among 10,000 men: Five year incidence and univariate analysis. *American Journal of Medicine.* 1973, *55,* 583–594.

Mitchell, K. R., & Mitchell, D. M. Migraine: An exploratory treatment application of programmed behavior therapy techniques. *Journal of Psychosomatic Research,* 1971, *15,* 137–157.

Moore, N. Behavior therapy in bronchial asthma: A controlled study. *Journal of Psychosomatic Research,* 1965, 257–276.

Multiple risk factor intervention trial (MRFIT). Journal of the American Medical Association, 1976, *235,* 825–827.

Norman, P. S., and Cluff, L. E. Asthma, hay fever and other manifestations of allergy. In T. R. Harrison *et al.* (Eds.), *Principles of internal medicine.* New York: McGraw-Hill, 1966.

Onions, C. T. (Ed.) *Oxford English Dictionary.* Oxford: Clarendon Press, 1933.

Ostfeld, A. M., & D'Atri, D. A. Rapid socio-cultural change and high blood pressure. In F. Reichsmann (Ed.), *Advances in psychosomatic medicine—Epidemiologic studies in psychosomatic medicine.* Basel, Switzerland. S. Karger, 1977.

Ostfeld, A. M., & D'Atri, D. A. Psychophysiological responses to the urban environment. *International Journal of Psychiatric Medicine,* 1975, *6,* 15–28.

Pavlov, I. P. *Lectures on conditioned reflexes* New York: International Publishers, 1928.

Rahe, R., O'Neill, T. O., Hogan, A., & Arthur, R. J. Brief group therapy following myocardial infarction. Eighteen month follow-up of a controlled trial. *International Journal of Psychiatric Medicine,* 1975, *6,* 349–358.

Rahe, R. H., Romo, M., Bennett, L., & Stiltanen, P. Recent life changes, myocardial infarction, and abrupt coronary death. *Archives of Internal Medicine,* 1974, *133,* 221–228.

Rainwater, L., & Yancy, W. L. (Eds.), *The Moynihan Report and the politics of controversy.* Cambridge: M.I.T. Press, 1967.

Rosenman, R. H. Role of type A behavior pattern in the pathogenesis of ischemic heart disease, and modification for prevention. *Advances in Cardiology,* 1978, *28,* 35–46.

Rosenman, R. H., & Friedman, M. Modifying type A behavior pattern. *Journal of psychosomatic research,* 1977, *21,* 323–331.

Rosenman, R. H., Brand, R. J., Jenkins, C. D., Friedman, M., Straus, R., & Warm, M. Coronary heart disease in the Western Collaborative Group study: Final follow-up experience of 8½ years. *Journal of the American Medical Association,* 1975, *233,* 872–877.

Saunders, E., & Williams, R. A. Hypertension. In R. A. Williams (Ed.), *Textbook of black-related disorders.* New York: McGraw-Hill, 1975.

Selye, H. The general adaptation syndrome and the diseases of adaptation. *Journal of Clinical Endocrinology*, 1946, *6*, 177.

Selye, H. *Stress in health and disease*. Boston: Butterworth, 1976.

Skinner, B. F. *Science and human behavior*. New York: Free Press, 1965.

Stuart, R. B. Behavioral Control of Overeating. *Behaviour Research and Therapy*, 1967, *5*, 357–365.

Stuart, R. B. Self-help group approach to self-management. In R. B. Stuart (Ed.), *Behavioral self-management*. New York: Brunner/Mazel, 1977.

Stuart, R. B., & Davis, B. *Slim chance in a fat world*. Champaign, Ill.: Research Press, 1972.

Stunkard, A. J. Behavioral treatments of obesity: Failure to maintain weight loss. In R. B. Stuart (Ed.), *Behavioral self-management*. New York: Brunner/Mazel, 1977.

Syme, S. L., Hyman, M. M., & Enterline, T. E. Cultural mobility and the occurrence of coronary heart disease. *Journal of Health and Human Behavior*, 1965, *6*, 178–189.

Turin, A., & Johnson, W. G. Biofeedback therapy for migraine headaches. *Archives of General Psychiatry*, 1976, *33*, 517–519.

Weiko, L. Risk factors and coronary heart disease—Fact or fancy? *American Heart Journal*, 1976, *91*, 87–98.

Weiss, M. Psychological factors in stress and disease. *Science America*, 1972, *226*, 104–113.

Weiss, M., Poherecky, L. A., Salonan, S., & Greenthal, M. Attenuation of gastric lesions by psychopathological aspects of aggression in rats. *Journal of Comparative and Physiological Psychology*, 1976, *90*, 252–259.

Williams, C. A. The relationship of occupational change to blood pressure, serum cholesterol, a specific overt behavior pattern and coronary heart disease. Dissertation, University of North Carolina, 1968.

Williamson, D. A., & Blanchard, E. B. Heart care and blood pressure biofeedback. I. A. review of the recent experimental literature. *Biofeedback and Self-Regulation*, 1979, *4*, 1–34.

Yager, J., & Weiner, H. Observations in man with remarks on pathogenesis. In H. Weiner (Ed.), *Advances in psychosomatic medicine—Duodenal ulcers*. New York: Krager, 1971.

13

Implementing Community Programs
The Black Perspective in Behavioral Community Psychology

RASHAD KHALIL SAAFIR

INTRODUCTION

The application of behavior modification principles in community settings has received considerable attention. Tharp and Wetzel (1969) reported several studies that provide documentation of the application of behavior modification outside of hospital settings. Studies by authors such as Boardman (1962), Williams (1959), Lovibond (1963), and Schwitzgebel (1964) represent a few of the successful applications of behavior modification principles with running away, lying and aggressive behaviors, bedtime problem behaviors, enuresis, and juvenile delinquency respectively. More recently, behavior modification principles have been applied in the treatment of neurotic behaviors, psychotic behaviors, mental retardation, and substance abuse problems (Fazio, 1972; Kondas & Scetnicka, 1972; Liberman, Teigen, Patterson, & Baker, 1973; Mahoney & Craighead, 1973; Sobell & Sobell, 1973). Also, behavior modification principles have been applied extensively in educational settings (Allen, Chinsky, Larcen, Lochman & Selinger, 1976; Allyon, Layman & Kandel, 1975; Birnbrauer, 1976; Jones & Kazdin, 1975).

The present chapter is concerned with the integration of behavior modification principles into community psychology and the utilization of behavior modification techniques in black communities. As indicated in the research cited so far, behavior modification has been traditionally concerned with changing specific behaviors of individuals. Community psychology, however, is concerned with changing social systems (Rappaport, 1977). According to Rappaport, "the aim of community psychology must be to identify and change those aspects of the social structure that degrade people" (p. 113). If we accept this as a goal of

RASHAD KHALIL SAAFIR ● National Institute of Mental Health, Rockville, Maryland 23857.

community psychology, then the question becomes: to what extent can behavior modification contribute to the achievement of objectives related to this end? The value of the behavior modification approach will be determined by the benefits derived from its application in community mental health and community psychology contexts. The distinction between community mental health and community psychology will become apparent through a discussion of community mental health and the emergence of the concept of community psychology.

Community mental health and community psychology are attitudes and ideologies that have their origins in the socioeconomic and political circumstances of the 1960s and the early 1970s. The war on poverty, the civil rights movement, protest against the Vietnam War, an upsurge in crime, pollution, and the landing of a man on the moon all contributed to the development of community mental health and community psychology.

President John F. Kennedy's message to the 84th Congress of the United States served to highlight the fact that treatment approaches to mental retardation and mental illness were inadequate and that greater attention had to be paid to the prevention of these problems (Task Force on Community Mental Health, Division 27 of the American Psychological Association, 1971). President Kennedy's message was based on a report by the Joint Commission on Mental Illness and Health (1961). The Commission recommended the establishment of comprehensive community mental health centers for the purpose of providing psychological services to persons in their local communities. The guidelines established for community mental health centers advocated programs that were designed to educate the community and prevent mental illness. The Community Mental Health Centers Act was passed by the United States Congress in 1963. Provisions were made for the establishment of community mental health centers across the nation. The availability of funds for construction and staffing of these centers contributed to the realization that serious problems existed regarding the availability and training of persons to provide community-based mental health services. Traditional models of service delivery were clearly inefficient, and traditionally trained service providers were not skilled to render many of the needed services. The civil rights movement of the 1960s alerted people to the need for minority representation in the health fields, in addition to highlighting the role of racism in mental health (Willie, Kramer, & Brown, 1973). A mandate to provide services to the mentally disturbed in their local communities and to reduce the number of persons being maintained in state mental hospitals emphasized a need to identify alternative models of service delivery to aid mental health personnel in solving a broad array of problems (Rieff, 1970). It was from this atmosphere that the concept of community psychology emerged. A conference was held in Swamscott, Massachusetts, in 1965 to address the issues of educating psychologists for roles in community mental health and community mental health program development (Zax & Specter, 1974). After several days of discussion, it became clear that the conferees were concerned with more than the traditional problems of mental illness. The roles of politics, education, poverty, and racism in the etiology and perpetuation of mental illness were discussed. Some of the participants were convinced that if community mental health was to become a reality, then political and economic issues would have to be addressed. What was needed was a psychology for the whole community, an orientation that would seek to identify and utilize all of the above-mentioned forces in the promotion of mental health and the reduction of mental illness. It was believed that mental illness was the result of social systems forces that contributed to the destruction of human potential and that these systems had to be studied and modified to make them more conducive to human development. Subsequently, beliefs such as these contributed to the emergence of the concept of community psychology.

CURRENT DEFINITIONS OF COMMUNITY PSYCHOLOGY

Several definitions of community psychology have been offered which variously describe it as what community psychologists do, as an orientation toward the prevention of social problems, and as the utilization of environmental forces to ameliorate human suffering (Rappaport, 1977; Scribner, 1970; Zax & Spencer, 1974). Generally, these authors emphasize movement away from psychodynamic views of human behavior and postulate that the causes for behavior problems can be attributed to socioenvironmental factors. Community psychology encompasses the prevention of behavior problems as well as the creation of social systems that are designed to promote and maintain healthy functioning. Its focus is away from the individual and incorporates the community as the "client."

Rappaport informs us: Community refers to a social group; psychology refers to the individual. Community psychology is by definition involved in the classic conflict between individuals and social groups. (1977, p. 1) He suggested that the aims of the community or society may not be the same as those of the individual and that community psychologists should be concerned with making social systems more responsive to individual needs. He also indicated that community psychology is characterized by an acceptance of cultural differences, ecology, human resource development, and a search for new paradigms to solve existing problems. More specifically, community psychology is concerned with the identification and utilization of social, political, economic, and environmental forces in the primary prevention of behavioral problems (Mann, 1978; Murrell, 1973; Myers, 1977).

The strategies by which psychologists attempt to intervene in social systems are many and depend upon the training of the psychologist as well as the dynamics of the social system. It is important for community psychologists to approach community situations from a social systems point of view and with the assumption that all problems of adjustment are the product of some rather complex interactions among persons and social-ecological systems. Halpert (1970) has defined a system as a "set of elements organized to perform a set of functions in order to achieve desired results" (p. 238). A social system is an open system in that it is continually exchanging inputs with the environment (Davidson & Seidman, 1974). An understanding of the properties of the open system may aid the community psychologist in choosing appropriate interventions (Rappaport, 1977).

For the present discussion, community psychology is defined as the study of the effects of social systems influences on human behavior and the utilization of social, political, economic, and environmental forces in preventing mental illness and in promoting human growth and adaptation. As implied in the definition, community psychology must develop a methodology for conducting systematic investigations, a data base from which to make sound decisions, and new paradigms for solving human behavior problems.

The behavioral strategies of data gathering identify functional relationships and attempt to quantify the occurrence of target behaviors and delineate the situations in which they occur. The community psychologists' concern over the identification of systems control variables and the specification of points of intervention into the system are closely aligned with a behavioral orientation (Harshberger & Maley, 1974). The difficulty with the behavioral approach involves the tendency of behaviorists to conclude that because they have impacted on the target behavior, they have solved the problem, and that behavior modifiers typically do not attend to the social-political implications of their interventions (Repucci, 1977). Repucci has warned us of the problems involved in implementing behavior modification programs without taking into account the politics of the system or institution in which the interventions are being planned. Willems (1974) is also of the opinion that behavior modification strategies will have only a minimal impact unless social policies are established to support them. This suggests a need for the behavior modifier to become more involved in the political process, as suggested by community psychology.

According to Repucci (1977), the acceptance of a social-ecological perspective has contributed to a merging of interest between behavior modifiers and community psychologists. He suggested that there are at least three implementation issues of which behavior modifiers should be cognizant when assuming the role of change agent. Repucci identifies entry into the setting, political realities, and problems related to existing institutional staff as issues of concern in planning strategies designed to facilitate institutional change. Furthermore, Repucci and Saunders (1974) suggested that the social application of behavior modification is not as trouble-free as some of the literature indicates. They identified several problems or issues that influence the effectiveness of behavior modifiers. These problems include institutional constraints, the problem of external pressure, language difficulties, the problem of using indigenous personnel, and limited resources. Behavior modifiers who are accustomed to working in controlled settings may overlook many of the systems variables impinging upon their projects and may consequently create more problems than they solve.

Community psychology advocates a broad range of strategies for intervening in social systems. The extent to which behavior modification principles are applicable to problems identified by community psychologists will be determined by an analysis of the compatibility of behavior modification at several levels of intervention, as well as its potential use in the primary prevention of behavior problems.

BEHAVIOR MODIFICATION AND COMMUNITY MENTAL HEALTH

Community mental health is concerned with the resocialization and/or rehabilitation of persons who have been identified as maladjusted. Community mental health centers provide services to outpatients, inpatients, persons who require partial hospitalization, and persons in need of emergency care or crisis intervention, as well as services to other community agencies in the form of consultation–education. Consultation–education services are designed to increase the overall effectiveness and responsiveness of mental-health-related systems in an effort to decrease the occurrence of mental disorders. The community mental health perspective suggests that the rate of mental disorders in the community can be reduced through the utilization of strategies of intervention that are designed to assist persons in adjusting to an already established norm.

Juxtaposed to this position, community psychology is concerned with the prevention of mental disorders and other problems of maladjustment. It seeks to alter social systems so that they are more responsive to individual differences and cultural diversity (Rappaport, 1977). There are several levels of prevention that differentially relate to community mental health and community psychology. Caplan (1964) explicated three types of prevention that are called tertiary, secondary, and primary.

TERTIARY PREVENTION

Tertiary prevention is aimed at reducing the rate of mental disorders in the community. The community is seen as the client, and such strategies as group therapy, family therapy, milieu therapy, and token economies are advocated. Behavior modification programs may be quite effective in dealing with problems at this level. Additionally, treatment strategies such as assertion training, behavior rehearsal in groups, group relaxation training, and systematic desensitization are applicable. The behavior modifier or behavior therapist must be cognizant of the fact that the strategies employed are only reducing the level of suffering and that while he is administering the treatment, other cases of similar problems may be occurring. One of the major advantages of using behavior modification at this level is that it is less costly than more traditional one-to-one psychodynamic approaches. The treatment sessions are usually fewer, and the techniques can be taught to paraprofessional level personnel (Suinn, 1974). By including paraprofessionals in the delivery of services, in addition to treating effectively larger groups or persons, the rate of problems in the community might be reduced.

SECONDARY PREVENTION

The goals of secondary prevention are to detect problems early and provide treatment which will retard their development in the community. Persons concerned with secondary prevention in the community must be able to diagnose accurately problems on a large scale. The use of existing diagnostic devices may meet part of the need, but the development of additional instrumentation is necessary (Rappaport, 1977). Early intervention attempts to reduce the prevalence of problems in the community. Approaches such as early intervention programs with children, crisis intervention, and consultation–education are recommended. For example, behavior modification techniques have been used in treating a wide array of childhood behavior problems. Behavior problems such as classroom disruption (Allen, Turner, & Everett, 1970), social withdrawal (Allen, Hart, Buell, Harris, & Wolf, 1964), studying (Broden, Hall, & Mitts, 1971), learning disabilities (Glavin, Quay, Annesley, & Werry, 1971), mental retardation (Birnbrauer, Wolf, Kidder, & Tague, 1965; Brown & Foshee, 1971; Hall, Fox, Willard, Goldsmith, Emerson, Owen, Davis, & Porcia, 1971), delinquency (Bailey, Wolf, & Phillips, 1970; Bedner, Zelhart, Greathouse, & Weinburg, 1970; Phillips, Phillips, Fixen, & Wolf, 1971), and psychosis (Lovaas & Simmons, 1969) have all been treated by using behavior modification techniques.

Social learning theorists assume that the child's behavior is influenced by those with whom he interacts. In order to facilitate change in the child's behavior, the significant others must be a part of the treatment (Patterson, 1971). Teaching parents to apply properly contingencies of reinforcement and punishment not only has an impact on managing the immediate behavior problem, but parents may also apply their knowledge of behavioral assessment and management in future situations with other children. Furthermore, modeling may extend the availability of reinforcement contingencies and systematize the acquisition of positive constructive behaviors while extinguishing negative destructive ones (Bandura, Jeffery, & Wright, 1974). Behavior modification principles show a great deal of promise in secondary prevention with young children, and such techniques as modeling and positive reinforcement are particularly attractive from a community psychology perspective.

Behavior modification approaches to crisis intervention involve taking advantage of an opportunity to have an immediate impact on the person in crisis by pointing out unsuccessful and destructive behaviors and seizing the opportunity to teach successful, constructive ones (Balson, 1971). Techniques such as positive reinforcement, negative reinforcement, shaping, modeling, prompting, and assertion training have been applied in crisis intervention (Golan, 1978).

Guidelines established for the operation of comprehensive community mental health agencies called for the development of consultation–education services in an effort to promote preventive interventions by the community mental health center. Typical approaches to consultation–education include providing services such as speakers' bureaus and technical assistance to school districts and other community mental-health-related facilities.

Caplan (1964) outlined several different types of consultation. He indicated that consultation is a process in which the consultant is at least one step removed from the client and imparts important knowledge or skills that focus on the consultee, the organization of the program, or administrative difficulties. In any case, the consultant seeks to improve the consultee's capability to provide a more efficient and effective service. By upgrading the consultee's skills, the consultant enhances the consultee's ability to handle similar cases effectively in the future.

Bellack and Franks (1975) suggested that behavior modification should play a major role in consultation within mental health systems. They indicated that behavioral principles can be instrumental in working through several problems associated with the consultation process. Such concerns as the formulation of consultation goals, the consultation format, and problems associated with the unwillingness of some consultees to accept a behavioral orientation can be facilitated through the application of behavioral principles. Such concepts as shaping, reinforcement, and modeling may be helpful in facilitating the development of consultation programs. The obvious advantages to this approach are that it can easily be taught to nonprofessional persons, the performance of trainees can be monitored, and feedback can be reliably generated regarding the effectiveness of consultation–education programs. Suinn (1974) reported the successful training of undergraduate students as behavior modification consultants. Mayer (1972) suggested that positive reinforcement, extinction, fading, and scheduling can be applied to assist consultees in selecting goals and in facilitating the consultee's acquisition and implementation of mutually agreed-upon procedures.

Behavior modification principles have been incorporated into other aspects of comprehensive mental health services which further demonstrate their value in promoting secondary prevention. Turner and Goodson (1977) described the use of behavior modification principles as a primary strategy of intervention for a community mental health center. The authors reported the successful implementation of a behavior modification approach in the Huntsville-Madison County (Alabama) Mental Health Center. Neitzel, Winett, MacDonald, & Davidson (1977) described the development of the Huntsville-Madison County Mental Health Center as an attempt to make the center's services more accountable to the public. The authors reported that initially the term *behavior modification* was not well received in the community and that the center staff had to devote a great deal of time to educating the community as to the term's actual meaning. Behavioral principles were used to extinguish criticism from the community. The center reported the successful application of behavioral principles in training all staff in the use of behavior modification techniques and in developing outpatient services for adults, procedures for managing staff, and a comprehensive evaluation program (Turner, 1975; Turner & Goodson, 1975; Turner & Pyfrom, 1974). Also, Liberman and Bryan (1976) demonstrated the use of behavioral principles in the development of a comprehensive community mental health center. Modeling, prompting, and positive feedback were used to motivate the clinical staff of a comprehensive mental health center to adopt systematic behavioral treatment and recording procedures. Innovations such as a credit–incentive system, educational workshops for community adaptation, and a goal-attainment method of evaluating treatment were implemented. Also, consultation–education programs were established for parents, schools, and other community agencies. Others have reported the successful use of behavior modification principles in community programs (Gambrill, 1975), and advocated the use of behavioral principles in the design of human service delivery systems (Malott, 1974).

Additionally, Stolz (1976) suggested that multiple baseline designs may be used in the evaluation of treatments administered in a community setting, as well as addressing the issue of accountability to the community. Stolz realistically argued that reversal designs are unacceptable to the public for use in evaluating the efficacy of behavioral interventions in the community mental health center. The requirement that treatment be discontinued in order to assess the potency of intervention is met with disapproval. She suggested that multiple baseline designs may be a viable alternative to the reversal procedure. The multiple baseline design procedure measures changes in consecutively treated behaviors and does not require interruptions in treatment.

The development and/or improvement of community organizations involved in the delivery of services to high risk groups is an important step in secondary prevention that has recently received attention by behavioral-oriented community psychologists. Problems such as the low rate of participation by poor people in community programs (Miller & Miller, 1970), a lack of participation of low-income persons in the decision-making processes of federal programs (Briscoe, Hoffman, & Bailey, 1975), and the use of dental services by low-income persons (Reiss, Piotrowski, & Bailey, 1976) have been successfully addressed by a behavior modification approach.

Miller and Miller (1970) used reinforcements such as donated clothing, household goods, and information about welfare services to increase the attendance rates of low-income persons at self-help group meetings from an average of three per meeting to 15 persons per meeting. The authors concluded that "practical forms of reinforcement" may be applied to effectively maintain the participation of disadvantaged populations in self-help groups. Briscoe *et al.* (1975) demonstrated the effects of training low-income adults to participate as board members in a federally supported community project. The participants were trained to make behaviorally defined statements which were designed to increase problem-solving behaviors in board meetings. The study showed that problem-solving responses during board meetings increased for participants following training and remained higher than baseline during a follow-up.

Reiss *et al.* (1976) investigated the effectiveness and cost efficiency of three techniques that were designed to encourage rural parents to seek dental care for their children. Three matched groups of parents were randomly assigned to one of three treatment conditions: (1) a "prompt only" group, (2) three prompts consisting of a note, a telephone call, and a home visit, and (3) a prompt plus a $5.00 incentive. The authors reported that the prompt plus the $5.00 incentive condition was effective in producing a slightly higher percentage of initial dental visits than the other conditions and that this condition was less costly than the three-prompt condition.

Thus, behavior modification principles have demonstrated their usefulness in tertiary and secondary prevention problems, as well as suggesting innovations in program development and evaluation in community settings. However, behavior modification principles have yet to prove their worth in primary prevention paradigms.

PRIMARY PREVENTION

Conceptually, community mental health and community psychology are different dimensions along the same continuum. Community psychology is concerned with primary prevention, and less emphasis is placed on tertiary and secondary prevention. Primary prevention is concerned with the prevention of problems before they occur by altering the circumstances that produce problems of maladjustment (Caplan, 1964). A social systems approach is called for, and community psychologists are required to address the political, social, economic, and environmental issues believed to have an impact on the development of human behavior problems.

It is at the level of primary prevention that behavior modification shows its major limitation. Very few studies have been published that demonstrate the efficacy of behavior modification principles in altering social structures and circumstances that contribute to maladaptive behavior. This is partly due to the fact that the traditional European perspective in which behavior modification principles were developed does not readily suggest the conceptualization of a comprehensive model of prevention. A proclivity toward the dichotomization of concepts (i.e., Descartes' mind–body, Plato's rational–irrational, man versus environment) has severely hampered the formulation of mental health policies that promote the development of highly integrated comprehensive mental health systems. This issue will be further explicated as we discuss the application of behavior modification in black communities and the black perspective in community psychology.

BEHAVIOR MODIFICATION AND BLACK COMMUNITIES

Community psychology is compatible with the black perspective. The focus on social systems, issues regarding power, community participation, racism, and prevention—all have particular significance for black psychologists. Due to the newness of the community psychology movement, few examples are available that demonstrate the efficacy of a systems approach in black communities. Taber (1970) described a project in which an ecological-systems approach was used in dealing with the problems of self-image and powerlessness in two black social systems— an adult social group and a teenage gang. The goal of the project was to develop models of service delivery that produced changes in existing social systems instead of focusing on individual pathology.

The main issues to be considered here are: (a) to what extent are behavior modification principles compatible with the black orientation toward treatment, and (b) to what extent has behavior modification been effectively applied with black populations?

A major concern regarding the implementation of behavior modification in black communities is the lack of participation on the part of black psychologists in conceptualizing and designing behavioral strategies of intervention (Bardo, Bryson, & Cody, 1974). A lack of input from black communities also contributes to the problem. Bardo et al. reported that the above concerns had not been adequately addressed because of the limited number of black persons trained in behavior modification, together with a lack of community awareness and sophistication. Bardo, Bryson, Scott, and Black (1973) suggested a moratorium on the use of behavior modification techniques with black populations when there is no input from black professionals. This situation was further highlighted by the President's Commission on Mental Health (1978). The Commission reported that chief among the complaints of minority persons seeking services in community mental health centers was feeling rejected, misunderstood, and abused by nonminority service providers. The Commission recommended that additional minority personnel receive training to provide culturally relevant mental health services in addition to increasing the number of minority professionals involved in the conceptualization of mental health service delivery systems. Apparently, the Commission assumed that there are meaningful differences between minority and majority populations that must be understood in order to improve the effectiveness of service delivery. These differences have to do with culture (Arewa, 1977) and world view (Clark, McGee, Nobels, & Akbar, 1976).

THE BLACK PERSPECTIVE IN MENTAL HEALTH

According to Arewa (1977), culture is a manifestation of human beliefs and is found everywhere. It also has local manifestations which are unique and contribute to variations in problem-solving from one group to the next. The solutions people develop for their problems are culture-bound, and the culture is bound by its belief system or world view.

Clark *et al.,* (1976) suggested that the differences between black psychologists and European-American psychologists are related to differences between African and European cultures. Nobles (1972) put forth the notion that black psychology is grounded in an ontology that is common to African people. The investigation of the relative merits of behavior modification programs must include an assessment of the expectations established by the black perspective as well as the particular cultural parameters that define behavior as normal or abnormal, adaptive or maladaptive.

The existence of a black perspective is based on the existence of an African ontology. The African ontology has been expressed in terms of African religions and philosophy (Mbiti, 1970). African philosophy is the understanding, attitude, perceptual set, and expectations that are common to African people. The philosophy is manifested in cultural traditions, ethics, a unique concept of time, a dedication to the survival of the tribe, and a belief in the oneness of being (i.e., that man and nature are one and that everything in the universe is interconnected). Life is viewed as a continuous process, beginning before birth and continuing after so-called death. According to Nobles (1972), African self-concept is a collective self-concept. Individual worth is a function of one's relationship to the collective worth of the community. In fact, the individual exists at the expense of the community. Thus, when an individual suffers, so does the community, and vice versa. The concept of kinship is central to the notion of community. Kinship lines are so extensive that it is often impossible to determine where a particular group begins and ends. Kinship lines extend horizontally to include every member of a local group and extend vertically to encompass the dead and those not yet born (Mbiti, 1970). The kinship lines contribute to a sense of community responsibility and establish a natural extended family network—much like the networks present in black communities.

The notion of unity or oneness of being prevents the dichotomization of the life process and contributes to a conceptualization of community problems that include physical and mental health within an ecological-systems framework. In contrast, dichotomization of physical and mental health is common within the European world view (Jackson, 1976). As noted by the President's Commission on Mental Health (1978), the separation of health and mental health systems is a major problem in the effective delivery of community mental health services.

The African concept of time (Figure 1) is fundamental to understanding the African ontology. Mbiti (1970) notes that Africans maintain a concept of time that includes past and present, but not the distant future. The words *zamani* and *sasa* are African words that refer to past and present respectively. *Sasa* encompasses the present and immediate future (i.e., the next minute, tomorrow, next week). *Zamani* and *sasa* also overlap to form the "here and now." Perceptions of the present reality are a function of our past and present perceptions. The notion of the hereafter or life after death is also essential to African reality. Death is a process by which a person moves from the *sasa* period to the *zamani*. Though the person is physically dead, he continues to exist in the *sasa* period. The fact that the deceased is remembered by relatives and friends

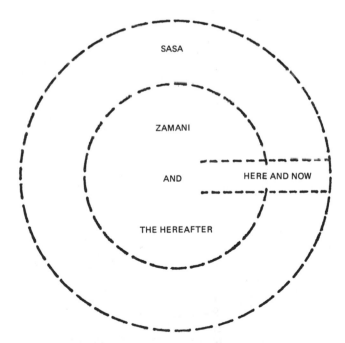

Figure 1. The interrelatedness of the African concept of time.

supports the continued existence of his spirit in the *sasa* period. The interrelatedness of the concept of time is presented in Figure 1. The practical aspect of the African concept of time and kinship involves interpersonal, family, and community relations and procreation. Because one's continued existence beyond physical death is tied to those who will be left behind to remember him, it becomes extremely important to cultivate healthy relationships as well as to produce children. Additionally, the concept of time has some important implications for mental health. One's sense of well-being is intertwined with events that occur in the *zamani* and *sasa* periods and with one's expectations for life after death. The physical, mental, and spiritual development of human beings is also thought to be related to one's participation in the community. In this sense, the African concept of self is interconnected with the concept

Figure 2. The concept of self as interrelated with one's spiritual, mental, and physical development within the context of the community.

of community (Nobles, 1972). The interrelatedness of the concept of self with the community is depicted in Figure 2. As the figure suggests, self-concept is related to how one feels about his community and his physical, mental, and spiritual development. In order to maintain a positive self-concept, the person must contribute to the community and engage in activities that contribute to his physical, mental, and spiritual growth. African self-concept is a collective self-concept. The expression "I am because we are and because we are therefore I am" (Mbiti, 1970) is the result of a community definition of self. Clearly, if we are to have an impact on the psychological well-being of members of the community, our interventions must be directed at or involve the community.

Nobles (1972) suggested that European preconceptions of family serve to distort their assessments of behavior and relationships within black families. He indicated that the African philosophical notion of survival of the tribe and oneness of being influences practices such as unofficial adoption, collective living arrangements, and maintenance of close ties with the elderly. In order to understand the nature of the black family, one must understand the "Africanity" (i.e., the influence of the African ontology), its basic philosophical fiber. Attempts to intervene in the black family from a purely European perspective may grossly distort the essence of the family and create more problems than are solved. The African concepts of unity and kinship have also influenced the development of a mental health delivery system that utilizes significant others in the client's environment in all phases of treatment, keeps the patient in the community, and utilizes the influences of indigenous mental health care providers (Lambo, 1978).

The black perspective of helping is characterized by actively seeking out those in need of help, using group approaches, being more focused, and providing treatment in the local community of the person(s) in need of assistance (Jackson, 1976). Lambo (1978) reported the development of a mental health center in Nigeria in which a significant other is required to accompany the identified client to the mental health center and remain with the client during the assessment phase and become involved in the treatment process. Other community resources are identified and included in the treatment, which is carried out in the person's local community. Behavior modification principles seem to be quite compatible with this orientation.

The preceding discussion emphasizes the importance of involving black psychologists in the conceptualization of behavior change strategies that are implemented in black communities. Lightfoot and Foster (1970) suggested that community psychiatry may be useful in dealing with psychological problems of black people but that leadership in programs aimed at black communities must be assumed by black Americans. Jackson (1976, 1977) also advocates the utilization of behavior modification principles by black psychologists. From Jackson's view, behavior therapy is suited to a variety of the needs of black people.

As indicated earlier, behavior modification is a particular approach to changing behavior. It is a tool to be used within the perspective maintained by the change agent. Unlike other systems of behavior change, behavior modification is a highly objective technology that can be applied at several levels within the community.

Traditional conceptualizations of behavior problems that rely on mentalistic explanations are inconsistent with the black psychologists' community perspective. The possibility of bias in the interpretation of behavior as well as in the application of therapy is too great when using a European conceptual framework. Behaviorism seeks to perform an objective analysis of behavior. Behavior is viewed as a specific response and is controlled by specific environmental events. Hayes (1972) states that black psycholgists should adapt a system called "radical black behaviorism" as a method of explaining the behavior of black people. He feels that much of American psychology has been detrimental to the well-being of black people because it is unscientific. Radical black behaviorism is based upon radical behaviorism (Skinner, 1964) and can be incorporated into the perspectives of black psychologists. In discussing the practical utility of this approach, Hayes suggested that it could be helpful in identifying, controlling, and predicting behaviors of black people that are crucial to our economic, social, and political struggles. The issue, according to Hayes (1972) is not whether control is to be exerted, but who will exert the control over black people. If black people are going to assume the responsibility for community control, then strategies designed to increase community participation are needed. At least two studies have been cited in the literature that employed behavior modification principles to increase participation in community programs (Miller & Miller, 1970; Reiss *et al.*, 1976).

MENTAL HEALTH MANPOWER IN BLACK COMMUNITIES: RECOMMENDATIONS FOR TRAINING

The issues of community control and participation in community programs by black people are very closely related to the issue of training personnel to provide services in black communities. A recent survey by the American Psychological Association estimated that only 0.9% of all doctoral-level health service providers in psychology are black. Additionally, a recent report indicated that although black people represent approximately 11.1% of the United States population, they comprised only 1.4% of the psychiatrists in 1978, 7.6% of the social workers in

1975, and 3.3% of the licensed nurses in 1972 (Johnson, 1979). While these data do not accurately represent the current numbers of black mental health service providers, they represent the best estimates available.

Furthermore, in 1972 it was found that only 7.3% (348) of the total population of doctoral-level clinical psychology graduate students were members of a minority group, and only 3.3% (41) of the clinical psychology faculty were black (Padilla, Boxley, & Wagner, 1973). This bleak picture suggests that a radical departure from traditional training models may be necessary to correct current imbalances in the number of black human service providers. Considering the wide range of specializations and orientations within clinical psychology, and the fact that social, political, and economic barriers impede the entry of black students into graduate programs, it seems doubtful that an adequate number of Ph.D.-level black psychologists will be trained in behavioral community psychology in the near future. Even if these barriers are lowered, the community will not be able to meet the costs associated with employing large numbers of Ph.D.-level persons in the delivery of mental health services. Therefore, training models must be developed that extend the knowledge and skills of behavior modification and community psychology to the Master's level and Bachelor's level degree, and to indigenous community workers.

Seidman and Rappaport (1974) have addressed the problem of manpower utilization and training by developing an educational pyramid which uses professional-level psychologists as consultants, researchers, and teachers of large numbers of graduate students. These students train and supervise a larger number of undergraduates and other paraprofessionals as direct service providers in schools, nursing homes, mental health facilities, and the court system. This approach is consistent with both community psychology and community mental health. The pyramidal structure enables large numbers of persons to participate in the delivery of services to diverse populations. With this conceptual framework in mind, departments of psychology should develop content areas that are consistent with behavioral community psychology. Faculty members with a behavioral orientation and training may find it useful to participate in postgraduate experiences in community psychology (i.e., workshops, seminars, lectures, independent study). These faculty could then teach courses in community psychology to graduate students who have backgrounds in behavior modification. The graduate students would in turn teach community psychology and techniques of behavior modification to undergraduate students and other paraprofessionals. Both students and faculty should participate in other disciplines (such as political science, sociology, city planning, and communications). An interdisciplinary orientation will aid the conceptualization of new paradigms of intervention and contribute to the development of an activist orientation among service providers at all levels.

It is extremely important that large numbers of black human service providers receive training at each level of the pyramid. These persons should have strong ties within black communities as well as a strong commitment to working with black populations. In addition to serving as human resources, they should participate in experiences that are designed to increase their understanding of black culture and of the effects of racism on mental health. Because many black students in predominantly white universities run the risk of losing touch with their communities as well as themselves, they should attend conferences and workshops that are sponsored by black organizations. It is also recommended that students spend their summers engaged in volunteer work or practicum agencies in black communities.

Internship and practicum experiences should be arranged with local, state, and national mental health agencies, political organizations, school systems, and criminal justice systems. Situations should be arranged by these agencies so that students will be exposed to the hardcore unemployed, chronically ill mental patients, children, youth, and elderly populations in black communities.

The ultimate success of the community psychology movement is contingent upon our ability to train large numbers of persons (Neitzel et al., 1977), particularly large numbers of black human service providers. Not only will involving large numbers of black people in the training process enhance black communities, but black students may contribute to improving graduate and undergraduate training programs at traditionally white universities (Moore, 1977). Moore suggested that minority students and faculty bring a different perspective to psychology and that their cultural perspectives will interact with the existing dominant ones in ways that will serve to improve social science and contribute to social change. Although the pyramidal structure allows for participation of large numbers of persons in the delivery of services to diverse populations, it is not consistent with the black perspective of service delivery. As demonstrated by Lambo (1978), and as suggested by Jackson (1976), the incorporation of community strengths and natural systems of mental health care that have been traditionally used by black people is essential. Training models must provide for the identification and utilization of persons considered to be natural care-givers by the community. Attitudes toward training must be open and flexible enough to include unconventional methods of healing, and research must address the effectiveness of these systems of care. I prefer a systems model which is depicted by concentric circles. Figure 3 depicts the interrelatedness among the

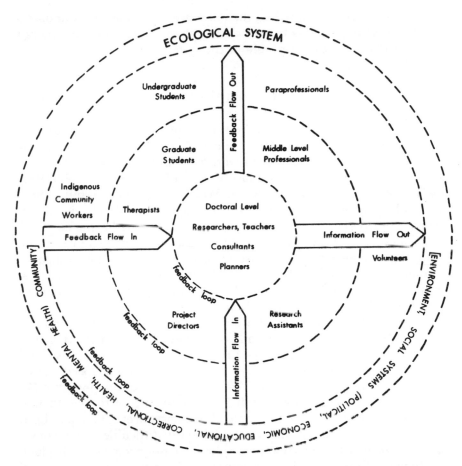

Figure 3. The interconnectedness of various levels of community psychology training program and the ecological system including the environment, social systems, and the community as viewed from an African-American world view. Systems boundaries are open, as indicated by broken lines.

various aspects of the training model (i.e., doctoral, middle, and under-graduate levels) and the ecological system. There are clearly defined boundaries for each aspect of the system. These boundaries are permeable, accepting inputs from all aspects of the system. Feedback is generated throughout the system so that training, research, and consultation do not occur in a vacuum. Decisions regarding training, research, and consultation are made in view of the needs and demands of the total system. Ecological requirements have an impact on training, as do political, economic, and other social systems. Although each aspect of the system has its primary function, the existence of permeable boundaries and feedback loops allows for the exchange of information and energy resources that permeate throughout the system.

CONCLUSION

Several authors have advocated the use of behavior modification in black communities (Jackson, 1977; Hayes, 1972). Principles of behavior modification have been employed with black populations (Chadwick & Day, 1971; Hart & Risley, 1968; Jacobson, Bushell, & Risley, 1969; Reynolds & Risley, 1968; Wasik, Senn, Welch, & Cooper, 1969). These authors have demonstrated the effective application of behavior modification principles with black students in school systems, having modified behaviors such as studying, speech problems, and classroom disruption. Others have demonstrated the use of behavior modification principles in community mental health (Gambrill, 1975), consultation (Bellack & Franks, 1975), crisis intervention (Golan, 1978), and in the secondary prevention of delinquency (Davidson & Robinson, 1975).

The fact that behavior modification techniques are easily combined with a variety of theoretical orientations suggests some interesting possibilities for their use in primary prevention. Behavioral analysis and modification procedures may prove useful in identifying specific environmental influences on behavior, as well as in the development of behavior settings that are more conducive to human growth and adaptation. The problem is that the area of primary prevention has been plagued with conceptual and methodological difficulties, and consequently, behavior modification principles have not been widely applied.

In view of the available alternatives, black psychologists will do well to investigate the efficacy of behavior modification. When combined with a social-systems and/or black perspective, behavior modification shows great promise in tertiary and secondary prevention. The fact that behavior modification can be easily taught to nonprofessionals (Suinn, 1974) makes it quite amenable for use in social-systems-oriented community psychology training programs. Its methodology seems promising in addressing the issue of community accountability. The fact that behavioral psychologists focus on overt behavior and direct their analyses toward the relationship between behavior and environmental events makes behavior modification an attractive approach to solving human behavior problems. This same degree of specificity has contributed to combining behavioral analysis with systems analysis (Harshberger & Maley, 1974).

Black psychologists should exercise caution in their reliance on the behavioral approach. Behavior modification programs should not be offered as substitutes for social-political activism. Problems facing black communities are integrally tied to social-political and economic processes that must be influenced if meaningful change is to occur. As Willems (1974) has suggested, behavior modification projects will only have minimal, short-lived positive results unless social policies are established to support them.

Change in black American communities is also related to the issue of training black psychologists. Steps must be taken to reduce social systems barriers to educating black Americans, and innovative approaches to training are necessary if sufficient numbers of black human service providers are going to be available to deliver mental health services in black communities. The various institutes of the Alcohol, Drug Abuse, and Mental Health Administration (ADAMHA) should make funds available for black psychologists who are involved in research on black perspectives in human service delivery, and additional training funds should be made available to stimulate the development of black mental health resources.

As recommended by the President's Commission on Mental Health (1978), black Americans must become more involved in the conceptualization and delivery of community mental health services. A black perspective in helping will facilitate the development of comprehensive systems of health care. This perspective needs to be investigated more closely.

REFERENCES

Allen, G. J., Chinsky, J. M., Larcen, S. W., Lochman, J. E., & Sellinger, H. V. *Community psychology and the schools.* Hillsdale, N. J.: Lawrence Erlbaum, 1976.

Allen, K. E., Hart, B., Buell, J. S., Harris, F. R., & Wolf, M. M. Effects of social reinforcement on isolate behavior of a nursery school child. *Child Development*, 1964, *35*, 511–518.

Allen, K. E., Turner, D. K., & Everett, P. M. A behavior modification classroom for Head Start children with problem behaviors. *Exceptional Children*, 1970, *37*, 119–127.

Allyon, T., Layman, D., & Kandel, H. J. A behavioral-educational alternative to drug control of hyperactive children. *Journal of Applied Behavior Analysis*, 1975, *8*, 137–146.

Arewa, O. Cultural bias in standardized testing: An anthropological view. *The Negro Educational Review*, 1977, *28*(3 & 4), 153–171.

Bailey, J. S., Wolf, M. M., & Phillips, E. L. Home-based reinforcement and the modification of pre-delinquents' classroom behavior. *Journal of Applied Behavior Analysis*, 1970, *3*, 223–233.

Balson, P. M. The use of behavior therapy techniques in crisis intervention: A case report. *Journal of Behavior Therapy and Experimental Psychiatry*, 1971: *2*, 297–300.

Bandura, A., Jeffery, R. W., & Wright, C. L. Efficacy of participant modeling as a function of response induction aids. *Journal of Abnormal Psychology*, 1974, *83*, 56–64.

Bardo, H., Bryson, S., Scott, H., & Black, A. *Black professionals discuss behavior modification techniques*. Paper presented at the meeting of the American Personnel and Guidance Association, Atlanta, Ga., May 1973.

Bardo, H., Bryson, S., & Cody, J. Black concern with behavior modification. *Personnel and Guidance Journal*, 1974, *53*(1), 20–25.

Bednar, R. L., Zelhart, P. F., Greathouse, L., & Weinburg, S. Operant conditioning principles in the treatment of learning and behavior problems with delinquent boys. *Journal of Counseling Psychology*, 1970, *17*, 492–497.

Bellack, A. S., & Franks, C. Behavioral consultation in the community mental health center. *Behavior Therapy*, 1975, *6*(3), 388–391.

Birnbrauer, J. S. Mental retardation. In H. Leitenberg (Ed.), *Handbook of behavior modification and behavior therapy*. Englewood Cliffs, N. J.: Prentice–Hall, 1976.

Birnbrauer, J. S., Wolf, M. M., Kidder, J. D., & Tague, C. E. Classroom behavior of retarded pupils with token reinforcement. *Journal of Experimental Child Psychology*, 1965, *3*, 219–235.

Boardman, W. K. A brief behavior disorder. *Journal of Consulting Psychology*, 1962, *26*, 293–297.

Briscoe, N., Hoffman, D., & Bailey, J. Behavioral community psychology: Training a community board to problem solve. *Journal of Applied Behavior Analysis*. 1975, *8*, 157–168.

Broden, J., Hall, R. V., & Mitts, B. The effects of self-recording on classroom behavior of two eighth-grade students. *Journal of Applied Behavior Analysis*, 1971, *4*, 191–199.

Brown, L., & Foshee, J. G. Comparative techniques for increasing attending behavior of retarded students. *Education and Training of the Mentally Retarded*, 1971, *6*, 4–11.

Caplan, G. *Principles of preventive psychiatry*. New York: Basic Books, 1964.

Chadwick, B. A., & Day, R. C. Systematic reinforcement: Academic performance of underachieving students. *Journal of Applied Behavior Analysis*, 1971, *4*, 311–319.

Clark, X. C., McGee, P. D., Nobels, W. W., & Akbar, N. *Voodoo or IQ: An Introduction to African psychology*. Chicago: Institute of Positive Education, 1976.

Davidson, W. S., & Robinson, M. J. Community psychology and behavior modification: A community based program for the prevention of delinquency. *Corrective and Social Psychiatry and Journal of Behavior Technology and Therapy*, 1975, *21*(1), 1–12.

Davidson, W. S., & Seidman, E. Studies of behavior modification and juvenile delinquency: A review, methodological critique and social perspective. *Psychological Bulletin*, 1974, *81*, 998–1011.

Fazio, A. F. Implosive therapy with semiclinical phobias. *Journal of Abnormal Psychology*, 1972, *80*, 183–188.

Gambrill, E. D. Role of behavior modification in community mental health. *Community Mental Health Journal*, 1975, *11*(3), 307–315.

Glavin, J. P., Quay, H. V., Annesley, F. R., & Werry, J. S. An experimental resource room for behavior problem children. *Exceptional Children*, 1971, *38*, 131–137.

Golan, N. *Treatment in crisis situations*. New York: Free Press, 1978.

Hall, R. V., Fox, R., Willard, D., Goldsmith, L., Emerson, M., Owen, M., Davis, F., & Porcia, E. The teacher as observer and experimenter in the modification of disputing and talking out behavior. *Journal of Applied Behavior Analysis*, 1971, *4*, 141–149.

Halpert, H. P. Models for the application of systems analysis to the delivery of mental health services. In P. Cook (Ed.), *Community psychology and community mental health*. San Francisco: Holden–Day, 1970.

Harshberger, D., & Maley, R. F. Behavior analysis and systems analysis: *An integrative approach to mental health programs*. Kalamazoo, Mich.: Behaviordelia, 1974.

Hart, B. M., & Risley, T. R. Establishing use of descriptive objectives in the spontaneous speech of disadvantaged preschool children. *Journal of Applied Behavior Analysis*, 1968, *1*, 109–120.

Hayes, W. A. Radical black behaviorism. in R. L. Jones (Ed.), *Black psychology*. New York: Harper & Row, 1972.

Jackson, G. The African genesis of the black perspective in helping. *Professional psychology*, 1976, *7*(3), 363–367.

Jackson, G. Community mental health, behavior therapy, and the Afro-American community. Paper presented at the 11th Annual Association for the Advancement of Behavior Therapy Convention. Atlanta, Ga., December 9, 1977.

Jacobson, J. M., Bushell, D., Jr., & Risley, T. Switching requirements in a Head Start classroom. *Journal of Applied Behavior Analysis*, 1969, *2*, 43–47.

Johnson, J. W. *Manpower development and training: Strategies for our future.* Report presented to the Minority Advisory Committee of the Alcohol, Drug Abuse, and Mental Health Administration, 1979.

Joint Commission on Mental Illness and Health, *Action for mental health.* New York: Basic Books, 1961.

Jones, R. T., & Kazdin, A. E. Programming response maintenance after withdrawing token reinforcement. *Behavior Therapy*, 1975, *6*, 153–165.

Kondas, O., & Scetnicka, B. Systematic desensitization as a method of preparation for childbirth. *Journal of Behavior Therapy and Experimental Psychiatry*, 1972, *3*, 51–54.

Lambo, T. A. Psychotherapy in Africa. *Human Nature*, March, 1978.

Liberman, R. P., & Bryan, E. A behavioral approach to community psychiatry. *Scandinavian Journal of Behavior Therapy*, 1976, *5*(2), 57–73.

Liberman, R. P., Teigen, J. R., Patterson, R., & Baker, V. Reducing delusional speech in chronic, paranoid schizophrenics. *Journal of Applied Behavior Analysis*, 1973, *6*, 57–64.

Lightfoot, O. B., & Foster, D. L. Black studies, black identity formation and some implications for community psychiatry. *American Journal of Orthopsychiatry*, 1970, *40*(5), 751–755.

Lovass, O. I., & Simmons, J. Q. Manipulation of self-destruction in three retarded children. *Journal of Applied Behavior Analysis*, 1969, *2*, 143–157.

Lovibond, S. H. The mechanism of conditioning treatment of enuresis. *Behaviour Research and Therapy*, 1963, *1*, 17–21.

Mahoney, M. J., & Craighead, B. K. Self-control techniques in behavior modification with the mentally retarded. Paper presented at the meeting of the American Association of Mental Deficiency, Atlanta, Ga., June, 1973.

Malott, R. W. A behavioral-systems approach to the design of human services. In D. Harshberger & R. F. Maley (Eds.), *Behavior analysis and systems analysis: An integrative approach to mental health programs*. Kalamazoo, Mich.: Behaviordelia, 1974.

Mann, P. A. *Community psychology: Concepts and applications*. New York: Free Press, 1978.

Mayer, G. Roy. Behavioral consulting. Using behavior modification procedures in the consulting relationship. *Elementary School Guidance & Counseling*, 1972, *7*(2), 114–119.

Mbiti, J. S. *African religions and philosophy*. Garden City, N.Y.: Anchor Books, 1970.

Miller, L. K., & Miller, O. L. Reinforcing self-help group activities of welfare recipients. *Journal of Applied Behavior Analysis*, 1970, *3*, 57–64.

Moore, T. Social change and community psychology. In I. Iscoe, B. Bloom, & D. D. Spielberger (Eds.), *Community psychology in transition*. Washington, D.C.: Hemisphere Press, 1977.

Murrell, S. A. *Community psychology and social systems: A conceptual framework and intervention guide*. New York: Behavioral Publications, 1973.

Myers, E. R. *The community psychology concept: Integrating theory, education and practice in psychology, social work and public administration.* Washington, D.C.: University Press of America, 1977.

Neitzel, M. T., Winett, R. A., MacDonald, M. L., & Davidson, W. S. *Behavioral approaches to community psychology.* New York: Pergamon Press, 1977.

Nobles, W. W. African philosophy: Foundations for black psychology. in R. Jones (Ed.), *Black psychology.* New York: Harper & Row, 1972.

Padilla, E. R., Boxley, R., & Wagner, N. N. The desegregation of clinical psychology training. *Professional psychology,* 1973, *4,* 259–264.

Patterson, G. R. *Families: Applications of social learning to family life.* Champaign, Ill.: Research Press, 1971.

Phillips, E. L., Phillips, E. A., Fixsen, D. L., & Wolf, M. M. Achievement place: Modification of the behaviors of predelinquent boys within a token economy. *Journal of Applied Behavior Analysis,* 1971, *4,* 45–49.

President's Commission on Mental Health. Washington, D.C.: U.S. Government Printing Office, 1978.

Rappaport, J. *Community psychology: Values, research, and action.* New York: Holt, Rhinehart & Winston, 1977.

Reiss, M. L. Piotrowski, W. D., & Bailey, J. S. Behavioral community psychology: Encouraging low-income patients to seek dental care for their children. *Journal of Applied Behavioral Analysis,* 1976, *9,* 387–398.

Repucci, N. D. Implementation issues for the behavior modifier as institutional change agent. *Behavior Therapy,* 1977, *8*(4), 594–605.

Repucci, N. D., & Saunders, J. T. Social psychology of behavior modification: Problems of implementation in natural settings. *American Psychologist,* 1974, 649–660.

Reynolds, N. J., & Risley, T. R. The role of social and material reinforcers in increasing talking of a disadvantaged preschool child. *Journal of Applied Behavior Analysis,* 1968, *1,* 253–363.

Rieff, R. The need for a body of knowledge in community psychology. In I. Iscoe & C. D. Spielberger (Eds.), *Community psychology: Perspectives in training and research.* New York: Appleton–Century–Crofts, 1970.

Schwitzgebel, R. *Street corner research: An experimental approach to the juvenile delinquent.* Cambridge: Harvard University, 1964.

Scribner, S. What is community psychology made of? In P. Cook (Ed.), *Community psychology and community mental health.* San Francisco: Holden–Day, 1970.

Seidman, E., & Rappaport, J. The educational pyramid: A paradigm for research, training and manpower utilization in community psychology. *American Journal of Community Psychology,* 1974, *2,* 119–130.

Skinner, B. F. Behaviorism at fifty. In T. W. Wann (Ed.), *Behaviorism and phenomenology.* Chicago: University of Chicago Press, 1964, 79–97.

Sobell, M. B., & Sobell, L. C. Individualized behavior therapy for alcoholics. *Behavior Therapy,* 1973, *4,* 49–72.

Stolz, S. B. Evaluation of therapeutic efficacy of behavior modification in a community setting. *Behavior Research and Therapy,* 1976, *14*(6), 479–481.

Suinn, R. M. Training undergraduate students as community behavior modification consultants. *Journal of Counseling Psychology,* 1974, *21*(1), 71–77.

Taber, R. H. A systems approach to the delivery of mental health services to black ghettos. *American Journal of Orthopsychiatry,* 1970, *40*(4), 703–709.

Task Force on Community Mental Health, Division 27 of the American Psychological Association. *Issues in community psychology and preventive mental health.* New York: Behavioral Publications, 1971.

Tharp, R. G., & Wetzel, R. J. *Behavior modification in the natural environment*. New York: Academic Press, 1969.

Turner, A. J. Behavioral community mental health centers: Development, management, and preliminary results. In R. A. Winett (chair), *Behavior modification in the community: Progress and problems*. Symposium presented at the 83rd convention of the American Psychological Association, 1975.

Turner, A. J., & Goodson, W. H. Behavioral technology applied to a community mental health center: A demonstration. *Journal of Community Psychology*, 1977, *5*, 209–224.

Turner, A. J., & Pyfrom, C. Evaluation and its use in a comprehensive community mental health center. Unpublished manuscript, Huntsville-Madison County Mental Health Center, 1974.

Wasik, B. H., Senn, K., Welch, R. H., & Cooper, B. R. Behavior modification with culturally deprived school children: Two case studies. *Journal of Applied Behavior Analysis*, 1969, *3*, 181-194.

Williams, C. D. The elimination of tantrum behavior by extinction procedures. *Journal of Abnormal and Social Psychology*, 1959, *59*, 269.

Willems, E. P. Behavioral technology and behavioral ecology. *Journal of Applied Behavior Analysis*. 1974, 7(1), 515–165.

Willie, C. V., Kramer, B. M., & Brown, B. S. *Racism and mental health*. Pittsburg: University of Pittsburgh Press, 1973.

Zax, M., & Specter, G. A. *An introduction to community psychology*. New York: Wiley, 1974.

Index